THE PROTESTANT WHORE

ALISON CONWAY

The Protestant Whore

Courtesan Narrative and Religious Controversy in England, 1680–1750

UNIVERSITY OF TORONTO PRESS
Toronto Buffalo London

© University of Toronto Press Incorporated 2010
Toronto Buffalo London
www.utppublishing.com
Printed in Canada

ISBN 978-1-4426-4137-2 (cloth)

Printed on acid-free, 100% post-consumer recycled paper with vegetable-based inks.

Library and Archives Canada Cataloguing in Publication

Conway, Alison Margaret
   The Protestant whore : courtesan narrative and religious controversy in England,
   1680–1750 / Alison Conway.

   Includes bibliographical references and index.
   ISBN 978-1-4426-4137-2

   1. English fiction – Early modern, 1500–1700 – History and criticism.
   2. English fiction – 18th century – History and criticism.   3. Courtesans in literature.
   4. Protestantism in literature.   5. Politics in literature.   I. Title.

PR437.C65 2010   823.409'353   C2009-907064-2

'The Protestant Cause and a Protestant Whore: Aphra Behn's *Love-letters*,' *Eighteenth-Century Life* 25.3 (2001): 1–19, copyright © 2001 College of William and Mary, used by permission of the current publisher, Duke University Press.

'Defoe's Protestant Whore,' *Eighteenth-Century Studies* 35.2 (2002): 215–33, copyright © 2002 American Society for Eighteenth-Century Studies, is reproduced with permission by the Johns Hopkins University Press.

This book has been published with the help of a grant from the Canadian Federation for the Humanities and Social Sciences, through the Aid to Scholarly Publications Programme, using funds provided by the Social Sciences and Humanities Research Council of Canada.

University of Toronto Press acknowledges the financial assistance to its publishing program of the Canada Council for the Arts and the Ontario Arts Council.

University of Toronto Press acknowledges the financial support for its publishing activities of the Government of Canada through the Book Publishing Industry Development Program (BPIDP).

For Katherine

Contents

Illustrations

Acknowledgments

The American and Canadian Societies for Eighteenth-Century Studies and the ASECS Women's Caucus have provided me with an intellectual community for many years now, and I wish to thank their members for the conversations I've enjoyed during sessions and over meals. I am happy to acknowledge those colleagues who have shared their expertise with me, listened to my thoughts as they unfolded, and read portions of the manuscript: Peter Sabor, Betty Schellenberg, Paul Hunter, Laura Rosenthal, Susan Shifrin, James Turner, Catherine Gallagher, Marcia Pointon, Helen Thompson, Al Rivero, John H. O'Neill, Mary Helen McMurran, Ruth Perry, and Rusty Shteir. April London lent me her support, and her research assistant, at a crucial moment. Kathy King read my introduction and spent time in the Manuscripts Room at the British Library on my behalf. When he befriended a graduate student at an ASECS conference in 1993, Tom Lockwood could not have known that years later he'd find himself chasing down obscure references for her in the British Library, even at the eleventh hour. My warmest thanks to him for his friendship and fine editorial skills. My thanks to Frederique Chevillard, Chris Roulston, and Jeff Tennant for their help with the translation of French material. Thanks are owed to the undergraduate and graduate student research assistants who worked with me on this project, especially to Tina Northrup. I'm grateful for the enthusiasm of my editor, Richard Ratzlaff, for the insightful and generous readings of the manuscript provided by the Press's readers, and for the care taken with the manuscript by Miriam Skey.

The seeds for this project were planted during month-long sojourns at the Henry E. Huntington and William Andrews Clark Memorial libraries, made possible by W.M. Keck Foundation and ASECS-Clark Library fellowships. My thanks to the librarians and staff at those libraries for all of their help and friendly hospitality. Thanks also to the librarians and staff at the British Library and to National Portrait Gallery curators Peter Funnell and Catharine MacCleod, as well as to the staff in the Gallery's archives and Emma Butterfield. I wish to acknowledge the financial support of the Social Sciences and Humanities Research Council of Canada, the University of Western Ontario, and the J.B. Smallman Fund. A portion of chapter 1 appeared in *Restoration* 29.1 (spring 2005): 47–63, and parts of chapters 2 and 4 appeared in *Eighteenth-Century Life* 25 (fall 2001): 1–19, and *Eighteenth-Century Studies* 35.2 (2002): 215–33. My thanks to those journals for permission to reproduce that material.

I am grateful for the hospitality offered by my mother-in-law, Martyn Belmont, the two summers I arrived on her doorstep, with my children and their caregiver, to work in the libraries of San Marino and Los Angeles. My family in British Columbia has always encouraged me from afar. My partner, Bryce Traister, provides the love that sustains me. Matthew Traister and Hannah Conway have taught me that while books progress slowly, children grow quickly, and their busy lives keep me grounded in the everyday. Thanks to Susanna Eayrs for dog walks in the park. Dawn McGoey and Sandy Lochead support me in countless ways, and I am privileged to have them as friends. For more than twenty years, Katherine Binhammer has offered encouragement and insight through thick and thin. This book is dedicated to her, with love and gratitude.

THE PROTESTANT WHORE

Introduction

We are votaries of pleasure.

The Town-Misses Declaration and Apology;
Or, an Answer to the Character of a Town-Misse (1675)

Can it be that pleasure makes us *objective*?

Barthes, *The Pleasure of the Text*

I became familiar with the mistresses who govern this study while
looking at Restoration portraits. Once noted, the names of these wom-
en – Barbara Villiers, Louise de Kéroualle, Hortense Mancini, and Nell
Gwyn, among others – appeared to me everywhere in my encounters
with the long eighteenth century. 'Nell Gwyn,' in particular, seemed
to circulate as a code name. The centuries between then and now have
made deciphering this code more difficult by reconstituting Nell Gwyn
as England's favourite *parvenue*, the face on a tea shop sign in Windsor, subject of *Town and Country* debutante news.[1] But she did not always appear so harmless, and this study seeks to restore her darker
side to view, to identify her place within a larger constellation of representations. It considers Nell Gwyn a touchstone for Restoration and
eighteenth-century reflections on women's relation to authority, part
of a Stuart royal mistress tradition that deserves close scrutiny as an
important strand of the period's cultural and literary history.[2]

The story that gives this book its title recounts Nell Gwyn's arrival in
Oxford at the time of the Exclusion Crisis in 1681. Confronted by an an-
gry mob that suspected the occupant of her coach to be the hated Louise
de Kéroualle, Nell Gwyn called out to the crowd, 'Pray, good people,

be civil: I am the protestant whore.'[3] If 'whore' appears the most obviously charged element of Nell Gwyn's self-branding title, 'protestant' also represents a loaded term, and its historical resonance introduces the second term – 'religious controversy' – governing this study. As I began my reading of Nell Gwyn's representations, what first appeared a simple opposition between an English 'good' courtesan and a legion of 'bad' mistresses – Catholic or French or both – soon emerged as a far more complex picture of a Protestantism rife with internal contradictions.[4] Anti-Catholic xenophobia was unable to protect Protestantism from its own self-doubt – a point driven home by the persistence of religious anxieties even after Protestant succession was secured by law in 1701. The Church of Rome, the Whore of Babylon, came to be imagined less as a singular threat than as part of a larger problem of Protestant self-division, a failure of England's national consciousness to unite its constituencies.

Seventeenth-century polemic filled thousands of tracts, broadsides, and ballads distinguishing between 'true' Protestants and 'false' Protestants, loyalists and hypocrites, martyrs and traitors. We see the kinds of tensions shaping Restoration religious controversy in the frontispiece to Edward Pettit's 1683 publication *The Visions of the Reformation* (figure 1). The image shows the Presbyterian as a two-faced rebel, visually representing what the text attributes to both 'true Papists' and 'true Protestants (as they call themselves)': 'you will find, that though they have two faces that look different ways, yet they have both the same Lineaments, the same Principles, the same Practices.'[5] The author's fear that the king and Church of England will fall to the Catholics and Dissenters articulates a widespread anxiety that another civil war was imminent. It also demonstrates the extent to which Whig demands appeared indistinguishable, for royalists, from treasonous plots. Indeed, in many cases the two *were* indistinguishable, as the Monmouth Rebellion of 1685 proved. The verse inscribed under the frontispiece image warns of the overthrow of English Protestantism through the Presbyterians' efforts toward a 'thorough Reformation': 'Thus when the Kingdom turns a Comon wealth / The Imperiall Crown will be the Popes by Stealth.' From the Dissenters' perspective, Charles II's on-again, off-again support for toleration suggested that their interests could never be secured through monarchical intervention and raised suspicions that the king's intermittent alliance with their agenda was motivated by political, rather than religious, principles. The sense that Protestant factionalism could, either consciously or inadvertently, advance the goals of both the

Roman Catholic Church and Louis XIV informed both Dissenting and Anglican apocalyptic, often incoherent, political narratives. As Kirsten Poole points out, 'the aim of many early modern authors was to express a profound sense of shapelessness, to convey the chaos of transforming and disintegrating communal categories, to paint a muddled world picture.'[6]

Cultural renderings of Protestantism's failure to unite the nation return again and again to the relation between sexual impropriety and religious heterodoxy. In 1707 Daniel Defoe described English Protestantism's fraught beginnings: 'The various turns in England under Henry VIII, about the Article of Divorce, the Regale, and other things, widened a Breach between him and the Pope; and those lucid intervals gave such breathings to the Reformed Religion, that it advanc'd exceedingly, till even in his Reign, it crept, first into his Cabinet, and then his bed.'[7] On the one hand, Defoe appreciates the 'lucid intervals' that allowed Protestantism to gain a foothold in England. On the other hand, he worries about the entanglement of religious and sexual politics, the corruption of state affairs by private interests. The reign of Charles II revived, in a particularly forceful manner, the concerns Defoe associates with Henry VIII, and it is the legacy of these preoccupations that I study here.

Critics writing about the Restoration have tended to describe its obsession with the courtesan as a by-product of court culture. Margaret Spufford, for instance, notes the popularity of stories about royal mistresses such as Fair Rosamund, mistress to Henry II, and Jane Shore, mistress to Edward IV: 'The chap-books about them were simply excuses for a good story of adultery, high life, and repentance in both cases, reinforced with a moral at the end.'[8] This study sets the courtesan against a larger cultural backdrop. A vast range of material represents royal mistresses and courtesans (women whose careers as prostitutes linked them mostly, if not exclusively, to aristocratic patrons): pornographic satire, history, political tracts, court manuscript poetry, memoirs, and plays. While sharing, importantly, traits with whore biographies, courtesan stories remain distinct in their focus on the unique position and powers courtesans enjoyed in France and England. Both whore biographies and courtesan stories draw on a long tradition of European writing about sex. They are distinguished in Restoration and early eighteenth-century England by the status afforded the courtesan in the Stuart court in the years leading up to the Revolution of 1688/9.[9] Whore biographies depend on the exposure of the prostitute's 'truth,' personal and sexual. Women who masquerade as something more than mere whores must be exposed, punished, and reduced to their proper place in the gutters of society. Sexually transmitted diseases may mar the face of a beauty, transforming her bodily exploits, conducted in the privacy of the genital arena, into a disfiguring, public pronouncement of disgrace. Even more menacingly, men who claim to have been infected by prostitutes may write this disfiguration themselves, with the point of a knife, on the face of the whore. While courtesan stories can, and often do, encompass the violence of the whore's biography and its desire to expose, punish, and socially humiliate its subjects, they also incorporate the possibility of an alternate tale.

The courtesan routinely appears embedded in 'high,' as well as 'low,' genres. So, for example, Whig polemicist Robert Ferguson supports the deathbed testimony of Charles II's first mistress, Lucy Walters, in an attempt to legitimate the Duke of Monmouth and name him the king's Protestant heir. The memoirs of Hortense and Maria Mancini participate in the popularization of French aristocratic forms in England. Their documentation of the involvement of Louis XIV in the sisters' negotiations of separation agreements with their husbands forms part of an ongoing dispute between French aristocratic families and the house of Bourbon in the late seventeenth century, a debate significant to antagonists of the Stuarts in the Restoration court. The long-standing European tradition of pornographic writing about the courtesan took on particular significance in Restoration England, exploring, through its meditations on female authority, the paradox sustained by women who, as James Turner observes, 'lived in open breach of the laws of Church and State, which forbade adultery and fornication in the name of the King.'[10] Personal and political stories converged around the figure of Charles II, whose informality rendered him open to observation and commentary and created ideal conditions for the emergence of new forms of narrative. The courtesan's proximity to the monarch allows her to function both as a sign of corrupting influence, a stand-in for the culture of favourites governing court circles, or, more positively, as a substitute for the monarch.

We see the possibilities afforded by the courtesan's representation in the voice adopted by the 'town miss' in a 1675 publication, *The Town-Misses Declaration and Apology*. The publication that provoked it, *The Character of a Town-Miss*, attempts to use the rhetorical force of 'whore' as a tool of social discipline: 'A Miss is a new Name, which the Civility of this Age bestows on *one*, that our unmannerly Ancestors call'd

Whore and *Strumpet.*' In a move familiar to readers of whore biography, the author predicts the prostitute's inevitable decline: 'Then her former *Adorers* despise her, the World *hates* her, and she becomes a *Loathsome* thing, too unclean to enter into *Heaven*; too *Diseased* to continue long upon Earth; and too foul to be *toucht* with any thing but a *Pen*, or a pair of *Tongs*.'[11] The town miss's response highlights the whore's right to public speech: 'We are now resolv'd to be our own Advocate; Tis not the first time that we have ventur'd to make our selves *Publick* & if our Rhetorick should prove too weak to make good our Cause, we have other Charms that we well know are Irresistable ... A Mistress is always fresh and sparkling, like a Glass of neat *Canary*, never unacceptable.'[12] The assertion of women's verbal prerogative and sexual authority challenges the moral and political orthodoxies governing both royalist and Puritan traditions. As a narrative subject, then, the courtesan moves beyond the historical limits to which the royal mistress was confined, embodying the contradictions of a period that produced both Margaret Cavendish's feminist revisioning of Stuart authority and the radicalism of Puritan women writers.[13]

The circulation of courtesan narrative allows us to test the temperature of the large political, religious, and cultural transformations that the period 1680–1750 witnessed: from a Catholic to a Protestant succession, from a libertine to a moral – at least rhetorically – court, from a culture of rudeness to a culture of politeness. After 1688 political and religious polemic repeatedly used the Stuart kings' mistresses as a foil to the eighteenth-century celebrations of the Revolution's legacy and a powerful, united Protestant Great Britain. Characterizations of the Restoration as a form of political and sexual pathology speak, not to a historical past, but to the issues immediately at hand for eighteenth-century authors, who continued to struggle with dissent, doubt, and aggression.[14] We witness, in Pope's representation of the Restoration as a time when '*Jilts* rul'd the State,' a common refrain – and one that registers, in this case, Pope's particular anxieties about female governance.[15] I do not study later royal mistresses – Melusine von der Schulenburg or Henrietta Howard, Lady Suffolk, for instance – who served, in different ways, as cultural barometers. A reading of the eighteenth-century, rather than the Restoration, courtesan would cast a different light on the Hanoverian period. It is the Protestant Whore's ability to draw together a constellation of meanings – about religion, politics, sexuality, and cultural authority – particular to the Restoration that enabled later authors to reflect on the Stuart legacy, both historical and literary. The darkness of the vision that shapes representations of the Restoration appears, to me, a forceful reminder of eighteenth-century England's uneasy sense that the past's spectral presence was haunting modernity's new edifices.

'Protestant Whore' stands as the marker of the early English novel's preoccupation with the Restoration, a signpost that directs us to literary encounters with that period's religious controversies and to the women who helped shape their representation. It is linked, of course, to Nell Gwyn, but it more broadly calls up the Stuart royal mistress and questions regarding women's relation to the public sphere and state affairs. 'Courtesan narrative' similarly marks an abstraction of stories about courtesans into a larger literary paradigm. Courtesan narrative folds reflections on sexual politics and religious controversy into England's new tradition of prose fiction. It inhabits the chronotope, to use Bakhtin's term, of the boudoir: 'Most important ... is the weaving of historical and socio-public events together with the personal and even deeply private side of life, with the secrets of the boudoir; the interweaving of petty, private intrigues with political and financial intrigues, the interpenetration of state with boudoir secrets, of historical sequences with the every day and biographical sequences.'[16] As an interpretive term, 'courtesan narrative' allows me to weave a common thread through my readings of a disparate group of novelists – Aphra Behn, Daniel Defoe, Henry Fielding, and Samuel Richardson.[17] These writers, I suggest, take up the lines of investigation pursued by Restoration polemicists: Upon what foundations should a national Protestant identity be built in the wake of civil war? What constitutes legitimate authority? Who has the right to speak? What is the right relation between public and private personae? How should literature engage with politics? Nell Gwyn, writ large as the nation's Protestant Whore, serves as a lightning rod through which the energy of Restoration anxieties travels into the ground of courtesan narrative.

Since Ian Watt, Protestantism has appeared a cornerstone in critical assessments of the novel's development of ideas about interiority, economics, and national identity.[18] This project draws attention to the cracks and fissures running through that cornerstone. If critical commentary often tells a story that highlights Protestantism's powers of demystification, common sense, and trustworthiness, as well as its ability to empower individuals to experience an enlarged world of action and thought, my reading of courtesan narrative emphasizes the modern subject's need for self-protection in a world whose violence is exacerbated, rather than diminished, by religious conviction. The Protestant Whore reminds us that there was no one Protestant discourse capable of sustaining an image of Britain as an 'elect' nation. We see, in the novels I study here, a Protestant agency oscillating 'between being and non-being,' a dynamic that reveals how, as Harold Mah observes, 'the inherent tendency of any projection of a mass subject is to collapse back into a spatialized image of conflicting social groups.'[19] Within this frame of reference, Protestantism buttresses neither the progressive vision of virtuous citizenry, nor a conservative vision of pragmatic restraint.

Watt writes: 'It is ... likely that the Puritan conception of the dignity of labour helped to bring into being the novel's general premise that the individual's daily life is of sufficient importance and interest to be the proper subject of literature.'[20] Courtesan narrative shows us what happens to the novel's conception of an individual life when the 'dignity of labour' is measured by sexual exploits, rendering the 'proper subject of literature' a scandal. Where, in *Moll Flanders*, the criminal appears a victim of circumstances 'which anyone might have experienced and which provoke the same moral conflicts between means and ends as those faced by other members of society,' the courtesan shocks precisely because she exceeds the limits of need.[21] She reveals the desire that both underpins modern conceptions of politics, religion, and economics and threatens to unravel the ideological tapestry used to cover conflicting social imperatives and competing interests.

Among literary historians, examinations of the intersection of Protestantism and gender have tended to focus on prose fiction's investment in female virtue as a source of cultural authority.[22] In attending to the power-hungry courtesan, I highlight an alternate modernity, one that stresses Hobbesian imperatives rather than those that shaped conduct books. My reading of the Protestant Whore, then, revisits Nancy Armstrong's thesis that 'the modern individual was first and foremost a woman.'[23] I stress how understandings of aristocratic authority shape representations of female governance in courtesan narrative, countering Armstrong's claim that the modern novel was instrumental in asserting a vision of power 'that would sweep aside an earlier form that inhered in the aristocratic body and depended on that body's power to hold the gaze of the people.'[24] But even as the courtesan insists on the relevance of the Restoration for an English public wanting to disown it, she revises Jacobite imperatives with her own understanding of sovereign power, drawing on a tradition of English female governance that extends back to the Tudors.

My reading of Restoration culture stresses the unstable nature of many of the representations that circulated in print and manuscript form, an instability that registers the historical contradictions that shaped Charles II's reign.[25] The traumas inflicted on England's collective imagination during the Civil War generated uneasy relations between the discourses of the body and faith, flesh and its metamorphoses into political and social signs. As Rachel Weil has observed, 'the lines between court and country, the regime and its opponents, and sexual puritanism and sexual libertinism were more hazy and complicated than the traditional stereotypes suggest.'[26] Charles II introduced new elements into a long-standing conversation on the subject of sexual corruption and politics, making it more difficult for opposition writers to gain a purchase on the ideological dimensions of his court practices.[27] But opposition writers were afforded new opportunities by the evolution of print culture in Restoration London, which rendered censorship a complex and often self-defeating program.[28] Like the royalists, they were able to draw on developments of the radical Enlightenment to advance their claims.

Sexual intrigue and religious controversy foster, in the works that narrate their mutual engagement, a scepticism unvarnished by the consolations of sensibility or sympathy. The scepticism I attribute to courtesan narrative is not the mitigated variety of latitudinarian or emergent liberal discourses, but a more corrosive threat of total dissolution, 'a potentially radical power never entirely under control.'[29] It establishes an interrogatory mode, both anticipating Enlightenment atheism and looking back to the origins of the term 'libertin,' first used to describe a heretical sect in northern France in 1525 and, soon after, a religious group that set itself against Calvin's authority in 1542.[30] The dynamism I attribute to courtesan narrative's sceptical impulse is derived from the mix of religious and sexual elements combined in the term 'Protestant Whore,' which brings together the anarchic spirit that governs Restoration street literature, libertinism's French and Catholic-inflected anticlericalism, and Protestantism's antinomian impulses. In stressing its ability to highlight the particular tensions governing Restoration culture and politics, I counter the association of scepticism with an evolution in taste that came to view literature as a space of 'epistemological leisure,' a form of cultural expression capable of ameliorating social and political conflicts by rendering literature a space apart.[31] Courtesan narrative remains committed to political engagement, recognizing that 'elevation above the fray [is] still a political geography.'[32]

My focus on the Stuart courtesan means that the connection I establish between prostitution and modernity looks different from that analysed by Laura J. Rosenthal in her insightful study, *Infamous Commerce: Prostitution in Eighteenth-Century British Literature and Culture*. Rosenthal explores 'the predicament of the prostitute for (in different ways) emerging middle-class and laboring-class subjectivities.'[33] My project traces modernity's obsession with the appropriation of monarchical power – its preoccupations draw the economic, for example, into meditations on state authority. Rosenthal's book describes a debate about capitalism that continued to develop through the nineteenth century – mine, a tradition whose end-point coincided with the last Jacobite rebellion. The two traditions overlap, of course, but I am concerned here to focus on the particularity of the earlier period and to attend to the novel's backward-looking moments.[34] Although I claim that the Protestant Whore disappears from view after 1750, I am not suggesting that women dwindled into passivity, nor that they were restricted to the domestic sphere in the latter part of the eighteenth century. As cultural historians Amanda Vickery, Elaine Chalus, and others have amply demonstrated, women exercised authority within the public spaces of Georgian England, and, as the parliamentary system developed, they were able to exploit new systems of patronage.[35] But the particular meanings attached to the Restoration courtesan lose their resonance in the aftermath of the Stuarts' defeat in 1746.

The novel after 1750 struggles with doubt, religious controversy, and the conduct of illicit women, to be sure. I stop at the point when Hume's 'common sense' begins to compensate for Hobbes's cynicism; when authors shift their focus from fears of Stuart invasions to revolutionaries in the colonies and the abuses of slavery; when women turn their attention to the realities dictated by a new marriage act; when Evangelicalism captures an audience; when the aesthetic proves capable of healing, if not the nation, at least individuals. Insofar as the novel continues to take up political questions, it attends to the hegemony that won out over Jacobitism.[36] That is, we see authors grappling, not with rebellious subjects and would-be monarchs, but with the limits of liberalism's new model of contractarian virtue.[37] Finally, as the novel attempts to claim status as a serious literary genre, its commitment to sociability guaranteed its disregard for unruly men and women alike.[38] The scandalous memoirs published by women like Lady Vane, Teresia

Constantia Phillips, and Laetitia Pilkington, continue the tradition of stories about courtesans, but these women are not the subjects of the later eighteenth-century novel.[39]

Rather than shoring up ideological boundaries or partisan identities, 'whore' signifies the difficulty of answering the questions raised by Restoration polemicists. Two principles governed my decision to keep 'whore' and 'whoring,' conventionally sexist and abusive terms, in play here. First, in Restoration debates, 'whore' refers to many subject positions – perjurer, Trimmer, Catholic, and traitor, for instance. By using it as a critical shorthand, I keep its multiple historical meanings in view to reveal how different definitions of whoring were pitted against one another by the period's authors. Within this context, the sexual content of 'whore' takes on multiple connotations. More particularly, 'whore' appropriates the freedoms that royal mistresses, by virtue of their status at court, enjoyed – a space outside the law, bawdy self-expression, material success, and sexual parity – for a larger community of women. By linking these freedoms to prostitution broadly defined, I identify the common ground of non-marital, non-monogamous sexual practices upon which courtesan narrative is built. While I do not want to glamorize the world of the royal consort, an impulse that more often than not has shaped biographies of Nell Gwyn and other Stuart mistresses, or, worse, advance a thesis that follows the 'jolly cavalier' line of thinking, I also refuse the characterization of Restoration culture and literature as only, or necessarily, misogynous.[40] Second, my use of 'whore' and 'whoring' challenges a tendency to invoke the terms as a means of foreclosing conversation, then and now. In his foreword to the exhibition catalogue *Painted Ladies: Women at the Court of Charles II*, National Portrait Gallery director Charles Saumarez Smith poses the question: 'Should mistresses be dismissed as whores or were they simply expressing an era of greater sexual freedom?' This study suggests that whores should not be dismissed under any circumstances and challenges the larger assumption governing Smith's statement – that sexual freedom and sex work are inimical.[41]

Lying (Silvia), murderous (Roxana), and willing to hatch rape plots against house guests (Lady Bellaston), the courtesans who populate the narratives this book reads engage in behaviour that has generated a fair amount of critical consternation. In advancing here what might be loosely described as 'the Satanist argument,' I hope to avoid what E.M.W. Tillyard identifies as 'the danger of sentimentalizing the rebel.'

But by highlighting the courtesan's contribution to English literary history, I counter a critical tendency that has governed readings of whores since novel criticism came into existence in the late eighteenth century – that of rendering the rebel 'too cheap.'[42] The doubtful protagonist raises a number of methodological issues, many of which fall into the category of determining authorial intention. Are the authors consciously or unconsciously siding with these 'bad' women? Do the courtesans have virtues as well as vices, or are the virtues they present to the world only vices masquerading as something else? Are the vices attributed to these women, in fact, vices? For example, is ambition a sin or a virtue? Do authors want to draw us into a sympathetic identification with these characters as a means of exposing our own moral depravity?[43] Those critics who sympathize with the courtesans studied here often do so by placing blame for their moral limitations elsewhere: with the exigencies of modernity and its alienating tendencies, for instance, or with systemic sexism. I climb out on a limb to suggest that Behn, Defoe, Richardson, and Fielding, as well as the less well-known and anonymous authors populating this study, exploit the literary opportunities afforded by the courtesan's amoralism.

I begin chapter 1 with a brief history of the late Restoration's religious controversies. The two decades leading up to the Exclusion Crisis of 1681 witnessed a series of reversals, with Charles II's twice announcing, for example, declarations in favour of toleration, only to withdraw them under pressure from Parliament. His tense relations with both Anglicans and Dissenters rendered the religious question a thorny and intractable problem. My history highlights the role played by the language of whoredom in disputes of the 1680s. The chapter then examines Nell Gwyn's Protestantism, which both reminded the nation of its divisions and offered an alternative to the Catholic mistresses and Charles II's Protestant bastard, the Duke of Monmouth. I close with an analysis of the representation of female authority in *The Whore's Rhetorick* (1683) and *The Parliament of Women* (1684). These satires reflect on the religio-political dimension of female subjectivity, laying the groundwork for an English prose narrative tradition that echoes and revises the political and philosophical discourses of the period.

Chapter 2 views Aphra Behn's characterization of the Protestant Whore and the scepticism that governs *Love-Letters* from two different vantage points. First, I examine Behn's dedications to Hortense Mancini, Duchess of Mazarin, and Nell Gwyn, in order to revisit Catherine Gallagher's analysis of Behn's identification with the figure of the whore.[44] How does this identification change when the prostitute stands not for a Nobody, but a prominent Somebody who, in the case of Mancini, appears as the subject of ghost-written memoirs and so, to a certain extent, as an author herself? Second, I analyse how Behn's courtesan narrative moves from the particularities of private interests to the public sphere of political action. Following the lead of her French contemporaries and their *chroniques scandaleuses*, Behn develops a narrative that enables both political commentary and philosophical speculation. In her representation of Henrietta Berkeley and James Scott, Duke of Monmouth, Behn exploits the idea of a competition between the interests of a Protestant Whore and the Protestant Duke in order to link gender, narrative, and historiography. I consider Behn's representation of the duke's plots (symptomatic of a larger problem of male aristocratic corruption) as ill-conceived stories of Protestant triumphalism, against which Behn sets the scepticism of courtesan narrative. The alternative historiography that Behn defines in this novel, I argue, both refuses Protestant nationalism and opens up historical discourse to include women's contributions to and commentary upon political affairs.

Chapter 3 serves as a bridge between Behn and Defoe and studies a broad range of texts – with special attention to secret histories – to consider how the Restoration courtesan's legacy was defined in the immediate aftermath of the Revolution of 1688/9. The figure of the courtesan unsettles distinctions that polemicists were eager to draw between the Restoration's Stuart kings and the Stuart queens (Mary and Anne) who succeeded them. Even as political discourse attempts to promote the idea of Protestant governance as morally renewed in the figure of Queen Anne, the figure of the courtesan challenges the claims of reform, reminding readers of the difficulty of establishing clear ideological distinctions and of the persistence of government corruption. *Queen Zarah* (1705), in particular, appears representative of the Restoration's uncanny afterlife: as much as it would like to discredit its satiric target, Sarah Churchill, by associating the Duchess of Malborough with the mistresses of Stuart kings, the narrative finds itself compelled by the efficacy of women's plots.

Chapter 4 analyses Defoe's representations of the difficulties that attended early eighteenth-century attempts to promote non-partisan religious sentiment. Defoe's *Roxana* takes us back to the Restoration to insist on the divisiveness of religious belief. Defoe evokes the Restoration's persecution of Dissenters, the Hobbesian ethos governing new forms of finance, and the spectre of female authority embodied by the

Stuart royal mistress. Roxana establishes a parity between Ottoman consorts and English kings, even as her refusal of Catholicism and its rites of confession deepen our sense of her inalienable Protestant identity. The conflict of cultures and religions that the novel stages does not, however, constitute its tragedy. Rather, I suggest, it is the domestic absolutism of Roxana's daughter, Susan, that puts the courtesan on a collision course with a modernity different from her own. In narrating this collision, Defoe shatters the illusion of English Protestantism as a refuge from the storms of social and religious schism.

Stuart monarchs and courtesans shape the ethical and formal meditations of *Clarissa* and *Tom Jones*, I claim in the final chapter of this study. Richardson's idealization of Clarissa relies heavily on seventeenth-century representations of monarchical power and court politics. It is the difficulty of naturalizing the female sovereign's powers of refusal, I suggest, that causes Richardson to resort to rhetorical violence in his representation of the prostitutes and courtesans who populate his finest novel. Fielding, by contrast, claims the courtesan's authority as his own, first by domesticating the courtesan in his representation of Sophia, and then, in a series of startling crossovers, by fashioning both his hero and his narrator as prostitutes. *Clarissa* and *Tom Jones* tap a vein of Restoration antinomian and free-thinking discourse that allows the novels to reframe mid-eighteenth-century cultural debates.

While I argue here that the controversies surrounding Protestantism and debates about women's authority intersect in important and compelling ways over the course of the Restoration and early eighteenth century, 'Protestant' and 'whore' do not always add up to 'Protestant Whore.' This study traces the sometimes tight, sometimes loose, bonds forged between multiple and varied discourses and so, at times, it takes one or the other term as its primary object for extended moments, rather than insisting on an exact correspondence between them. At a time when 'whore' is as likely to refer to the Roman Catholic Church as a woman and when 'Protestant' can signal treachery (James Scott, Duke of Monmouth) or integrity (Queen Anne) or both (William and Mary), new constellations of meaning shine and fade, creating in their allusiveness and echoes patterns of association whose significance develops cumulatively. This book provides a 'thick description' of a culture, to use Clifford Geertz's term, and its reading of that culture's semiotic systems is shaped by an interpretive practice attentive to the short- and long-term effects of the Restoration's performative acts of self-definition. It is primarily a literary history, although it does not imagine the novel's development as an evolution in the forward-looking sense. That is, the English novel, here, emerges as much a product of historical contingency – of local debates and accidental discoveries – as of broad cultural transformations.

In his compelling reading of the eighteenth-century novel's resistance to closure, J. Paul Hunter reflects on the conditions that fostered narrative's desire to dwell in its 'full, subjective uncertainty': 'In the mid-eighteenth century ... the signs no longer meant what they had, the forms no longer contained it all, and there were stories, stories, stories – new and particular stories – everywhere.'[45] *The Protestant Whore* looks back to an earlier moment, when there were plots, plots, plots – new and frightening plots – everywhere. The narratives I read take their epistemological cues from the political disorder birthed by the Restoration and the Revolution of 1688/9, and from the convergence of sexual and religious discourses, of private and public meanings, that was the Restoration's cultural legacy. Courtesan narrative uses the seventeenth century's heterodox traditions to challenge the social and political imperatives that surfaced in the Restoration's wake. In doing so, it grants us, most immediately, a sense of the novel's historical acumen.

1 The Invention of the Protestant Whore

And hereupon it was my Mother Dear
Did bring forth Twins at once, both Me, and Fear.

Thomas Hobbes[1]

How much weight, exactly, did the king's courtesans carry in political debates? How did the cultural commentaries of the period gender and sexualize their representations of Catholic and Protestant authority? How was Nell Gwyn able to sustain an image of a united Protestant interest in the face of Church of England and Dissenting factionalism? Why did the language of Protestantism as self-protection work for Nell Gwyn, when it so clearly damaged the case of Stephen College, the Protestant joiner hanged for treason in Oxford only a few months after Nell Gwyn's proclamation? The answers I provide to these questions place the Protestant Whore at the centre of the Restoration's and early eighteenth century's preoccupation with Protestantism's relation to power and identity, both national and personal.[2] A range of discourses, religious, political, legal, and sexual, circle around the figure of the courtesan throughout the period. These discourses overlap at a number of points, but their convergence rarely receives sustained analysis.[3] Tim Harris has argued that 'the distinction between high and low politics – if by that we mean a distinction between the political and the sub-political nation, or between the rulers and the ruled – ... seems of questionable value for seventeenth-century London.'[4] When one author – Andrew Marvell, for example – writes both scandalous and sober treatises on the state of the nation, when articles of high treason drawn up against a royal mistress rehearse the complaints voiced by obscene literature, when polite women authors champion the world of female rule satirized by libertine misogynists, we discover the difficulty of distinguishing genres along conventional lines. Read together, 'high' and 'low' genres demonstrate how the commentary on courtesans that emerges in the Restoration speaks directly to, and forms part of, the period's religious controversies and political debates, identifying both the figurative and practical uses of 'whore' as an organizing principle of late seventeenth-century English culture. The cross-pollination that occurred between texts created a new iconic status for the courtesan.

This chapter begins by analysing the language of the Restoration's religious controversies in order to understand how concerns about whoredom and the Protestant polity were twinned in the public's imagination. The rhetorical use of 'whore' took on an added urgency in the face of the king's commitment to maintaining his mistresses as court subjects and his brother's open attachment to the Whore of Babylon – i.e., the Roman Catholic Church. The second part of the chapter turns to the figure of the historical mistress, beginning with Lucy Walters, mother of Charles II's first child, James Scott, the Duke of Monmouth. The Black Box affair placed the question of Lucy Walters's sexual integrity at the heart of the nation's most pressing political matter: the question of a Protestant succession. Was Lucy Walters a whore or a wife, and was her son a bastard or the legitimate – and helpfully Protestant – heir to the throne? In political satires of the period, Nell Gwyn serves as the counterpoint to the Protestant duke, as well as figuring more broadly as both an extension of, and departure from, the standard of corruption wielded by the French and Catholic mistresses of Charles's court. Nell Gwyn, in her most benign manifestations, stands for a principle of Protestant disinterestedness, but she also always carries the shadow of political influence cast by her nefarious counterparts. Finally, I close the chapter with a reading of two Restoration satires: *The Whore's Rhetorick* and *The Parliament of Women*. These two narratives illustrate how closely intertwined stories about England's sexual and religious interests had become by the late Restoration. More broadly, their reflections on the art of storytelling serve as a starting point for the work this study as a whole undertakes: to investigate how the writing of courtesan narrative contributed to the evolution of the English novel.

'Infidelity, Popery and raging sensuality': Protestantism and Its Discontent, 1680–8

'It is worth asking,' Tony Claydon and Ian McBride observe, 'whether the reformed faith could ever have been a sound basis for a unifying national identity.'[5] Religious historians have long stressed the doubt that attended those seeking to define, in general terms, Protestantism's national and international character, and, more specifically, the Church of England's and Dissenting traditions' agenda. Their work suggests that the debates surrounding England's faith after 1660 reveal that competing demands could never adequately be satisfied by a single discourse of Protestantism. Two concerns underpin my overview of different Protestant responses to the challenges posed by the later years of Charles II's rule.[6] First, how did Protestants understand the king's moral debauchery? The problem of the king's sexual appetite set the stage for the increasingly intense scrutiny of the monarch's courtesans, especially as it became clear that the queen would produce no heir.[7] Second, how did the charges of Catholicism circulating within Protestant communities heighten the nation's anxieties? Stuart licentiousness not only raised questions about the integrity of the monarchy's conduct, but also drew the public's attention to the ways in which the body natural, which ought to serve as the material reminder of the polity's commitment to a uniform Protestant faith, functioned rather as a duplicitous source of internal corruption and self-division.

John Spurr has argued that 'atheism and apathy, rather than any brand of religion, appeared to be the true victors of 1689.'[8] How did Protestant rhetoric devolve to this point in the 1680s? While it is beyond the scope of this study to examine the details of the religious question from 1660 onward, it is important to note that its persistence posed – and continues to pose – a series of hermeneutical challenges.[9] On the subject of Charles II's relation to toleration, for instance, Annabel Patterson asks: 'Was he genuinely in favor of what he called "indulgence" for all "tender consciences," for leaving the laws elastic and subject to exception? Or was he rather seeking primarily to improve the lot of his Roman Catholic subjects?'[10] The issues of the king's body politic and of Protestant sectarianism were inextricably linked in the Restoration: 'When we would destroy *this* [Popish influence], something we must set up; the *Church of England* is that which our Protestant Law-givers have erected, and by so many Laws confirmed; *This* now is twisted with our *Monarchy*, and the whole frame of our Civil Government: so that the overthrow of one, will be the destruction of both,' Anglican Joseph Glanvill perceptively remarked.[11] Radical Stephen College named the situation more bluntly when he declared that 'The Head o' th' English Church, / Had left the body in the lurch.'[12] Restoration Protestant commentators never did solve this problem, and by 1688 it was clear they never would without engaging in some kind of treachery. While the invasion of William III enabled a revolution, his rule only nominally eased tensions between Protestants.[13] The Restoration became a sore point for later English writers, not just because it needed repeated discrediting, but because it revealed the difficulty, indeed impossibility, of integrating faith, nationalism, and authority into a coherent ideology.

'To remove all reasonable fears that may arise from a possibility of a Popish Successor's coming to the Crown, if means can be found, that in such a case the Administration of the Government may remain in Protestant Hands, I shall be ready to hearken to any such expedient, by which the Religion may be preserv'd and the Monarchy not destroy'd': these were hollow words indeed by 1681, when Charles II spoke them.[14] The Church of England imagined itself the institutional bastion guarding English interests against incursions of the Roman Catholic Church. Its political work involved keeping the king attached to his national interests. A large part of the efforts of Anglican ministers to achieve this goal was directed toward inspiring the king, and the nation, to moral reform: 'The foundation of our peace and agreement must be laid in the reforming our selves and our own Tempers,'[15] wrote Benjamin Calamy. John Tillotson, future archbishop of Canterbury, alluded to the difficulty of sustaining the monarch's symbolic relationship with the Church in the face of the king's propensity for vice in a 1680 sermon delivered to a royal audience:

> I wish it were as easy for us to justify our Lives as our Religion. I do not mean in comparison of our Adversaries (for that, as bad as we are, I hope we are yet able to do) but in comparison of the Rules of our holy *Religion*, from which we are infinitely swerv'd; which I would to God we all did seriously consider and lay to heart: I say, in comparison of the Rules of our Holy Religion, which *teach us to deny ungodliness and worldly lusts, and to live soberly, and righteously, and godly in this present World, in expectation of the blessed hope, and the glorious appearance of the great God, and our Saviour Jesus Christ.*[16]

Tillotson evokes 'the Rules of our holy *Religion*' – first as a general principle, and again as a term that introduces a list of particular moral mandates – but the knowledge of Charles's attachment to French customs and mores draws our attention to a less abstract frame of reference at work in the passage: the behaviour of England's Catholic 'Adversaries' in the monarch's inner sanctum. By attributing the standard of moral corruption to the French (as bad as Charles is, he is not yet as bad as

Louis XIV), Tillotson maintains the ideal of the king's two bodies. Both the 'Rules' and the king remain recognizably English within this configuration. But in a more apocalyptic vein, Zachary Cawdrey, Anglican author of *A Preparation for Martydom*, wrote: 'Hath not also the most Pious, Learned, and Reverand Prelate ... Dr. Fell, Lord Bishop of *Oxford*, in his Sermon then before the Lords, set it out with the Zeal of a Prophet, how Lust, and Uncleanness are Rampant amongst us? For indeed Adultery hath not only taken the *place*, but Usurps also the *Title* of *Marriage*. And *Whoredom* claims to be *Honourable* amongst all Men.'[17] Here the rules are no longer recognizable, as adultery usurps the title of marriage and the corruption stemming from the court infects the nation. Sexuality serves as the focal point for the argument, the incarnation of sin, birthed by the king's corrupt bedroom practices. Unlike Tillotson, Cawdrey does not imagine reform but rather degeneration, perhaps all the way to Catholicism; the pamphlet's title evokes Foxe's *Book of Martyrs*. As in Tillotson's sermon, the jeremiad retains the link between king and country: for better and for worse, his fate mirrors the nation's. Charles II has allowed the body natural to compromise the body politic, bringing the frailties of the flesh into the arena of governance and rendering the nation, like the natural body, subject to decay and death.

Presbyterian Richard Baxter takes up this apocalyptic voice in *The Second Part of the Nonconformists Plea for Peace*, in which he warns of the civil unrest that must follow from Charles II's bad example: 'If Princes will ever set up Epicurisme, Atheisme and Infidelity, they shall set up Rebellion with it, and expose their Lives to every man that hath but [life] to venture upon a secret or open assault.'[18] The king's corrupt body courts its own destruction by reducing the monarch to the status of mere mortal, unprotected by the sanctity of office. The Dissenter no longer recognizes the king as separate from his constituency. By adopting the life of an infidel, Charles II becomes merely one man among many. In the aftermath of the Civil War, the threat of rebellion, however undesirable, could never be taken back, and the English Dissenters, however disenfranchised, recognized the power afforded by the discourse of the rule of law and Protestant national integrity. Meditations on the Catholic Church's priests and practices served as thinly veiled commentary on Charles II's character:

Is not the Apostate Church of *Rome* commonly Intituled in Sacred Oracles, *The Whore*, yea, *The Mother of Harlots*, and *Abominations of the Earth*,

Rev.17.5? Which though principally intended of her Spiritual Fornications
and Adulteries ... Yet it is also true in a Literal sense; what *Fulsome Brutes*
have most of their Popes been?[19]

The Dissenters' criticism of the king expanded to include the Church
of England. Baxter concludes his plea for toleration by remarking: 'we
leave their Principles and ours to the judgement of posterity, wishing
(in vain) that those Conformists who are thought sufficient for the sacred work without us, and have access to those whom we may not converse with, had proved more sufficient to have preserved Cities and
Corporations and the Land from Infidelity, Popery and raging sensu-
ality.'[20] Circling back to the king's corruption, Baxter notes the failure
of ministers like Tillotson to reform the monarchy, recording each individual insufficiency as a reflection on the Church's weakness as an
agent of Protestant faith.

The Church of England responded to attacks of this kind by linking
the Dissenters to treasonous plots, evoking the Puritans' regicidal past:

> The Brethren associated for that end are actually to perform *Themselves*
> what they (inhumanely) forced upon *Others*; And whilst mens fancies are
> filled with (false) Ideas of Popish Treasons, Murders, and Massacres, the
> same Exploits (that is, *bloody Villainies*) must be really committed by the
> *Dissenters* on the Sacred Person of the King; on the Duke of York; on the
> *Papists*; and on *Orthodox-Protestants*, (*viz. Church-of-English men*) as *Popish-
> ly-affected*.[21]

Just as the Dissenters used the Anglicans' institutional authority against
them, so too the Church of England pointed to Dissent's myriad associations as the hotbed of sedition and Catholic interference: 'I have been
credibly informed,' wrote Tory propagandist John Nalson, 'that a St.
Omers Jesuit declared, that they were twenty years hammering out the
Sect of the *Quakers*; and whoever considers the *Positions* of those People,
will easily be induced to believe them forged upon a *Popish* Anvil.'[22] The
fear of infiltration of Catholic interests through unorthodox channels
stems from the idea of a wilful people – Dryden's 'Headstrong, Moody,
Murmuring Race' – incapable of making informed judgments.[23] Any
departure from the structure of the Church opens the door to endless
error, argues William Saywell: 'there are too many examples of profane
ignorant persons, rolling from Presbyterians to Independents, then to
Anabaptists, afterward to Quakers, and at length to Papists; and many

times when the former Devil is gone out, seven worse enter in.'[24] Where the Dissenters saw specious Anglican rhetoric replacing the substance, the 'matter,' of Protestant faith, Anglicans identified verbal mania with the dangerous, seditious acts of ambitious men. As Dryden observed in his preface to *Religio Laici*, "'tis to be noted by the way, that the Doctrines of King-killing and Deposing, which have been taken up onely by the worst Party of the Papists, the most frontless Flatterers of the Pope's Authority, have been espous'd, defended, and are still maintain'd by the whole Body of Nonconformists and Republicans.'[25]

It was simple enough for both Dissenters and Anglicans to accuse each other of Catholic tendencies and treasonous plotting. Less simple was defining what English Protestantism ought to look like.

For a Nation divided against it self in Religion, how can its Religious Interest stand?

The *Religious* Differences that are amongst them as Churches, do weaken the *Political* Interest of Protestants.

We who profess our selves Protestant, have stood a great while at some distance, and of late our Difference has been exceedingly heightened, nay it is to be feared many attempts have been made by some sort of People, to render us wholly unreconcileable ... *We must either unite, or we must perish.*

Popery we will not have; so far we are *right*, but what are we for?[26]

More often than not, the question 'what are we for?' went unanswered. While hardliners of both Anglican and Dissenting communities imagined various solutions to this complex problem (usually involving the aggressive repression of opposing viewpoints), more subtle thinkers found it intractable. 'The way to make National Religion most National, is by comprehending all the differences, that can be reconcil'd with true Religion; while they that dissent in some things receive one another with a good, peaceable, holy, and publick temper of mind,' wrote Independent Thomas Beverley, author of *The Whole Duty of Nations*.[27] But how might this 'publick temper of mind' be realized?

By 1687, the problem had become acute. A question posed only rhetorically by John Nalson in 1680 suddenly took on real urgency in the face of Louis XIV's revocation of the Edict of Nantes and James II's attempts to reinstate Catholicism as a legitimate faith in England: 'Now who is to be Judge of the goodness and fitness of Laws, Religious, Moral or Political? Either the Prince or the People.'[28] The Church of England mounted political opposition to James's impositions even as those who hoped for a constitutional resolution to the crisis retreated into the language of passive obedience. While warning Dissenters against James II's peace offerings, George Savile, Marquis of Halifax, argued this line in his 1687 *Letter to a Dissenter*: 'We all agree in our Duty to our Prince; our Objections to his Belief, do not hinder us from seeing his Vertues; and our not complying with his Religion, hath no effect upon our Allegiance; we are not to be Laughed out of our Passive Obedience, and the Doctrine of Non-Resistance, though even those who perhaps owe the best part of their Security to that Principle, are apt to make a Jest of it.' The problem with this stance – 'Let us be still, quiet, and undivided' – was that action was insisted upon by the king himself.[29] When James II ordered Anglican ministers to read the Act of Indulgence in 1688 from their pulpits, maintaining a posture of passive obedience alongside Church of England standards required careful contortions. The bishop of Hereford asked, 'Should I read a Paper in the Church declaring the Kings Toleration of Sectaries, doth it any way declare my Consent unto it? No certainly.'[30] The defiance of the seven bishops who refused to read the declaration revealed most glaringly the schism that divided church and state in the years between 1685 and 1688.[31]

Meanwhile, Dissent distanced itself as actively as it could from both the Church of England's attempts to return the king to the policies of his brother and James II's overtures, turning up the volume of its already virulent anti-Catholic discourse. Church of England ministers fearful of James II's incursions on their prerogative and Dissenters alike feared that the Whore of Babylon was setting up residence in England, reducing those who supported James II to prostitutes of the great Bawd. Within this frame of reference, Samuel Parker, the bishop of Oxford (who had suggested that the Test Act be abrogated) could appear as a streetwalker:

> Certainly, his ways of Discourse are like those of the Whorish Woman in the Proverbs, so moveable, one cannot know them ... Now he is in the Streets of the Strange Religion, and layeth in wait in every Corner with a New sort of Ecclesiastical Polity, or in a New Edition, and his great Temptation is, I have, saith he, Peace-Offerings with me, that carry at the same Time Reconcilableness to Rome, and likewise a Blessing himself in a design'd Indulgence to his own Genius, and caressing himself in the thoughts of his comfortable Magdalen Importances.[32]

The author, capitalizing on Marvell's earlier sexualized satirizations of Parker's phrase 'comfortable importance' in the *Rehearsal Transpros'd*, transforms the bishop into a Magdalen luring innocent Protestants into dark alleys for illicit encounters.[33] The bishop's metamorphosis speaks to fears that the English polity was shape-shifting. And indeed it was. What was clear, by 1688, was that there could be no resolution to the political and religious crises facing the nation that would not involve compromises of various stripes. No religious conviction could secure its practitioner from the label 'whore,' even as each party claimed to act disinterestedly. For the fact remained that each had something political to gain from the path he chose to pursue.

Protestant divisiveness and the corruption most often associated with the court's debauchery were paired in the English imagination in the mid-1680s. Gilbert Burnet observed: 'Nor have our Divisions with the heats, animosities, revilings, & persecutions that have ensued thereupon, proved only an occasion for the seduction of several from our Religion, and of their Apostacy to Popery, but they have been a main spring & force of the debauchery, irreligion and Atheisme, which have overspread the Nation.'[34] England's long-standing identification of the Roman Catholic Church with lewdness took on renewed zest as fears surrounding the Stuart brothers' religious habits crystallized into a political crisis. But even when Catholicism constituted a palpable threat to English Protestantism, some recognized that the problem was larger than Charles II's libertinism and James II's imminent ascent to the throne. No *one* Protestantism, the Restoration had proved, could secure the faith of the nation, and from this limitation flowed innumerable sins.

'Let us be governed by an English C–t': Reading Nell Gwyn

In courtesan representations of the period, 'whore' became the fleshly universal, to modify a New Critical term, of Protestant England's sexual, political, and religious imagination. Four polemical 1680 publications on the subject of the Duke of Monmouth's claims to the throne demonstrate this point. Rumours that the court had in its possession a black box that contained evidence of Charles II's marriage to Lucy Walters, mother of James Scott, Duke of Monmouth, became the touchstone for controversies concerning the claims of the Protestant duke, the quality of Charles II's rule, and the future of the English nation. In the aftermath of Charles II's public denial of a marriage with Lucy Walters on 26 April, Robert Ferguson, Whig ringleader of the period, sustained an extended commentary on the subject in two pamphlets:[35]

> In truth, the whole referring to the *Black Box*, is a meer Romance, pur-
> posely invented to sham and ridicule the business of the Marriage, which
> indeed hath no relation to it. For they who judg'd it conducible to their
> present business to have the *D. of M.*'s Title to the Crown not only dis-
> credited but exposed, thought it necessary, instead of nakedly enquiring
> whether he be the *Kings Legitimate* or only *Natural* Son; to bring upon the
> Stage a circumstance no way annexed with it, supposing that this being
> found a Fable, the *Marriage* it self of the *K*. with the said *D.'s Mother*, would
> have undergone the same Censure. But by what I do perceive they were
> mistaken in their measures; seeing most men know how to separate what
> they endeavoured so artificially to have interwoven.[36]

Ferguson's attribution of the Black Box story to the enemies, rather
than friends, of the Duke of Monmouth takes the affair's narrative in
an interesting direction: we discover, through his explication, that conspiracy theories concerning the duke's birthright belong to the realm
of 'meer Romance' and that the 'fact' of the duke's legitimacy might be
obtained through 'naked enquiry.' Fiction-making becomes the prov-
enance of the Catholic Duke of York and sympathetic judges, to whom
Charles II uttered his declaration (made public by its authorized appearance in the *Gazette*). Ferguson attributes significant interpretive
powers to the English public, for how the truth might reveal itself in the
absence of any known facts remains a mystery here. But determining
the truth appears somewhat beside the point, as Ferguson pits the public's powers of discernment against royal mystifications. Epistemology
constitutes the real bone of contention. Even more specifically, literary
criticism organizes the frame of reference, as Ferguson encourages his
reader to recognize the romance conventions adopted by the court to
discredit the facts at hand. Dismissing the idea of the king's words as
Word, divinely inspired and hallowed by custom and status, Ferguson
characterizes the king and his men as artificers whose fictions must be
laid bare by parliamentary law and, more generally, the laws of empirical investigation.

Ferguson encourages the English public to relinquish its romantic
thinking about both the king and his son in favour of clear-thinking
pragmatism. Ferguson's second pamphlet on the subject deepens the
republican tone of the first volley, suggesting that 'the denyals of Kings
are not to be subscribed unto with an implicite Faith, but that we ought

to use the same discretion in believing or not believing what they say, that we esteem our selves priviledged to use towards others in the credit which they require we should give unto them.' The king's personal character, rather than his public crown, will either vouch for the integrity of his words or – as in the case of this particular monarch – not: 'If ... neither the Eye nor Dread of God, nor the Faith of a Christian, are effectual to restrain a person from Adulteries and promiscuous Scatterings, Can we have any security that they will prevent such a one from the guilt of other Crimes?'[37] Here we come to the crux of the matter: what significance does the king's sexual behaviour have for the legitimacy of the Stuart regime?

The Duke of York's betrayal of his own wife serves as evidence against the claim that King Charles was never married to Lucy Walters:

> Now we all know, not only with what Asservations the *D.* disclaimed his Marriage with *Mrs. Hide*, but with what reflexions upon her Chastity he did it. And yet the Proofs of the said Marriage were so evident, that he was necessitate at last to acknowledge it; and to own her for his Wife, after he had by himself, and many others, Proclaimed her for no better than a Common Whore. And I'm sure it left this Impression upon most Persons, That his Faith to Men was not very far to be relied on, seeing he made so slight of that Faith which he had plighted in an Ordinance of God to a harmless Lady.[38]

James Stuart's willingness to brand his own wife a 'Common Whore' renders him particularly odious and untrustworthy. Although many satiric works of the period characterized all the court women as whores, Ferguson recuperates Anne Hyde as a member of an abused English public against whom the Stuart brothers conspired. Ferguson uses her ability to represent both public and private interests to heighten the tone of indignation that characterizes his appeal to the nation. Anne Hyde was only 'a harmless Lady,' and her reputation deserves the public's protection. The Stuart brothers' private abuses speak to a personal corruption with far-reaching consequences, Ferguson implies, refashioning the court bedroom as a microcosm of the nation.

Ferguson objects to the Duke of York's insult not so much because it undermines the sanctity of the marriage vow as because it uses Anne Hyde's birth against her. Here we encounter the question of social status, important not only for determining the reputations of women like Anne Hyde and Lucy Walters, but also for measuring claims made by all members of the English public, especially with regard to possible future heirs to the throne. Ferguson counters charges that the king would not have married Lucy Walters because of her low birth by pointing to precedent: 'Whereas the Partisans of the *D. of Y.* would have it judged too great a reproach upon the King, that ever he should be thought to have married a person of so low a quality as *Madam Walters*; they do but in that discover at once their small acquaintance with History ... Your Lordship doth very well know, that *Edw. 4*, though actually in the Throne, and withal a Magnanimous and Victorious Prince; yet he Married an ordinary Gentlewoman.'[39] In the end, however, Ferguson aims less at proving that a marriage between Lucy Walters and Charles Stuart did take place in 1650 than that the claims of 'ordinary' gentlewomen and gentlemen ought to be upheld against exercises of royal prerogative: ''Tis of no great concernment, who is the immediate apparent Heir in the *Regal Line*, if we do but consider that the *Parliament of England* hath often provided a Successor to the Government, when the Interest of the Publick hath required it. ... Nor hath *Bastardy* it self been an Obstruction to the confering of the Crown upon a person, provided all things else have corresponded with the desires and Humours of the People.'[40] Legitimacy devolves, not through marriage laws, but through the will of the people, here figured in the ill-used Lucy Walters and Anne Hyde. In their abuses of these women the Stuart princes enact their neglect of a nation. Their singular desires, Ferguson argues, must be pitted against England's collective desire for a secure Protestant succession.

Two works by Whig polemicist William Lawrence, published together in 1680, broaden the import of the terms introduced by Ferguson's discussion of Lucy Walters. Both *Of the profound Popery of the Common Lawyers, in Transubstantiation of two persons into one person* and *Marriage by the Morall Law of God Vindicated* promote the Duke of Monmouth's claims to legitimacy by advancing a radical argument in support of divorce. Unlike Ferguson, who argues first for Lucy Walters's spousal rights, then for the rights of bastards (thereby hedging his bets in rather different discursive and legal registers), Lawrence undertakes a wholesale condemnation of marriage ceremonies and the laws that devolve from them. In particular, Lawrence uses the logic informing Protestant assaults on the doctrine of transubstantiation to attack the church's assertion that men and women become one flesh when they marry:

In like manner may be said of the foppery of Sacramental Transubstantiations of the Bread into the Body, or one Body into another, or making many persons in Society or Communion one person, because the Scripture calls them one Body, as it is said, I *Cor.* 10. 16 *The bread which we break, is it not the Communion of the Body of Christ? For we being many are one Bread, and one Body: for we are all partakers of that one Bread.* This is intended a figurative but not a natural Body; and it were very ridiculous to make allusions, conclusions or similitudes, to run on four Feet, or to say, Because all these Communicants being Men and Women are by the Scripture call'd one Body, Figurative or Politick: Therefore to conclude that they are one Body natural, and one Person natural ... I shall not dispute which is the greatest Absurdity of Transubstantiation, of Bread into Flesh in the Mass, or of the Flesh of a Woman into the Flesh of a Man in Marriage.[41]

As in Ferguson's account of the Black Box affair, Lawrence places emphasis on the interpretive moment; how we read scripture's language determines how we believe. Protestantism requires that we understand 'This is my body' as figurative rather than literal language. To understand it so renders language more, rather than less, transparent, by aligning it with the evidence of the senses. Given that this assertion serves as the mainstay of Protestant attacks on Catholic doctrine, Lawrence argues, Protestantism ought to renounce its marriage ceremonies, which replicate Catholicism's belief in transubstantiation by insisting that one entity stands before the priest after a marriage ceremony has been performed, despite ocular evidence to the contrary.

Lawrence goes on to suggest that sexual relations and consent constitute a marriage, and that marriages and divorces ought to be undertaken in private. According to this logic, all of the king's sons are legitimate heirs. In its desire to unite sons and fathers, the treatise upholds patriarchal privilege above all other claims. Nonetheless, a feminist polemic emerges alongside this assertion of patrilineal bonds when Lawrence argues explicitly that women always retain their right to the property they bring to marriage and the right to protect themselves against theft and assault by their husbands. Significantly, the prostitute stands as the example who proves Lawrence's point on this subject:

I shall not need to answer any place of Scripture making the Husband and the Wife but one Person: for there is not one word in the whole Scripture which affirms a Man and his Wife to be one person, or if it were, it must be a figurative and not a natural person. If it be objected, That they are called one Body, or one Flesh, I say the same words are said of an Harlot. I *Cor.* 6.16. *Know ye not that he which is joined to an Harlot is one Body?*

for two (saith he) *shall be one flesh.* Yet was never any Divine or Lawyer, I have met with, so absurd as to infer from hence, That the Harlot and her Mate are one person, or that they are transubstantiated into one another, but remain two distinct Substances as they were before; much less that the Harlot hath no property in her Goods, and that every Customer she hath may rob her Shop, take all her Goods, and beat her, and she have no Action or Remedy against him ... because he and she are in Scripture call'd one flesh.[42]

Separate bodies designate separate property lines, a fact that judges and divines grant prostitutes, at least theoretically, but not wives. Lawrence recognizes the imbrication of private and public identities that marriage involves, departing from his more famous Whig colleague, John Locke, whose treatises on individualism distinguish between men, who can champion their rights through their claims to property, and women, who, designated merely private persons, can only assume those rights – and their property – through their spouses.

Like Ferguson, Lawrence attacks aristocratic men's uses and abuses of common women: 'By the unquestionable law of God, if the greatest Peer lie with a Beggar, whom he may lawfully marry, and get her with Child, he lawfully makes her his Wife.'[43] While disavowing the idea of a transubstantiation of man and woman into one flesh, Lawrence upholds an alternative kind of transfiguration, whereby the miracle of birth transforms a man into a husband, regardless of his consent. The flesh, in other words, utters both the performative 'I do' and 'You do.' As Rachel Weil has pointed out, Lawrence never casts into doubt the legitimacy of women's claims regarding their children's paternity.[44] Here we find an alternative form of mingling word and flesh, one that refuses the royal oath – of innocence or marriage to a queen – as a safeguard against the metamorphosis of bastards into princes. Instead, we find the stories that circulate in public about those bastards, including the stories told by their mothers, granted legal authority and aligned with the will of the people:

And, my *Lord*, Is it not strange, if there was never any Marriage, that *Mrs. Walters* should not only when in travel with the said D. but at many other times, particularly in her last hours, when in the Prospect of approaching Death and ensuing Judgement, affirm it with that positiveness which she did? And is it not more surprising, if there had been no such Marriage, That *Dr. Fuller*, late *Bishop of Lincoln*, should so often, and in *Verbo Sacer-*

dotis, declare to divers worthy Persons, *That he married them.* Nay, What should byass the *Inkeeper* at *Liege* to make it the great Mystery with which he entertained his *English Guests, That the Marriage was cellebrated and consummated in his House, and that both he and his Wife were eye and ear Witnesses of it.*[45]

Ferguson's narrative provides a marriage plot that moves backward in time from the sanctity of Lucy Walters's death-bed vows to the eyewitness reports of a bishop and an innkeeper, creating an ever-expanding circle of storytelling that reaches out to encompass the nation in its rhetorical appeal. We have an indication, in this narrative moment, of how a stone like 'Protestant Whore' might later create a ripple in the narratives that contain it, one that moves outward from the private commitments it describes to the public identities both created and implicated in those contracts.

Ferguson and Lawrence wrote on behalf of the Duke of Monmouth, supporting Parliament's cause against the king, who was increasingly viewed with suspicion and hostility after the Exclusion Crisis of 1681. Their writings reflect concerns shared by many, if not all, members of an English public deeply connected to the political debates that evolved after 1660. If the harlot somewhat accidentally became the heroine of writings by polemicists like Lawrence and Ferguson, the literary imagination of the late Restoration period and its aftermath used this accident to foster its own ambitions.

Weil has perceptively commented on the difficulty of defining the contours of the relationship between Restoration libertine literature and political attacks on Charles II. Unlike France, where libertinism emerged as a form of religious and political critique, English authors did not use sexual libertinism 'as the basis for an antiabsolutist political stance.'[46] But the abjection associated with the label 'whore' maintained its polemical force in political pornography of the period, diminishing the appeal of Charles's libertinism while using all the sexual energies associated with the term to harness an effective critique of the Stuart regime.[47] The idea of Charles II as a monarch willing to prostitute his duty to his private appetites – primarily for sex and for excessive amounts of power – fuelled the inflammatory rhetoric of the Whore of Babylon in obscene literature of the period, which exploited the literalization of 'whore' to great satiric effect.[48] A poem addressed to the Duchess of Portsmouth outlines the threat to the nation posed by the king's flirtation with Catholicism and France:

You treach'rous Whore of France, may Rabble's rage
Seize thee, & not till thou'rt destroy'd aswage.
The People's Cross, misfortune, constant Pest,
The Milstone whelm'd upon this Nation's breast;
Brittain's impairer of her honour & Fame,
The Festring Soar of Majesty, the Shame
Of English Councils; the Crowns costly load,
And Prince's thriving Infamy abroad;
The Commons hater, & false France's Friend.
Lord, from this Basilisk Loyalty defend!
Permit a change, our ruins to confront,
Let us be govern'd by an English C–t;
The kingdom can't by whoring suffer want
If prince swives concubines that's Protestant.[49]

The French mistress brings to England all the misery conventionally associated with the prostitute's body – disease, shame, despair – and deserves the mob punishment routinely inflicted on brothels and their inhabitants. The religious allegory implies that vengeance wrought upon the courtesan will rid the nation of its cross, 'misfortune,' and restore 'honour & Fame' to the long-suffering nation. The poem's closing lines imagine an alternative to Charles II's French-infected rule, drawing on both the satiric and utopian literature of women's parliaments that appeared in the Interregnum and Restoration periods: 'Let us be governed by an English C–t.' Here English female rule, rooted firmly in the comfort of genital slang, replaces the diffuse 'Festring Soar' of a French, emasculated, Stuart regime. Were Charles II to swive 'concubines that's Protestant,' rather than a Catholic mistress, he would bear less of a resemblance to a whore himself, these lines most simply suggest. But in a more sinister register, the lines' easy slide between allusive references imply that the monarch and Portsmouth may be indistinguishable, two sides of the same French coin.[50]

In the last fifteen years of Charles II's reign, the Duchess of Portsmouth presided over court affairs both symbolically and practically. Nancy Klein Maguire has argued convincingly for the importance of Louise de Kéroualle as a political actor, noting that while historians have paid scant attention to Charles II's favourite mistress, 'Portsmouth's own contemporaries could not afford to ignore her.'[51] Over the course of her reign at court, Portsmouth effectively established an English version of the French office of *maîtresse-en-titre*, controlling courtiers' access to the king and presiding over key patronage appointments while serving as a spy and negotiator for Louis XIV. The articles for treason drawn up against Portsmouth in 1680 detail, from inside English court and parliamentary circles, how Portsmouth was perceived as a political operator and an enemy of the Protestant religion (almost all of the twenty-two articles come back to this theme). Of particular interest to us is the representation of Portsmouth as mother to the king's son:

> XX. That she has by her creatures and friends given ont [*sic*] and whispered abroad, that she was married to His Majesty, and that her Son the Duke of *Richmond* is His Majesties Legitimate Son, and consequently, Prince of *Wales* ... to that great dishonour and reflection of His Majestys and the manifest peril and danger of these Kingdoms, who may hereafter by such false and scandalous Storys and wicked practises be embroyled in distractions if not in Bloud and Civil Wars, to the utter ruine of His Majesties Subjects, and subversion of the Protestant Religion, it being manifest, she being a *Papist* her self, will breed her Son in the same Religion however she may pretend to the contrary.[52]

Unlike the Lucy Walters of Ferguson's tracts, as well as the anonymous commoners of Lawrence's polemics, Portsmouth, as a mother, acts as her own worst enemy in the unfolding public relations war. The family drama plays out not as female innocence pitted against royal libertinism, but as political and religious subversion bred in the Catholic whore's corrupt body. Religion passes 'naturally' from mother to son, and Portsmouth's claims to the contrary only highlight her hypocrisy.

Portsmouth wielded considerable influence, but the representations that vilify her take on additional weight by melding together portraits of several important mistresses of the period. Before Portsmouth there was Barbara Villiers, Duchess of Cleveland, Catholic convert and the subject of the satiric *Whores Petition* in the aftermath of the Bawdyhouse Riots in 1668. As one of the period's most notorious female libertines, Villiers did not restrict herself to betraying English dreams of Protestant renewal, as the 1663 portrait that now hangs in the National Portrait Gallery suggests (figure 2). In this portrait Villiers poses as Mary with the infant Jesus (Charles Fitzroy, son of Charles II), mocking Catholicism's veneration of the Virgin Mother by placing a courtesan in her place. In the 1680s, Hortense Mancini, Duchess of Mazarin, entered into the mix as a powerful patron of the arts and promoter of French culture. Within this context, Portsmouth comes to symbolize the political authority of a group of women whose associations with the most feared elements of the Stuart regime – its Catholicism and ties to France – created a vision of monstrosity and threat summed up in the idea of an emasculating virago.

Because she was a royal mistress, and therefore capable of distracting the king from his political obligations, Nell Gwyn was viewed as a member of this group – 'his Cleavelands, his Nells and his Carwells' – although, as we shall see, she also came to represent its opposition party.[53] James Turner claims that Gwyn and Portsmouth function as 'an indispensible pair, defining two kinds of contaminating Other' in satiric and pornographic literature of the period and, indeed, understanding the weight that the term 'Protestant Whore' came to bear requires an acknowledgment of the darkness this icon contained within it.[54] The fears surrounding Nell Gwyn appear writ large in a Richard Tompson engraving that circulated in the period (figure 3). Here Gwyn appears as Cupid, her arrow pointing to the seat of power in a nation ruled by a monarch addicted to women. The hermaphroditic image suggests what power reversals occur when monarchs relinquish authority to their mistresses: 'Showing that she is herself capable of full sexual penetration, the female Cupid nevertheless threatens to reduce her potential lover to the level of a passive catamite,'[55] Clive Hart and Kay Gilliland Stevenson observe. Not only has Gwyn inappropriately claimed the king's sceptre for herself, that is, but she threatens to turn it back against the king, reducing him to a level below both men and women, a place reserved, within the Restoration sexual economy, for Rochester's infamous 'sweet, soft Page.'[56]

Like Portsmouth, Nell Gwyn serves as a starting point for many of the attacks on the king's abdication of his responsibilities:

How poorly squander'st thou thy seed away,
Which should get Kings for nations to obey,
But thou, poor Prince, so uselessly hast sown it,
That the Creation is ashamed to own it:
Witness the Royal Line sprung from the Belly
Of the Anointed Princess, Madam Nelly:
...
Look back, & see the People Mad with Rage,
To see the Bitch in so high Equipage;
And every day they do the Monster See,
They let Ten Thousand Curses fly at thee.[57]

Charles's refusal to honour the conventions of monarchy implicate him in the social disruption figured in the rise of Nell Gwyn from pit to royal bed, an ascent that unleashed real violence when the king's men attacked Sir John Coventry, the people's representative, on behalf of Nell Gwyn:

> If the sister of Rose,
> Be a whore so anointed
> That the Parliament's nose,
> Must for her be disjointed,
> Should you but name the prerogative whore [the Duchess of Cleveland],
> How the bullets would whistle, the canon would roar![58]

That the Duke of Monmouth ordered the attack in his capacity as captain of the King's Life Guard of Horse intensified the disruption Nell Gwyn represented, extending it into the future with the introduction of violent bastards into the House of Lords:

> Thrice happy Nell that had'st a King so gracious
> To poke for Princes in thy Dust & Ashes
> And well done Charles when thou can'st get no Heirs
> To stock thy Peerage with St. Martin's Peers.[59]

As we have seen, that princes were appearing where they ought not to have became an issue of enormous import in the years following the Exclusion Crisis. The idea that attention to a mistress and her children encourages neglect of the nation – the monarch's rightful heir – appears over and over again in literature of the period: 'Nell's in again, we hear, though we are out. / Methinks we might have met to give a clout [diaper].'[60]

As the years passed, this idea encompassed increasingly more symbolic territory, as both Gwyn and Portsmouth served as particular instances of the monarch's moral and political bankruptcy:

> From *Those* that like the *Spider* spin,
> And also think they have no *Sin*:
> From *Chastity* in *Orange-GWYN*,
> And bloody *Bonners* of Squire THYN,
>   *Libera nos*, &c.
> From all upon a *Papal Bench*,

With all the *Masquerading French:*
And also from that Foreign WENCH,
Who leaves behind her such a Stench,
    Libera nos, &c.[61]

Here the language of moral reversal that also governed more conventional descriptions of the nation's degeneration tells a familiar story: lewdness overtakes chastity and corruption replaces justice in the narratives of decline set in motion by the monarchy. We find the admonishment seen in *A Preparation for Martyrdom* – 'Adultery hath not only taken the *place*, but Usurps also the *Title* of *Marriage*' – rehearsed in the cheerful satire that imagines a dialogue between Portsmouth and Gwyn:

> [Gwyn:] Marry! bless me at these years, to whom? for what? what would be the effect of Marraiage [*sic*]? ... I am not so old but I can Skip to *Newmarket* as nimbly as the youngest lass in *Town* and whilst any Royal sport is stirring hope to come in for a snack.
> *Whilst any thing is stirring for the Belly,*
> *The best [in the]Land will give a piece to Nelly,*
> *And comfort her old age with Royal jelly.*[62]

Gwyn's ability to claim the king's attention whenever she pleases, and at whatever moral, economic, and political cost, confirms the fear of female rule that underpins these representations. 'I wholly will abandon State affaires,' the king vows as he assumes the throne in a satire of the period, 'And pass my time with Parrasites and Players, / And visit Nell when I should be at Prayers.'[63] That Nell was not as expensive, in any register, as the Duchess of Portsmouth or her predecessor, the Duchess of Cleveland, did not exempt her from the general condemnation of the royal mistress as an institution.[64]

And yet even the representations critical of Gwyn as the 'dunghill wench'[65] anticipate the emergence of an icon capable of drawing together sexuality, religion, and politics in potentially restorative ways. Over the course of two decades, Gwyn evolved into a Protestant vaginal antidote to the Catholic distemper lodged in Portsmouth's 'pocky bum.'[66] The public's admiration of Gwyn appears evident in sources as different as Pepys's diary entries in the 1660s and newspaper accounts of 1681, which follow her journey to Oxford: 'Madam *Gwyn* was very liberal to the Ringers and Poor all the Road, and especially at *Beconsfiedl* [*sic*] and *Wickam*, where she distributed much money'; 'Madam *Gwyn* has been very liberal here [in Oxford] upon all occasions, and out of her charitable inclinations, has released three Prisoners for Debt out of the Castle, and Two out of *Bocardo*.'[67] The same newspaper, by contrast, implicates the Duchess of Portsmouth and the Duchess of Mazarin in the Rye House Plot. Dryden anticipated, and helped to produce, Gwyn's celebrity in the early days of her career as Charles II's mistress. In the mock-eulogy, spoken by Gwyn herself, written into the epilogue to *Tyrannick Love, or the Royal Martyr*, he plays on the conflation of actress and 'princess' that the office of royal mistress enabled, as well as Gwyn's willingness to brand herself 'whore': 'Here *Nelly* lies, who though she liv'd a Slater'n, / Yet dy'd a Princess, acting in S. *Cathar'n*.'[68]

The mock-competitions that contrasted the powers of Gwyn and Portsmouth often focussed their attention on Gwyn's sexual ascendency:

> Long days of absence, dear, I could endure,
> If thy divided heart were mine secure;
> But each minute I find myself without thee,
> Methinks I find my rival's arms about thee.
> She perhaps her interest may improve
> By all the studied arts of fraud and love;
> Whilst I, a poor, kind, harmless creature,
> A plain true passion show and trust good nature.
> In her white hand let thy gold sceptre shine,
> And what I must not name be put in mine.
> Crowned and in purple robes to her I'll fling thee,
> But naked every night let Nell unking thee.[69]

While the poem sustains the usual criticism of the king's willingness to abdicate political responsibility and his mistress's role in this abdication (both Portsmouth's ambition and Nell's nakedness 'unking' the monarch), these lines also situate Nell in the register of the more purely sexual adventure, outside of the scheming world of court politics in which Charles II and Portsmouth blend together as an ambiguous unit of power.[70] This separation of Gwyn from the political fracas of the day emphasizes her commitment to whoring as a career. Nell Gwyn comes to represent the courtesan whose sexuality renders her impervious to political corruption, a court agent whose integrity the nation might trust because of, not despite, her sexual character:

Hard by Pell-mell lives a Wench called Nell.
King Charles the Second he kept her;
She hath got a trick to handle his p—,
But never lays hands on his sceptre;
All matters of state from her soul she does hate,
  And leave to the politic bitches.
The whore's in the right, for 'tis her delight
To be scratching just where it itches.[71]

Mme de Sévigné reconstructs Nell Gwyn's objection to the social pretensions of Louise de Kéroualle in a letter of 1675: '"If she be a lady of
such quality, why has she become a whore? She ought to die of shame.
As for me, it is my profession. I don't pretend I'm anything else."'[72]
Because of the clarity of focus that allows her to scratch 'just where it
itches,' Gwyn is able to claim a superior moral standpoint to that of
the Catholic courtesan, who uses her sexuality for social and political
advancement alone.

The idea of Nell Gwyn's work ethic appears in several lyrics of the
period:

This to evince, it were too long to tell ye,
The painful trick of his laborious Nelly –
While she employs hands, fingers, lips, and thighs
To raise the limb which she each night enjoys.[73]

'Nelly' focuses her attention on the king only in order to grant him sexual pleasure and herself an honest livelihood, not in order to insinuate
herself in his political life. Gwyn's public display of her sexuality, that
is, her professionalism, renders her sexuality less, rather than more,
threatening. It is the secrecy of the Catholic mistresses' intentions that
transforms their sexual activities into treasonous engagements with the
king. By emptying out her sexuality of all but its bodily performances,
Nell becomes, paradoxically, less dangerously embodied, a suitable ci-
pher of public admiration.

The story of Nell Gwyn's Oxford pronouncement in 1681 draws on a
history of association between Nell Gwyn and Protestant integrity, an-
chored in the body of a whore whose Englishness provides the mark of
authenticity. Harold Love identifies an explicit reference to Nell Gwyn
as the 'Protestant Whore' in an anonymous satire, 'A satyr upon the
mistresses,' datable to 1678: 'The Protestant Whore I cannot here leave

out; / Fam'd for not wearing of the double Clout.'[74] In *A Pleasant Battle Between Two Lap Dogs of the Utopian Court*, the royal bitches substantiate this point:

> Snap-short [Portsmouth's dog]: Ha, good *Tutty*, rather than my Lady should be ruined, I will perswade her to turn Protestant too, I am confident she will do anything to serve her own Interest.

> Tutty [Gwyn's dog]: But *Snapshort* let me tell you that a *French* Whore will never make a good Protestant Lady, for if she should turn Protestant, and make a Whore of Religion, as she has of her Body, the whole World will set a mark upon her for a notorious murtherer both of Religion, Honesty, and common Reason.[75]

'Religion, Honesty, and common Reason' accrue to Nell Gwyn's 'natural' Protestantism and her lack of 'interest' renders her the repository for one form of religious integrity.[76] As I have argued, the dream that England could rid itself of its problems with the banishment of Catholic interlopers – 'now the Protestants cry out, blessed be God our Plague is removed!' – only partially addressed the nation's anxieties about the state of its national faith.[77] A more positive champion of Protestant renewal needed to emerge, and Gwyn, however unlikely a heroine, came to fit the bill.

Gwyn's status as an icon whose popularity matched that of the would-be Protestant king, the Duke of Monmouth, produced a competition between 'the Protestant Whore' and 'the Protestant Duke' in poems of the period:

> She's now the darling strumpet of the crowd,
> Forgets her state, and talks to them aloud;
> Lays by her greatness and descends to prate
> With those 'bove whom she's rais'd by wond'rous fate.
> True to the Protestant interest and cause,
> True to th'established government and laws;
> The choice delight of the whole mobile,
> Scarce Monmouth's self is more belov'd than she.
> Was this the cause that did their quarrel move,
> That both are rivals in the people's love?
> No, 'twas her matchless loyalty alone
> That bid Prince Perkin pack up and be gone:

'Ill-bred thou art,' says Prince. Nell does reply,
'Was Mrs. Barlow better bred than I?'
Thus sneak'd away the nephew overcome,
By aunt-in-law's severer wit struck dumb.[78]

In the notes to this satire, Elias F. Mengel, Jr. states, 'I can find no evidence of a quarrel between Monmouth and Nell.'[79] But the poem does not need to document an actual historical breach between Gwyn and Monmouth, because it more simply recognizes that the two figures are rivals for the English public's attention. True to the 'Protestant Cause' understood in the most general sense, Gwyn is first and foremost loyal to Charles II and her loyalty to the monarch, in the final instance, sets her against his son. The tone of the poem is sarcastic, as is 'The Ladies March,' which describes Gwyn as 'A saint to be admired the more / Because a Church of England's whore,' but in both cases, the satire documents the courtesan's popularity as a figure connected to both the people's interests and the king's.[80] The Duke of Monmouth, as a representation, is confronted with Gwyn's ability to represent both loyalty and Protestantism, however nominal, simultaneously. Amidst the dangerous titles of the 'True Protestant,' 'the Protestant Joyner,' and 'the Protestant Duke,' 'the Protestant Whore' emerges as a refuge, and not because the woman wearing the title was innocuous by virtue of her sex and occupation.[81] Gwyn provided the fiction of a loyalty that could serve a national cause; she represents the difference between affiliation and obsession. (And indeed, her will bequeathed what little money her estate left to Catholics impoverished by English laws.) Gwyn's Protestantism, perhaps *because* nominal, became substantial enough a point of identification so that no less a figure than Dr Tenison of St Martin-in-the-Fields preached her funeral sermon.[82]

'A great pretender to Religion': From Nell Gwyn to Protestant Whore

Different genres produce a spectrum of courtesan representations. The power the courtesan exercises as a spectacle, for example, is best displayed by dramatic performance. Poetry heightens her erotic charge through the compressions of metaphor and metonymy. The expansiveness of prose fiction allows its practitioners to weave the courtesan's story together with threads taken from other prose traditions: the moral seriousness of sermon jeremiads, for example, and the chicanery of plots circulated by Tory and Whig propagandists. *L'Escole des Filles*, translated into English in 1680 as *The School of Venus*, fantasizes a world in which women rule both world and church, indulging as a pornographic dream the nightmare evoked, in England, around the figure of the Duchess of Cleveland in the *Whores Petition* of the late 1660s. In the closing years of Charles II's reign, English writers, inspired by their French contemporaries and preoccupied with the royal consorts' power and the legacy of Puritan women's political activism in the Interregnum period, turned to narrative repeatedly to explore the dynamic tension between sexual, church, and state politics.[83] *The Whore's Rhetorick* (1683) and *The Parliament of Women: Or, a Compleat History of the Proceedings and Debates, of a Particular Junto ... with a Design to Alter the Government of the World* (1684) take the sexual misconduct of women as their starting point, figuring England's political crises as the product of anarchic women willing to sell what they should not. But if the representations in these narratives start out as a form of misogynous humour aimed at reducing, rather than legitimizing, women's claims to authority, they take on a more complex cast as the works unfold, to the point where the satiric thrust of the works gives way to a more generalized scepticism about the operations of power in Restoration England.[84] The illicit woman embodies this sceptical principle, I claim, and she anticipates the Protestant Whore's evolution as a literary figure capable of transmuting Nell Gwyn's various significations into a more abstract interrogatory mode. The Protestant Whore acts outside the conventions of church and state, but not, as the real royal mistress did, simply by flouting those strictures. Instead, she sets a standard of her own, exercising a mode of self-governance in her imaginative acts.

The young heroine of *The Whore's Rhetorick*, Dorothea, faces imminent descent into whoredom as a direct result of Charles II's licentiousness. The king's mistress has consumed the portion that should have been bestowed on the girl's father, a royalist seeking compensation for loyalty and services rendered after the Restoration: 'from him [Charles II] he found a reception full of mercy, goodness, and generosity, even like the Fountain from whence it flowed: but there casually happened a fair *Danae* in the way, that received some part of the Golden Shower, and intercepted for some time the rays of that sacred influence.'[85] At the other end of the political spectrum, the Puritans appear as eager citizens of the infamous bawd Cresswell's 'amorous Republick' even as they imagine themselves 'the Elect, the Children of Adoption, who believe they cannot fall' (26). Their private hypocrisy mirrors their political dishonesty: 'What the World calls rebellion, is in them taking the Sword out of the hands of the Mighty; and the Plunder, Rapine, and Sequestration are in the Saints only, civil ways of Borrowing as the *Israelites* did from the *Egyptians*' (148). Equally bankrupt of authority, court and city incite the carnage of moral ruin.

The Parliament of Women similarly indicts male rule: 'We find how that under the Reigns of Men your Monarchs are nothing but wars and destructions: the Divines are at daggers drawing with the Divines; the Philosophers at Mortal Enmity with the Philosophers; nothing but confusion in the World.'[86] The women's condemnation of masculine imperatives takes us back directly to the radical politics of William Lawrence in its identification of the link between private and public forms of tyranny. Just as Lawrence challenged English marriage laws' ability to strip women of their legal identities, the satire's women disavow their status as men's property:

'Tis very true that while men had the Reines and Bridle of Government in their own hands, they have all along endeavour'd to impale the Female Sex to themselves, and by Matrimony and custom to make marry'd Women their particular Properties, as if they had an absolute power of disposing of Women as they pleas'd, and that they were their own as their Gloves and their Canes; or else by a kind of Pye-corner Law. This chump of Beef is mine because I have put a Scewer into it. (126)

The parliament's attack on matrimony extends to a critique of adultery and legitimacy laws, again echoing the kinds of argument made by William Lawrence and other polemicists of the period: 'Adultry [*sic*] can never be committed where no Property can be claimed ... A Woman may have as many Fathers for one Child as she pleases, since the Birth alwaies follow'd the Belly, nor was it an Acorn matter, who was the Father' (132–3). Even as the satirist mocks the women's efforts to free themselves from the conventions governing marriage and maternity, the proximity of their ideas to those circulating within mainstream political philosophies of the period gives an edge to their proclamations, allowing them to cut against the grain of the satire's ostensibly conservative plank.

In its satiric advocacy of restraint and the quiet pursuit of profit, *The Whore's Rhetorick* grants the courtesan the power to shape public affairs while remaining detached from their investments: 'I have, as it is well known,' Cresswell tells Dorothea, 'made it my business to quell all insurrections, appease all unlawful emotions, to keep the Kings peace, both by Night and by Day: and to satisfie all men according to their several exigencies' (62). But as much as Cresswell idealizes the whore's space as free from political strife, we know the bawd's career has gained prestige from its association with London's most powerful men: 'I have at this day some worthy and eminent Debtors, who have been the Kings Lieutenants, Lord Mayors, and Sheriffs of the City of *London*' (29). Rather than presiding over politics as the royal mistress, hand-maiden to the king's desire, the whore serves her own interest in her capacity as spy. These powers of observation in turn serve the fiction-making that goes on in the boudoir, which allows the whore to delight her client 'with a real, or at least an imaginary pleasure' in the tales she narrates (165). Presumably these tales are primarily pornographic, but Cresswell intimates that pillow-talk also includes more worldly news in its stimulation of sexual appetite. Both knowing and detached, the whore circulates among the populace, gathering information – sexual *and* political – that will produce a narrative capable of inciting desire in its rehearsal. Remarking on Charles II's – and his sons' – propensity for London's whores, Dorothea notes that 'it is an intrigue might afford matter for a Novel, which would in part take off the scandal of translat-ing daily such numbers of *French* ones, that are in my mind, fitter for the necessary House than the Closet' (182). An English tradition emerges out of the whore's narrative, one capable of providing a new vantage point from which to view the workings of power.[87]

'Interest is the subject of this art,' Cresswell declares (39–40), but so integral is the relation between the two that Creswell could as eas-ily announce, 'Art is the subject of this interest.' Over and over again, the whore's artifice appears as a species of fiction, the rendering of a pleasing narrative that will ensure client loyalty. Purged of all linger-ing traces of 'what the World calls vertue' (181), the whore becomes a character as empty as type-face, but also an author whose imagination spawns multiple narratives and identities: 'Invention is principally necessary in this Art, to frame new pretexts, and a diversity of expres-sions, with reference to the circumstances of person, time, and place: and to impose probabilities, or even things utterly false, as certain, and true ... Your whole life must be one continued act of dissimulation' (39–40). Anticipating Locke's *Essay*, *The Whore's Rhetorick* stresses the func-tion of memory in the creation of the persona the whore presents to the world: 'A good memory is requisite to avoid contradictions, and those inconveniences, the repetition of the same frauds and artifices would infallibly produce'; 'In as much as all her discourses in conformity to her manners, are a medley of lyes and fictions; it is requisite she should have a faithful remembrance to hinder tripping and contradiction' (39, 160).[88] The whore's memory bears no resemblance to the larger capacity that creates interiority in Locke's theory, but rather takes on a functional property as 'an artificial ready remembrance,' its powers associated with the organization and dissemination of details crucial to the maintenance of the whore's mask and her seduction narrative (164).

In *The Parliament of Women*, artifice stands as the principle of right rule. Women have proven themselves 'the greatest dissemblers in the World, and it is a Maxim, that they who cannot tell how to dissemble, can never tell how to Govern; it follows then than they who can best dissemble are most fit to rule' (50). It also follows that art, in this utopia, might replace war as a national preoccupation:

> I bless myself to consider, were our Noble Sex restor'd to that Right which nature has bestow'd upon it, what quiet and serenity the Common-weal would enjoy, there would be no Room for Factions and Underminings, but all things would flow into Liberty and pleasure; Instead of raking every Corner of the land for Armies, there would be nothing but preparing for Masques, and Amorous Appointments, Men should then follow their Handy Crafts. (53)

'Liberty' evolves through the exercise of appetite within the conventions of art, which in turn provides the space for entertaining alternative political scenarios to 'Factions and Underminings.' And while the author uses the triviality of masques, intrigues, and handy crafts to undermine the legitimacy of women's activities here and to satirize the women's claim that 'if the Reins of Government were delivered into our hands, it would go much better with the world then it does' (7), elsewhere the stories that women tell of female rule offer a more serious vision of what happens when the female imagination encompasses ideas of political reform:

> This Great *Moguls* Mistress commanded him to let her have the full and absolute Rule and Government of the whole Empire, for four and twenty hours ... She turn'd out all the Emperors evil Ministers, put wise and Able in their Places, she cut off all her Enemies, she built five hundred Almes-Houses in several parts of the Empire for the Relief of the poor ... and the

story tells ye farther that she did more good in that four and twenty hours
then in all the Raigns of ten *Moguls* before. (65)

Women's storytelling, in this narrative moment, takes on the full import of sustaining an alternative to the destructive political regimes in
which the women live.

Both *The Whore's Rhetorick* and *The Parliament of Women* stress the literary aspect of women's proximity to fiction-making in their meditations on the types of reading women take up as children and adults.
The Parliament of Women describes the boarding schools where girls discover the pleasures of *L'Escole des Filles* and Aloisia Sigea: 'it is not for
nothing Latin is call'd the *Language* of the *Whore* ... I lost my Virginity
with only hearing it read – And I am perswaded that were it translated there would not be a Virgin in the Town, by that time a Girl had
read her Primmer out' (31–2).[89] *The Whore's Rhetorick*'s Dorothea is well-
versed, despite her self-presentation as ingenue, in Restoration come-
dies. While encouraged to draw on the language of the French romance
tradition – 'from those Romantick Ladies [thou] mayest say something
more heroine and gallant than I can at present suggest' (66) – Dorothea
is warned against its excesses. Echoing Robert Ferguson's attack on the
mystifications of romance, Cresswell steers her young charge clear of
from representations of emotional states as a lure that could draw Dorothea away from more pragmatic realities: 'I am against your reading
Romances, where constancy in love is cryed up as a vertue, and dying
Lovers make up a great part in the Pageantry' (150).[90]

How do these questions of whoring, politics, and fiction-making return us to the institutional crises facing England's religious community
in the 1680s? 'We shall wont dissembling Females to deal with Male
Hypocrites', *The Parliament of Women* announces (33), anticipating the
religious scepticism, and its gendering, that came to characterize the
Protestant Whore. 'I am as ready once more to offer up my Bodkin and
Thimble to the support of this glorious Cause, as ever I gave them formerly to the *Publick Faith*,' the Lady Speaker tells a cheering assembly
(11). Their willingness to donate silver to support the cause (as did the
women of civil war London) aligns these women with the rebellious
impulses of the Puritans. But the text as a whole more profoundly registers a disenchantment with all forms of religious orthodoxy: 'Quo the
Lady *Voluble*, why such a deal of stir about Religion? The less we have,
the better – 'tis that which still sets the men together by the Ears, and
alwaies had done ever since there was ever Religion in the World; and

therefore, said she, we have but little Reason to be so fond of Religion – a little of that will go a great way – we Women are not so sharp upon cutting one anothers throats' (108–9). The morally dubious idea of religion as merely 'outward ornament' appears preferable to the violence spawned by the kinds of commitments claimed by Puritans and Royalists alike. The 'liberty in Spirituals' advocated by Lady Voluble echoes the call for a 'publick temper of mind' we encountered earlier in this chapter, the dream of an alliance that could enable England to avoid both civil war and a French invasion.

The Whore's Rhetorick integrates religion into its larger masquerade: 'You must not be unprovided of the *Whole Duty of Man*, *Practice of Piety*, and such like helps to Devotion; as having been from the beginning a great pretender to Religion' (63). Religious conviction serves as one fiction of interiority among many, including that of 'immoderate passion' (65). The whore engages them only to win the prize of financial security. The broader satire sustained by the text, however, suggests a similar insincerity among the clergy for whom personal conviction stands as the guiding principle of a religious life. Cresswell dwells at length on the lessons to be learned from 'the gifted Preacher':

DOR. What is that?

M.C. That is one inspired with a double portion of the Spirit of hypocrisie, one who hath served seven years to the Trade of Gerning, putting on a starched countenance, an edifying look, and the white innocence of a Soul-saving eye. (186)

The preacher's success, like the whore's, depends on producing the idea of interiority for an audience through the manipulation of signs that remain both recognizable and repeatable even as they create the illusion of a uniquely individual and spontaneous desire: of the preacher's for God, of the whore's for her client of the moment. That the preacher often *is* the whore's client deepens the sense that only self-deception – on the side of the minister – differentiates the two professions.

Explicitly drawing on the association between sexual and religious practices, Cresswell characterizes the whore's client as 'the hypocritical and the cowardly Lover, him that thinks to cheat the eyes of Heaven, as well as those of the World' in the 'dark Conventicles' of the bawdy-house's rooms (75). Through the panopticon of the whore's perspective, the client, who imagines he has purchased a deeply private moment, is relentlessly exposed. Casuistry, in other words, is challenged by a world in which an ethical standard remains in place (for the bawd does not refute the presence of heaven's gaze) but operates as a formal principle rather than a moral content.

Cresswell advises Dorothea to hang pornographic images around her room, as 'all Men are of a Romish perswasion; in as much as their devotion at the Shrine of *Venus* is extreamly enlivened by the prospect of a naked Saint' (170). By contrast, whores are 'of a *Geneva* stamp, all militant, but mortal enemies to that Bugbear, called *Passive Obedience*' (171). The statement establishes an interesting contrast between Protestantism as part of England's political program, which allows Anglican clergy to accommodate the Catholic leanings of the Stuarts by adopting the stance of passive obedience, and a more anarchic Protestantism that maintains its radical, anti-authoritarian roots. Dorothea asks Cresswell if the Protestant narratives regarding England's fall from grace accurately reveal the state of the nation in the 1680s: 'You think ... there is no difference between the wickedness practised nowadays, and the honest sincerity of our Fore-Fathers so much talked of?' (206–7). Cresswell responds with a relativist's perspective – 'I believe that Vertue and Vice are at all times both triumphant in the World, though not in the same place or region' – while conceding that in Restoration England 'the Fops are a degree more exquisite, and the Ladies a thought more tender-hearted than they were in King *Edgar's* days' (208). Instead of dwelling on the question of sinfulness Dorothea's questions raise, Cresswell recasts the jeremiad's moral lament as a story about the origins of fiction. Dorothea understands Ovid's representation of Astrea's flight from earth and the resulting 'rapine and oppression' as an allegory of the world's decline (208). In response to this reading, Cresswell asserts that 'it is possible the Poet was induced to tell the World of Astrea's flight, in that he found all the dispensations of Fortune so partial and unjust: he thought it was no eaven hand that intailed poverty on him and all his fraternity, whereas those he called dull and insipid (I take it for granted there were Lawyers and Aldermen in those days) could lead the World in a String' (208–9). Narrative serves as an antidote to the machinations of civic leaders, the place where an insistence on vice can pit the poets against the 'dull and insipid' statesmen's claims of civil benevolence in the face of the social inequalities that leave writers poor. In contemporary England, however, it is the 'dull and insipid' clergymen who write the jeremiads. Cresswell's comment enables a distinction between different kinds of stories about vice. Because the courtesan stands outside social convention, her authorial acts, like Ovid's, incite stories of vice as a mode of fictional pleasure and professional advancement. Cresswell uses the example of Ovid to advocate storytelling *as* storytelling, as artifice whose truthfulness resides somewhere other than in the moral absolutes it sustains.

When we recall the Dissenter's denunciation of the Anglican minister – 'certainly his ways of Discourse are like those of the Whorish Woman in the Proverbs, so moveable, one cannot know them' (p. 24 above) – we recognize the whore's corruption, here signalled by her abuse of language, as the key to the author's attack. *The Whore's Rhetorick* and *The Parliament of Women* draw on this understanding of the whore's pathology when they satirize England's political and religious degeneration as 'whorish.' But in the final instance the authors seem more interested in pitting their transgressive women against the whorish status quo than aligning them with it, recognizing the narrative opportunities afforded by the audacity of a female bid for power. Even the specific satirizations of women's claims to social and political authority that the works represent give way to a more general identification between illicit female speech and the modes of authorship the works advocate. The whore's scepticism establishes a concrete sense of the distance between the authors of these underground texts and the patrons of both court and city interests. It also links the authors to the French seventeenth-century libertine tradition and its rebellion against religious authority, to which I will return in my consideration of Aphra Behn's *Love-Letters* in the next chapter.

The Restoration's religious controversies reveal the deep divisions and conflicts that eroded confidence in England's ability to secure a Protestant hegemony capable of carrying the nation into its future. Royal mistress iconography highlights the role played by the courtesan in the sexual drama that unfolded over the reign of Charles II. Restoration satire shows how the period's narrative traditions shaped the reading public's understanding not only of the political crises at hand, but also of literature's role in responding to those crises. The chapters that follow argue that these three systems of meaning together made a profound contribution to the evolution of the English novel. In the figure of the Protestant Whore, the courtesan is transformed into a literary subject capable of carrying the symbolic weight – political, sexual, and religious – of the Restoration. Nell Gwyn's Protestantism set her apart from Charles's Catholic mistresses even while allowing an English encounter with them, a way of knowing the Catholic sensibility lurking at the heart of court circles. Unlike the Puritan hero of spiritual autobiography who disavows corruption by attempting to escape the world altogether, the Protestant Whore remains connected to England by sleeping with its leaders, commenting on its history as it unfolds, and sustaining a political perspective that neither renunciation nor attachment can afford.

2 'No Neuters in Treason': Aphra Behn's *Love-Letters between a Nobleman and His Sister*

There are no Neuters in Treason, as there are no luke-warm persons in Heaven.

Nicholas Adee, *A Plot for the Crown* (1685)

Mr. Just. *Jones.* You are, Madam, to answer only such Question[s] as are asked you pertinent to the Issue that the Jury are to try, and if the Counsel will ask you no Questions, you are not to tell any Story of your self.

The Trial of Ford, Lord Grey of Werk (1716)

Aphra Behn's status as a court operator and observer provided England's first professional woman author with a unique vantage point from which to recognize the narrative potential of courtesan iconography. *Love-Letters between a Nobleman and His Sister*, first published in three installments (1684, 1685, 1687), writes a courtesan narrative that contemplates the political ramifications of religious conviction and the role that sexual knowledge plays in the shaping of national history. As a royalist, Behn seeks to maintain the status quo, and the novel's sharpest dart directs itself at the heart of James Scott, Duke of Monmouth (the 'Protestant Duke') and his failed rebellion of 1685. But its satiric particularity, like that of *The Whore's Rhetorick* and *The Parliament of Women*, gives way to a more pervasive scepticism regarding the operations of power in late seventeenth-century England. Behn's refusal of the Duke of Monmouth's Protestant triumphalism becomes part of a larger interrogation of the dangers that attend a court and a public that refuse to direct their gazes outward toward a broader understanding of community and culture.

As a personality, Nell Gwyn does not serve as a model for Behn's

Silvia, although each of the women's stories neatly inverts the other's: Gwyn began as an orange girl and lover to several men and finished her career as a royal courtesan, while Silvia is born into aristocratic privilege and spends a period of her youth as a peripatetic mistress to various members of Europe's aristocracy. Silvia's characterization does draw, however, on the kinds of desires attributed to all of the Stuart mistresses, and, as Janet Todd has noted, on the portrait of the prostitute drawn by *The Whore's Rhetorick*.[1] In particular, it highlights the vision of political and personal independence that Restoration representations of Nell Gwyn sustain, one that Behn deepens through her representation of an authorial persona that actively distances itself from male aristocratic privilege. In maintaining this distance, Behn both exploits and inverts the period's political and religious epistemologies, which render explicit the idea of treason as social contagion: 'No man will trust a Traitor ... Sedition is one of the works of the Flesh, a sin that keeps a man out of Heaven without Repentance.'[2] Like *The Whore's Rhetorick*, Behn's courtesan narrative describes the desire that fuels political ambition and religious zealotry and sets its ability to enslave both individuals and nations against the whore's disinterestedness. The courtesan stands as the sign of detachment and her negotiations with the world demonstrate an ability to pursue power without stooping to mania or treason.

In designating the novel's heroine a Protestant Whore, I also draw attention to the way that 'whore' unites the different political, socio-economic, and literary registers in which the novel dwells, in order to show how representations of courtesans engaged larger cultural debates. For instance: historically, both Henrietta Berkeley's and her sister's extra-marital affairs were exploited by Tory propaganda as a species of 'whoredom.' Behn uses this association to explore the difference between political and sexual forms of self-alienation. In the novel, Silvia must learn the economic realities that govern the sexual lives of lower-class women – those most likely to be named 'whores' – in her bid for independence. And Silvia's sister, Mertilla, in warning her sibling about the life of infamy that awaits her, draws on the familiar moral tenets governing whore biography. Placing Silvia against the backdrop of these different conventions allows Behn to broaden the hermeneutical horizon of courtesan iconography and in doing so, establish a continuum linking the mistress and the common woman, aristocratic and populist understandings of sexual exchange. 'Protestant Whore' more abstractly defines the narrative's critical stance. Rachel Weil has argued that 'it is not an accident that novels emerged as a form of political writing in this period. Many people responded to morally ambiguous political situations not by applying abstract principles to fixed and known events, but by shaping their stories about what happened in ways that allowed them to feel that their actions suited their principles.'[3] By this account, the scepticism Behn sustains in *Love-Letters* appears simply cynical, an expedient methodology in a confusing moment. But we can approach the novel more positively by examining how the literary, for Behn, encompasses an expansive view of English historical narratives and controversies, and brings the category of sexual difference to bear on the religious and political discourses that shaped the radical Enlightenment.[4]

Behn's creation of the character Silvia, the fictional stand-in for the historical Henrietta Berkeley, most markedly defines the literariness of *Love-Letters*.[5] Unlike Ford, Lord Grey, who both testified at his trial and wrote a confession regarding his role in the Rye House Plot, we know little to nothing about Henrietta Berkeley, save the physical descriptions of her appearance and clothes provided by witnesses at the trial of Lord Grey.[6] In her discussion of historical narration focalized through a fictional character, Dorrit Cohn observes 'the sense of presentness it creates and the ensuing impression that it opens on an unknown future.'[7] The imaginative aspect of Behn's work marks the place where aesthetics intersect with politics. As Michael McKeon notes, 'Crucial to Behn's hermeneutics is not the direct "political" correlation of character and personage (e.g., Philander and Lord Grey) which is soon known and accepted, but the construction of a broad, "ethical" grid of private possibility – or probability – for reading "public" events.'[8] In contrast to Robert Ferguson, the Whig propagandist we encountered in chapter 1, who demanded that the English reading public recognize the 'facts' of the Black Box affair, Behn allows the poetics of her narrative to develop a truth of their own. Following Lucretius, she demonstrates how 'acts of reading can serve to make us up – to constitute and reconstitute our bodies in their persistent, intimate reactivity to language.'[9] Writing in response to the political events of the 1680s, Behn recognized the uncertain future England faced, and her historical fiction moves from the immediacy of political debate to larger contemplations of ethics, individualism, and patterns of historical change.[10]

Verbal Icons: Behn, Gwyn, Mancini

What Curtizan, why 'tis a Noble title and has more *Votaries than Religion*.
                                    Behn, *The Feign'd Curtizans*

In his reading of *Oroonoko*, Srinivas Aravamudan remarks the narrator's habit of 'wilfully rearranging political identities to make her role more central,' including 'perhaps a fantasy identification as one more of Charles [II]'s numerous mistresses.'[11] Behn's engagement with the Stuart courtesans follows a complex trajectory of identification and appropriation. Against a decade of political attacks on the royal mistresses, Behn's dedications to Nell Gwyn and Hortense Mancini, Duchess of Mazarin, maintain the ideal of the courtesan's timeless fascination and enduring authority. The sublime courtesan, of course, was not new, and James Turner has shown how it maintains one end of both graduated and binary systems of whore discourse in the early modern period.[12] Behn invokes this figure in order to reinscribe it in an alternative register, one fundamentally about authorship. The largest challenge facing Behn, in her representation of women's illicit conduct, involves rewriting contemporary sexual ethnography so that the lawbreaker might assume, as fully as possible, the privileges of libertine culture – including its aesthetic elitism – and in turn confer them on the English woman author. Integral to this process is the identification of the courtesan with the literary principles governing the writer's craft.

The literariness of Behn's dedications appears in their proximity to the French tradition of the verbal portrait that emerged in post-Fronde culture.[13] The literary portraits circulated first by Scudéry functioned initially as a kind of social game for the aristocracy – i.e., guess who the subject of this portrait might be – but soon developed, in the works of Lafayette and others, into a means of experimenting with different kinds of psychological realism.[14] They also enabled new modes of thinking about the author's relation to her subject, imagined not simply as a social relation forged in the salon, but as a proximity to forms of truth-telling that rely on both critical distance and intimate proximity. Behn uses the French model to imagine her relation not only to the court's courtesans but also to the male aristocrats she addresses in *Love-Letters*.[15]

In 1659, Lafayette wrote a portrait of her close friend Sévigné that was published as part of *Divers Portraits* and again in an expanded collection of portraits a few months later. This portrait's reflections on female intimacy and the rhetorical modes best suited to its representation bear a striking resemblance to Behn's and suggest that both women were preoccupied with similar questions as they carved out positions for themselves in their respective literary worlds. In her portrait, Lafayette writes under the cover of a male speaker she names Inconnu. The mask of anonymity presents itself as the means by which a disinterested representation of the subject might appear: 'thanks to the privilege of Unknown I have in addressing you, I'm going to paint you boldly, and tell you all your truths at my leisure, without fear of attracting your anger.'[16] Lafayette announces a particular kind of knowledge gained by observation and by a psychological insight unique to the author: 'if I am unknown to you, you are not unknown to me, and I must have had the honour of seeing you and speaking to you more than once in order to unravel what in you makes this charm that takes the world by surprise' (10). The world may be astonished by Sévigné's appeal, but the speaker knows exactly what makes it tick. Even as Lafayette argues for the necessity of authorial distance and new modes of observation, she announces the dedication's open secret: 'You are naturally tender and passionate, but to the shame of our sex, this tenderness has been useless to you, and you have withdrawn it to yours [that is, your sex] in giving it to Mme. de Lafayette'(10). When the speaker asks, 'What happiness to be the master of a heart likes yours,' we know that 'he' knows some version of this happiness. The portrait's closing citation brings female intimacy to the brink of desire: 'to give praise that is worthy of you and worthy to show: It would be necessary to be your lover, / And I don't have the honour of being one' (10–11). Lafayette locates the sexual precisely at the place where citation takes over – the portrait's closing couplet is a quotation – in order to enmesh sexual knowledge in a web of artifice.

Behn's dedications intensify the dynamics at work in Lafayette's portrait in a way that enables the commentary to expand beyond the subject and the author to the larger political events unfolding around them.[17] Behn's address to Nell Gwyn was the author's first published dedication, appearing with *The Feign'd Curtizans* in 1679. Johnson secured its eighteenth-century fame by attacking, in *The Life of Dryden*, Behn's hyperbole. While, most generally, the dedication's effusive rhetoric counters satiric attempts to dip Gwyn in the social gutter of her origins, its energies go beyond simple recuperation or defence, and move toward the creation of an art/artist/courtesan analogy that also governs Behn's representation of Mancini and the fictional Silvia in *Love-Letters*.

Behn begins the Gwyn dedication in a strain that borders on the profane (and one wonders if it wasn't this rhetoric that set Johnson's teeth on edge): 'Tis no wonder that hitherto I followed not the good example of the believing Poets, since less faith and zeal than you alone can inspire, had wanted power to have reduc't me to the true worship.'[18]

'True worship,' that is to say, patron-worship, only appears attractive
to Behn when the figure of Gwyn presents itself to her, a vision who
inspires 'Adoration.' Immediately Behn attaches this adoration to the
particular conditions of Gwyn's status as a royal mistress, a woman
for whom gifts constitute much of her pay for services rendered. It
is this materialism, Behn insists, that alone distinguishes Gwyn from
God: 'so Excellent and perfect a Creature as your self differs only from
the Divine powers in this; the Offerings made to you ought to be worthy of you, whilst they accept the will alone; and how Madam, would
your Altars be loaded, if like heaven you gave permission to all that
had a will and desire to approach 'em' (86). In marking the division
between a providential desire for a willing heart and the courtesan's
insistence on goods, Behn strikingly points toward a defining charac-
teristic of courtesan narratives: their preoccupation with things and a
corresponding lack of regard for intentionality expressed independ-
ently of those things.[19] Here Behn's dedication stands as the gift that
bridges the enormous divide separating 'those distant slaves' whom
Gwyn conquers with her fame alone and those court intimates who
'boast the happiness' of beholding Gwyn 'dayly.' Long since removed
from the theatre where she began her career, Gwyn now inhabits the
remote world of London's West End. But having noted this cultural divide, Behn immediately eradicates it, placing Gwyn at the centre of the
English public's sense of itself. It is not the 'distant slaves' who bemoan
the courtesan's aristocratic remoteness, but rather those 'succeeding
ages' who 'shall Envy us who lived in this, and saw those charming
wonders which they can only reade of' (86). The 'we' Behn establishes
here enjoys, at least occasionally, the immediacy of Gwyn's presence, a
monarchical spectacle appearing among the commoners:

> You never appear but you glad the hearts of all that have the happy for-
> tune to see you, as if you were made on purpose to put the whole world
> into good Humour, whenever you look abroad, and when you speak, men
> crowd to listen with that awfull reverence as to Holy Oracles or Divine
> Prophesies, and bear away the precious words to tell at home to all the
> attentive family, the Gracefull things you utter'd. (86–7)

The English public reverentially consumes Gwyn's 'good Humour,'
orally circulating the 'Gracefull things' the courtesan speaks. Within
this culture, Behn functions as a scribe, one who will ensure Gwyn's
words appear in a 'History' that future ages will read. The author

serves not simply as handmaiden to the courtesan, however, but also as her proxy, one who, like Gwyn, elevates good humour to the status of 'Holy Oracles,' and in doing so confirms the pleasure principle associated with the king's royal sport, official and unofficial. But Behn takes this principle further, into the realm of social critique. Gwyn's speech acts not only please, they teach. Testimony to the courtesan's 'undeniable self,' Gwyn's declarations to the crowd witness women's abilities, calling up cultural memories of Elizabeth I, whose speeches – most notably to the troops at Tilbury – drew attention to her gender while confirming her singular powers.[20] Most immediately, Gwyn's words put to shame 'those boasting talkers who are Judges of nothing but faults.' The inflated egos of men and their conventional misogynous attacks appear in stark relief to the courtesan's confidence and generosity.

Behn does not stop at cowing misogynists, but proceeds to set the courtesan in the place of absolute power: 'And who can doubt the Powers of that Illustrious Beauty, the Charms of that tongue, and the greatness of that minde, who has subdu'd the most powerfull and Glorious Monarch of the world' (87). Relying on the conventions of amatory discourse to speak the courtesan's authority, Behn alleviates, in one register, concerns about Gwyn's political influence: we are safely in the arena of love, here, and should not mistake the courtesan's desire to secure her place in the king's heart for an attempt to maintain a proxy seat in his cabinet. But in setting the idea of Gwyn's amatory control alongside the portrait of her public authority over the mob, a rather different idea of authority appears, one that identifies Gwyn as an alternate monarch. Importantly, by representing Gwyn in this way, Behn differentiates her rendition of the courtesan's political authority from hostile portraits of the *maîtresse-en-titre*. For here Behn imagines Gwyn wielding her powers over the public *and* the king, rather than over the public *through* the king. In this regard, Gwyn represents a new kind of nobility, most immediately figured in the illegitimate offspring of her union with the king: 'Nor can Heaven give you more, who has exprest a particular care of you every way, and above all in bestowing on the world and you, two noble Branches ... whom you have permitted to wear those glorious Titles which you your self Generously neglected, well knowing with the noble Poet; 'tis better far to merit Titles than to wear 'em.' God, like the monarch, comes to the courtesan bearing gifts. The sons wear their titles through the mother's, rather than the father's, intervention. Nell Gwyn, however, remains title free, relying on her iconic status in a larger English public to determine her cultural capital.[21]

Behn achieves two significant goals with this dedication: first, she establishes the author's rights of access to the courtesan through the elevation of her dedication to the status of both gift and historical record; second, she creates the courtesan in the likeness of the woman author whose merit reflects an alternative register of cultural value. Behn could have drawn on Gwyn's career as an actress and her own work as a playwright to forge a bond with the courtesan, but chose, instead, to create a more abstract social and literary discourse to represent the woman author and courtesan as peers. As in Lafayette's portrait of Sévigné, both distance and proximity are carefully measured for best cultural leverage.

Behn's dedication to Hortense Mancini, Duchess of Mazarin, returns to the sexual intimacy that Lafayette suggests in her portrait of Sevigné, deepening the connection between French and English literary traditions and broadening the conception of the courtesan/author relation. When Behn wrote her dedication to Mancini, the royal mistress's patron was dead, the courtesan was aging, at least by Restoration standards, and she was, as usual, up to her neck in debt. Behn, too, was living in debt and watching the Stuart regime crumble. The points of contact must have seemed historically measurable to Behn, but, as in the Gwyn dedication, Behn pursues a different logic of identification than that afforded by empirical evidence.

Hortense Mancini was one of three nieces of Cardinal Mazarin, Louis XIV's most powerful minister and the individual instrumental in defeating the Fronde's anti-absolutist rebellion (1648–53) during the prince's regency (figure 4).[22] With her sister Marie, Hortense arrived from Italy as a child, just as her uncle was celebrating his victory over the Fronde in the mid 1650s. She was married to the Marquis de Meilleraye in 1661 at age sixteen and assumed, with her husband, Mazarin's title and his vast fortune when he died shortly after her marriage.[23] The description of Cardinal Mazarin's death, recounted in Mancini's memoirs, establishes a close correspondence between political and domestic arenas:

> It is a remarkable thing that a man of that merit, that all his life had laboured to raise and enrich his Family, should never receive other Thanks from them, than apparent signs of hatred and aversion even after his Death. But if you knew with what severity he treated us in all things, you would be less surprised at this. Never man had so sweet a behavior abroad and in publick, and so harsh and severe at home[;] all our humours

and inclinations were point blank opposite to his. Add to this the Tyrannical Subjection we were kept in.[24]

Mancini draws on her audience's familiarity with the cardinal's political career to discredit his generosity toward her family and represents
Mazarin's politeness as a mask concealing a social aggression more
nakedly on display in the privacy of the home. Civility's success depends on rigid conformity to a set of codes, which in the Mazarin
household was maintained with brutality in order that the family might
appear a seamless whole in the public sphere.

   With this family drama in mind, one can read the very public rebel-
lions that both Hortense and Maria Mancini staged a few years into
their marriages as allegories of the Fronde's resistance to Cardinal
Mazarin's political tyranny.[25] Indeed, the Mancini sisters enacted their
flights from home as the princess rebels did before them, cross-dressing
and arming themselves when necessary as they fled their husbands'
militia. In a moment that links the sisters both to the Fronde's celebrated heroines and to the romances of Scudéry, Hortense Mancini's
Memoirs recount: 'Madam *de Grignan* was so Charitable, as to send us
some Shifts, adding, *That we travelled like True* Roman Heroines, *with
abundance of Jewels, but no clean Linnen*' (109). Mancini's representation
as a latter-day *frondeuse* in her use of its most famous rallying slogan,
'Point de Mazarin,' against her husband is suggestive of aristocratic
wit, but it also reflects the historical acumen of French women writing in the wake of the Fronde's defeat.[26] As Joan DeJean has observed,
Louis XIV's regime regulated marriages as insurance against another
uprising by the powerful families surrounding the king.[27] Although
Louis XIV tried to stay out of the affairs of the Mancini sisters (having
initially counselled both women to return to their husbands), he was
placed, at various moments, in a compromised position by their demands for pensions and for sanctuary, both in France and neighbouring
states. Their legal claims matched the literary ambitions of the memoirs, confirming DeJean's thesis that a desire for 'increased economic
control' over the institutions of marriage and authorship set women of
the Mancinis' generation against the house of Bourbon.[28]

   The Duchess of Mazarin arrived in England in 1675 trailing not only
clouds of scandal, but also French literary traditions preoccupied with
questions of sexual politics and authority.[29] Her *Memoirs*, penned by
her friend and perhaps lover César Vichard, abbé de Saint-Réal, were
published that year and immediately translated into English. Mancini's

closest friend in England, the French libertine Saint-Evrémond, had fled France after Louis XIV ordered his arrest for a retrospective attack on Cardinal Mazarin's policies. Maria Mancini's memoirs appeared soon after her sister's, authored by Gabriel de Brémond, who lived in exile in Holland for his antigovernment writings. Both Saint-Réal and Brémond provide sympathetic accounts of the French women they write about, and while we might consider their rhetoric a matter of financial expediency, it is worth considering that Brémond also wrote a strictly satiric portrait of Charles II's English-born mistress, Barbara Villiers. Hostile satire, in other words, could be as profitable as sympathy. In creating heroic figures in their representations of the Mancini sisters, Saint-Réal and Brémond declare their social alliance with the women, and by extension, with French women writers preoccupied, in the literary arena, with the relation of marriage to state politics.

In both France and England, Hortense Mancini represented a form of heresy, Protestant and Catholic, respectively. Upon hearing of Hortense Mancini's departure to England, Sevigné observed: 'Madame Mazarin roams the fields in England, it is believed. There is neither faith, law, nor priest there, as you know. But I believe that she would not have wanted, as the song says, to see the King driven away' (1:951).[30] The idea of England as a space of religious lawlessness identifies Mancini's conduct with libertinism in its broadest sense.[31] In England, Mancini's installation as royal mistress immediately touched the nerve of a nation already sensitive to the imbrication of sex and politics in the wake of Charles II's liaison with the Duchess of Portsmouth and James II's treatment of Anne Hyde. Dubbed the 'Italian Whore,' the Duchess of Mazarin's status was defined through the prism of her international and peripatetic past, her 'experience'd and well-travel'd lust': 'For tell me, in all Europe, where's the part / That is not conscious of thy lewd desert?'[32] The convent surfaces as a suitable house of correction for the courtesan; to 'cloister up fulsome Mazarin,' one poet suggests, would 'once more make Charles King again.'[33] Figured less as an agent of Louis XIV than an instance of insidious European sexual contagion, Mazarin represents a diffuse form of cosmopolitan corruption in court satires of the period.[34]

Like Nell Gwyn, Hortense Mancini used religion to further her own cause. In particular, she set her narrative against the backdrop of her husband's religious mania: 'The most sacred Tyes of Nature and Reason, become the most horrible Crimes when Jealousie and Envy comes to descant upon them: and there is nothing impossible to a man that makes Profession of Piety and Devotion, rather than he shall be thought in the wrong; the most Innocent and Upright Persons in the World, shall be thought the most infamous, and the most Abominable' (76). Glossing over the various scandals that followed her to England, including that of her affair with a gentleman servant (a plot line echoed in Love-Letters), Mancini presents herself as a woman only interested in securing her children's fortune and her own independence from a spouse whose zealotry constitutes a form of insanity. She stands as the principle of civility, the defender of polite and artistic culture against the mania of belief.

Behn's dedication to the Duchess of Mazarin announces the author's desire for Mancini in no uncertain terms: 'Madam, when I survey'd the whole Toor of ladies at court, which was Adorn'd by you, who appear'd there with a Grace and Majesty peculiar to Your Great Self only, mix'd with an irresistible Air of Sweetness, Generosity, and Wit, I was impatient for an Opportunity, to tell Your Grace, how infinitely one of Your own Sex adored you, and that among all the numerous Conquest[s] Your Grace has made over the Hearts of Men, Your Grace had not subdu'd a more intire Slave.'[35] Behn uses this desire to distinguish her address from conventional modes of sycophancy: 'there is neither Compliment, nor Poetry, in this humble Declaration, but a Truth, which has cost me a great deal of Inquietude' (208). Since convention includes declarations of love as part of the dedication's repertoire, Behn's claim to her own desire's uniqueness as 'truth' only appears in its singularity, that is, its same-sex nature. The fact of Mancini's well-established bisexuality enables this particular address, although Behn couches the courtesan's desirability in an aesthetic of universal appeal: 'how few Objects are there, that can render it so entire a Pleasure, as at once to hear you speak, and to look upon your Beauty?' (208).[36] Mancini's example allows Behn to exploit English libertinism's preoccupation with sexual freedom, which here enables the courtesan's sexuality to emerge as a literary principle that links the woman author's craft to the courtesan's beauty and 'surprising wit.' As in Lafayette's portrait of Sevigné and Behn's earlier dedication to Gwyn, the dedication's intimate address appears alongside a representation of the speaker's distance from her subject: 'Fortune has not set me in such a Station, as might justifie my Pretence to the honour and satisfaction of being ever near Your Grace, to view eternally that lovely Person, and hear that surprising Wit' (208). The distance Behn acknowledges here marks the difference between the kind of authority she claims, and that assumed by Lafayette. For as much as Lafayette asserts the primacy of her representation's disinterestedness, rendered by the male persona the text both creates and disavows, her portrait of Sévigné can always be read back into the friendship the author has with her subject and as a result an aura of aristocratic clubbiness remains in place.

Behn, of course, had no such social relation upon which to draw. When she asks her leading questions they remain, unlike Lafayette's, strictly rhetorical. Todd claims that Behn wrote her dedication to Mancini with an awareness of her inability to penetrate court circles, despite her long-standing loyalty to the Stuart regime: 'For years Behn had desperately wanted to be of the royal court. Perhaps, now that her hopes of this were fading, she set her sights on [Mancini's] more louche, ambiguous and achievable one in Chelsea.'[37] I suggest that Behn's emphasis on the gap that separates her from the courtesan acknowledges the author's garret as a place where a significant amount of cultural capital might accumulate. That is to say, Behn uses the idea of a social difference that only her writing can bridge to keep our focus on the author's work: '[My homage], Madam, can only be exprest by my Pen, which would be infinitely honor'd, in being permitted to celebrate your great Name for ever, and perpetually to serve, where it has so great an inclination' (208). The author as historical chronicler appears once again as the sign of permanence, the means by which the courtesan can escape her precarious status.

In the figures of Gwyn and Mancini, Behn finds English folk-charm and European urbanity, Protestant integrity and French anticlericalism, popular appeal and aesthetic elitism: and it is the yoking of these qualities in the figure of Silvia that allows Behn to advance a political vision committed both to English national stability and a broader European Enlightenment. The Protestant Whore, in *Love-Letters*, advances the cause of a cosmopolitan author, educated in modern languages, conversant in political and philosophical debates, and committed to a literary discourse capable of drawing together insights both particular to the crisis at hand and general to the condition of early modern European culture. She remains loyal to her monarch while learning to temper her idealism with pragmatism – a pragmatism that fosters not only self-interest, but also the ideals of tolerance and awareness.

The Protestant Cause and a Protestant Whore

The uncertainties of philosophy are scarcely larger than those of history, and those that have read them much say that one approaches history as one does the preparation of meat in a kitchen. Each nation prepares it to its own taste, just as the same thing is cooked in as many stews as there are countries in the world; and almost always one finds most agreeable those that conform to one's custom. One would have to be truly simple, says a fine mind, to study history with the hope of discovering what happened; it's enough that one knows what such-and-such an author believes, and it's not so much the history of facts one needs to look for as the history of men's opinions and accounts.

César Vichard, Abbé de Saint-Réal, '*Lettre.*
Sur l'Étude & Sur les Sciences'[38]

Behn was not interested in riding on the courtesan's petticoats to power. Instead, she hazarded her bid for patronage on establishing an association between her own claims to representational authority and those she attributes to the courtesan. This association shapes her representation of the debates about Protestantism and Protestant identity that gave rise to the events that serve both as the backdrop to, and the subject of, *Love-Letters between a Nobleman and His Sister*. We have seen, in chapter 1, how satire of the period distinguished Nell Gwyn's Protestant popularity from the political threat of the Duke of Monmouth's appeal.[39] In *Love-Letters*, Behn dramatically expands the scope of this casual distinction in order to render her Protestant Whore a figure of cosmopolitan scepticism uniting the best features of Behn's favourite courtesans, Gwyn and Mancini, against Whig conspirators and their leader, a credulous and self-deceiving duke.

In writing *Love-Letters*, Behn developed a hermeneutics that discredits the impulse to read human affairs against a divine plan and foregrounds the desire to do so with self-deception and, most important, treason. Tory satire in the Restoration period frequently promoted the idea of Whig credulity, linking it to Puritan habits of mind and identifying seditious impulses behind the veil of prophetic discourse. The 'mystery' of Henrietta Berkeley's disappearance and whereabouts received several satiric treatments in 1682: 'Let Divines and Phylosophers say what they will of Oracles and Witches, they shall never beat out of my Brains the Doctrine of Spirits and Visions ... Was not my own Sister but Spirited away t'other Day?' asks 'Lady Grey,' abandoned wife and also, importantly, the Duke of Monmouth's ex-lover. The satire goes on to identify dreams of national resurrection with the sexual misconduct of Lady Grey: 'The next Night coming from an Entertainment in the Land of Promise, which the Tories call Whigland, I had no sooner laid me down upon my Pillow, but straight (methought) my Genius appear'd; nay, tho' I were dead asleep, this Prophet [the Duke of Monmouth] by laying Mouth to Mouth, Brest to Brest, Thigh to Thigh, and Foot to Foot, would even raise me to new Life.'[40]

The Duke of Monmouth serves as the most immediate point of reference for the critique Behn undertakes. Significantly, Nell Gwyn is said to have dubbed the Duke of Monmouth 'Prince Perkin' around 1679, a name that proved disastrously accurate, as Monmouth's predecessor (1474–99), an illegitimate son with pretensions to the throne, was eventually executed for his treasonous ambition.[41] Echoing Gwyn's prescience, Behn registered her dislike of the duke in the 'Epilogue' to *Romulus and Hersilia; or, the Sabine War* (1682), an act that landed Behn and the actress who spoke the lines in custody. The lines explicitly allude, like Gwyn's Perkin reference, to the crime of treason:

And of all Treasons, mine was most accurst;
Rebelling 'gainst a KING and FATHER first.
...
Not my Remorse, or Death, can expiate
With them a Treason 'gainst the KING and *State*.[42]

Angeline Goreau has argued that the lines seem to contradict Behn's usual leniency on the subject of rebellion against fathers: 'such a statement ... seems strangely inconsonant with the personal politics she had defended from the outset of her career as a writer. To present rebellion against a *father* as the highest moral sin was out of character indeed when the whole of her literary work was implacably committed to the promotion of disobedience to parents, particularly fathers, in the matter of marriage.'[43] But Behn's attack on Monmouth stems from her hatred of rebellion in the name of a false cause, a stance that appears in all of her characterizations of Cromwellian Puritans and, more generally, Whig politics.[44]

Behn's indictment of the Duke of Monmouth (to which we will return below) serves as one instance, however, of a larger antagonism Behn sustains toward aristocratic men in *Love-Letters*. This larger antagonism reflects the uneasy sense, in Behn's prose fiction, that the nation is being misled not only by zealous and credulous Whig fanatics, but also by cynical and power-hungry loyalists – loyalists who would, eventually, become turncoats in the Revolution of 1688–9. In an essay on Aphra Behn and patronage, Deborah C. Payne explores the sardonic and irreverent posture Behn assumes in her plays' dedications to various members of the aristocracy throughout the 1670s. Identifying Behn's aggression as part of a larger pattern of tensions, Payne suggests that 'for this generation of writers, caught between a regressive system of patronage and an emergent marketplace of print at the close of the seventeenth century, the relationship of dramatist to patron was difficult indeed. Was the patron to be implored, emulated, or surpassed?'[45] After 1680, Payne argues, Behn's tone changes from one of challenge to accommodation, a shift that Payne identifies as the result of Behn's increasingly secure place within the world of the Royalist theatre. But if Behn learned to mask her aggression in her later plays, she found ways to express it in another medium: namely, the novel. The heady mixture of satire, scandal, and fiction that *Love-Letters* concocts provides ample room for shifting the terms of a relationship that, within the playhouse, had stricter, or more readily definable, conventions. *Love-Letters'* dedications take us back to the dynamics at work in Behn's representations of Gwyn and Mancini, adding to the desires Behn announces in those portraits a scepticism that governs the narrative of *Love-Letters*. Most immediately, the dedications interpellate author, patron, and reader, establishing the literary and social paradigms at work in each volume. The dedications, together, achieve a cumulative effect of their own even as they become integrated into the courtesan history Behn recounts.

Claiming to have translated a 'little Book of Letters' from French, Behn opens her first dedication to Thomas Condon with a declaration of esteem that mimics the 'soft and amorous' qualities of the letters Behn pretends to have discovered: 'I think it no where so proper to address so much tender passion, as to a man whom Heaven and Nature has so well form'd both for dispencing and receiving of Love as your self.'[46] Using a language of exchange, whose sexual logic will become more pronounced as the letter unfolds, Behn links her amatory fiction to the life of the aristocratic man. That the narrative is penned by a woman does not distance it from his interests. The comparison assumes a less flattering aspect when Behn links Philander, the figure of Lord Grey in the narrative to follow, and Condon: 'Sir, I wou'd fain think that in the Character of *Philander* there is a great resemblance of your self as to his Person, and that part of his Soul that was possest with Love: he was a French Whigg, 'tis true, and a most apparent Traytor, and there, I confess, the comparison fails extremely' (5). Political affiliation disrupts the comparison, but only momentarily. Philander remains a positive model of love's instincts, and his symbolic capital as a libertine allows Behn to admonish Condon's failure to act on his own beauty, a withholding that can only lead the young aristocrat to take on the worst qualities of Behn's hero: 'Pray Heaven you be not reserv'd like our Hero for some Sister, 'tis an ill sign when so much beauty passes daily unregarded, that your love is reserved to an end as malicious as that of our *Philander's*' (6). The comparison works strangely here: Condon is like Philander, whose appetite does not know its proper limits, politically or sexually, because Condon loves too little. Withholding is as damaging as excess. The comparison also infers that a patron's failure to respond generously could signal a dangerous lack of social intelligence, an inference that Behn draws by positioning herself as a would-be lover, the instigator of a relationship with an aristocrat who can grant all favours if he is – as he should be – so inclined.

The second dedication initially seems more straightforward than the first. In it, Behn lauds the political success of Lemuel Kingdon against the Duke of Monmouth and his followers. But the problem of misrecognition structures this dedication, just as it does the first. 'Tho the World storm and reel with mad confusion, still from the serenity of your looks we read the fair weather in your mind, which times or seasons can never discompose, while all goes well with your King and Country,' Behn declares (118). The apparent confidence of this description is undercut by a tension that circulates through the dedication as a whole. The world's 'mad confusion' has resulted from political upheavals, so the idea that Kingdon's admirers can read contentment in the midst of this confusion does not rest easy with the idea of Kingdon's dissatisfaction when all does not go well with king and country. Furthermore, the idea that Kingdon might appear transparent to the world at any time is belied by Behn's concern, which she declares earlier in the dedication, that the good man 'is not as well understood by every body as by myself,' a refrain that takes us back to the first dedication and the need for Behn's intervention as an author and translator of aristocratic men for the English public (117–18). Finally, the dedication marks its temporal strangeness in the assertion of its own belatedness. The narrative, it seems, is overdue: ''Tis only what was long since design'd you, when possibly it might have found something [of] a better wellcome, by its having made (as then it must have done) a voyage to have kist your hands, and might perhaps then have contributed in some small degree to your diversion, in a place where there is found so little' (117). Rather than shoring up political resolve, the narrative appears as an antidote to the vexations and distresses of the battlefield, the imaginary escape from the pressures of historical crisis. One might imagine that it is only through the consolations of Behn's fiction that Kingdon can imagine that 'all goes well' with king and country, that it is in the instruction and delight provided by the narrative, rather than in the immediate pressures of shifting political sands, that Kingdon's 'fair weather' features might be composed. However, the dedication's belatedness more fundamentally alters the idea of history writing's temporal impulses. Kingdon will learn, through Aphra Behn's fiction, that history inhabits the repetitive and episodic rhythms of a new form of narrative, that its resolutions are only temporary, and that political attitudes are developed not only on the battlefield but also in the bedroom.

The third and final dedication registers most viscerally the issues raised by its predecessors. Writing to the young Lord Spencer, a known rake, Behn claims to dedicate the narration of the Duke of Monmouth's fall to him as an example of 'the Misfortune of heedless Love, and a too Early Thirst of Glory' (254). She then goes on to assert:

> I hope no One will imagine I intend this as a Parallel between your Lordship and our mistaken brave Unfortunate, since your Lordship hath an unquestioned and hereditary Loyalty, which nothing can deface, born from a Father, who has given the World so evident Proofs, that no fear of threatened danger can separate his useful Service, and Duties from the Interest of his Royal and God-like Master. (254)

The assertion of the difference between the Duke of Monmouth and Lord Spencer flies in the face of the striking similarities between the men and the fatalism built into both of their narratives. As surely as the duke's rebellion led him to the scaffold, Spencer's dissipation led him to the grave in September 1688. The irony of Behn's statement is rendered even more acute by the statement's swerve to the father as the guarantor of difference. Within Behn's historical moment, the Earl of Sunderland, Lord Spencer's father, could hardly be read as a stable figure of political loyalty, having saved Ford, Lord Grey, from the scaffold and having previously been suspected, by some, of supporting the Duke of Monmouth.[47] Todd argues that the strangeness of Behn's dedication suggests 'some ambiguity of political message.'[48] I would go further, to stress Behn's conscious creation of an interpretive problem that she alone can resolve. Readers must engage with the terms of her narrative and the portraits it draws in order to discern the political imperatives governing her dedications. What is most clear from the dedications is that Behn suspends any assurances about the reliability of aristocratic male character in order to create anxiety about their conduct as lovers and politicians. Rather than insisting on the victorious outcome of the history about which she is most immediately writing, Behn opens up her narrative to a temporal moment of a much longer, and less reassuring, duration. The most resilient figure, within this moment, is the courtesan. The best reader of her narrative's import is the courtesan's proxy, the woman writer.

As these dedications suggest, Behn's preoccupation with male libertine character follows a number of different, but related, streams. When we turn to the novel itself, male privilege, political and social, undergoes a radical refashioning in the figure of the aristocratic woman who leaps from the socially sanctioned space of her father's home into the unknown territory of disrepute and desperation. The gratifications afforded by this leap unfold and explore the intimations of Behn's dedications, including their reworking of class relations and the assertion of authorial power. Sexual difference marks not only the social double-standard regarding conduct and consequences, but also differing relations to the question of belief.[49] The examples of the male libertines Silvia encounters invite her to compare different modes of desire against a backdrop of social and political affairs and to draw conclusions that take on significant historiographical import by the end of the novel.

Silvia begins her narrative a true believer in every sense, investing political loyalty and personal fidelity, in particular, with metaphysical significance. On learning of Philander's engagement with Cesario's treasonous plots, she argues:

> I have a fatal prophetick fear, that gives a check to my soft pursuit, and tells me that thy unhappy ingagement in this League, this accursed Association, will one day undo us both, and part for ever thee and thy unlucky *Silvia*; yes, yes my dear Lord; my Soul does presage an unfortunate event from this dire ingagement; nor can your false Reasoning, your fancy'd advantages reconcile it to my honest, good-natur'd heart. (38)

In fact, neither Silvia nor Philander is undone by their proximity to the prince's failed rebellion. Nor does it have any bearing on the outcome of their affair, as Philander abandons Silvia long before he is called to battle on Cesario's behalf. Neither are the couple parted forever by his-

torical events; the narrative closes with an account of the close friendship they develop after their passions have subsided. In other words,
Silvia's overblown rhetoric invokes a view of history driven by an igno-
rance the narrative actively criticizes.

The first two volumes of *Love-Letters* recount Silvia's fall from belief
into disbelief, from sexual innocence to illicit experience. Curiosity is
the attitude that guarantees personal freedom in Behn's courtesan narrative. Kathryn R. King, following J. Paul Hunter, describes curiosity
as the habit of mind that best sums up the impulses of an 'emerging
novelistic consciousness,' and Barbara M. Benedict, expanding on these
themes, links curiosity to a sexualized reading experience: 'Novels link
the idea to find something out, curiosity, with the desire to be aroused,
and they plant both firmly in the social sphere.'[50] The novel's first mention of curiosity appears in a scene of illicit reading, one that threatens
to expose Silvia while she is still living at her father's house: an exposure only prevented by the timely intervention of Silvia's servant and
confidant, Melinda. Melinda retells the story in a letter to Philander,
and starts with the discovery of a letter Silvia has written to Philander
by a curious countess, who declares,

> Nay I am resolved to see in what manner you write to a Lover, and whether
> you have a Heart tender or cruel; at which she began to read aloud, My
> Lady to blush and change Colour a Hundred times in a minute; I ready to
> dye with fear; Madam the Countess in infinite amazement, my Lady inter-
> rupting every word the Dutchesse read by Prayers and Intreaties, which
> heighten'd her Curiosity ... My Lady, whose wit never fail'd her, Cry'd, I
> beseech you Madam, let us have so much complisance [*sic*] for *Melinda* to
> ask her consent in this affair, and then I am pleas'd you should see what
> Love I can make upon occasion. I took the hint, and with a real confusion,
> Cry'd – I implore you Madam not to discover my weakness to Madam
> the Dutchess ... My Lady after this took the Letter, and all being resolv'd it
> should be read, she her self did it, and turn'd it so prettily into Burlesque
> Love by her manner of reading it, that made Madam the Dutchess laugh
> extreamly. (52–3)

The moment of reading initially threatens to become a moment of scandalous exposure, a revelation of truth about Silvia's private conduct.
The countess's curiosity is piqued by the scandalous allure of a love letter, for we are introduced to it as 'heighten'd' by Silvia's visible distress
at the letter's discovery, a bodily revelation that adds to the countess's

desire to read the letter aloud. She wants to enter into the scene of reading as a moment of pleasure tied to knowing the heart's secrets and the pleasure of Silvia's writing; the illicit nature of this knowledge does not, in her mind, immediately conjure up its opposite, the need for discretion. The scene stages a moment of female community that takes licence as its privilege, a moment fantasized about by men and, perhaps, experienced by women as readers and writers during this period.[51]

Intuitively inhabiting a libertine convention, Silvia has the intelligence to transform the truth into fiction by representing the lover in the letter as Melinda, for whom she pretends to have served as an amanuensis. The language of consent that organizes the fiction first depends on Melinda's ability to anticipate the scene that Silvia is creating; once the two women have signalled to each other their mutual awareness of the fiction, Silvia can take control of the moment. But while Silvia's transformation of her own ostensibly sincere love letter into a burlesque comedy may seem to depend on the exploitation of class difference, Silvia's gesture also involves a careful manipulation of the countess's expectations, including a rather crude curiosity about the love lives of servants. Indeed, it appears that Melinda and Silvia jointly author the scene – Melinda appears the shy retiring maid, Silvia the mistress – and they give their audience what it wants to hear. But we, knowing the fiction of the fiction, are set at a remove from the dynamic, and our curiosity is piqued, not by the class conventions that are played out, but by the text's self-consciousness in relation to those conventions. Melinda's careful recounting of the scene in her letter to Philander places her in the most powerful position of all, as the author capable of knowing what it is about this scene that must be retold to the lover after the fact. That the story is told on the eve of Philander's and Silvia's first sexual encounter, and that the letter has been written as an antidote to Silvia's last moments of resistance to seduction only sharpens our sense of its significance and of Melinda's power as an actor in the scene as it unfolds.

Both King and Benedict highlight the extent to which the trope of female curiosity deepened, in the Restoration and eighteenth century, the association of women with the early modern novel, 'the genre of the questions of Eve.'[52] Behn triangulates the Eve/curiosity dyad, however, in the narration of the Genesis story that accompanies Silvia's first recognition of Philander's treachery:

here again she read *Philanders* Letter, as if on purpose to find new torments out for a heart too much prest already; a sowre that is always mixt with the sweets of Love, a pain that ever accompanies the pleasure. Love else were not to be number'd among the passions of men, and was at first ordain'd in Heaven for some divine motion of the Soul, till *Adam* with his loss of · *Paradise* debaucht it, with jealousies, fears and curiosities, and mixt it with all that was afflicting; but you'l say he had reason to be jealous, whose Woman for want of other Seducers listen'd to the Serpent, and for the Love of change wou'd give way even to a Devil, this little Love of Novelty and knowledge has been intail'd upon her daughters ever since, and I have known more Women rendered unhappy and miserable from this torment of curiosity, which they bring upon themselves, than have ever been un-done by less villainous Men. (191)

Behn attributes humanity's downfall, not to Eve's curiosity, but to Adam's, and the passage goes out of its way to counter the conventional – 'you'l say' – misogynous account of the Genesis story before reverting to standard narratives regarding the moral debauchery that inevitably attends women's desire to know. Behn's version of the story places adultery – and the cuckolded husband – at the roots of humanity's fall from grace, but immediately undermines the idea of this fall as tragedy in its representation of the education it affords Silvia. Her curiosity *is* sated by her reading of the letter, and she writes a response to Philander calculated to inspire his jealousy. Against the vision of women's unhappiness the narrative affords us, we witness the heroine's movement from weakness to strength, an evolution accompanied by increasingly sophisticated ways of reading the world. Both developments rewrite biblical stories and their applications.[53]

The second volume of *Love-Letters* moves behind the watch-glass of vow-breaking to examine its inner workings in the psychological portrait it draws of Silvia's descent into whoredom. In order to transcend the sexual double standard that governs the code of male libertinism and her own initial seduction by Philander, Silvia must transform the sexual curiosity that drove her into her lover's arms into a curiosity about how the world functions economically, a knowledge that, beyond the parameters of the aristocratic marriage plot with which she is familiar, Silvia can only glean from someone outside her social corner. In particular, Silvia must learn the facts of prostitution. Silvia's servant in Holland, Antonett, transforms Philander's betrayal of his lover into an opportunity for her mistress's economic advancement. The reversal of power this scene involves is anticipated by Antonett's relation to Silvia's secrets, circulated through the exchange of letters:

Antonett was waiting at [the] reading of that Letter, nor was there any thing the open hearted *Silvia* conceal'd from that Servant; and Women, who have made a breach in their Honour, are seldom so careful of their rest of Fame, as those who have a Stock intire; and *Silvia* believ'd after she had trusted the Secret of one Amour to her discretion, she might conceal none. (183)

Silvia's transformation into a courtesan figure takes place through the sharing of a private letter, a revelation that includes a redefinition of the social codes governing the aristocratic woman's relation to her servant. Having relinquished her honour – the fetishized sexual status that separates her from a lower-class woman – Silvia has nothing to lose by joining forces with Antonett. Behn's identifications work in both directions, toward the downwardly mobile aristocrat and the upwardly mobile servant. As a woman writing scandal fiction for an eager public, the author depends on the sharing of secrets, on her ability to extract narratives for her readers. Having discovered that spying for the king was financially ruinous, Behn found an alternative form of profiting from her connection to court circles.

In the passage that follows the letter's exposure, Antonett's recipe for success in love sounds like a formula for good fiction-writing:

[Antonett:] I am indeed of that opinion, that love and int'rest always do best together, as two most excellent ingredients in that rare Art of preserving Beauty. Love makes us put on all our Charms, and int'rest gives us all the advantage of dress, without which Beauty is lost, and of little use. Love wou'd have us appear always new, always gay, and magnificent, and money alone can render us so, and we find no Women want Lovers so much as those who want Petticoats, Jewels, and all the necessary trifles of Gallantry. (186)

We can link the two moments – the disclosure of the letter and the advocacy of prostitution – as part of a movement toward rendering the illicit both attractive and available to a large group of consumers. Antonett's pronouncements take on a particular resonance when compared to the dismal prophecies of Silvia's sister, who explicitly addresses the fate of the prostitute:

Consider, oh young noble Maid, the infamy of being a Prostitute! ... Alas, consider after an action so shamefull, thou must obscure thy self in some remote corner of the world, where honesty and honour never are heard of: No thou canst not shew thy face, but 'twill be pointed at for something monstrous: for a hundred ages may not produce a story so lewdly infamous and loose as thine. (74)

Mertilla's narrative takes on the rhetorical conventions that ensure a predictable outcome of Silvia's adventure, with its 'must' and its 'canst' and its 'will' and its elevation of Silvia's tale as the most remarkable of moral exempla. But Behn's curiosity takes us in a new direction, rejecting the haunting realism of disease for the pleasures of a courtesan narrative in the making. As a response to the conventional letter, Behn insists on the indestructibility of Silvia's beauty, which never fades but only becomes more powerful as the story unfolds. She also insists on rendering the story more and more attractive as it moves along. The more self-consciously lewd Silvia's narrative becomes, the more it tightens its hold over the reader, as the intrigues of mastery and deception heighten the pleasures of amatory fiction. We are compelled to read by our curiosity about Silvia's plots, plots hatched, significantly, with the help of Antonett.[54]

The tidy oppositions the narrative sets up through its various speakers – between nature and incest, providence and materialism, singularity and repetition, wife and whore – break down in the moments of and around their articulation. Silvia's earnest commitment to the king gives way to desire for Philander, and Mertilla writes her diatribe against adultery as a cast-off mistress. Simply exposing the hypocrisies of the speakers inclined to utter moral pronouncements, however, only interests Behn up to a point. The larger issue at stake involves exploring the damage sustained by those who refuse, if only theoretically, the fall into experience. Competing versions of 'whore' appear as the signs of an opposition between idealism and pragmatism.

As Ros Ballaster has noted, 'By the third part [of Love-Letters], Sylvia has graduated to the narratorial complexity of Behn herself, drawing upon multiple fictional identities and languages in order to secure her control over a lover/reader as sophisticated and cynical as herself.'[55] Silvia develops habits that enable her to survive outside of the protection of her family and marriage, and her resilience and willingness to engage in the narrative of seduction, conquest, and abandonment more than once sets her apart from the idealism both of Octavio, whose treatment at Silvia's hands inspires him to monastic life, and of Cesario. Critics tend to read Silvia's Bildungsroman as either apolitical, or as strictly allegorical in its relation to the political narrative that reappears in the novel's concluding volume –i.e., Silvia's corruption mirrors Cesario's treason.[56] But I suggest Silvia's narrative teaches us modes of reading that prepare us to view the Monmouth Rebellion and its aftermath from a sceptical standpoint. Against the backdrop of her evolution, that is to say, we witness Cesario's tale as inversion, rather than recapitulation, of the courtesan's narrative. '[Cesario] was resolved to be a King or Nothing,' Philander is told, not once but twice: 'he is resolv'd to win or be nothing' (327, 336). From these statements alone we can anticipate the duke's fate, having learnt, by this point, the necessity of a more pragmatic relation to desire if social and political nothingness is to be avoided.

If Silvia's evolution can be charted along a curiosity curve that moves sharply upward, turning the courtesan outward to the world she seeks to exploit for personal gain, Cesario's interest in the events he directs turns him inward, away from exploration and toward zealotry: 'he stops at nothing that leads to his Ambition; nor has he done all that lies in the Power of Man only, to set all *France* yet in a Flame, but he calls up the very Devils from Hell to his Aid' (397–8). While Silvia evolves from innocent girl to libertine sceptic, Cesario evolves into a fanatic, developing modes of thinking that evoke the religious libertinism of the Ranters (or of Hortense Mancini's husband), juxtaposed against the Hobbesian attitudes adopted by Silvia and Philander. Cesario's commitments, both political and sexual, mark the distance between him and Silvia and Philander, who happily forfeit personal and political relations in their pursuit of self-interest. While Behn's satiric vision may include all of the characters, one cannot claim that the terms of the satire equally apply to each. Cesario, in particular, is singled out as a failure.[57] Behn's interrogation of male aristocratic character takes on a philosophical dimension in its pursuit of the 'truth' behind the veil of one man's pursuit of Truth.

We hear echoes of seventeenth-century philosophical examinations of providential historiography in Behn's meditation on the Duke of Monmouth's and Henrietta Wentworth's obsession with the supernatural: 'There is no Man fam'd for Negromancy, to whom he does not apply himself; which, indeed is done by the Advice of *Hermione* [Wentworth] who is very much affected with those sort of People, and puts a very great Trust and Confidence in 'em' (398).[58] Unlike Silvia, Cesario refuses to take responsibility for the plots he instigates, looking to the stars for authority: 'They [the sorcerers] have, at the earnest Request of

Hermione, calculated his Nativity, and find him born to be a King; and that before twenty Moons expire he shall be crown'd in *France*' (398). In a protracted midnight scene, Cesario witnesses a dumb show staged by the evil wizard Fergusano, in which, against a backdrop of sublime effects, the prince appears destined for triumph on the shores of 'France.'[59] Fergusano is able to deceive and manipulate Cesario through the idea of the oracles' constitutive obscurity. When Cesario complains that the final outcome of his narrative is not made plain by the dumb-show, the wizard reassures him that 'what was left unreveal'd, must needs be as glorious and fortunate to him, as what he had seen already, which was absolutely to be depended on' (408). Albert J. Rivero has noted perceptively the extent to which Behn is able to satirize both the Whig plotters and the credulous duke in this moment. Behind the scene, Rivero claims, stands the figure of the 'impartial' historian – i.e., Behn – who does not need to resort to artifice because she is 'telling the truth' in her narrative: 'Her reading of history must be correct because the Monmouth rebellion failed. God, the Author of History, underwrites her historical account.'[60] My own sense of this episode's relation to the narrative as a whole moves in a different direction, toward a representation of history in which Providence plays no role, or at least none recognizable to the reader of historical events. How does sexual difference inform the sceptical historiography that the novel represents?

Cesario's chief weakness, the narrative suggests, resides in a willingness to be ruled by a woman. Hermione allows the prince to appear to her 'in any Condition and Circumstances' (321), extracting, in turn, a promise that she will become queen to Cesario's Protestant king, 'in spight of all former Ties and Obligations' (324). Hermione serves as 'the Oracle of the Board' for Cesario, dictating the political plot as it unfolds while consolidating her own authority (397). Hermione's authority stands in for the corruption associated with Louise de Kéroualle, a woman whose power offended not only because it claimed what most assumed to be a male prerogative, but also because its motivations were suspect. In Behn's narrative, we are never certain whether Hermione wants power so that she might become queen or only so that she might bind Cesario more tightly to her. Her interests, in other words, lack the autonomy Behn attributes to both Gwyn's and Mancini's claims to authority.

Cesario's superstition bears a direct correlation to his willingness to misname his relationship with Hermione, whom he marries in a sham wedding ceremony reminiscent of the mock marriage staged between Portsmouth and Charles II:

> He pleaded impatiently for what she long'd, and would have made her Petition for, and all the while she makes a thousand doubts and scruples only to be convinced and confirmed by him; and after seeming fully satisfied, he leads her into a Chamber ... and Married her: since which, she has wholly managed him with greater power than before; takes abundance of State; is extreamly elevated, I will not say Insolent; and tho they do not make publick Declaration of this; yet she owns it to all her Intimates; and is ever reproaching my Lord with his lewd course of Life; wholly forgetting her own; crying out upon infamous Women, as if she had been all the course of her Life an innocent. (412)

When Silvia learns of Hermione's newly discovered moral integrity, she can only observe the situational irony: 'At this *Silvia* laughed extreamly, and cry'd, Hermione *would be very well content to be so mean a Sinner as myself, to be so young and so handsome an one*' (402). Silvia also recognizes the political implications of Hermione's and Cesario's stance: '*However*, said she, *to be serious, I would be very glad to know what real Probability there is in advancing and succeeding in this Design, for I would take my Measures accordingly*' (402). In contrast to Hermione's manic over-investment in Cesario's schemes, Silvia remains detached but observant. Cesario's and Hermione's willingness to assume a moral high ground around the topic of sexual conduct maps directly onto their rationalization of treason, Behn implies. Both gestures involve a wilful misrecognition of the imperatives of civil society. It is not Silvia's ethical ambiguity that stands allegorically for the principal of political anarchy, that is to say, but rather the abstraction of political action into a providential intention, one that recasts both private and public acts as singular in their significance even while insisting on their collective application. Hermione proclaims herself the champion of female virtue and Cesario declares himself the hero of Protestant nationalism, and they both imagine themselves most true to moral standards just as they embark on their most significant departures from the rule of law.

Silvia's response to the narrative of Cesario's ambition contributes to the narrative's sceptical tone: '*Silvia* laughed, and said she prophesied another End of this high Design than they imagined; but desperate Fortunes must take their Chance' (401–2). This assessment is reiterated by

Philander: 'he verily believed they would find themselves all mistaken; and that instead of a Throne the Prince would meet a Scaffold' (423). Philander's and Silvia's political views reflect a dearth of passion, a lack that also governs their relation to each other: 'it was now that they both indeed found there was a very great Friendship still remaining at the bottom of their Hearts for each other' (425). By contrast, Cesario and Hermione endure a terrible parting: 'a Hundred times they swounded with the apprehension of the separation in each other's Arms, and at last the Prince was forced from her while he left her dead, and was little better himself' (425). The couple's tendency to cast themselves as heroic players on the world's stage leads directly to the prince's will- ingness, however reluctant, to assume the title of king after his invasion of 'France': 'those about him insinuated into him, that it was the Title that would not only make him more Venerable, but would make his Cause appear more just and awful; and beget him a perfect Adoration with those People who liv'd remote from Courts, and had never seen that glorious thing called a King' (427). Of course, it is not the people who live remote from court who make and unmake kings, and Cesa- rio's error in judgment alienates him from the powerful men whose aid he needs and who quickly abandon the cause, leaving the prince only the humiliation of defeat.

'Nothing but the immediate hand of the Almighty ... could have turned the Fortune of the Battle to the Royal side,' the narrator asserts at the plot's climax (432). This pronouncement barely lasts the moment of its utterance.[61] In the wake of Cesario's defeat we find ourselves im- mediately facing a court organized around more cynical principles than that of divine right. God may be willing to intervene on the battlefield to preserve the status quo, but he is nowhere to be found at court. The idea that Behn only affords temporary consolation, in this moment, to the reader looking for political or historical assurances takes us back to the dedicatory letter that opens the third volume of *Love-Letters* and the suspicions it raises about the conduct of those aristocratic men who shifted or hid their allegiances in the Monmouth affair. By 1687, when Behn published the final volume of her novel, the crisis surrounding James II's increasingly open Catholic ambitions had been building for at least a year. In January of 1687, Laurence Hyde was dismissed from his post of Lord Treasurer; in the spring, James issued his Declaration of Indulgence, paving the way for Catholics to hold public office. The possibility of future treachery on the part of England's prominent aristocrats appears in the novel's closing sentence, concerning Philander's lucky escape from the scaffold:

> *Philander* lay sometime in the *Bastile*, visited by all the Persons of great Quality about the Court; he behaved himself very Gallantly all the way he came, after his being taken, and to the last Minute of his Imprisonment; and was at last pardoned, kiss'd the King's Hand, and came to Court in as much Splendour as ever, being very well understood by all good Men. (439)

The satirical comment appears in the contrast between Philander's recent cowardice on the battle field and his ready gallantry as a prisoner. Most darkly, it envelops the whole court and its willingness to accept Philander back into its circle, echoing the court's earlier decision not to follow through on its guilty verdict in the 1682 case against Ford, Lord Grey. Who are the 'good Men' capable of discerning Philander's real character, and what is the nature of their understanding? Were we to believe in the idea of the court's divinely ordained authority, we would assume that the good men accept Philander's reentry into court culture while guarding themselves against him. But how good are the good men? As we know from the case of Sunderland, who posted the bond that allowed Lord Grey to go free, the monarch's closest allies always had the potential to betray him, and Behn understood this as well as we do after the fact. Behind these figures lurks James II himself, a man who also betrayed England in his refusal to maintain a moderate stance on the subject of religion in the political arena.[62]

In 1682, at his trial for the abduction of Henrietta Berkeley, Ford, Lord Grey exclaimed, 'My Lord, were I guilty of the Villainies that here are lay'd to my Charge, I certainly should need no other Punishment: I am sure, I could not have a worse, than the Reflections of my own Conscience for them, and I ought to be Banish'd [from] the Society of Mankind.'[63] Three years later, Nicholas Adee indicted the clergy who showed signs of wanting to challenge the authority of James II: 'they who make no bones of Oaths, will make no scruple of Treason.'[64] This chapter has traced Behn's representation of vow-breaking in the moment before the invasion of William III gave shape to the Monmouth Rebellion and James II's abuses of his office. For Behn, I believe, the problem was more intractable than either Whig or Jacobite historiography would later admit, encompassing a larger European concern about religious factionalism and the role played by personal belief – of all varieties – in political narratives.[65] It should not surprise us to find that, in the world as Behn draws it, 'there is no poetic justice.'[66]

A year after publishing the final volume of *Love-Letters*, Behn wrote, in the letter of dedication that opens her translation of *The History of Oracles*:

> 'Tis a Discourse of *Religion*, in a time when we have scarcely any other Theme; 'tis grown so general a Mode, that even the Sword-men are now fiercer disputants than heretofore the lazier Gown-men were, while every Spark of noise enough, (sometimes the best of the Argument) shews his Wit and Learning on that subject. But since the stream runs that way, I believ'd it as ridiculous to appear in good company drest like Mrs *Abigail*, as (at this time) not to be arguing some points of Religion, tho' never so *Mal à propo*. But least, by such an undertaking I should, as many do, but the more embarass the Mystries of it, we shall treat here only of the *Pagan Religion*, and of the abominable Cheats of the *Oracles* and their *Priests*.[67]

Embedded in the wit of these remarks lies the density of the controversy at hand and its import for politicians and writers, as well as gownmen. The subject circles back to the woman author in the metaphor of female fashion it introduces and we can recognize, in Behn's desire to appear à la mode, a deeper preoccupation with proving her status as a philosopher and translator of substance. 'Some points of Religion' may take Behn into deep waters, both theologically and politically, but she limits her risk by restricting her attention to the 'abominable cheats' of the pagan tradition's oracles and priests. Such commentary constituted a central strand of seventeenth-century anticlerical discourse, but Behn protects herself from charges of atheism by adopting the veil of historical and linguistic difference.

That these remarks were addressed to George, Lord Jeffereys, whose judgments as Lord Chief Justice condemned the enemies of James II to execution and transportation after the Monmouth Rebellion, proves that Behn's sceptical tendencies did not preclude her support of Tory hardliners after 1685. The political poems Behn wrote in the years between Charles II's death and her own routinely evoke the divine right of kings to support Stuart hegemony. But the prose fiction that Behn produced during this period tells a different story.[68] In her reading of *Love-Letters*, Ellen Pollak has remarked that 'the irony of Behn's political defense of royalism is that it ends with the triumph not only of the king but also of the woman who most quintessentially embodies unrecuperated female defiance of male supremacy.'[69] If we remember the authority Behn invested in the figures of Nell Gwyn and Hortense Mancini, however, and consider the way those figures shape her characterization of Silvia, *Love-Letter*'s conclusion appears less ironic than revealing of the way that the novel, as a genre, afforded Behn with a means of uniting her understanding of sexual relations and the political crises that faced England in the 1680s. In the unconventional narrative *Love-Letters* tells, we see reflections on the 'cheats of Priests' intertwined with meditations on marriage and whoredom. Prose fiction affords Behn a space in which to weave an intricate tapestry of allusion and association, and also a vantage point from which to view the pattern as it unfolds.

3 The Secret History of Women's Political Desire, 1690–1714

> Madam Mazarine is dead, may her Faults die with her; may there be no more occasion given for the like Adventures, or if there is, may the Ladies be more Wise and Good than to take it!
>
> Mary Astell, *Some Reflections Upon Marriage, Occasion'd by the Duke & Duchess of Mazarine's Case; Which is also consider'd*[1]

England's last two Stuart monarchs attempted to bridge the chasms dividing the nation in the 1690s and early eighteenth century. Both Mary II and Queen Anne acted as champions of the Protestant cause and their supporters identified the monarchs' piety as a political principal. Rather than alleviate the anxieties that surrounded the royal mistresses of the Stuart brothers' courts, however, the reigns of Mary and Anne only further complicated the question of female rule. Mary's Jacobite opponents routinely characterized her as a parricidal whore and destroyer of principled governance. Anne's attachment to the powerful women of her court, not all of whom shared her high Anglican loyalties, resurrected the ghosts of Charles II's desires and the mistresses who exploited them.[2] Both queens' self-identification with the goals of the moral reform movement paradoxically deepened their political alienation and isolation. As the modern party system evolved in the wake of the Revolution, parliamentary practice wedded conventional understandings of political rule as inherently male with the newer limitations of monarchical authority – the only kind of authority, in England, legally accessible to women.

Proponents of this configuration of gender and religio-political authority worked hard to render the Protestant Whore both dangerously anachronistic *and* harmless. Nell Gwyn appears in popular culture as libertine hedonist, associated with Restoration court excesses, and folk heroine, harbinger of the Glorious Revolution. The Protestant Whore's representations signal the repetition compulsion that governed the period's obsession with the Restoration.[3] The desire to return to the reign of Charles II over and over again in debates about England's national identity articulates two modes of historical repetition. The first of these seeks to establish a bedrock 'truth' of Restoration history against which modernity can be defined. The second understands the way in which the Restoration has moved forward through history into the present, providing an alternate vantage point from which to view the operations of modernity.

This chapter traces the evolution of this historical dialectic in the cultural moment spanning the publication of the final volume of Behn's *Love-Letters* (1687) and Defoe's *Roxana* (1724). In the first half of the chapter, I track debates over the meaning of the Revolution in the 1690s, paying particular attention to the new dimensions these debates added to the religious controversies that were carried forward from the 1680s. Representations of Queen Mary map political and religious debates onto a sexual geography that the decade's secret histories mine for profit and polemic. Even as the court of William and Mary attempted to distance itself from the immediate past, secret histories kept that past alive, using the space of prose fiction to interrogate political motivation, sexual appetite, and religious conviction. Within this frame of reference, the Stuart royal mistress's spectral presence intimated foreignness, scepticism, and political critique in the period's new cultural edifices. The second half of the chapter turns to Queen Anne's reign and examines how debates about religious toleration were sexualized in the first decade of the eighteenth century. Representations of Queen Anne and Sarah Churchill, Duchess of Malborough, added new dimensions to the Restoration's debates concerning Protestantism's future in England and the role played by women in advancing its agenda. Tory satire *Queen Zarah* (1705) illuminates this point in its rendering of modern politics and the place of the 'female favourite' in a court ruled by a queen. Its author appears to be a champion of a beleaguered monarch and defender of the faith called to protect English institutions from the corrupting influence of Sarah Churchill, a latter-day Louise de Kéroualle. But Sarah Churchill's pursuit of power generates a narrative that ends up overshadowing the passive queen's, whose moralism proves largely ineffectual in the arena of modern politics. I conclude with an analysis of the Whig attack, in the years leading up to 1714, on Jacobite dreams of a Stuart restoration, an attack enabled through representations of the dangers of female misrule against which Nell Gwyn's political inefficacy stands as a salutary principle. We see the displacement not only of the royal mistress but also of the female monarch in the Whig narratives that anticipate George I's accession.

The Amphibious 1690s[4]

[It is] a severe Jest that the common people have got up against the Clergy, That there was but one thing formerly which the parliament could not do, that is, to make a Man a Woman: But now there is another, that is, to make an Oath which the Clergy will not take.

> Charles Leslie, *An Answer to a Book Intituled, The State of the*
> *Protestants in Ireland Under the late King James's Government* (1692)

The Revolution of 1688 did little to assuage distrust between Dissenters and Anglicans in the 1690s. The Church of England was divided over the question of swearing allegiance to England's *de facto* king and the willingness of most clergy to secure their futures under William III led William Stephens to observe, in 1696, that 'there is now no need of going over the Water to discover that the name Church signifieth only a Self-interested Party ... The Clergy have no Godliness but Gain.'[5] At stake was not only the identity of England's rightful king, but the Church of England's political future. As William forged alliances among a range of Protestant interests, both at home and abroad, Anglicans fought to establish a Church of England hegemony against the encroachments of Dissenters granted freedom of worship by the Toleration Act of 1689.[6] On the other side, William's appointment of Tory members of the Church party to office in the early 1690s enraged his Whig supporters. *A Dialogue Betwixt Whig and Tory* records a conversation on this subject:

WHIG ... Was ever any Government in so promising a Condition, as ours was at the time of the Revolution? Were we not the Hopes of all our Allies, and the Terror of our Enemies? And is not the case alter'd with us? I fear it is: To be plain, a Ministry from *Wapping* could not have made worse work on't than yours have done ...

TORY. And do you think the Government would be better serv'd at this time by Novices, and Strangers to Business?

WHIG ... I think it would be much better serv'd by ignorant Friends, than understanding Enemies.[7]

After the honeymoon of the Revolution had ended, Craig Rose observes, 'whig true believers came to despise King William every bit as much as die-hard Jacobites.'[8] That Whig moderates were able to exploit opportunities afforded by the new regime only exacerbated tensions by severing ties between different Dissenting constituencies. Gary S. de Krey notes, 'The radical bond that had transcended urban social divisions in the 1680s snapped in the face of the conflicting needs of different social elements.'[9] Schism was the defining mark left by the 1690s on Dissenters and Anglicans alike.

The Act of Toleration heightened, rather than diminished, tensions among Protestant constituencies even as it provided a legal framework for their peaceful coexistence.[10] One contemporary remarked on the factionalism that greeted the new regime's initiatives:

These Moderation hate, and these no less
Immoderately for Moderation press:
...
Some think the Breach too great, and some too small
To admit or need a Cure, some loudly bawl
That Int'rest, Int'rest is the Cause of all:[11]

While enabling a tentative alliance between Dissent and the Church of England, toleration was most markedly defensive.[12] As such, it darkened, rather than dissipated, the clouds of intolerance and paranoia hanging over the nation. Locke responded to the crisis in authority by advocating for a shift from the exercise of top-down ecclesiastical power to a more broadly based and communally defined moral sensibility as the grounds of social conformity:

Now, though the divisions that are amongst sects should be allowed to be ever so obstructive of the salvation of souls, yet, nevertheless, 'adultery, fornication, uncleanness, lasciviousness, idolatry, and such like things, cannot be denied to be works of the flesh'; concerning which the apostle has expressly declared, that 'they who do them shall not inherit the kingdom of God', Gal.v.21. Whosoever, therefore, is sincerely solicitous about the kingdom of God, and thinks it his duty to endeavour the enlargement of it amongst men, ought to apply himself with no less care and industry to the rooting out of these immoralities, than to the extirpation of sects.[13]

Locke was not alone in calling for the reformation of manners in the 1690s. The 'moral revolution' appears as an ideological compensation for the continued disintegration of intra-Protestant alliances. While Dissenters pursued their goals in the freedom of their own meeting houses, the Church of England developed organizations that it hoped would regenerate its cultural authority: the Religious Societies, the Society for Promoting Christian Knowledge (SPCK), and the Society for the Propagation of the Gospel in Foreign Parts (SPG). The Society for the Reformation of Manners (SRM) was the only group to emerge from the Anglican constituency that would allow Dissenting members. As Tina Isaacs has observed, the SRM eventually became a competitor with Church of England orthodoxy for jurisdiction over the governance of moral conduct, and those who hoped that the call for moral reform would unite Protestants were destined to disappointment: 'fear of nonconformity and lay encroachment on church authority, along with distaste for those who accepted toleration, divided churchmen over how to reform manners, and placed obstacles in the way of any institutional alliance between Church and lay reformers.'[14] Eventually the more liberal branch of the moral reformation movement would win out against the Church of England, in part because the SRM advocated personal morality as a political and social, rather than strictly religious, goal, thereby uncoupling the conventional identification between ecclesiastical and moral concerns.[15]

The sexual politics of the Revolution were actively shaped by Queen Mary. Two portraits were drawn during the period, one by the Revolution's propaganda machine, the other, more covertly, by the Jacobites.[16] The Williamites drew attention to Mary's long-standing reputation for piety – '*Urania* [Mary] to the Stars does show / What Beauty Crown'd with Piety can do,' declared a 1688 celebratory ode – and her resolve to reform the nation's morals.[17] Gilbert Burnet, among others, celebrated Mary's religious conviction publicly and often:

> I cannot without a particular joy see that Person, whose present Circumstances mark her out to be both the defender and perfecter of that blessed work, to be such in all the parts both of her private Deportment and the publick administration of the Government that she seemeth to be in all points fitted for the work for which she seems to have been born.[18]

Mary's commitment to the nation's moral improvement coincided with her belief in the providential role she and her husband had played in saving the nation from a Catholic king in 1688:

> As We cannot but be deeply Sensible of the great Goodness and Mercy of Almighty God (by whom Kings Reign) in giving so happy Success to our Endeavours for the Rescuing these Kingdoms from Popish Tyranny and Superstition, and in Preserving Our Royal Persons, Supporting Our Government, and Uniting the Arms of most of the Princes and States in Christendom against Our Common Enemy; So We are not less touched with a Resentment, that (notwithstanding these great Deliverances) Impiety and Vice do still abound in this Our Kingdom.[19]

This providential rhetoric was politically crucial to the post-Revolutionary regime and found active support in Anglican sermons of the period. William Lloyd, bishop of Saint Asaph, wrote:

> I cannot without ingratitude to God, but mention that mercy of the late Revolution; and those of our deliverances since; especially that of this present time: All these being so visibly the effects of Gods continued care of us; being all for the same Church and Nation, all in times of great and near danger, and all with the like Evidence of Gods hand in them; so that whosoever considers them severally, cannot but see reason enough to acknowledge, that each of these was *the Lords doing*.[20]

Whigs linked William and Mary to the unfolding of providential history in order to reinvest the monarchy with the status it sorely lacked, and this rhetoric was a crucial element in the establishment of new grounds of monarchical authority. Mary's piety served as a sign of election, both political and personal.

Mary's death in 1694 prompted an outpouring of praise for the queen by Williamite propaganda. Mary's piety – 'The Pious MARY She is gone on High, / And Seated in the Heavenly Hierarchy' – was a theme often repeated, as was the idea of Mary as England's saviour:

Say, *Happy Man*, Inhabiter of Earth,
On that Great Day MARIA had her Birth,
Did not the Balmy Aspect of the Morn
Portend the Budding Glory of our Realm?

The transformation of Mary's piety into a political principal enabled a fictional, if not actual, reconciliation of church and state:

> In a hot Ferment [she] found the State
> Perplex'd with Factions, Jarring, and Debate;
> ...
>   Yet still encourag'd by celestial Aid,
> The Royal Shepherdess divinely sway'd,
> Held out Her Crook, and the rude Herd obey'd.

One poem links her death to that of John Tillotson, archbishop of Canterbury, who died the same year: 'By these two great Examples we may see, / The State goes Hand in Hand with Piety.' 'She better knew / What milder Paths Religion shou'd persue,' William Walsh observed.[21] Commentators used the opportunity of Mary's death to reflect on Mary's particular brand of female governance:

> It is not a Cruel Athaliah, an Idolatrous Maachah, an Incarnate Devil of a Jezebel, an Inhumane Irene, a Lascivious Marozia, a Heterodox Theodora, a Blood-thirsty Mary that we are speaking of; but another second Christian Queen, like Helena, (tho' alas without a Constantine to her Son) ... possessing the Virtues, Religion and Constancy, of the Illustrious Queen of Navarre, and dazling the Glory of the Renowned Elizabeth Her Protestant Predecessor: Since, I say, we are called to behold such a Person; and of so near a concern to us and our Religion, so great an enemy to the Mother of Harlots![22]

Juxtaposing Mary II and her namesake, the Catholic Bloody Mary, the speaker establishes a strict opposition between the whores of Babylon and the champions of Protestant integrity. The exceptional nature of female monarchy shines through, its status as depraved or ideal highlighted by the urgent assignation of positive value to Mary II's reign. Gilbert Burnet highlights this discourse of singularity in his account of Mary's rule: 'Female Government has had its peculiar Blemishes, with fewer Patterns to compensate for the Faultiness of others. The fierceness of Semirami's Character, does lessen her Greatness: And the Luxuries of Cleopatra does more than balance her Beauty ... Female Government has seldom looked so great as it did in Isabel of Castile. But if she was a good Queen, she was but an indifferent Wife.'[23] Isabel's failings as a wife, Burnet implies, qualify her success, rendering a queen's personality an important component in any consideration of her fitness to exercise political authority.

Jacobites used the same starting point in their attacks on Mary.[24] Dubbed 'Tullia' to William's 'Tarquin,' Mary appears a whorish parricide in satires of the period. A 'lustful Goneril,' Queen 'Molly' alienated, like a whore, her most intimate relations in the name of profit and self-advancement, according to Tory satires of the 1690s. In these satires, Mary's iniquity announces itself in the daughter's attack on the father's body politic, a sin deepened by the queen's willingness to conceal the truth of both her intent and her actions. Her promotion of moral reform appears as little more than the expression of an occasionally felt remorse: 'Yet when she drunk cool tea in liberal sups / The sobbing dame was maudlin in her cups.'[25] Mary's famed piety, likewise, appears only a question of sexual preference; while William engages with Bentick 'at the old Game of Gomorrah,' 'Wise Tullia his wife, more Pious of Life, / With Shrews—y drives away Sorrow.'[26] The sceptical attitude these Jacobite attacks sustain toward the language of female piety takes us back to Silvia's critique of Hermione in Behn's *Love-Letters*. Indeed, Behn's 'Congratulatory Poem' to Mary announces its disapproval of the new regime in its refusal to read the queen as anything more than 'daughter of a king,' whose 'god-like attributes' have been passed on to the daughter genetically, rather than by providential fiat. An imitation of the original, Mary appears the consolation prize for a public mourning 'all the ills the ungrateful world has done' in deposing the rightful king.[27]

More generally, the providential narrative so eagerly advanced by Anglican clerics and others in their treatments of Mary could not adequately absorb the facts of the queen's death. Indeed, her death could support a very differently inflected – i.e., Jacobite – view of Providence's interests. As Rachel Weil notes, 'the fact that Mary died young from a disfiguring disease did not say much for God's providential support of the Glorious Revolution.'[28] At best, then, Mary's rule appeared a well-intentioned and well-supervised exercise of authority; at worst, a profound corruption of Stuart (male) hegemony.

The ideological gap between the Williamite court's claim to moral supremacy and the licentiousness of England's recent past provided the authors of secret histories with an occasion ripe for exploitation, and narratives describing the decadence of Stuart kings appeared through the 1690s. Their descriptions of Charles II's arrival in England in 1660 describe, not his ascent to the throne, but rather his descent into the boudoir, a fall away from the standard of Protestant masculine heroism the histories identify with the nation's new-found integrity: 'Soon after he arrived into *England*, where he was received with all the Pomp, Splendour, and Joy that a Nation could express; but then, as if he had left all his Piety behind him in *Holland* care was taken against the very first Night, that his Sacred was to lie at *White-hall*, to have the Lady *Castlemain* seduced from her Loyalty to Her husband, and enticed into the Arms of the happily restored Prince.'[29] From this point forward, the histories assert, Charles's rule was shaped entirely by the royal mistresses: 'He derived, they said, his desires of Peace from the desire he had to possess [women], and that Women rendered him the merciful Prince he was.'[30] Courtiers wanting to influence Restoration policy soon discovered that the way to the king's policy was through his genitals: 'What all the Arts of the most refin'd Politicks and Rhetorick could never have been able to bring about in a long Succession of Time, was done with ease and Diligence by a Woman's Tongue and Tail.'[31] The Stuart royal mistresses stand as signs of a despotic past of female absolutism, an aberration corrected by the Revolution's principles and principal players.

The royal mistress's iconic status also reveals itself in her association with French interests. The secret histories recount how Charles's appetites rendered him the dupe of France, easy prey to Louis XIV's machinations, facilitated by Charles II's sister, the Duchess of Orleans: '[Henrietta] presented our King, her Brother, with her Woman, known then by the Name of Madam *Carewell*, but much better since by the Title of Dutchess of *Portsmouth*, to serve the French King as a Heifer afterwards to Plow withal ... So that if they failed in their Ends of furnishing the King with a French Wife, they were resolved to make it up, by supplying of him with a *French* Whore.'[32] This French threat extends into the post-revolutionary decade; one series of secret history narrative devotes all of its attention to the misdeeds of Mary of Modena, who appears reconstructed as a courtesan in her representation as mistress to Louis XIV. Together, the pair appear as libertine tyrants in secret histories detailing their alleged affair: 'why should thy lofty and unbounded Soul, stoop to the mouldy prescripts of doting feeble Age, or which is worse of crafty whining Priests: Great Monarchs to themselves should be a Rule, and virtues from *their wills* should have their Denominations,' declares 'Polydorus' to 'Messalina.' The French king's plans to back James II's invasion of Ireland are founded on the prospect of having Mary to himself: 'Yes, to *Ibernia* he'll send him, and with assistance too, but with the irrevocable Fate of falling there ... The

Gothic Government so suspected by the *Ibernians*, the very disgusted Pagans themselves shall fall from his Cause, whilest with the certain Destruction and Fate of *Lycogenes* [James II], the certain *Messalina* is his own.'[33]

These satiric accounts of the Stuart brothers and their unruly women pay close attention to the dynamics governing the courtesan's rise to power. In these accounts, the act of storytelling as an exercise of political authority serves as an important trope and marks the place where the interests of the secret history and those of the women they seek to discredit converge. *The Amours of the Sultana of Barbary* (1689) includes two embedded narratives that trace the personal histories of mistresses. The practice of storytelling is linked explicitly to the advancement of a political agenda:

> He [Henry Bennet, Earl of Arlington, Secretary of State] will know if he finds her ready to follow all he should advise; if she will, then he is absolute Monarch of the Sultan [Charles II] ... The Grand Vissier believes it necessary for his Designs, that he should be acquainted with the life of *Indamora* [Portsmouth], (for so was the fair Christian call'd), she had confusedly related to him some of the particulars when he first ransomed her, but that does not satisfie; he goes to her then, conjures her to give him that satisfaction, since he assured her it was for both their Interests, he should be ignorant of nothing that concerned her.[34]

The intimacy Indamora's story recounts is mirrored in the storytelling moment shared by the mistress who tells the story and the courtier who listens, as sex, narrative, and political opportunism coalesce. The secret history repeatedly turns to emergent techniques of the novel, in particular those adopted by contemporary French narratives, to describe the minds and motivations of its principal characters. In this secret history, for instance, the second embedded narrative, 'The Amours of Mustapha [James II] and Zayda,' which is recounted to Barbara Villiers, Duchess of Cleveland, proves an end in itself. Originally solicited to provide the Duchess with information she might use against her rivals, the story ends up narrating a revenge tale already enacted, leaving the Duchess with the story itself as proof of her enemies' defeat. The habit of storytelling expands into a biographical essay in *The Secret History of the Dutchess of Portsmouth*, one that recounts the courtesan's psychological development and considerable talents. By way of conclusion, the narrative asserts that 'it is certain, that her sound Judgment, accurate

Apprehension, her happy Memory, her smart Wit, and insinuating Way was sufficient to Captivate the Mind of so Amorous a Prince as was the Prince of the Isles, especially, when all those Accomplishments were accompany'd with some share of Beauty and Love, though but in an outward appearance.'[35]

The propensity to linger over the lives and careers of the courtesans as important cultural subjects draws the secret history's logic close to pornographic satires of the 1680s that we encountered in chapter 1. In both *The Parliament of Women* and *The Whore's Rhetorick*, the whore's bid for power mirrors the writer's act of self-authorization. In this regard, the whore's illicit acts of narration, recounted so often in the secret histories, link her to the imperatives governing modern authorship. Both whore and secret history writer attempt to undermine conventional understandings of authority, emphasizing the 'elsewhere' of the underground writer's knowledge as an alternative location for the production of cultural legitimacy. Eve Tavor Bannet claims that 'by virtue of carrying out to the public secret letters, memoirs, and documents concealed in the closet, as well as stories of private conversations and intrigues, secret historians ... placed themselves in an apparently dishonorable position. They appeared to occupy the role of those *unfaithful* secretaries in which the long eighteenth century abounded – those untrustworthy servants, vengeful intimates, and secret spies who betrayed their masters for gain.'[36]

The mandate of the secret history, Annabel Patterson has argued, is 'to speak the unspeakable.'[37] But, if my sense of the secret histories' proximity to pornographic and satiric discourses of the 1680s is correct, the 'unspeakable' had been repeatedly spoken since the inception of libertine discourse in England. The historical irony, I believe, is that the Whigs who authored the secret histories were writing on behalf of a regime whose providential historiography their own satiric impulses and narrative practices undermine as thoroughly as the Jacobite critiques circulating in the period. The sharp contrast that mainstream discourse was so keen to establish between legitimate and illegitimate instances of female rule depended on a model of political authority originating in divine right – not the divine right claimed by James Stuart and his defenders, but a more general divine right of Protestant election. The world that the secret history describes defeats this mythic impulse, leaving a Hobbesian narrative in its stead.

In emphasizing the secret history's reliance on the conventions of Restoration pornographic narratives and of French prose fiction and memoir, I counter Robert Mayer's assertion that two different secret history practices appeared in the late seventeenth and early eighteenth centuries, one that readers understood as fact, the other as fiction.[38] The dross of fictional pleasure that Mayer identifies as the distinguishing feature of Delarivier Manley's work, in particular, appears in all secret histories.[39] Indeed, fiction appears as a source of readerly pleasure, the representational practice that mitigates the starkness of the ideological agenda governing the court of William and Mary. John Sheffield, Duke of Buckingham, writes that 'a bewitching kind of pleasure called Sauntring, and talking without any constraint, was the true Sultana Queen he [Charles II] delighted in.'[40] 'Talking without constraint' aptly describes what secret histories do best; its pleasures provide the link between the Restoration's cultural practices and the evolution of narrative modes in the early eighteenth century.

Toleration's Sexual Politics

By the end of [the seventeenth] century, the Scarlet Woman, at long last, had made her protesting exit over the remains, not of broken hearts, but of lost souls; and her place was taken, in silent dignity, by Natural Man, the embodiment of those sterling qualities which civilization was now striving to regain.

David Ogg, *England in the Reigns of James II and William III*[41]

Queen Anne's attachment to the Church of England has often been remarked in histories of the period, but the role played by that attachment in the scandals of her reign has received less attention, despite the fact that the most powerful woman of Anne's court, Sarah Churchill, named it as the cause of her downfall.[42] Defending her decision to publish her memoirs, Churchill wrote, 'It was to give an account of my conduct with regard to parties, and of the successful artifice of Mr. Harley and Mrs. Masham, in taking advantage of the Queen's passion for what she called the Church, to undermine me in her affections.'[43] In popular culture, the connection between Anne's religious obsessions and her affairs of the heart also seemed plain:

When as Queen Anne of great Renown
Great Britain's Sceptre sway'd,
Besides the Church she dearly lov'd
A Dirty Chamber-Maid.[44]

Debates about religious toleration that emerged in the first decade of
the eighteenth century juxtaposed the female favourite against Queen
Anne's attempts to claim the political and moral high ground.

Like her sister, Queen Anne supported the moral reform movement.
On 25 February 1702/3, Anne issued a proclamation, 'For the Encouragement of Piety and Virtue, and for the preventing and Punish-
ing of Vice, Prophaneness, and Immorality.'[45] But the divisiveness of
debates between High and Low Church Anglicans, the activism of
Dissent, and the political exploitation of religious fervour as irrational
enthusiasm by Whigs and Tories alike made a stable identification between church and state interests difficult to maintain. One of Anne's
earliest speeches to Parliament records her attachment both to the Act
of Toleration and to the Church of England: 'I shall be very careful to
preserve and maintain the Act of Toleration, and to set the Minds of all
my People at Quiet; my own Principles must always keep me entirely
firm to the Interests and Religion of the Church of England, and will
incline me to countenance those who have the truest Zeal to support
it.'[46] These goals proved elusive. Toleration was anathema to the majority of High and Low Anglican Church members alike, for, as Frederick
Wilson points out, 'the accession of Anne seemed to the Church to be
a pledge that all unclean connection with Dissent would cease.'[47] To
the Dissenters, on the other hand, Anne's 'Zeal' was cause for concern,
implying, in their minds, an excessive attachment to High Anglican
ideals. Both ends of the spectrum and all colours in between, in other
words, shaded Anne's attempts to assume a disinterested commitment
to Protestant hegemony.[48]

Anne quickly realized that the Protestant cause was being used
against her by both Dissenters and Anglicans. The rallying cry of High
Church zealots (often Jacobites), 'The Church in danger,' provoked a
pointed response in her speech to Parliament in October of 1705:

> I cannot but with Grief observe, there are some amongst us, who endeav-
> our to foment Animosities; but I persuade my self, they will be found to be
> very few, when you appear to assist me in Discountenancing and Defeat-
> ing such Practices.
>
> *I mention this with a little more Warmth, because there have not been wanting
> some so very malicious, as even in Print to suggest the Church of England, as by
> Law Establish'd, to be in Danger at this time.*
>
> I am willing to hope, not one of my Subjects can really entertain a Doubt
> of my Affection to the Church, or so much as suspect that it will not be my

Chief Care to support it, and leave it secure after me: And therefore we may be certain, that they who go about to insinuate things of this Nature, must be mine and the Kingdom's Enemies; and can only mean to cover Designs which they dare not publickly own by endeavouring to distract us with unreasonable and groundless Distrusts and Jealousies.[49]

The recognition that the language surrounding Protestant integrity had assumed an allegorical dimension, cloaking commitments to treasonous causes, required Anne to distance herself even from the moral reform movement when she recognized that charges about the licentiousness of the age had become a political code:

> The suppressing Immorality, and profane and other wicked and malicious Libels, is what I have always earnestly recommended, and shall be glad of the first Opportunity to give my Consent to any Laws that might effectually conduce to that End: But this being an Evil complained of in all Times, it is very injurious to take a Pretence from thence to insinuate, that the Church is in any Danger from my Administration.[50]

This reading of religious discourse as party propaganda involved Anne in the acts of interpreting and shaping the master narrative governing England's Protestant future. But a number of circumstances conspired against her attempts at political authorship, including, as Toni Bowers observes, her own failure to produce a Protestant heir: 'Anne's "provision" for the Protestant succession was anything but the manifest, indubitable accomplishment the queen purported to consider it. On the contrary, it was a gaping absence, a festering wound, the site of perennial contention and anxiety.'[51]

During the War of the Spanish Succession, Bowers argues, Anne's political authority was undermined by reflections that found her lacking in comparison to the prowess of her general-in-chief, John Churchill, Duke of Malborough.[52] But in the early years of Anne's reign, challenges to the queen's authority were as likely to consider her weakness in relation to Sarah Churchill as they were her reliance on the duke, so that the debates surrounding the monarch came to be refracted through a cultural lens focused on a more general debate about female governance. One lampoon, titled 'On the Duchess of Malbrough' [sic], puts it succinctly: 'Burn but the witch, and all things will go well.'[53] The question of Anne's authority repeatedly encompassed a contemplation of the monarch's female favourites: most famously the Duchess of Malborough, but also Abigail Masham and, in the final years of her regime, the Duchess of Somerset. Not surprisingly, these debates frequently circled back to the Restoration as their point of departure. Churchill, as part of her ongoing attack on her rival, Abigail Masham, drew parallels between Anne's affections and those of Charles II: 'You cannot but remember ... how many affronts King Charles had, that was a man, upon account of the Duchess of Portsmouth; and I think I need not say a great deal to show how much worse it is for your Majesty, whose character has been so different from his, to be put in print and brought upon the stage perpetually for one in Abigail's post,' she wrote to the queen in 1708.[54]

But the Restoration royal mistress – and the prostitute more generally – did not provide a point of reference any more stable than did the term 'Protestant,' as popular culture engaged in continuous reimaginings of her significance. The Preface to *A Collection of all the Dialogues Written by Mr. Thomas Brown*, which includes a series of whore vignettes, warns that 'a Poet is as unfit to manage the Serious Part of Controversie, as an Irishman is to write the Miracle Part of Church History: For besides, that his Integrity is as much to be suspected as his Judgment, the least Thought, or extravagant Fancy, is apt to lead him a hundred Pages out of his way.'[55] And, indeed, the early eighteenth century's representations of the Restoration's royal mistresses, like those of the secret histories of the 1690s, varied widely in their allegiance to 'fact.' The fictional reconstructions of the Restoration imagined, among various scenarios, Nell Gwyn's career as exemplary in its financial acuity, despite the public's knowledge of her will, which suggested the opposite. In Brown's dialogues N-ll G–n admonishes Peg Hughes:

> I, you see, through the whole course of my Life, maintain'd my Post, and I was Mistress to a King, liv'd as great as a Dutchess to my last Minute; and you like an Extravagant Concubine ... Game[d] away an Estate in few Years, large enough to have maintain'd a score of Younger Brothers at your Ladiships Service ... Fie upon't, I am asham'd to think, that a Woman who had Wit enough to tickle a Prince out of so fine an Estate, should at last prove such a fool as to be bubled on't by a little spotted Ivory, and painted Paper.[56]

In a similar vein, 'Beau Feilding's' elegy on the death of the Duchess of Cleveland laments the fortune lost when Feilding threw over his banker/benefactor for a new lover:

It was the Loss of a good Yearly Pension,
Which makes me thus with grief and Sorrow mention
For I who always honestly did mean,
Think a fat Sorrow better than a Lean.[57]

Echoing the popular literature of the Restoration, the courtesan appears as the consummate economist, rather than the hedonist of court culture described in the secret histories of the 1690s. Indeed, 'Moll Quarles' bemoans the licentiousness of the present and hopes for the resurrection of a Puritan standard that will generate business for the trade:

We have nothing to hope for, but that the National Senate, through their wonted wisdom, will find out, without shamming on't, some real expedient to restrain the looseness of the Age, and promote the practice of Morality and strict observance of Religion; for through all the Experience I have had in the Mistery of Intrigueing, I have ever found the Lady Students in the School of *Venus*, attended with the most prosperity when the People are most Pious.[58]

The satires dismiss both the teleology and the substance of the moral reformists' arguments concerning England's progress out of the darkness of the Restoration and uncouple the link between prosperity and virtue in a manner that anticipates Mandeville's *A Modest Defence of Publick Stews* (1724).

These examples provide a backdrop against which to read *Queen Zarah*'s searing 1705 portrait of Sarah Churchill, whose narrative, I suggest, represents a particular kind of courtesan story. Churchill was resolutely modern in her approach to politics, particularly in her manipulation of an emergent party system. Powerful within the court as the queen's keeper of the privy purse, groom of the stole, and mistress of the wardrobe, Churchill also considered herself representative of court interests even as she distanced herself from the queen's religious convictions and attempted to separate the queen from the High Church Tories, whose rhetoric appealed to Anne on a number of levels. Criticized a decade earlier by Queen Mary for her laxness in religious matters, Sarah, in turn, described Anne's zeal as 'that darling phantom which the Tories were ever presenting to her imagination, and employing as a will-o'-the-wisp, to bewilder her mind and entice her ... to the destruction of her quiet and her glory.'[59] Juxtaposed against a queen whose religious attachments rendered her at once trustworthy and politically vulnerable, Sarah Churchill's amoral pursuit of power summed up, in her detractors' eyes, the danger and efficiency of the new century's politics.[60]

Written in 1705, *The Secret History of Queen Zarah and the Zarazians* and its continuation (published the same year), capitalized on the few Tory victories that interrupted the Whig sweep of the spring elections of that year.[61] *Queen Zarah* made public the hatred of Sarah Churchill shared by many court intimates and hastened the decline of a star already falling in 1705. In a conventional fashion, it identifies Sarah Churchill's pursuit of power with the epithet 'whore': 'How great a Shame it is,' writes one detractor in the narrative, 'for Albigion [England] to see Albania [Anne] the Mother of her Country, a Princess who loves Goodness, and the Repose of her Subjects, sacrific'd to the Ambition of a —, who renders her the weakest of all Women.'[62] But *Zarah* adds a new dimension to the familiar configuration of sex and corruption in its treatment of religious affairs. Rather than associating the Whore of Babylon with the French and the Catholic Church, as did the Whig secret histories of the 1690s, *Zarah* points to the enemy at home: the Low Anglican Church and Dissent support for toleration. The secret history adopts the 'Church in danger' rhetoric, which, in 1704 and 1705, was used to bemoan recent defeats of the Act of Occasional Conformity.[63] The 'Church in danger' rhetoric particularly countered the discourse of 'Moderation' that emerged after Anne admonished Parliament, in her speech of April 1704, to 'go down into your several countries so disposed to moderation and unity, as becomes all those who are joined together in the same religion and interest.'[64] *Zarah* rewrites the discourse of moderation so that, in the case of the queen, it stands for private virtue, while in the case of the Whigs it disguises an appetite for power, as when a young courtier confronts Volpone (Godolphin) about his affair with the duchess: 'these last words [of Aranio] had like to have ruin'd his L–ds–p's Pretentions to *Moderation*, for he was forced to summon all his Conduct and his Reason to support himself' (158).

The narrative begins with a meditation on the Restoration, the reign of *Rollando*, and the period's sexual politics, drawing on the premise that the court of Charles II rewarded both its men and women for their willingness to prostitute themselves. Zarah's mother, 'Jenisa,' displays 'some little arts ... peculiar to some sort of women, by which means she gain[s] the hearts of all the men who convers[e] with her'; John Churchill, 'Hippolito,' pleases women and is reputed 'to make his fortune that way' (4–5). Directly quoting (without acknowledging) Gabriel

de Brémond's 1683 satire, *Hattigé* – a portrait of Barbara Villiers, Duchess of Cleveland – *Zarah* dwells on the figure of the courtesan, and, in
particular, on her ability to divest the monarch of his power: 'Such is the
Fortune of Monarchs in Love; when they are with their Mistresses they
commonly lay aside that Majesty which dazzles the Eyes and affects the
Hearts of Mankind; they go undress'd into their Chambers and make
themselves so familiar with their Mistresses, they afterwards use them
as other Men' (8–9). The narrative does not berate this practice, but
rather uses the psychological paradigm it provides – that is, sex's ability to reconfigure power relations – as a template for its consideration
of Sarah Jenyns – technically a 'nobody' – and her rise at court through
her marriage to another opportunist, John Churchill.

The plot includes the story of young Zarah's triumph over Barbara
Villiers and makes a significant break with the facts of the Sarah Jenyns's
and John Churchill's courtship and marriage: the historical record suggests that the courtship lasted over a year and was neither aided by
Sarah's mother, nor interfered with by Villiers, who was living in Paris
at the time.[65] But the narrative's reconstruction of the marriage plot focuses entirely on a fabricated competition between the Jenyns women
and the duchess. ''Tis easie,' Zarah's mother announces to her daughter,
'to think of such Measures as will bring about what is agreeable, both
to your Wishes of Love and my Desires of Ambition' (11). Interrupting
a seduction scene between Zarah and Hippolito (John Churchill) at an
opportune moment, Zarah's mother manages to force a marriage on
the unsuspecting libertine. When Hippolito attempts to ward off the
mother with declarations of love to Zarah, the daughter defers to maternal rule: 'Zarah answer'd, She ow'd that duty to her Mother, and
that Virtue to her self, she wou'd not betray for the whole World; and
since he had profess'd such a Passion for her, and her Mother was now
become a Witness of it, she did not know how he cou'd part from her
without giving her such Satisfaction as Parents in those Cases expected'
(21–2). The mother promptly produces a priest and the couple is married. The duping of the male libertine, as well as his mistress Clelia
(Villiers), generates much of the narrative excitement that colours this
scene: 'The Consideration of being Outwitted and as it were forced into
such a Compliance grated upon [Hippolito] exceedingly, and seem'd to
be the chief Thing that troubled him' (24–5). Clelia's surprise at finding
Zarah and Hippolito together is eclipsed by the horror she experiences
when Jenisa and the priest appear: 'What Confusion and a Trembling
seiz'd Clelia, when she saw them! This was a Scene more shocking that

what her Thoughts and Jealousies could ever have suggested to her'
(29). The marriage plot, here, revels in the fall of those who take their
social and sexual authority for granted.

At this point the narrative circles back to Charles II, who, it appears,
has ushered in a new era, in which challenges to aristocratic prerogative appear acceptable, even to the monarch himself:

> Being a Personage of admirable Wit and Pleasantry, he began to be very
> facetious and rally [Hippolito]: 'What would become of Men and Women
> of gallantry,' says he, 'if when they engage in Kindness with one anoth-
> er, they should absolutely sell themselves, and not be allow'd to change
> when they grow weary, or have a greater Inclination for another ... And
> you know, Hippolito,' continued the king, 'I glory in those Maxims; for if
> Clelia had not been of my humor I fancy I shou'd not have loved her so well,
> and perhaps I love her for nothing more than that she loves Inconstancy.
> (32–3)

The king goes on to imagine cuckolding Churchill: '"Now, Hippolito,
would you take it ill the King shou'd do as much for you as you did
then for him?" "Yes, without a Doubt," says he, "Sir, for I did it not
for the Purpose that you shou'd do as much for me." "Well," answers
the King prophetically, "if I do not, another may"' (33–4). Charles II's
commitment to female inconstancy – and his prediction that Zarah will
prove as sexually promiscuous as he – bridges the gap between the
Restoration and the early years of the eighteenth century, a continuity
more broadly confirmed by the narrative's observation regarding the
conventional role of favourites in England: 'This great Rise of [Zarah's],
and her Power at Court gain'd her the title of Queen Zarah among foreigners, who knew not the constitution of Albigion, where it has been
a usual Thing for Kings to uncrown themselves, and place it on their
Favorites' (100–1). Sarah Churchill's promiscuity and political rise form
part of a tradition that *Zarah* both attacks and naturalizes.

Young Zarah quickly learns how to gratify her desires for 'love and
ambition' simultaneously: 'though she was resolved to gain the Last,
she was one who left no Stone unturn'd to secure to herself the First,
which has always made her life one continued Scene of Politick Intrigue'
(41). 'For Zarah,' John Richetti notes, 'sexual experience is a desirable
result as well as a method of political power.'[66] The shuttling between
objectives – political power and personal pleasure – stands as the sign
of ethical vacuity. But this vacuity takes on an ambiguous valence in the

challenges posed to ethical standards by the events of 1688–9. On the one hand, the emptiness at the core of the Churchills' identities manifests itself in their pragmatic approach to religion, which informs the betrayal of their king in 1688. The subject is introduced as one might expect, with an attack on the Churchill cabal as unscrupulous in matters of faith: 'He [Robert Spencer, second Earl of Sunderland] was a man of Zarah's Principles and Volpone's Politics, [and] *wou'd sell his Master for a Groat, change his Religion for Policy, and betray his Country for nought'* (58, emphasis in text). Religious affiliation takes on a somewhat different character when viewed in relation to the conflict it creates between Princess Anne's Protestant commitment and her father's Roman Catholicism. Zarah addresses the dilemma directly in her address to the princess: '"consider, Madam, the Zeal you have express'd for the Religion of your Country, which you must leave, without [unless] you leave the King ... If you depend upon Honour, I hope you never expect to succeed to the crown of Albigion"' (64–5).

The plot thickens as the narrative turns to the reign of William and Mary. *Zarah*'s characterization of the 1690s, like the Whig secret histories, attempts to fix a stable account of the decade. On the one hand, the narrative continues to insist that the Churchills act only out of self-interest in their support of the younger Stuart princess; on the other, it idealizes Anne as an Anglican and properly English opponent to the Calvinist Dutch import, William III. Insofar as Anne appears neither negligent in her duty to Protestantism, like her father, nor mercenary in her timing, like her sister and brother-in-law, she appears distanced from the squalor of the Revolution, a legitimate successor to the throne – a true queen in waiting. The Churchills prove instrumental in criticizing the Williamite regime and in instigating a larger collective revolt against the king. After the failure of his second attempt to invade France, the narrative remarks on William's inadequacy: 'the whole Nation began to take Notice of it as a Miscarriage that redounded much to the dishonour of Aurantio, who had more people about him, some said, than Zarah that studied to confound all his Devices, and render him Odious to the People, who then began to murmur grievously against his Reign' (96–7). In her capacity as informant between the court and the public, Zarah serves as a figurehead for popular revolt – a position the narrative as a whole also assumes.[67]

The Tory rhetoric of 'the Church in danger' that emerged after Anne's succession enables the story to divide Anne from Zarah and attack the Churchills' embrace of the Whig policies they had criticized during the rule of William and Mary. It draws extensively on the language of High Church zeal to advance its critique: 'The Ecclesiasticks of Albigion were very Restless and Uneasie at this Tide of Government, which like a Torrent threatened the Destruction of their Constitution, which, as all Wise Men of the Nation thought, was the foundation of Albigion's Future Peace and Tranquillity' (104–5). The Whigs' attempts to ridicule the extremists among the Anglican divines backfire when 'the Wise, Disinterested, and Unprejudiced people of Albigion' transform the High Church clergy into 'Darling Patriots' (107). The clergy and their supporters appear both an abstract principle of Protestantism's constitutional integrity and the unruly mob that will prove, the narrator hopes, 'a Thorn in the Sides of those Men who thought to stab them to the Quick' (108). The violence of the language links this moment of popular unrest to the earlier protests associated with Zarah's attack on William's foreign policy. Here, however, the narrative pits Zarah's ambition against the stubborn intractability of the English, whose religious affiliations take the form of a tenacious resistance to the idea of female misrule: 'Nothing griev'd Zarah like this ungovernable spirit of the Albigionois, who would not bear to think of being rid with Side-Saddle, having had their Backs galled so much before in the female reign of Rolando' (110). The allusion to Charles II's royal mistresses sets clerical prerogative and England's constitutional liberty against the tyranny of she-rule, rather than against, more specifically, the idea of religious toleration, a swerve made possible by the cultural memory of the Catholicism of Charles's mistresses.

By defining female rule so broadly as antithetical to English liberty, *Zarah* runs the risk of diminishing the queen's authority. The narrative can overcome this obstacle only by relying on Zarah's association with the epithet, 'whore.' In bracketing off Anne's rule from the perverse articulation of power that Zarah's career represents, the narrative draws on a misogynous rhetoric common to Whig and Tory propaganda alike. To shore up its indictment of bad female political ambition, the first part of *Zarah* concludes with a glowing account of Queen Anne's singular moral purpose and virtue. Volpone notes, 'amongst so many Illustrious Qualities as we have observed in *Albania*, I will not omit the Supream Virtue of *Moderation*, wherewith she favours her Friends, and her very Enemies too, and which we both know by Experience she possesses in the highest Measure' (114). The discourse of moderation is de-politicized, becoming a paradigm of moral excellence instead of a slogan in a religious controversy. While this appropriation effectively denies the Whigs their political platform, it only works insofar as Anne's private integrity takes precedence over her public authority.

The second part of *Queen Zarah* returns to the religious conflicts of 1703–5 as the focus of its political commentary: 'These disputes rais'd great Heats and Feuds everywhere, which were supported and carry'd on by Means of *Zarah's* Partizans, who were very Numerous, tho' of little Account in respect of the others who were the Chief of the Gentry and Ecclesiasticks of *Albigion*; a Country where the Better Sort were always fast Friends to the C—' (197–8). Reflecting on the Whigs' manipulation of popular opinion, the narrator dwells at length on the uses and abuses of religion in the field of politics:

> How many are they who affect [Religion] from a Principle of Vanity and Presumption, and do all they do out of Design and Vain-glory? Some pretend to it in order to be Statesmen, and make a Mystery of all Things, and by a certain counterfeit and studied Art labour to pass for great Men; others dispose of themselves by Interest, and insinuate with the Multitude to be protected by them, that so they may exact upon the world: All these People make Religion the highest Point of their Politicks; for by this Pretence they Reign imperiously over many, and captivate the obstinate and unthinking Vulgar, who are charm'd with their promising outside ...
> But to return to Zarah. (210–12)

The passage points to religious sloganeering as the sign of political corruption and in doing so assumes an odd stance, given the narrative's endorsement of the clerical attacks on Whig power in earlier moments of the narrative. But this logic assumes that the Whigs seek to alter, fundamentally, the order of society in their manipulations of religious discourse, whereas the Tories merely defend the natural order of things. The Whigs, in other words, put the cart before the horse in advancing the cause of religious toleration. In its assessment of religion's place in culture, *Zarah* looks to religious conformity as the bedrock of political and social arrangements:

> It has been judiciously decided, that Religion is the Principle and Foundation of Policy; and that those States are always in Danger and Disorder in which it is not firmly settled: So that the *Bees*, which never go out of their Hives, according to Tradition, without first crossing their Legs, and kiss-

ing them, by an Instinct as it were of Religion, shew us what we ought to do before we undertake any Business; and we ought of Necessity to Worship aright before we can know how to govern so. (222–3)

The rote behaviour of bees serves as an analogy for the established customs of the Church of England, which shore up the nation's political culture. The commentary does not interrogate what the content of these rituals should be, but rather presumes an identical fit between religion's imperatives and those of the Anglican Church. We are 'instinctively' committed to rituals, the passage suggests, and the Church of England shapes them correctly.

When the narrative reflects on the question of female character, a similar logic unfolds. Noting women's preferences for rich men over poor, the narrator remarks: 'I know no Reason why the Women shou'd be reproach'd with being *Mercenary* and *Coquettish*, 'tis a piece of Injustice done them. I think they shou'd be so, and at all times make use of their Charms to please Men; we may find the same Desires in both Sexes' (230).[68] 'Character' consists not of obedience to a moral code, but rather a set of desires matched more or less well in men and women. *Zarah* contrasts women who recognize this principle against those who remain rigidly attached to cultural standards regarding female chastity:

> Those Women that take a Fancy to Severity are generally too formal, and the Affectation of Wit which they shew when their Conduct is not entirely regular, renders them much more despisable; we should have much more Charity for them if they did not so absolutely set up for *Nuns*; their *Reputation* does not depend on the Capricious Notions of Men, and the Applauses they give them, but on their *Merit* and *Virtue*. (232)

The moderation here advocated draws on French anticlerical rhetoric, with the nun standing as the sign of an enforced and possibly fraudulent sexual character that women should take pains to avoid imitating. Unlike the earlier association of religious integrity with masculine Protestant rule, this moment advances women's interest against both clerical and male standards. A woman's reputation does not stand on 'the capricious notions of men' but rather on women's 'merit and virtue.' 'Merit and virtue,' it appears, depend not on what the substance of a woman's sexual conduct might be, but rather on a woman's right relation to that conduct. As the Church gives shape to our instinct for religious ritual, so too a woman's conduct articulates her sexual desires. But what is the connection between the church and social conduct, between religious and sexual desire?

The connection appears in the satisfaction each grants us. This satisfaction, as a social principle, finds expression as civility that does not use prejudice or bigotry to sustain its imperatives: 'Knowing how to Converse, is knowing how to Oblige; in fine, it is the best Method of pleasing, the shortest Way of gaining the Good-will of every Body' (250–1). When we return to Zarah in the narrative, it is her failure to please others that isolates her both politically and socially: 'But it is high time, after this long Digression, to return to our Story again, where we shall find *Hippolito* acting the most generous thing, and *Zarah* the most Niggardly Unfriendly Part in the World' (252). As the narrative recounts Zarah's acts of unkindness toward friends and family, it reflects on her wilfulness. But it does not take issue with the idea that society is organized around the commercialization and commodification of human relations. When one lady offers Zarah a broach as a bribe, the narrator comments not on the practice of bribing, but on Zarah's greed: '[Zarah] knew the Jewel cou'd not be worth above a Thousand *Florins*, and that was as much as was thought fitting by the Lady to offer for the Favour she ask'd of her; for she knew beforehand it was necessary to bid a Market Price, but cou'd not believe *Zarah* had been so unconscionable as to overstand the Market' (2:259–60).

When we consider these moments in relation to the narrative's earlier condemnation of Zarah as a Restoration whore, we are granted a different perspective on that epithet. It is not whoring that renders female rule unbearable to the English public, but rather whoring that fails to please. The Restoration appears neither as the pathologized Other of a post-revolutionary present, nor as an idealized Golden Age of a lost past, but rather as the origin of contemporary practices. Zarah emerges as both representative of those practices and as a social aberration. She sells herself, but she sets her price too high; she brings together religion and politics, but she sets them in the wrong relation to each other. And yet the narrative does not dispense with the terms her example provides. As in the secret histories, the narrative's commitment to a broad exploration of cultural dynamics and the pleasures of storytelling exceeds its political intention, and in the final instance, *Zarah* does not go the distance with High Church Tory zealotry – nor with its misogyny. Attacking Sarah Churchill, the narrative takes for granted the duchess's power, even at the moment when its decline was apparent to all court observers. In contrast to Queen Zarah, Queen Anne appears oddly inef-fectual. Indeed, only Anne's attachment to Zarah renders her recogniz-ably political in the first part of the narrative and she disappears from view entirely in its continuation.

Jacobites and Whores

> It is Childrens play, for any men to hold the first Posts in a government & not have it in their power to remove such a Slut as that.
>
> Arthur Mainwaring to Sarah Churchill,
> on the subject of Abigail Masham[69]

The year 1710 marked the downfall of the Whig ministry and the politi-cal disgrace of the Churchills. But the Tory victory was short-lived and conditions for an eighteenth-century Whig oligarchy began to emerge out of social, political, and economic developments of the period. The decline of Anne's powers, represented viscerally in her failing health and symbolically in the imminent end of the Stuart reign, signalled a shift toward a larger evolution in cultural understandings of the mon-arch's role. As R.O. Bucholz observes,

> in presiding over a court that embodied the middle-class virtues of thrift, sobriety, moderation, and decorum, [Anne] ... anticipated a time when the monarch's greatest service to the state would be to represent it, and when the perpetuation of even that limited role would depend upon popularity with the masses in general and with a politically significant middle class in particular.[70]

The threat of a Jacobite rebellion accelerated this shift toward a limited monarchy and helped to steer debates surrounding the monarch's and the nation's faith in a new direction. In particular, those who supported the Hanoverian succession were at pains to challenge claims that the Old Pretender would protect England's Protestant faith. Presbyterian James Kirkpatrick warned:

> Our greatest Danger is from the Protestant Jacobites, the Monsters of our Age, and those who are blindly led into their Measures ... Shall we be so vain and credulous, as to believe that the Pretender, who, if he comes to the Crown, must come fraughted [sic] with all the Vengeance that enrag'd

Resentments of his suppos'd Father's being unjustly dethron'd, and himself injur'd, will ever protect the Religion and Liberty, which he has been taught from his Infancy to destroy?[71]

To counter the Jacobites' strategic and explicitly political Protestant discourse, Whigs advocated a doctrine of nonpartisan spiritual renewal, used to counter the idea that religious affiliation could be self-divided – as in the example of a king whose personal faith might differ from that of the nation's. The moderate Gilbert Burnet argued:

> Politicks and Party eat out among us not only Study and Learning, but that which is the only Thing that is more valuable, a true Sense of Religion, with a sincere Zeal in Advancing that for which the Son of GOD both lived and died, and to which those who are received into Holy Orders have vowed to dedicate their Lives and Labours.[72]

Of course, the 'true Sense' of religion could only be expressed by Protestantism, but Burnet's statements indicate the extent to which clergy attempted to heal the divisive battles between Protestant factions by using a language of personal faith carefully emptied of political content.[73] Religion should not serve as a political tool (for the Stuart cause), these critics argued, as they sought new ways to represent how religious sentiment might demonstrate its disinterestedness.

Against a backdrop of shifting state-church relations, the figure of Lady Jane Grey, a Protestant queen for a brief moment in the sixteenth century, might have appeared, initially, a perfect candidate for the role of national icon. Nicholas Rowe and others were quick to capitalize on her appeal, especially with the threat of a Jacobite rebellion looming. Helpfully, the figure of Mary I could stand for the Old Pretender: 'They urg'd her [Mary] to declare whether she would alter the Protestant Religion; to whom she gave solemn Assurances, *That she would make no Innovation or Change, but would be satisfy'd with the private Exercise of her own Belief.* And being possess'd with a Belief in her Sincerity, they resolv'd to hazard their Lives and Estates in the Cause of the Queen, who had given them such faithful Promises.'[74] The dedication to Edward Young's *The Force of Religion; or, Vanquish'd Love* (1715), which tells Grey's story, signals the way in which Grey's iconography could be harnessed to a vision of a private and pious aristocratic woman. In his address to the Countess of Salisbury, Young writes:

There is not in Nature a more glorious Scene, than he enjoys, who by Accident oversees a Great, and Young, and Beautiful Lady in her Closet of Devotion, instead of Gaiety, and Noise, and Throng, so natural to the Qualities just mention'd; all is solemn, and silent, and private. Pious Meditation has carry'd her away into a Forgetfulness of her lovely Person, which no one but herself can forget! All her exquisite Features are animated with Religion in such a Manner, as to make any licentious Thought in the Beholder impious and shocking![75]

But contemporary commentary on Nicholas Rowe's play, *The Tragedy of Lady Jane Gray*, recognized the degree to which the political aspect of Jane Grey's character, however much attenuated, interfered with the play's aesthetic appeal. As a defeated usurper, Grey was not, perhaps, the ideal vehicle for a celebration of the Hanoverian succession, despite her Protestant credentials. Charles Gildon's *Remarks on Mr. Rowe's Tragedy of the Lady Jane Gray* notes that '[Rowe] has made the Lady her self argue enough against the *Usurpation*, to make her guilty of so horrid a Crime; but it was to save her Country and Religion. If he brings this as a Christian example, he should not have made her whom he designs a *Saint*, doing *Evil* that *Good* might come of it.' Another commentator viewed the play as crassly opportunistic, pointing out its flaws while observing, 'I don't doubt, you were convinc'd the whole Attention of your Readers would be engag'd in hearing the Case stated betwixt Popery and Protestantism.' Gildon concludes his remarks by noting that the play, 'with all its faults ... is not worse than *Jane Shore*; but the *Whore* found more favour with the Town, than the *Saint*.'[76]

How could a whore generate more applause than a saint? To recount briefly the Jane Shore plot to which the period returned so often: the narrative replays the relationship between Edward IV and his middle-class mistress, Jane Shore, who became a political target for the Duke of Gloucester, future Richard III, after the king's death. Although history provides us with few details of Jane Shore's story, we do learn from Renaissance accounts that she became mistress to Lord Hastings, enemy to Gloucester, after Edward IV's death – a detail that, for obvious reasons, does not appear in Rowe's she-tragedy. Most important, for our purposes, Jane Shore's early eighteenth-century representations bring Nell Gwyn back into view.[77] The Preface to *The Unfortunate Concubines*, represents Nell Gwyn as a latter-day Jane Shore:

It is yet recent in the Memories of most, that we have had Royal Misses who have liv'd in that Pomp and Splendor ... as if their Honours had legitimated their Crimes ... I have not heard that any of them ever did so much Good, in the time of their Favour with those Princes [Charles and James], as Jane Shore did in that of hers with King Edward the Fourth, unless it was Madam Gwin; who (how mean soever her Extraction was) bore [her] Exaltation with less Pride, and did more Good in her Station, than any of the rest; being exceeding Charitable to them that were in Want, and often refreshing the Prisoners with her Bounty; and for that reason was more acceptable to the People, than all the other Court-Mistresses, however dignify'd and distinguish'd with their high-flown Titles.[78]

The emphasis placed on Nell Gwyn's charitable impulse produces the possibility that a courtesan might redeem herself in one register, should she sufficiently distance herself from the pursuit of political power. The authority exercised by aristocratic title and its attendant wealth is measured against the influence gained by Gwyn's charity and found wanting. 'The People' recognize a moral, rather than political, leader in Gwyn. Another commentator stresses the significance of Gwyn's Protestant affiliation even as he emphasizes her relative political ineffectiveness in the comparison he draws between Gwyn and Shore:

When I read this Account of her [Sir Thomas More's], I thought it bore some Resemblance to that we have receiv'd by Tradition of *Nell Gwin*, who was the merriest and best natur'd Mistress, of a very merry and good natur'd King, the Memory of whose Amours is not yet forgotten. The difference in their Characters seems only to arise from the difference of the Times, and which is a little hard, the difference of their Religion; for if King *James* told us true, his Brother King *Charles* was a Papist, and 'tis very well known *Nell Gwin* was in the Protestant Interest; and whether, tho' she had as good a Disposition to do all friendly Offices as *Jane Shore*, she was as successful is much to be doubted. [79]

Gwyn appears an icon of 'Protestant Interest' stripped of any political import. As in the resurrection of her reputation through the turn to charity, the advocacy of 'the merriest and best natur'd Mistress' depends on Gwyn's political inefficacy. The mistress who merits sympathy, then, is the mistress who has learned not to meddle in state affairs.

Whig doctrine committed itself to deposing the Stuart royal mistress, sign of monarchical absolutism and tyranny. One of its most effective critiques appears in John Dunton's 1714 pamphlet, *King Abigail: or, The*

Secret Reign of the She-Favourite, Detected and Applied; in a Sermon Upon these Words, 'And Women rule over them.' Abigail Masham's influence over Queen Anne, and by extension Oxford and Bolingbroke, serves as a model for the dangers of female political activism, especially damaging to religious principal: 'It is this She-Favourite, and the rest of her Creatures, that I here speak of, as the Chief Authors of all our Calamities ... It was by their pernicious Advice, that Religion had like to have received its mortal Stab; and their Maxims of Fire and Blood were just ready to be put in Execution.'[80] *King Abigail* identifies the corruption of the nation with women's manipulation of state-church relations: 'In the Reign of Henry the Second, King of France, *Anno* 1554, many were burn'd for their Religion, as they said, but indeed it was to satiate the Covetousness, and support the Pride, Pomp and Luxury of Diana Valentina, the King's Mistress, to whom he had given all the Confiscation of Goods made in the Kingdom, for the Cause of Heresie, and then let her alone to look out for the Prey' (10–11). Jacobitism appears as a problem organized around the predatory female whose unnaturally masculine aggression and ambition lead directly to other political ills: 'All the Noise about the Churches Danger, indefeasible Hereditary Right, Passive-Obedience, &c. was but the subtil Intriegue [*sic*] of our late Court-Favourites, only to fit you for Popery and French Slavery' (11).

Dunton traces Abigail Masham's pathology back to the figure of Charles I's queen and his mother-in-law, and in doing so brings the female monarch into the fold as a site of political corruption:

> Story tells us, that in the Reign of Charles the First's Queen, *before she had attain'd the Age of Twenty, began of a Pupil to be his Regent*, and the fatal participant with him in most of his Counsels, and his directrix in the Government, and after her Mothers Arrival both of them gain'd an Interest in his inmost Secrets, and principal Transactions of State, an evident Truth, and more then stood with the King's Honour, the Nation's Welfare, and his own Personal Safety, for *the Rule of these Women cost him his Head*, besides a Million of Innocent Lives, in *England* and *Ireland*. (16–17)

The proliferation of victims of female rule – not just the king but 'millions of Innocent Lives' – raises the stakes considerably in considering the threat posed by Abigail Masham and other female court favourites. Unsurprisingly, the narrative ends with a celebration of George I as a phallic saviour of the nation's integrity: 'Blessed art thou O Britain, who hath such a King upon the Throne, that will no more suffer *Women*

and Children to Rule over thee ... Now our Princes or Officers of State ...
are modest and abstemious, not dissolute and debauch'd. Great Men
shou'd not Cater for the Flesh, *Rom.* 13.14. but to serve the Body, that
the Body Politick may be serv'd by it, and the Lord by both' (20). Significantly, neither Abigail Masham nor Queen Anne signifies in this
account. The virtues of the 'modest and abstemious' queen become
the *king*'s attributes, to which the corruptions of Masham's 'rule' in the
years leading up to his reign serve as a foil.

We have seen, in this chapter, how the questions of governance raised
by the figure of the Restoration courtesan took on a new significance in
relation to the reigns of two female sovereigns, Queens Mary and Anne.
Concerns about the legitimate and illegitimate exercise of power – central to the religious debates that shaped Jacobite, Tory, and Whig ideologies – circulated through the representations of both licit and illicit
acts of female rule. The tension between monarchical commitments to
moral reform and the exigencies of modern politics afforded writers a
rich literary opportunity, and prose fiction narratives of the 1690s and
early eighteenth century were able to draw their own preoccupations
about authorship and cultural agency into a larger analysis of national
affairs. Despite efforts to pathologize the Restoration past, its example
proved a valuable resource to those contemplating the potential for corruption and nepotism within a modern political system. As we shall see
in the next chapter, the religious controversies that plagued the nation
after 1714 provoked another round of debate on Protestantism's future.
In Defoe's final novel, the Protestant Whore takes us back to the Restoration to meditate on the cultural challenges faced by England in the
1720s.

4 'A House Divided': Defoe's *Roxana* and the Protestant Body Politic

Believe that these very Creatures who would incense you against the Tolleration of Dissenters are Her Majesty's only Enemies; all Foreign Resistance has been hitherto of no Effect; nor ever will be, if you lay not aside differences one among another: But if you will be *a House Divided against it self, you cannot, nay, shall not stand.*

> *An Appeal from the City to the Country, for the Preservation of*
> *Her Majesty's Person, Liberty, Property, and the Protestant Religion* (1710)

Our Fathers of old took Oaths, as their Wives,
To Have and to Hold, for the Term of their Lives;
But we take Oaths, like a Whore, for our Ease,
And a Whore and a Rogue may part when they please.

> 'The Sense of the Tories,'
> *A Collection of State Songs* (1716)

George I's assumption of the throne in 1714 and the English army's victory over Jacobite rebels at the Battle of Preston a year later did little to assuage religious controversies of the period. Indeed, the doubts that plagued English Protestantism in the seventeenth century deepened in the years immediately following the Hanoverian succession. Benjamin Hoadly, bishop of Bangor, brought internal conflict within the Church of England into sharp relief when he preached 'The Nature of the Kingdom, or Church, of Christ' before the king in 1717. The sermon, almost certainly motivated by a political desire to deny authority to High Church – both Tory and Whig – doctrine, espouses a radical individualism:

As the *Church* of *Christ* is the *Kingdom of Christ*, He himself is *King*: and in this it is implied, that *He* is himself the sole *Law-giver* to his *Subjects*, and himself the sole *Judge* of their *Behaviour*, in the Affairs of *Conscience* and *eternal Salvation*. And in this Sense therefore, *His Kingdom is not of this World*; that He hath, in those Points, left behind Him, no visible, humane *Authority*; no *Viceregents*, who can be said properly to supply his Place; no *Interpreters*, upon whom his Subjects are absolutely to depend; no *Judges* over the Consciences or Religion of his People.[1]

The immediate political fall-out from the ensuing controversy was the crown's decision to prorogue the Anglican convocation that sought to discipline Hoadly in February 1718. The convocation did not reconvene for over a hundred years.[2] The Church's failure to manage any kind of damage control in the months between the sermon's publication in the spring of 1717 and the Anglican synod's meeting early in 1718 suggests the press's increasingly powerful role in shaping English public opinion.[3] The expansion in the press's coverage of religious affairs had implications not only for the Church of England's authority, but also for the Dissenting community. The Salters' Hall controversy of 1719 emerged when a convocation of Dissenting ministers was asked to sign a declaration of belief in the Trinity: a majority refused.[4] Like the Bangorian crisis, the Salters' Hall dispute received much attention in the press. The nation's communities were divided both against each other and within their own ranks, and the violence of 1715 served as a reminder that Protestant nationalism had yet to secure its terms.

The legacy of the on-again, off-again relation between Dissent and the Church of England and its monarch appears in the range of responses Daniel Defoe registered in his writing on the subject. In 1702 Defoe launched a scathing attack on Anglican clergy in *The Shortest Way with the Dissenters*. Yet, only five years later, with a different wind in his sails, he could write, 'No Man then can deny, but that the Dissenters in *England* would *gladly come into* the Church of *England*, and become one Body with them again, and ought to do so, would they abate, alter, or remove all those things in which they differ from them, which do not appear warranted by the Word of God.'[5] By 1714, in his attack on Jacobites and High Church Tories, Defoe was anticipating arguments advanced by Hoadly's 1716 pamphlet, *Preservation against the Principles and Practices of Non-Jurors in Church and State*, writing, 'The Vulgar entertain a Superstitious Reverence and Esteem for the Clergy, and account all for the Oracles of God, that drops from their Mouths, especially in the Pulpit ... The Clergy abound with indigent Persons, of restless and uneasie Minds, who are more violently set to compass their Designs than the Laity are.'[6] Defoe's defence of Dissenting clerical orthodoxy in debates arising from the Salters' Hall controversy spoke less to a conviction regarding the justness of its authority than a rearguard attempt to maintain the community's political viability: 'most of all, he was horrified that the Dissenters would match those involved in the Bangorian controversy in making a public display of their basic disagreements.'[7]

The proximity of Defoe's and Hoadly's views (an association shared by other Dissenters and Low Church Anglicans) at this particular historical juncture manifests the fluidity of theological and ecclesiastical discourses in the period, as well as the important role political considerations played in shaping religious arguments. Defoe's deep involvement in early eighteenth-century religious controversies provides evidence to support G.A. Starr's view that 'the leading religious ideas in Defoe's fiction were in fact commonplaces of the English Protestant tradition, not merely crotchets of his much-discussed Dissenting milieu.'[8] The difference between reading the Protestant content of Defoe's fiction through the lens of an ongoing controversy, rather than as an English Weltanschauung, is that the Protestant identity so often assumed to serve as a stable foundation upon which Defoe rests his representations proves fractured, a divided subject open to a kind of radical doubt more often attributed to Augustan satire.[9]

This chapter asks: why did Defoe return, in his final novel, to a historical moment that offered no answers to the questions raised by religious conflict? His evocation of the Restoration, I suggest, allows Defoe to achieve three related goals. First, by tracing the controversies of the Hanoverian regime back to an earlier inception, one more explicitly identified as a political crisis, Defoe emphasizes the public aspect of religious discourses. Where the eighteenth century increasingly imagined individual conscience as a category separable from the political, the persecution of Dissenters during the Restoration collapsed the personal/political distinction. In returning his readers to this historical frame of reference, Defoe argues that the production of conscience remains a social issue. Second, by returning to the Restoration moment, Defoe uncouples Protestantism's relation to emergent capitalist discourses, demonstrating the Hobbesian imperatives governing both formal and informal economies of the period. By bringing together the spectacle of monarchical power with the workings of modern finance, Defoe counters early eighteenth-century accounts of modernity's financial acumen as an antidote to the Restoration's tyrannical excesses.[10] Third, the Restoration foregrounds women's relation to public authority. Through the figure of the courtesan Defoe demonstrates at once his utopic dreams of the prostitute's unlimited ability to create wealth (she houses the means of production in her very body) and the dystopic sense that new forms of social regulation and control encroach in profound ways on the individual. I emphasize Defoe's sceptical relation to progressive ideology's understanding of sexual difference, and in doing so, I refuse the associations of realism, interiority, and moral rectitude that tend to cluster around critical representations of Roxana. Lincoln B. Faller, for example, asserts: 'So Roxana lives, her discourse carrying her away not only from duty but, finally, from a proper sense of the real ... But the novel ... directs its readers to a sense of things as they really are – or should be – behind the screen of language, offering in particular a full, rich sense of the human mind and heart amidst other human minds and hearts.'[11] The 'proper sense of the real' is what, I contend, Defoe most forcefully calls into question. Instead of imagining how things 'should be,' Defoe raises a series of questions unresolvable within the confines of the historical discourses that shape them.

'Conscience, *or something else*': Desire Abroad

Money ... wou'd make a Woman go any-where.

Defoe, *Roxana*

A Prophet's Honour is not in his own Country.
    Defoe, *Royal Religion; Being some Enquiry after the Piety of Princes* (1704)

Roxana's description of herself as a 'Protestant Whore' appears as she negotiates her second liaison, in France with a prince. As she debates the ethical stakes with herself, Roxana considers consulting a Catholic clergyman:

This I had a strong Inclination to try, but I know not what Scruple put me off of it, for I could never bring myself to like having to do with those Priests; and tho' it was strange that I, who had thus prostituted my Chastity, and given up all Sence of Virtue, in two such particular Cases, living a Life of open Adultery, should scruple any thing; yet so it was, I argued with myself, that I could not be a Cheat in any thing that was esteem'd Sacred; that I could not be of one Opinion, and then pretend myself to be of another; nor could I go to Confession, who knew nothing of the Manner of it, and should betray myself to the Priest, to be a Hugonot, and then might come into Trouble; but, in short, tho' I was a Whore, yet I was a Protestant Whore, and could not act as if I was Popish, upon any Account whatsoever.[12]

Roxana's integrity here initially appears in her refusal to extend the scope of her corruption to include the realm of the 'Sacred,' in her ability to maintain a purity of standard that would allow some ethical universe to remain intact even in the face of an active commitment to whoring. But, in a move that recurs throughout the novel, practical considerations almost immediately come to bear on this ethical absolutism when Roxana realizes that she cannot risk exposure of her true identity as a French Protestant. This secondary factor – or is it primary? – adds a double-edged nuance to her final declaration, 'I ... could not act as if I was Popish,' a phrase that, given the practical concerns that the heroine has just voiced, could reveal either an unwillingness or, more problematically, an inability not connected to moral objections to perform a 'Popish' confession. Indeed, what remains with us is the powerful attraction of confession, opposed not by a more rigorous standard of Protestant moral investigation, but by pragmatism.

The conditions governing Roxana's self-definition radically alter the meaning of Nell Gwyn's Oxford pronouncement. Instead of evoking a communal standard, one capable of uniting a public with the figure of the whore, Roxana's Protestant identity puts her at odds with the Roman Catholic society in which she is living; its public articulation could only lead to exposure and prosecution. In this context, 'Protestant' and 'Whore' appear analogous: both identities must be concealed and both require subterfuge for their survival. That is, 'Protestant' serves not as a corrective to 'Whore,' as it did when Nell Gwyn sought to distinguish herself from her Catholic counterpart, but rather as an intensifier. The pronouncement is further transformed by its articulation as a private reflection, rather than a public statement.[13] But the private conscience that 'Protestant' ostensibly names remains linked to the public sphere Nell Gwyn was able to control: Roxana fears social and political, rather than divine, censure here.

As a Protestant and an Englishwoman, Roxana is a foreigner during her residence in France. But as a French Huguenot by birth, she also remains something of a resident alien in England, an identity she will exploit in her seduction of the king. By denaturalizing Nell Gwyn's xenophobic pronouncement and foregrounding 'Protestant' as a vexed geopolitical category, Defoe reminds us of the ways in which Gwyn was read not only as an English folk heroine but also as one of a group of corrupting foreign women. Defoe draws on popular representations of both Louise de Kéroualle and Hortense Mancini in his characterization of Roxana, refusing to let the Nell Gwyn allusion secure her meaning within the frame of reference the popular icon, most immediately, would seem to provide.[14] While in France, Roxana's relation to her community mirrors that of Louise de Kéroualle's to England. Both pass as naturalized subjects, but as courtesans they remain open to interrogation. Where that interrogation functioned, throughout Louise de Kéroualle's career, as a public discourse, Defoe stages it as an interior monologue. By turning the pronouncement inward, Defoe links the performative element at work in Gwyn's theatrical gesture into the construction of personhood itself. Roxana imagines herself *essentially* 'a Protestant Whore,' but that essence, it turns out, speaks to contingent, rather than fixed, considerations.

Defoe's political writing argues both sides of the debate regarding the potential for Protestantism to provide a transnational point of identification. His celebration of William III, published in 1704, suggests that it can serve in this capacity: 'As to the Memory of King *William*, it needs no Addition from my Pen; it lives with a profound Esteem in the Mind of every true *English-man*, that has a Value for the Protestant Religion, and the Peace of his Native Country; it lives abroad in the Hearts of all Nations, where he has made good the Saying of our Saviour, *That a Prophet's Honour is not in his own Country*.'[15] But in a letter written to Robert Harley the same year, Defoe argues the opposing line. Commenting on the war in Europe, he observes: 'If it be Objected why Not as well the Swede against the Pole and the Hungarians Against the Emperor Since Otherwise you fight Against the Protestant Religion, I Return *This is Not a War of Religion*. The Present Question is Not Protestant or Papist But Liberty Or Universall Monarchy.'[16] Defoe's refusal to place religion ahead of political considerations draws attention to the Hobbesian tendency at work both in this letter and in *Roxana*, which similarly questions transnational Protestantism's ability, as a religious discourse, to unite English and European subjects. Instead, it suggests a more practical understanding of 'Protestant,' one closer to the definitions offered by Pierre Bayle than those dreamt of by Bunyan.

Roxana's first page announces the suspicion that Huguenot refugees may not always have come to England in pursuit of religious freedom:[17]

> my Father was in very good Circumstances at his coming over, so that he was far from applying to the rest of our Nation that were here, for Countenance and Relief: On the contrary, he had his Door continually throng'd with miserable Objects of the poor starving Creatures, who at that Time fled hither for Shelter, on Account of Conscience, *or something else*. (37, emphasis in text)

Roxana represents the Huguenot refugee both as 'natural' to England – her father immediately flourishes as a commercial subject upon his arrival from France – and as a potential threat, a drain on resources. One Huguenot is pitted against another, the conflict waged along economic, rather than religious, lines. Further, Roxana links integrity to the commercially successful father, while attributing the power of deception to the subject who lacks his financial acumen. Those who flee France on account of '*something else*' seem willing to become economic subjects outside of the normal channels, by begging for their support. Financial security guarantees that conscience can be read *as conscience*; a lack of it suggests the presence of an inner vacuity or opacity, difficult to interpret.

Roxana's investment in the economic as the paradigm defining her self-understanding has been well-documented as one instance of many in Defoe's novels. For Ian Watt, Defoe's attachment to narratives of capitalist enterprise obliged him to unload some moral luggage as social and economic progress gained priority over religious concerns in the early eighteenth century: 'the heritage of Puritanism is demonstrably too weak to supply a continuous and controlling pattern for the hero's experience.'[18] But *Roxana*'s language returns repeatedly to moral and biblical precepts and to intimations of ruin and damnation – so much so that critics, as we saw in the citation that closed this chapter's introduction, are inclined to adopt moralizing language themselves when engaging with the text. Viewed within the context of a conventional moral epistemology, Roxana's career falls into two phases, the first of which links sin and necessity, the second, sin and vanity. In the early days of her career, we are encouraged to read Roxana as a victim of circumstance, driven into prostitution by an abusive husband and the limited economic opportunities open to women. As her servant Amy suggests, 'Poverty is the strongest Incentive; a Temptation, against which no

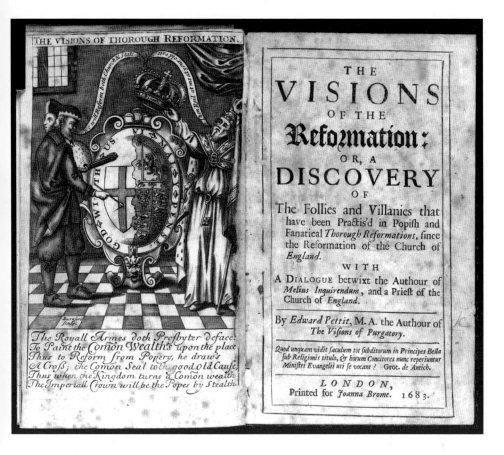

THE VISIONS OF THOROUGH REFORMATION.

The Royall Armes doth Presbyter deface:
To Paint the Comon Wealth's upon the place
Thus to Reform from Popery, he draws
A Cross; the Comon Seal with good Old Cause;
Thus when the Kingdom turns a Comon wealth,
The Imperiall Crown will be the Popes by Stealth.

THE
VISIONS
OF THE
Reformation:
OR, A
DISCOVERY
OF
The Follies and Villanies that
have been Practis'd in Popish and
Fanatical *Thorough Reformations*, since
the Reformation of the Church of
England.
WITH
A DIALOGUE betwixt the Authour of
Melius Inquirendum, and a Priest of the
Church of *England*.

By *Edward Pettit*, M. A. the Authour of
The Visions of Purgatory.

*Quod unquam vidit sæculum tot subditorum in Principes Bella
sub Religionis titulo, & horum Concitores nunc reperiuntur
Ministri Evangelii uti se vocant ?* Grot. de Antich.

LONDON,
Printed for *Joanna Brome.* 1683.

1 Frontispiece, Edward Pettit, *The Visions of the Reformation*, 1683. © British Library Board. All Rights Reserved 3936.b.20.

2 Sir Peter Lely, *Barbara Palmer (née Villiers), Duchess of Cleveland with her Son, Charles Fitzroy, as Madonna and Child*, c. 1664. National Portrait Gallery, London.

3 Richard Tompson, *Nell Gwyn*, 1675–9. National Portrait Gallery, London.

4 French school, seventeenth century, *The Three Nieces of Cardinal Mazarin.* Bridgeman Art Library.

5 Benedetto Gennari, *Hortense Mancini, Duchess of Mazarin*, c. 1684. Private Collection.

6 Pierre Mignard, *Louise de Kéroualle, Duchess of Portsmouth, with an unidentified servant*, 1682. National Portrait Gallery, London.

7 Unknown engraver, *Françoise d'Aubigné Maintenon*, date unknown. National Portrait Gallery, London.

8 Giovanni Battista Tiepolo, 1696–1770, *The Empire of Flora*, c. 1743. Oil on canvas, 28 1/4 × 35 in. (71.8 × 88.9 cm). Fine Arts Museums of San Francisco. Gift of the Samuel H. Kress Foundation.

9 Jacob-Ferdinand Voet, *Portrait of Gabriela Mancini* (?)(identified here as a portrait of Hortense Mancini), 1670s. The State Hermitage Museum, St Petersburg.

Virtue is powerful enough to stand out' (61). Like Rowe's Jane Shore, Roxana views herself as a pawn of systemic sexism, particularly as it appears in the habits of the aristocracy: 'Unhappy Women are ruin'd by Great Men' (100). 'Protestant Whore' evokes the wounded nation in need of rescue, a fallen version of Andrew Marvell's Brittannia, victim of Charles II's blindness to all but sexual gratifications:

> Naked as born, and her round Arms behind,
> With her own Tresses interwove and twin'd,
> Her mouth lockt up, a blind before her Eyes,
> Yet from beneath the Veil her blushes rise;
> And silent tears her secret anguish speak,
> Her heart throbs, and with very shame would break.
> The Object strange in him no Terrour mov'd:
> He wonder'd first, then pity'd, then he lov'd:[19]

This sexual epistemology subsumes politics into a naturalized language of difference, and sentiment serves as the antidote to tyranny. The association of aristocratic privilege and sexist abuse had become commonplace by the time Defoe wrote his final novel, a central tenet in the Whigs' ongoing attack on the Stuart kings.

Roxana begins her career of crime with 'Eyes open' (79), and she keeps them open against possible surprises throughout the narrative. As her career progresses, Roxana's self-consciousness and her fear of detection appear in the narrative's obsession with the figure of the spy. Defoe's language of spying draws on conventional religious calls to spiritual vigilance, but it also identifies the social and political stakes governing ways of seeing, anticipating modernity's use of visual discipline as a means of internalizing state authority. Defoe's activities as a spy for Robert Harley provided him with the experience to claim that 'Intelligence is the Soul of all Publick bussiness [sic].'[20] Roxana's private life constitutes her 'Publick bussiness' and her narrative recounts both the prostitute's habits of self-surveillance and her ability to protect herself by watching others: Roxana hires a spy in France to watch over the activities of her brewer husband, and Amy repeatedly serves as a spy to gather intelligence, both at home and abroad. Roxana's spying stands, however, not for the particular requirements of her profession, but rather for a more general condition of transnational, political modernity. Roxana's second client, the French prince, is not, in fact, a French subject, but a German working as a spy in France. As Roxana and the prince plan their travels to Italy, Roxana discovers that her costs will be absorbed by the government: 'as for the Expence, that was not to be nam'd, neither, indeed, was there room to name it; for I found, that he travell'd at the KING's Expence, as well for himself, as for all his Equipage; being upon a Piece of secret Service of the last Importance' (136). If the courtesan appeared a species of Restoration royal sport in libertine ideology, here the mistress functions as part of a modern state apparatus of surveillance, a cog in a larger, invisible wheel.[21]

Significantly, becoming a cost to the state allows Roxana to avoid setting her travel expenses against a professional fee as she contemplates the journey abroad. The invisibility of the spy mirrors the invisibility of material gain that, despite Roxana's obsession with listing items she has accumulated, remains most powerful when it appears most abstract and mobile. The prince's business – *'whatever it was'* (138) – also allows him, and Roxana, to traverse national boundaries with ease, gathering information, luxury items, and capital along the way. It is in Italy that Roxana purchases the 'little Female Turkish Slave' and the costume that will garner her power in England (140), a power Roxana anticipates in her self-description as the Prince's mistress: 'I may say, I was sure, the Queen of Whores; for no Woman was ever more valued, or more caress'd by a Person of such Quality, only in the Station of a Mistress' (119). The political title of 'Queen' is made possible only by the fact that Roxana is able to incite the excessive spending that makes her a 'very chargable [*sic*] mistress' (144). As the profits of whoring accumulate, Roxana's meditations on the iniquities of her practice increasingly draw on a language of excess and waste: 'I could not but sometimes look back, with Astonishment, at the Folly of Men of Quality, who immense in their Bounty, as in their Wealth, give to a Profusion, and without Bounds, to the most scandalous of our Sex, for granting them the Liberty of abusing themselves, and ruining both' (110). But for all of her language of financial ruin, we never encounter a client whose wealth is compromised by his involvement with Roxana. Instead, it becomes clear that the liberty to ruin oneself also constitutes the freedom to generate wealth in new and unprecedented ways. Roxana and her German Prince appear as two sides of the same bank note.

Roxana will only fully claim the status of an 'imperial whore' once she has demonstrated her ability to bring her accumulated capital home to England, but Europe serves as the training ground for her economic and personal transformation. The transformation of the Protestant Whore into a power-broker is marked in the evolution of Roxana's relation with the Dutch merchant who appears as Roxana prepares to leave France, where she has resided for several years, and return to England. Looking to secure her wealth, Roxana turns to the Dutch financial advisor, who in turn finds a Jewish merchant to dispose of her jewels. The Dutch merchant treats Roxana 'very kindly' (151), we learn, and the commission he takes from Roxana's 12000 pistoles in his capacity as her financial advisor appears as 'nothing but what was his Due': that is, as invisible, naturalized money (160). His capacity to secure Roxana's wealth finds expression as a paternalistic, protective concern in the face of the threat that immediately appears in the figure of the Jew, whom the novel characterizes as violent and uncivilized, incapable of regulating his passion.[22] Suspecting that Roxana has gained her jewels illicitly, perhaps by murdering her lover, the Jew sets about persecuting her. But,

> the Malice of his Thoughts anticipated him, and the *Dutch* Merchant was so good, as to give me an Account of his Design, which indeed, was wicked enough in its Nature; but to me it would have been worse, than otherwise it wou'd to another; for upon Examination, I cou'd not have prov'd myself to be the Wife of the Jeweler, so the Suspicion might have been carried on with the better Face; and then I shou'd also, have brought all his Relations in *England* upon me; who finding by the Proceedings, that I was not his Wife, but a Mistress, or in *English, a Whore*, wou'd immediately have laid Claim to the Jewels, as I had own'd them to be his. (153)

The fear of prosecution for murder and the fear of losing her wealth to the hands of the English jeweller's 'true' family appear as versions of each other. Significantly, both fears involve having to abandon French, the language of politeness, for the blunt honesty of '*Whore*,' the term that as a form of self-identification allows Roxana to sustain a lucrative career – '"I am a Whore, *Amy*, neither better nor worse, I assure you"' (74) – but that in public signifies her lack of title to all that she has earned. The narrative never discredits the Jew's suspicions, even when his own self-interest (using blackmail to obtain the jewels) is revealed. The jeweller has good reason to suspect Roxana of murder, and the narrative dwells at length on the fate that awaits her should she fall into the French state's hands:

> [They will] put you to the Question, that is, to the Torture, on Pretence of making you confess who were the Murtherers of your Husband.

> Confess! *says I*; how can I confess what I know nothing of?
> If they come to have you to the Rack, *said he*, they will make you confess
> you did it yourself, whether you did it or no, and then you are cast. (156)

The violence of the French state manifests itself in its ability to extract
confessions through the use of torture, the flip-side of the earlier portrait of the consolations afforded by Catholicism's rites. Now the Catholic state appears as uncivilized as the Jew as it threatens to unleash
its powers against Roxana. By contrast, the Dutchman and Roxana
together represent Protestant integrity, a principle of justice that finds
expression in the gender ideology at work in the Dutchman's desire
to protect Roxana, despite the evidence against her: 'I cou'd not but
approve all his Measures, seeing they were so well contriv'd, and in
so friendly a Manner, for my Benefit; and as he seem'd to be so very
sincere, I resolv'd to put my Life in his Hands' (158). And yet it is not
so much the Dutchman's sincerity that, in the end, saves Roxana, but
the violence wreaked upon the Jew by the 'gentleman' of her German/
French prince: 'Two men ... carried him into a more private Place, and
cut off both his Ears, telling him, It was for talking impudently of his
Superiours' (172). The Dutch merchant, in turn, brings 'Information
against him for a Cheat ... so he was sent to the *Concergerie*, that is to
say, to *Bridewell*' (173).

That the Jew should end up mutilated like a whore whose nose has
been cut and incarcerated in a prison reminiscent of England's house
of correction for prostitutes marks him as inhabiting the space of social
punishment Roxana dreads. But, as it turns out, she fears this space
less than that of marriage, and it is the refusal of marriage that, in turn,
undermines the vision of Protestant integrity that both the initial stages
of Roxana's career, and her brief alliance with the Dutch merchant, sustain. The Dutchman's desire to claim Roxana as a wife expresses itself
in the language of debt and repayment:

> [He told me] that I cou'd not think so hard of him, as to suppose he wou'd
> take Money of me, *a Widow*, for serving me, and doing Acts of Kindness to
> me in a strange Country, and in Distress too; but, *he said*, he wou'd repeat
> what he had said before, that he kept me for a deeper Reckoning, and that,
> as he had told me, he would put me into a Posture to Even all that Favour,
> as I call'd it, *at once* ... (179)

Instead of marrying the Dutchman, Roxana seeks to redress the debt she
feels she owes him through her ability to alienate her sexual favours –

in this case, to give them away for free. Importantly, Roxana's ability to discharge her debt is only made possible by the Dutchman's conception of women's sexual integrity and the function of shame in the marriage plot: 'he thought of a Way, which, he flatter'd himself, wou'd not fail ... this was, to try if he cou'd take me at an Advantage, and get to-Bed to me, and then, *as was most rational to think*, I should willingly enough marry him afterwards' (181, emphasis in text). Roxana uses this system against the Dutchman and in doing so secures her estate, symbolized in the money she owes him: 'so I granted him the Favour, as he call'd it, to ballance the Account of Favours receiv'd from him, and keep the thousand Pistoles with a good grace' (184).

Roxana's refusal of the Dutchman's marriage proposal places her in the same position as the Jew: that of social pariah. In particular, the Dutchman uses the language of maternal failure to highlight Roxana's distance from 'the general Practice' (193): 'I cannot, therefore, *says he*, but beg and intreat you, as you are a Christian, and a Mother, not to let the innocent Lamb you go with, be ruin'd before it is born, and leave it to curse and reproach us hereafter, for what may be so easily avoided' (196). Roxana recognizes that the production of conscience is, however, part of the manufacturing of consent to her own disenfranchisement, and she chooses, against the imperatives of domestic ideology, a Hobbesian position: 'if no-body was trusted, no-body wou'd be deceiv'd' (193). To assume this position is to forgo the consolations of conventional gender roles in marriage and to claim, instead, the power belonging to a single woman, 'Masculine in her politick Capacity' (188).

The Dutch merchant promises Roxana the life of a trophy wife: 'the Woman had nothing to do, but to eat the Fat, and drink the Sweet; to sit still, and look round her' (187). Within the confines of such a marriage, Carol Flynn has observed, Roxana 'would become an object of his well-earned conspicuous consumption, as symbolic in her indolence as one of Usbek's wives locked up in his seraglio.'[23] The Dutch merchant, in other words, upholds the sexual economy that governs prostitution without guaranteeing the economic independence that accrues to the independent sex-trade worker. His vision of marriage maintains that women do not have to work in the home or outside of it, but simply remain sexually available to the husbands who support them. The economic contract legally belongs to him, however, as Roxana points out: 'you can take the Helm out of my Hand when you please, and bid me go spin' (190). Roxana's understanding of prostitution, by contrast, keeps the power in her hands. Throughout the negotiations between Roxana and the merchant, the 1000 pistoles the merchant lost in his endeavours to protect her against the Jew's attacks, and which Roxana offers to repay before offering sex instead, stays in view: 'I had some Reason to believe, [he] repented that he had refus'd the Money,' Roxana observes (183). The money remains a material reminder of what is at stake in the negotiations – namely, the economic, which the merchant seeks to absorb into the realm of morality.

Where the narrative earlier linked 'conscience' and financial stability in its account of the French Huguenot refugees, Roxana's refusal of the Dutch merchant suggests that, for women, conscience – defined in conventional terms – and financial ambition are mutually exclusive categories. Roxana may exercise economic autonomy as a single woman, but in doing so she places herself outside of the categories of 'woman,' 'Christian,' and 'mother,' leaving her close to the space inhabited by Jews and infidels. In assuming the alienating title 'whore,' Roxana defines conscience as not only 'something else,' but also as a condition existing 'somewhere else,' a subjectivity open to the possibility of geopolitical alterity. Just as Hoadly's contentious sermon reads Christianity as a religion of salvation open to all of 'sincere faith' (an interpretation that critics read as potentially limitless in its inclusiveness),[24] so too Roxana's ethical relativism, made evident in her refusal to separate conscience from social, political, and economic factors, identifies her as the kind of free-thinker John Foxe grouped with 'Turkes, Jewes, [and] Anabaptistes [sic]' when he introduced 'libertine' into the world of English religious controversy in the Renaissance.[25]

Imperial Whores: Desire at Home

These penal laws of England and France are in perfect conformity with each other. It is as if the same spirit had dictated them. How comes it then that what is sacred in Paris is impious in London and what is just in London is not legitimate in Paris? Could it be that the sea serves as a boundary to confine equity and justice, as it serves as a frontier for the two states? No, but rather that men judge things only according to their own interests; they sacrifice everything to them, truth, justice, religion and God himself.

Anon., c. 1687[26]

Mrs Salisbury being then asked; *And what are you?* She replyed, *good enough for a* Garter, *I am a Who–.*

The Genuine History of Mrs. Sarah Prydden,
Usually Called Sally Salisbury (1723)

As we saw in chapter 2, Hortense Mancini, Duchess of Mazarin, inhabited most fully the contours of the 'imperial whore' persona. Figured as the 'Italian Whore,' her ability to move between different European nations and England and to secure economic independence as a mistress in her various locales rendered her particularly hateful, a figure of a new cosmopolitan female sexuality resistant to regulation. Mancini flaunted her unorthodox sexual practices in the portrait she commissioned during her residence in England (figure 5). Srinivas Aravamudan notes that the representation of the black slaves in the image 'suggests an erotic complicity and uneasy violence that leads transitively through the black bodies to the figure of the king himself.'[27] The portrait indicates how only the Stuart monarchy's aspirations to absolute power reflected not so much the trappings of an outdated feudal legacy as an extension of political authority made possible by imperialism's bounty. We see this extension in the famous Mignard portrait of Louise de Kéroualle, now housed in the National Portrait Gallery (figure 6). Where Louise de Kéroualle appears with a child slave whose blackness stands in for both the courtesan's illicit sexuality and her powers of consumption, Mancini's appetite more forcefully takes the body of the slave as its object of pleasure.[28] The value of the Mancini portrait, in this regard, is that it exposes the way that empire consumes slave labour, including its sexual labour. Further, it exposes the pleasures – both sexual and aesthetic – afforded to white consumers by that labour and the power that oversees it.[29]

But the portrait also tells another story about empire. The neoclassical allusion takes us back into the Mediterranean, to Greece and Africa as the cradles of civilization.[30] Rather than establishing a link between England and Mediterranean cultures through an Apollonian discourse, the portrait emphasizes a Bacchanalian culture of excess. Mancini's Italian skin marks her as non-white and non-English, as part of the continuum of dog-black-woman that represents a challenge to the 'civilizing' mission England imagined it brought to the 'new' world. Mazarin sets herself in the monarch's place, drawing on Diana's authority within the classical tradition while mocking the idea of sexual abstinence upon which that authority conventionally depended. As Susan Shifrin notes, 'In having herself literally and figuratively "pictured" as Diana ... Mazarin courted perceptions of herself as chaste (that is to say, virginal) and chaser, all-powerful in her ability simultaneously to compel and defeat the attentions of her male audience and thereby ... to manipulate and dominate an implicitly male court politics.'[31] The black slaves appear not as play things, but as play-mates, companions in the hunt. That the slaves are boys – and in one case, at least a teenager – suggests another level of play, one that alludes to the common perception that Mancini had engaged in an affair with her servant, Mustapha. 'Rochester's Farewell' documents the duchess's transgression: 'And having all her [Rome's] lewdnesses outran, / Takst up with devil, having tir'd out man; / For what is else that loathsome filthy black / Which thou and Sussex in your arms did take?'[32] 'Nor was our monarch such a cully, / To bear a Moor, and swingeing bully,' observes another satire.[33] That Mancini's promiscuity reputedly outstripped the king's and indeed took one of the king's daughters as its object suggests how far removed Mancini appeared to set herself from the constraints of social convention.[34]

Roxana's transformation into an 'imperial whore' marks the novel's shift away from the moral system that had earlier facilitated an uneasy accommodation of sin under the cloak of necessity. Once necessity is taken out of the equation we are confronted with the problem of desire that, in fact, attends the entire narrative and articulates itself in Roxana's repeated admission that she is vain. In recounting the steps by which she descends into whoredom early in the narrative, Roxana notes that, in addition to, and inseparable from, the very strong incentive of avoiding poverty and destitution, vanity impels her: 'I was young, handsome, and with all the Mortifications I had met with, was vain, and that not a little' (73). Roxana organizes her selfhood around the emptiness of vanity, the vessel into which all of the courtesan's 'content,' in the form of moveable goods and credit, places itself. Conquest for Roxana depends not only on her ability to put her best face forward, it appears, but also on her own interest and attachment to that face. As she sets up her second liaison, with the prince in France, Roxana announces: 'I was now become the vainest Creature upon Earth, and particularly, of my Beauty; which, as other People admir'd, so I became every Day more foolishly in Love with myself, than before' (97). Only by inhabiting the structure of vanity's narcissism can Roxana prepare herself for the accumulation of wealth upon which her economic and social survival depends.

This sense of self appears in the masquerade of 'French lady' (204) that Roxana assumes as she plans her next conquest: 'nothing less than the KING himself was in my Eye; and this Vanity was rais'd by some Words let fall by a Person I convers'd with' (212). Even as Roxana looks to capitalize on her status as a sexually desirable object, however, she also imagines herself as deeply unsexed as an economic and political subject. Contemplating the socially advantageous marriages she turns down, Roxana observes: *'I was happier than I cou'd be in being a Prisoner of State to a Nobleman;* for I took the Ladies of that Rank to be little better' (207, emphasis in text). Robert Clayton, unlike the Dutch merchant, is willing to support Roxana's bid for power as a *'Man-Woman'* (212) and helps Roxana establish a link between the informal economy her work participates in and the formal economies of banking and the stock market. At the moment of appearing most anachronistic in her desire for a 'court appointment,' Roxana proves herself most modern.[35]

Roxana's use of a Turkish costume to advance her goals yokes sovereign power and modern economics, and in depicting the authority it grants the courtesan, Defoe draws on the cluster of meanings attached to the Stuart royal mistress.[36] The costume, we discover, was purchased for Roxana during her travels abroad:

> in less than half an Hour I return'd, dress'd in the Habit of a *Turkish Princess;* the Habit I got at *Leghorn,* when my *Foreign Prince* bought me a *Turkish* Slave, as I have said; the *Malthese* Man of War had, it seems, taken a *Turkish* Vessel going from *Constantinople* to *Alexandria,* in which were some Ladies bound for *Grand Cairo* in Egypt; and as the Ladies were made Slaves, so their fine Cloaths were thus expos'd; and with this *Turkish* Slave, I bought the rich Cloaths too. (214–15)

Roxana's transformation into an exotic object fit for a king is only made possible, as Felicity Nussbaum points out, by the exploitation of foreign women.[37] It is worth observing that this exploitation involves not only the form of appropriating the culture attached to Turkish dress, but also the labour of the young Turkish slave who has dressed Roxana before in this costume: 'little did I think, when I bought it, that I shou'd put it to such a Use as this; tho' I had dressed myself in it many times, by the help of my little *Turk,* and afterwards between Amy and I, only to see how I look'd in it' (215). Roxana's vanity has created the conditions of possibility for this moment, but the moment's manifestation is only made possible through the work, and diminishment, of others. The syntax of the passage confuses the distinction between the 'fine ladies' who are rendered slaves by their capture and the 'little Turk' – whom we later discover is a girl – Roxana purchases when she buys the ladies' dresses. The figure of the 'Turkish Princess' is reduced both to a commodity and to the stature of a child.[38] Roxana further consolidates her English national supremacy over a degraded Eastern rival by assuming the political power that accrues to the name 'Roxana.' The name alludes both to the Ottoman Roxolana and to the Greek Roxana, women whose ability to exercise authority captured the attention of several seventeenth-century writers.[39] That Defoe's Roxana should appropriate this power announces the author's anxious hope for a European victory over the Ottoman Empire.[40] Roxana transforms its culture, by way of French dance, into a commodity item for consumption by an English aristocracy, becoming her own 'Turkey merchant.'

But just as Hortense Mancini entertained the possibility of an identification of her own foreignness with that of her black slaves in the portrait she commissioned, so too Roxana deepens her attachment to her alien status when she adopts the disguise of the French/Ottoman princess. The aristocratic culture in which Roxana gains her footing not only sets the stage for England's imperial conquests, but it also allows for an equivalency to appear between foreign and English sovereigns:

> I was now in my Element; I was as much talk'd of as any-body cou'd desire, and I did not doubt but something or other would come of it; but the Report of my being so rich, rather was a Baulk to my View, than anything else; for the Gentlemen that wou'd, perhaps, have been troublesome enough otherwise, seem'd to be kept off; for *Roxana* was too high for them. (223)

The king's willingness to walk where other aristocrats fear to tread is marked, however, not by bags of gold, but by the purchase of privacy: 'There is a Scene which came in here, which I must cover from humane Eyes or Ears; for three Years and about a Month, *Roxana* liv'd retir'd, having been oblig'd to make an Excursion, in a Manner, and with a Person, which Duty, and private Vows, obliges her not to reveal, at least, not yet' (223). The king's ability to sequester himself serves as an objective correlative to the secrecy Roxana has maintained throughout her career, a secrecy that has been so private it must necessarily become public again, in the form of an identity known to some, and as susceptible to investigation by others, later in the narrative. The culmination of Roxana's career marks its alienation in the narration's use of the third-person to describe its first-person subject, but it also marks its power in the allusion to the monarch's habits of speaking of himself in the first-person plural, 'we.'[41]

As much as Roxana's ascent marks a crowning achievement in her career as a mistress, the moment *after* her affair with the king more properly defines the apotheosis of her courtesan identity:

> At the End of this Time I appear'd again; but I must add, that as I had in this Time of Retreat, *made Hay*, &c. – so I did not come Abroad again with the same Lustre, or shine with so much Advantage as before; for as some People had got at least, a Suspicion of where I had been, and who had had me all the while, it began to be publick, that *Roxana* was, in short, a meer *Roxana*, neither better nor worse; and not that Woman of Honour and Virtue that was at first suppos'd. (223)

The explanation of the courtesan's mystery coincides with Roxana's acknowledgment of her beauty's reduced power, but the way that Roxana describes that diminishment is not entirely straightforward. The expression 'made Hay, &c' implies that Roxana has gained, rather than lost, from her excursion's excesses; the *OED* defines the expression 'to make hay while the sun shines' as 'to lose no time, to seize or profit by opportunities.'[42] In abbreviating the expression, Roxana implies the presence of the king as the sun who has shone on her. Even as she locks his name away from the public glare of prose, Roxana incorporates the monarch's attentions into her own sense of aristocratic entitlement, and, in the rhetorical wink provided by the '&c.,' includes the reader in the intimacy of her scandalous privilege. The shorter expression that Roxana actually uses, 'to make hay,' more simply suggests, and this is the *OED* again, 'to make confusion.' Confusion appears in the curious dearth of concreteness in Roxana's description of her time with the king and the public's response to her excursion: Roxana's engagement has taken place in a space of retreat removed from the public gaze of London, a geographically vague land of pleasure. The demotion Roxana suffers in her public status places her in a position that she defines as morally neutral, as 'neither better nor worse' than that of a courtesan. And, finally, Roxana's assumption of incredible wealth appears, in narrative time, to coincide with her acquiescence to a public branding. Indeed, her success seems coterminous with that exposure:

> You are now to suppose me about seven Years come to Town, and that I had not only suffer'd the old Revenue, which I hinted was manag'd by Sir *Robert Clayton*, to grow, as was mention'd before; but I had laid-up an incredible Wealth, the time consider'd; and had I yet had the least Thought of reforming, I had all the Opportunity to do it with Advantage, that ever

Woman had; for the common Vice of all Whores, I mean Money, was out of the Question, nay, even Avarice itself seem'd to be glutted. (223)

The hardening of Roxana's identity as a whore, paradoxically, appears in the spectacle of a wealth that exceeds all questions of need and avarice. Roxana is an exceptional whore, one capable of transcending the limitation of the 'common Vice' associated with her profession. Roxana's identity appears as a fantasy unchecked by any conventional empirical markers. At the moment when Roxana becomes a 'mere' Roxana, she achieves her greatest powers by identifying unauthorized practices with economic transcendence.

Roxana uses the cultural capital she has gained as the king's mistress to bargain hard with her next client. To the extent that it wishes to emulate the trajectory of a successful career, Defoe's narrative must embrace the most illicit aspects of its heroine's conduct. What appears as a species of royal sport in Roxana's dalliance with the king reveals its true colours in this final liaison: a prostitute's sex is work, and as such, has both pleasant and unpleasant dimensions. The vice that grows 'surfeiting and nauceous [sic]' (241) to Roxana over the course of her relationship with a peer expresses itself in the very architecture Roxana and her patron inhabit:

My Lord came readily into this Proposal, and went farther than I expected; for he found out a Lodging for me in a very handsome House, where yet he was not known; I suppose he had employ'd somebody to find it out for him; and where he had a convenient Way to come into the Garden, by a Door that open'd into the Park; a thing very rarely allow'd in those Times.

By this Key he cou'd come in at what time of Night or Day he pleas'd and as we had also a little Door in the lower Part of the House, which was always left upon a Lock, and his was the Master-Key, so if it was twelve, one, or two a-Clock at Night, he cou'd come directly into my Bed-Chamber. N.B. I was not afraid I shou'd be found a-Bed with any-body else, for, in a word, I convers'd with no-body at-all. (227–8)

The idea of the private entrance that conceals the comings and goings of Roxana's client fantasizes unlimited access to both the psychology and sexuality of the courtesan.[43] There are two ways to read the idea of Roxana's position as it appears in this passage. First we should consider Defoe's characterization of Roxana's vulnerability and the enforced passivity brought on by her precarious social position. Here I follow Cynthia Wall's astute analysis of the role that architecture plays in *Roxana*. Wall points to the way in which Roxana 'draws *all* her rooms around her to generate and consolidate forms of power' only to find that 'all her inhabited space – psychological as well as architectural – becomes haunted space.'[44] According to this reading, we should look at the way in which Roxana disappears from the passage describing her residence. Roxana's lover demonstrates his authority over the home by remaining anonymous within its space, an anonymity that he guarantees both by having someone else negotiate the lease and by finding ways of arriving invisibly at the house. The verb 'to come' appears three times in the passage in a pattern of reiteration that moves us, through the lover, from the abstraction of Roxana's proposal to the intimacy of her bed-chamber. The lover's key is the 'Master-Key,' one that presumably can open the gates of the park onto which Roxana's house backs, as well as the various doors to the house. We are told that 'a little Door in the lower Part of the House ... was always left upon a Lock,' a detail that suggests that the door is left locked but not bolted. This image heightens the sense of entitlement the lord claims over his mistress by making her seem vulnerable, always penetrable by him. The lord appears, then, as a master of both Roxana's space and her time, indulging the sex they have according to his, rather than her, desires. The courtesan's sexuality, by this account, necessarily only finds expression through male imperatives and prerogatives, in contrast to the enticements of the companionate marriage offered to Roxana by the Dutch merchant. Even more insidiously, Defoe's account of Roxana's availability links his characterization to the misogyny of conventional tropes that brand the courtesan's sexuality.[45]

But such a reading only partially captures the significance of the representation of Roxana's home. The passage takes us immediately back to the figure of Nell Gwyn, for whom Charles II leased a residence on Pall Mall. The house backed on to St James's Park. In a diary entry of 1671, John Evelyn notes: 'I had a fair opportunity of talking to His Majesty in the lobby next to the Queen's side, where I presented him with some sheets of my History. I thence walked with him through St. James's Park, where I both saw and heard a very familiar discourse between him and Mrs. Nellie, as they call an impudent comedian; she looked out of her garden on a terrace at the top of the walk, and he standing on the green walk under it. I was heartily sorry at this scene.'[46] Evelyn's words register a dismay at the informality of the scene, which both places the king physically below his mistress and exposes his intimacy in the public space of St James's Park. While Charles's infidelities were no secret to his subjects, Evelyn apparently objects to the king's willingness to take his affair beyond the bounds of private royal prerogative, out of the boudoir and into the park. Charles's libertinism, from Evelyn's standpoint, undermines his authority as a monarch and inappropriately elevates an actress into the ranks of the aristocracy.

In reminding us of Nell Gwyn and 'those times' – i.e., the Restoration – Defoe returns us to the conventions of scandal narrative that govern the earlier moment of Roxana's retreat, with its mysterious suppression of the king's identity and the location of the love-nest Roxana shares with him. Indeed, the allusion to Nell Gwyn's Pall Mall home actually brings the earlier moment forward, so that the time spent with the king works as a palimpsest to the interlude Roxana describes here; the retreat is relocated from its presumably pastoral location at the margins of London's cultural life to the urban centre. When we return to the passage from this vantage point, another reading of the residence appears, one that brings Roxana's earlier pleasure as the mistress of a Pall Mall home and as the seducer of the king into this residence, which very well could be located in the same neighbourhood. In particular, Roxana's curious note – 'I was not afraid I shou'd be found a-Bed with any-body else, for, in a word, I convers'd with no-body at-all' (228) – immediately suggests that the courtesan could, in fact, entertain other male guests when her patron is not at home (as did, most famously, Hortense Mancini and Barbara Villiers).[47] The description of the door as remaining 'always upon a Lock' reminds us of the more common expression, 'left upon a latch' – an expression that implies that the door has been left unlocked and is capable of being opened from the outside without a key.[48] The confidence and intimacy with which Roxana renders her aside alerts us to the salacious content of the detail she is rendering; we enter, in the note, the realm of gossip and assume the authority of its speaker, which in turn colours the passage as a whole. Beyond the horizon of the allusion to Nell Gwyn's apartments, we glimpse the political discourse of back-door interlopers gaining access to the king's residence in secret: Jesuit priests, foreign diplomats, and other secret agents.[49]

The narrative's devolution into a space of claustrophobic entrapment begins when Roxana relinquishes control over locks, replacing her ability to handle real latches with the pleasures afforded by her husband's ability to purchase titles for her after their marriage:

I was now my LADY –, and I must own, I was exceedingly pleas'd with it; 'twas so Big, and so Great, to hear myself call'd *Her Ladyship*, and *Your Ladyship, and the like*; that I was like the *Indian* King at *Virginia*, who having a House built for him by the *English*, and a Lock put upon the Door, wou'd sit whole Days together, with the Key in his Hand, locking and unlocking, and double-locking the Door, with an unaccountable Pleasure at the Novelty; (290–1)

In the last issue he wrote of the *Review* eleven years earlier, Defoe remarked: 'What a Whoring Generation is this! *F.* is newly made a Baronet, and never tires with looking at his new Coat of Arms; like the *Indian* King at *Virginia*, who being presented with a Locke to his House-Door, pleas'd himself with locking and unlocking it a Thousand times a Day.'[50] The potential for desire to distract individuals from the world around them takes on a political significance in the example of the Indian King, whose delight in a door lock blinds him to the loss of a nation. The comparison between Roxana and the Native American marks the political aspect of marriage: Roxana becomes the Indian subject granted trinkets in exchange for a continent and she no longer pursues wealth of her own, but only the social status afforded her by her husband's acquisition of titles. Further, the house of marriage is not one Roxana can freely exit, unlike the previous lodgings she has inhabited.

Roxana, Inc.

They [Dissenters] abhor subjection to Bishops, because every Individual will be himself more than a Pope.

Anon., *Fanatick Loyalty* (1716)

As Roxana recounts the wealth she accumulates as mistress to Lord —, she pauses, and takes us back again to the moment of her arrival in England after her travels abroad: 'I must go back here, after telling openly the wicked things I did, to mention something, which however, had the Face of doing good' (230).[51] The 'something,' as it turns out, is Roxana's progeny, whom she locates and attempts to help financially while advancing her career as a courtesan. Roxana's sons take her wealth back out into the arena of British trade and empire, where they are able to follow in their mother's footsteps. Amy, passing as the children's benefactor, circulates the story that she has recently returned from India: 'it was not a strange thing for young Women to go away poor to the *East-Indies*, and come home vastly Rich' (235). Roxana imagines the children as part of a larger corporation developing the wealth she has amassed, extending through its channels the domain of her estate. She entertains, for several years, the idea that the 'home' she has made of England as a whore and the 'home' she once inhabited as a wife and mother can converge, however tentatively. As she describes her efforts to launch one son's career, Roxana remarks: 'it put me upon thinking how to put an End to that wicked Course I was in, that my own Child, when he shou'd afterwards come to *England* in a good Figure ... shou'd not be asham'd to own me' (247). But the bid for power the courtesan's career has involved necessarily excludes Roxana from consideration by the imperatives of the domestic. While recognizing that 'whore' and 'mother' are mutually exclusive categories, Roxana fails to see that money cannot bridge the gap.[52]

The question Roxana asks as she shifts her attention to her children, *'What was I a Whore for now?'* (243), signals the end of desire as it relates to her work. Not surprisingly, it is the ability to say 'no' to sex acts that Roxana no longer feels economically motivated to allow for that marks the end of her career: 'I was much more sick of his Lordship, than he cou'd be of me; he grew old, and fretful, and captious, and I must add ... he grew worse and wickeder the older he grew, and that to such a Degree, as is not fit to write of' (241). What appears as a devolution from pleasure to aversion is more acutely rendered in the shift in Roxana's material circumstances: 'as I had good Leisure now to divert and enjoy myself in the World, as much as it was possible for any Woman to do ... so I found that my Judgment began to prevail upon me to fix my Delight upon nobler Objects than I had formerly done' (242).

But Roxana's attempt to reenter the world of 'nobler Objects' reveals the gendered fault-line that runs through eighteenth-century discourses of conscience: for women, conscience requires an abdication of the kinds of authority invested in the Stuart courtesan. And Roxana discovers that she is not willing to entertain these abdications when challenged by one of her daughters. Significantly, the story returns to the problem of this daughter, Susan, after it takes a pause to meditate, once again, on the attractions of Catholic confession: 'it was well, *as I often thought*, that I was not a *Roman-Catholick*; for what a piece of Work shou'd I have made, to have gone to a Priest with such a History as I had to tell him? and what Pennance wou'd any *Father-Confessor* have oblig'd me to perform? especially if he had been honest and true to his Office' (310–11). Here the enormity of her crime seems to make it impossible to confess, even hypothetically, to the Catholic priest in whom Roxana dreams of confiding. Roxana's dream of absolution can be read two ways: first, as the end point of a narrative defined more by a habitual than a primal sin, a pattern of sinfulness more readily forgiven within a Catholic than a Protestant register; second, as a moment that would serve the opposite end, that of licensing everything: Roxana's dream perhaps imagines a self freed, in the moment of absolution, to pursue further sinful gratifications. Catholicism appears, in both formulations, as a fantasy of escape from the rigours of Protestantism, from its relentless hounding of the self into a moment of recognition and final transformation. But it is a fantasy from which Roxana resolutely turns away.

As in Roxana's earlier dream of absolution, pragmatic considerations colour the moral imperatives governing the moment. That a priest might *not* be 'honest and true' to his office, but rather might be bought off (as when Roxana was able to purchase a Catholic burial for her English Protestant jeweller 'husband' in France), introduces the economic into the moral once more, and suggests one of the reasons why Roxana finds it difficult to express a 'thorow effectual Repentance' (167). The structure of this repentance, we discover, cannot absorb the nature of Roxana's sin unless it, too, has been corrupted by illicit materiality. Roxana can never achieve repentance in its 'sincere' form as long as she claims personhood as an economic subject. Only the consolations afforded by a Catholic priest open to bribery appear available to Roxana. Instead of indulging in these consolations, she consigns herself to eternal self-damnation – 'I went about with a Heart loaded with Crime' (311) – a gesture that grants Roxana an interiority otherwise out of reach. In a similar fashion, Roxana carefully secures her wealth away from the Dutch merchant's when she finally marries by riddling it with disease: '*shall my ill-got Wealth, the Product of* prosperous Lust, *and of a vile and vicious Life* of Whoredom and Adultery, *be intermingled with the honest well-gotten Estate of this innocent* Gentleman ... I'll *keep them asunder, if it be possible*' (304).

The story of Roxana's daughter, Susan, most often is read as the anti-Roxana narrative, as the hook that unravels the courtesan's identity. In terms of the novel's dénouement, this is certainly true. But what I would like to draw attention to here is the structural similarities that link Roxana's and Susan's narratives. What we encounter in Susan's narrative is a retelling of the heroine's story in its purest form, for Susan's quest is most fundamentally about desire and the dream of self-recognition that, in my discussion of Roxana's vanity, I have identified as the organizing principle of the courtesan's identity. Once it becomes clear that

Roxana is not going to acknowledge her daughter, Susan might very well ask herself, *'What was I a Daughter for now?'* Susan's repetition of Roxana's narrative allows Defoe to avoid the conundrum of how to end his libertine heroine's career without capitulating to the demands of the marriage she finally enters into, allowing the narrative both to turn back toward its heroine and to consider the larger implications of the Protestant Whore's desire as a narrative pattern and principle that Susan both embodies and perverts in her relentless pursuit of truth.[53]

Susan's story begins at the moment when Roxana's narrative has ostensibly ended:

> I went about with a Heart loaded with Crime, and altogether in the dark, as to what I was to do; and in this Condition I languish'd near two Years; I may well call it languishing, for if Providence had not reliev'd me, I shou'd have died in little time: *But of that hereafter.*
>
> I must now go back to another Scene, and join it to this End of my Story. (311)

In announcing the need to go back into the story she has already told, Roxana both introduces a new subject and the idea that we are going to encounter an alternative perspective. And we do. Susan embodies an extended and exaggerated form of the identity and narrative her mother has directed up to this point in the novel. Her desire immediately defines itself through its hyperbolic and excessive nature. When Amy announces that she is not the young woman's mother, Susan responds hysterically: 'The Girl fell a-crying, and *Amy* had much ado to keep Life in her ... She said still, *But O do not say you a'n't my Mother! I'm sure you are my Mother*; and then the Girl cry'd again like to kill herself' (312). The young woman's desperation propels her toward the self-annihilation she will eventually bring upon herself as either real or symbolic, and it marks her inability to control and regulate, to pattern as cycle rather than insisting on a telos, the imperatives governing the courtesan identity. As much as we may want to sympathize with the daughter's desire, the narrative marks it as dangerous and, after a point, suicidal, unlike Roxana's desire, which only courts destruction because of the social context in which it is forced to remain secretive.[54]

Susan, like Roxana, is ambitious, but her empire-building energies are directed toward the family: in particular, toward the mother who shares her name.[55] The search begins as a material ambition when

Susan discovers, on a visit to her uncle, that her brother has been provided for: 'I had not let them know where I liv'd; and the Lady would have taken me, and they say, wou'd have provided for me too, as she has done for my Brother, but no-body cou'd tell where to find me, and so I have lost it all, and all the Hopes of being any-thing, but a poor Servant all my Days' (238). Like Roxana, whose fears of ending up as vulnerable as she once was as a young abandoned wife drive her to pursue massive amounts of wealth, Susan never forgets this first moment of being 'lost.' Having finally discovered her mother, she pursues her at the cost of her life. Susan's desire to reconstitute her family ties represents an expression of familial affect that domestic ideology brought into view in the early eighteenth century. Within an emergent capitalist economy, Susan represents the progression by which, as Deleuze and Guattari observe, 'the family ceases to give social form to economic reproduction: it is as though disinvested, placed outside the field.'[56] Susan imagines the family as separable from the economic conditions of its creation and sustenance and seeks to hive her mother off from these conditions as well.[57]

Susan's insistence on desire's satisfaction, rather than deferral, marks her for death. At the moment when Susan, thinking Amy is her mother, is confronted with the prospect of economic ruin, Susan, like her mother, embraces her abjection: 'The Girl, a passionate Wench, *told her*, she knew the worst of it, she cou'd go to Service again, and if she wou'd not own her own Child, she must do as she pleas'd; then she fell into a Passion of crying again, as if she wou'd kill herself' (314). Despite her age and her status as an economically independent young woman, Susan claims the dependency of a child. But her self-identification as an 'innocent' requires, for its compensation, Roxana's willingness to abandon the power she has earned. The Turkish dress reveals the secret of Roxana's identity, but the question of whose claims to that identity are paramount governs the tragedy that ensues. Susan recognizes the role that secrecy is playing in her quest from the outset – 'I can keep a Secret too, especially for my own Mother' – but she refuses to acknowledge that the secret cannot include both her and her mother simultaneously (313). Roxana has created a version of maternity that does not grant her children unlimited access or the end-game of total revelation. Susan's desire for an unmediated and transparent moment of mother-daughter recognition reflects the dream of absolution that Roxana entertains in her fantasies of a Catholic moment of confession.

It simultaneously brings home the impossibility of reconciling those fantasies with Roxana's need to sustain the identity she has forged, an identity that lives, for better and for worse, in a singularly Protestant register.

The emotions that Roxana experiences when she encounters her adult daughter for the first time threaten to obliterate distinctions, separateness, and even the self's integrity: 'I felt something shoot thro' my Blood; my Heart flutter'd; my Head flash'd, and was dizzy, and all within me, *as I thought*, turn'd about, and much ado I had, not to abandon myself to an Excess of Passion at the first Sight of her, much more when my Lips touch'd her Face' (323).[58] Unlike Susan, however, Roxana has learned to harden herself against her emotions, and her children, in order to survive, and knows that her secret self is the only chance at independence she might have. Contemplating Susan's unlocking of the mystery that surrounds her, Roxana can only imagine the intimacy of her daughter's understanding as a violation: 'I must for-ever after have been this Girl's Vassal, *that is to say*, have let her into the Secret, and trusted to her keeping it too, or have been expos'd, and undone; *the very Thought fill'd me with Horror*' (326). The syntax here renders the 'Thought' ambiguous as a point of reference – is it the threat of exposure, or more simply the possibility of her daughter's knowing her true identity, that fills Roxana with horror? David Marshall notes Roxana's repeated references to her fear of being 'undone' by Susan, and observes that 'To be *undone* means more than to be ruined; it means to be opened, unlocked, uncovered, unfastened.'[59] Susan, too, imagines her mother's refusal to own her as a species of violation: 'O! Says she, stand my Friend, if you have any Charity ... for I am utterly undone!' (352). We are reminded of the narrative's reflections on locks and latches – and of the power vested in those who hold the keys.[60]

Marshall also argues that Susan stands as a prototype of *Roxana*'s reader, from whom secrets must be hidden.[61] But I would suggest that an alternative figure for the reader appears in the figure of the Quaker, whose home provides Roxana with a safe refuge from her past while keeping alive, in the curiosity she reveals about that past, the vanity that fosters Roxana's sense of self. It is no surprise to this reader that the keeper of Roxana's secret should inhabit the fringes of Protestant identity and bring us full circle to the problems with which Defoe continually grappled in determining who and what should count as spiritual authority. Unlike Susan, the Quaker does not rely on a master narrative in her reading of Roxana: 'she thwarted the Girl so cleverly, that if she had known the whole Affair, she cou'd not have done it better' (327). Roxana, recognizing that trust vested in the Quaker will not necessitate her self-destruction, notes: 'I cou'd more freely have trusted her, than I cou'd the Girl, by a great-deal; *nay*, I shou'd have been perfectly easie in her' (331). We see in the narrative's representation of the Quaker's delicate negotiations with her conscience the admiration of casuistry that G.A. Starr has defined as a guiding principle of Defoe's narratives.[62] Most important, the Quaker's curiosity, while strengthening Roxana's sense of self, never threatens to violate that self by insisting on revelation, and abets Roxana in her desire to avoid Susan's prying investigations. Like Susan, the Quaker is drawn to Roxana's courtesan past, fixating on the costume that will ultimately expose Roxana's true identity. But her curiosity allows itself to indulge the fantasy without needing to destroy the secrecy upon which the courtesan's survival depends.

In protecting Roxana's past as an imperial whore, the Quaker reveals the political dimension of her community's respect for secrecy, one that was linked to Jacobite activism by Defoe's contemporaries and the Hanoverian state:

> In spite of the merits of their religious policy ... the banished Stuarts were constantly frustrated by the conservatism of institutionalized religious bodies ... Jacobitism had to rely on the Catholic gentry, the Nonjurors, independent or isolated Anglican clergymen and Quakers ... For these oppressed religious minorities, survival required that the Church and government exist apart, except at the highest level, in the person of the sacred and divinely ordained king.[63]

Roxana's recognition of the Quaker as her ally suggests an affinity between the two women, between Roxana's dreams of power and the Quaker's membership in a persecuted community. When the story of the Turkish dress resurfaces, Roxana knows the Quaker will grasp its implications and recognize Roxana's identity: 'it was impossible but the QUAKER, who was a sharp penetrating Creature, shou'd receive the Impression in a more dangerous Manner, than the Girl; only that indeed, she was not so dangerous a Person' (331). Roxana's material generosity toward the Quaker does not account for the trust Roxana invests in her. Rather, it is the Quaker character itself that seems to inspire confidence. The Quaker becomes Roxana's 'faithful SPY' *'upon the meer foot of her own Sagacity'* (357, emphasis in text).

If the Quaker's commitment to the integrity of secrets provides the basis for her attachment to Roxana, it is Susan's commitment to the principle of maternal recognition that produces Roxana's antipathy toward her daughter. 'It was a sad thing she wou'd not let her call her Mother, who was her own Child,' Susan laments when she believes that Amy is her mother (313). But while using the language of affect to characterize her quest, Susan nonetheless is as interested in power as Roxana. To have the secret of her past revealed to her daughter, Roxana realizes, will involve the mother's subjugation by her child, as when she imagines herself as Susan's 'Vassal' (326). In contrast to the Quaker and Amy, Susan appears as an enemy spy, watching the door 'Night and Day': 'for she was so bent upon a Discovery, that she spar'd no Pains' (365). She uses the language of the judiciary in her quest: 'If I cou'd but speak to her,' she tells the Quaker, 'I wou'd prove my Relation to her, so that *she* could not deny it any-longer' (369). Her torment of Roxana is such that she becomes the punishment Roxana more typically inflicts on herself: 'I was continually perplex'd with this Hussy, and thought she haunted me like an Evil Spirit' (358).

Most dangerously, Susan proves as mobile as Roxana has been in her own career:

> She was resolv'd ... that she wou'd visit all the Airing-Places in the Nation, and even all the Kingdom over, ay, and *Holland* too, but she wou'd find me; for she was satisfy'd she cou'd so convince me that she was my own Child, that I wou'd not deny it; and she was sure I was so tender and compassionate, I wou'd not let her perish after I was convinc'd that she was my own Flesh and Blood. (356)

Susan's mobility demonstrates the long reach of domestic ideology. Its consignment to the private sphere does not render the family a private affair, but one that permeates all spaces of the nation, even travelling abroad. Susan proves disastrously wrong in her assumption that maternal love follows recognition, but her error masks another truth: that Susan represents a new version of social authority.

In the end, Defoe sacrifices the daughter and saves the mother, and in doing so, insists on the economic conditions of agency that the prostitute so compellingly represents. James Thompson's claim, that 'Roxana is Defoe's one protagonist who does not know when to give over, when to quit the game safely,' overlooks the fact that modern economies sustain a game no one can quit or, indeed, even play 'safely' – a fact pointedly represented in the fate that awaits those rendered most vulnerable by its operations.[64] Trapped between the imperatives of domestic ideology, capitalism's economic vicissitudes, and an increasingly masculinized political arena, Roxana's quest for personhood can produce nothing *but* guilt. Indeed, we can say the narrative's conclusion produces the event needed to stage the guilt. We are never presented with an eye-witness account of Susan's murder, or, in fact, any explicit confirmation that the murder has taken place, but we never doubt that the narrative must lead, ineluctably, to this point of exposing Roxana's 'pathology.'[65] Anticipating the revelation that will ruin her, Roxana concludes: 'What a glorious Testimony it is to the Justice of Providence ... that the most secret Crimes are, by the most unforeseen Accidents, brought to light, and discover'd' (345).

In the final instance, however, Roxana's dark deeds are not brought to light. If, on one level, the narrative depends on our conviction of Roxana's guilt to anchor its moral epistemology, its commitment to exposing the social conditions that produce this state and to releasing Roxana from the punishments that attend it sustains an amoral counter-narrative, generated in the tension that appears between the Roxana who narrates the tale and her younger self. Critics err, I believe, in imagining that the novel's conclusion suggests that a final blow has been administered to Roxana's pride, for if it has, what do we do with the narrative voice which, through the novel's 'Relator,' expresses as much delight as it does dismay in recounting the heroine's past life? Starr has argued that 'there are fairly early indications that Defoe means to consign Roxana to the devil, and ... that the technical difficulty of making an unregenerate malefactor her own critic is the book's undoing,' but I suggest that only by having the unregenerate malefactor tell her story can Defoe's scepticism regarding the separation of political, economic, and moral spheres come to light.[66] As when Roxana cannot resist encouraging her daughter to speak of the secret life she wants to closet – 'I cou'd not help being pleas'd and tickl'd with it; and put in Questions two or three times, of how handsome she was? and was she really so fine a Woman as they talk'd of?' (334) – so the narrative endlessly loops back into the life it ostensibly condemns, undermining, each time it does, the integrity of the conventional moral wisdom served up intermittently in the narrative and in the novel's concluding paragraphs.[67] And it is not only pleasure that we find in the younger Roxana's tale, for, as Malinda Snow observes, 'Often the reader may find that the younger Roxana's arguments to herself have sufficient merit to undercut the old narrator's counterarguments.'[68]

Jesse Molesworth argues that 'at the end of the novel, Roxana does not reflect on the singular path of her life story ... retrospectively working all events into a providential scheme ... Instead she faces a swirling ocean of contingency and uncertainty.'[69] In aesthetic terms, the conditions for the possibility of narration become inseparable from the novel's willingness to suspend judgment. 'I am not to preach, but to relate,' declares Roxana (83), confirming the link between narration, scepticism, and the prostitute's marginal status established by Behn's *Love-Letters*. If social discourses require Roxana to meditate on 'the opposite Circumstances of a *Wife* and *Whore*,' courtesan narrative takes her in a different direction: 'my Business is History' (171). Roxana imagines her story as 'a piece of Work' incapable of fitting within the interpretive epistemology of confession – it is linked, rather, to the material conditions of labour. Her courtesan 'work' renders her part of a trade that cannot, ideologically, reconcile economics, morality, and selfhood. Only 'something dark and dreadful brings us to our selves again,' Roxana notes early in the narrative, anticipating the crime that will draw together the strands of her narrative (105). But coherence is not, finally, the same as judgment.[70]

Julian Hoppit claims that

> the quiescence of the 1720s ... reflected a mood of conservatism born of bitter experience. Attempts by the State to promote religious homogeneity and orthodox spiritual intensity that had begun at the Reformation had now reached their limit and, to a certain extent, were tacitly acknowledged to have failed ...
>
> It was not so much that God, Christ, or the Church were less significant by 1727, rather that there was more uncertainty as to just what their significance was.[71]

To set *Roxana* against this backdrop is to provide a local view of the author's Protestant commitments, to witness his Protestantism in its least sanguine mode. Michael McKeon describes Defoe's desire to reconcile Protestantism's moral imperatives and 'worldly activity' in *Robinson Crusoe* thus: 'Robinson's long isolation schools him into the psychological necessity needed to transform his activity into his calling ... He is a great exemplar not only of the Weber thesis but of progressive ideology.'[72] But *Roxana* tells another story, refusing to commit to the discourses and practices of the early eighteenth century, pacing back and forth, rather, over Restoration terrain as if to find an alternate path forward, there. Defoe evokes Nell Gywn's legacy and the Restoration's struggle to sustain the dream of Protestant community to plumb the narrative opportunities afforded by the title 'Protestant Whore.' In responding to the Restoration's central question –'*Popery* we will not have; so far we are *right*, but what are we for?'– Defoe refuses the idea that the answer could reside in any theological or moral abstraction, insisting rather on the embodied status of the individual who responds to the challenges it poses.[73]

5 A World of One's Own: *Clarissa,*
Tom Jones, and Courtesan Authority

> Women signify nothing unless they are the mistress of a prince or a first
> minister, which I would not be if I were young; and I think there are very
> few, if any women, that have understanding or impartiality enough to
> serve well those they really wish to serve.
>
> Sarah Churchill, Duchess of Malborough, 1737–8[1]

> Though I cannot be *Henry* the Fifth, or *Charles* the Second, yet I endeavor
> to be *Margaret* the *First*; and although I have neither power, time, nor occa-
> sion to conquer the world as *Alexander* and *Caesar* did; yet rather than not
> to be mistress of one, since Fortune and the Fates would give me none, I
> have made a world of my own.
>
> Margaret Cavendish, *The Blazing World*[2]

Sarah Churchill's lament regarding the rise of the mistress in the 1730s
seems curiously anachronistic. As this study has shown, references to
the Stuart mistress provided a shorthand for descriptions of the abuse
of power after 1660. Latter-day accusations of sexual corruption in the
Hanoverian court drew on two generations of cultural commentary.
But the Duchess of Malborough's remarks place their emphasis on the
political acumen of the women with whom she shared the limelight in
her younger days. Twenty years after the death of Queen Anne, Sarah
Churchill's key no longer unlocked the cabinets of power. New models
for women's engagement in the public sphere were emerging in the
1730s, but these differed substantially enough from the practices of the
Restoration and the early eighteenth century to render them invisible to
the aging eyes of the Duchess.[3]

Even as new forms of state power evolved, Restoration discourses and iconography continued to circulate widely, shaping, in particular, the language of Jacobite resistance to an emergent Whig oligarchy. Margaret Cavendish's seventeenth-century dreams of creative authority as consolation for political disenfranchisement provide us with a model for thinking about courtesan narrative's response to the failure of the Jacobite rebellion of 1745, and the larger cultural implications of that failure. Both *Clarissa* and *Tom Jones* are saturated in Restoration iconography. *Clarissa*'s characterization confirms Catherine Gallagher's reading of 'the paradoxical connection between the *roi absolu* and the *moi absolu*' that governed seventeenth-century Tory feminist discourse.[4] Richardson develops his reflections on sovereignty, power, and the body to foster a radical critique of the status quo, drawing on the language of Jacobite mysticism and, in the novel's concluding volumes, Protestant antinomianism.[5] *Tom Jones* similarly engages the Stuart legacy, refashioning the Protestant Whore in the likeness of a bastard – and his whore-like (male) author. To read Richardson's and Fielding's greatest novels as 'Restoration' texts is to emphasize the common ground they share, rather than their well-documented differences, and to link their achievements to earlier aesthetic practices. Reading *Clarissa* and *Tom Jones* as courtesan narratives helps us to see the extent to which the early novel does not necessarily, or in any straightforward way, lead up to late eighteenth-century modernity. These novels mark, here, the end of a road.

'The inconvenient situation of royalty': Clarissa *Rex*[6]

> He has not had reason to think me weak.
> Clarissa to William Morden, Letter 448, *Clarissa*

Over the past thirty years, feminist criticism has celebrated *Clarissa*'s ability to protest the misogyny of the rake's creed – 'every woman is at heart a rake.'[7] Richardson's narrative ennobles female character, generating, through its formal innovations, a new depth of sexless interiority.[8] The novel challenges not only libertinism's erotic misogyny, but also the more pervasive sexism of mid-eighteenth century England: Clarissa refuses the base designs of a family that would reduce her to chattel on the marriage market, the seductive blandishments of a man for whom she has feelings, and, in the aftermath of her rape, the paltry consolations offered as compensation. The novel's tragedy registers the loss, to the world, of a woman like Clarissa Harlowe. Less often re-marked, however, is the extent to which other women in the novel are made to carry some of the burdens – economic alienation, embodiment, spiritual compromise – that Clarissa sheds in her quest for emancipa-tion. This chapter asks: how much does the representation of Clarissa's freedom depend upon the vilification of her will to power in the figure of the courtesan? And: to what extent does Richardson's willingness to exploit cultural antipathy toward illicit women compromise the En-lightenment vision of the novel?[9]

Striking parallels appear when the transcript of the trial of Ford Lord Grey, seducer of Henrietta Berkeley, is placed alongside Richardson's novel. In both we discover a clandestine correspondence between a rake and a young woman, interfering family members, an alternative suitor, plans for a secret meeting, an elopement, a London secret house, and meddling servants. Lady Henrietta's courtroom declaration, 'I have been very much reflected upon here today, and my reputation suffers much by the censure of the world,' captures Clarissa's sense of personal injury and her fear of public condemnation.[10] The difference, of course, is that Aphra Behn's fictional rendering of Henrietta Berke-ley represents a young woman who willingly participates in the seduc-tion plot hatched by her lover and then actively shapes the narrative that follows. The connection between *Love-Letters* and *Clarissa* nonethe-less remains compelling if we consider the ways in which both Behn's and Richardson's heroines contemplate power and its exercise. Both, I maintain, imagine themselves as sovereigns in ways that evoke a Stu-art configuration of monarchical authority. Whereas Silvia's representa-tion draws out the Hobbesian implications of this conceptualization of power, Clarissa's characterization invokes an eighteenth-century Jaco-bite. Behn's Tory feminism becomes, in Richardson's novel, a discourse that hovers between radical critique and misogynous conservatism. The sovereign power Clarissa claims over life and death is balanced by the abjection to which Richardson consigns those women who engage with power in the world and live to tell the tale. The idea of the courte-san's agency as a collective pathology, in particular, comes to stand as the obverse of Clarissa's singular claim to authority, although each, in fact, can be viewed as a logical extension of the other.

'There is no evidence that Richardson was ever opposed to the House of Hanover,' T.C. Duncan Eaves and Ben D. Kimpel observe.[11] There is plenty of evidence to suggest, however, that Richardson harboured strong Tory sympathies and that *Clarissa* speaks directly to the post-

1688 problem of monarchical legitimacy, as well as to the more immediate crisis of the Jacobite Rebellion of 1745.[12] Margaret Anne Doody's
understanding of Clarissa as a 'new Tory in a Whig environment' takes
on an added dimension in relation to the mystical strain of Jacobitism
that arose in the eighteenth century.[13] This discourse places its emphasis
on the proximity of divinity to kingship, to the idea that political events
could be read in cosmic terms. The hermeneutics of Jacobite mysticism
involve reading national and personal integrity in relation to the restoration of the divinely sanctioned monarch – and the devolution of that
integrity as a sign of oppression and usurpation. In opposition to the
Whigs, who set their claims to authority against the backdrop of Restoration tyranny and sexual corruption, Jacobites identified a 'national
malaise' at the heart of eighteenth-century culture and attributed it to
the illegitimacy of the Hanoverian regime.[14] Moral reform depended
on the proper symmetry of the king's two bodies, and only a Stuart
restoration could resolve the nation's conflicts, they argued. For Richardson, Jacobitism's reflections on the moral dimension of power, as
well as its frequent use of the tropes of virginity and rape, rendered it a
fertile soil in which to plant novel reflections on authority.[15]

The analogies that *Clarissa* draws between the family and the state,
and between its heroine's abuse and that endured by the subjects of
arbitrary tyrants, have been noted.[16] After the rape, Clarissa objects to
Lovelace's abuse of 'the freedom which is my birthright as an English
subject' (934), and throughout the narrative those who oppress Clarissa
are characterized as corrupt prime ministers or tyrannical monarchs.
Whig oligarchy and monarchical absolutism meet in the pursuit of self-
interest and self-gratification, the refusal of moral claims, and the corruption of communal standards by individuals willing to manipulate
or override practices that, hypothetically, ensure the safety and security of society's most vulnerable members. What is less often observed
is the extent to which Clarissa pits herself against arbitrary power by
claiming her status, not as an abused subject, but as a monarch in her
own right. Despite her protestations that she only seeks a life of re-
tirement and Anna Howe's recognition that she has been 'pushed into
blaze' (40), Clarissa is figured as monarchical throughout the narrative
– not only irreverently, as Lovelace's 'GLORIANA' (542) – but in her own
mind and those of her sympathizers. 'I know my power; but have not
the least thought of exerting it,' Clarissa declares early on, before discovering, tragically, that her power is circumscribed to the point where
only its most sovereign manifestation – the power to choose life or

death – remains in her grasp (200). (As Mrs Harlowe observes, 'What a torment is it to have a will without power!' [586].) Anna Howe sets Clarissa apart from her family as 'an alien' (237) and marks, over and over again, Clarissa's singularity – a pattern later repeated by Belford. Lovelace describes the difficulty of approaching Clarissa in the days after her seduction from Harlowe Place in monarchical terms: 'by her good will my access would be as difficult to her as that of the humblest slave to an eastern monarch' (399).

Clarissa refers repeatedly to her 'sturdy will' (e.g., 54, 181, 210) and marks her independence from material considerations that would bind her to a larger familial imperative: 'I have often reflected with a degree of indignation and disdain upon the thought of what a low, selfish creature that child must be, who is to be reined in only by what a parent can or will do for her' (243). Before the narrative begins, the much-disputed grandfather's will has already established Clarissa's exemption from the standards that limit others by asking that the bequests to Clarissa not be contested, 'although they should not be strictly conformable to the law, or the forms thereof' (53). Clarissa's exemption from the law represents a larger antinomian ideal, one organized most cogently around a battle over moral authority that unfolds within the Harlowe family.[17] In response to Clarissa's request to live single, Arabella Harlowe remarks: 'What a triumph would her obstinacy go away with, to delegate her commands, not as from a prison, as she called it, but as from her throne, to her elders and betters; and to her father and mother too!' (256). As Carol Kay notes, 'the Hobbesian battle of divided authority and competing moral claims is not set in motion by a struggle for tangible property as much as by the love of fame.'[18] Clarissa maintains that her pursuit of justice represents a higher law, one that takes precedence over the crass materialism driving her family's desire for an alliance with Solmes.[19] A sense of aristocratic entitlement grounds her understanding of this social law, which is why, in part, Clarissa cannot recognize Lovelace's true character. 'How impolitic in them all to join two people in one interest whom they wish for ever to keep asunder,' Clarissa remarks of her family (84), although the 'interest' she imagines she shares with Lovelace can draw only on a metaphoric aristocratic association on her part. She views Solmes as an 'upstart man' (81) and imagines Lovelace's pedigree will guarantee his eventual reformation: 'We shall conclude in his favour, that he knows what sort of behaviour is to be expected from persons of birth, whether he act up to it or not. Conviction is half way to amendment' (182).[20] When Lovelace urges Clarissa to claim his family's protection, she objects to the social ambition on her part that it implies while establishing her moral sovereign imperative: 'I said that I should not be affected by the splendour of even a royal title. *Goodness* I thought was *greatness*' (169). As the novel unfolds, Clarissa distinguishes herself by manifesting a 'sovereign contempt' (712) toward Lovelace's material and social inducements to accept his various corrupt offers. Her refusal of Lovelace's encroachments draws on the idea that to accept his offers would be to alienate what can never be separated: her sense of self and her body's integrity as inalienable property. When Clarissa comes to realize that Lovelace's desires are, in fact, inimical to her own, she claims the monarchical 'one interest' for herself.[21]

The novel's ability to turn sexual assault into a cue for voluntary death depends on its alliance of Clarissa's body with a mystical, monarchical body whose rape upsets the symbiotic relation between the body politic and the body natural that Richardson's heroine maintains as her birthright. Clarissa's interpellation as a virgin queen establishes women's right to self-sovereignty, but the perfect chastity of the body remains the condition of its authority.[22] The mere thought that the public might discover signs of desire in her relationship with Lovelace prompts Clarissa, imagining herself abstractly as 'a woman,' to remark, 'how much more eligible would she think death itself to such a discovered debasement!' (546). An intimation of the scandal that her elopement will unleash prompts Clarissa to reflect, 'I would sooner make death my choice than take a step which all the world, if not my own heart, will condemn me for taking' (350). Clarissa's oft-noted fantasy of wedding herself to her 'shroud' rather than 'to any man on earth' (514) highlights the difficulty of reconciling the exercise of power and the vicissitudes of embodied experience.[23] As Clarissa notes to her cousin Morden, 'when chastity is the crown of a woman ... shall your cousin stoop to marry the man who could not attempt upon *hers* but upon a presumption that she was capable of receiving his offered hand, when he had found himself mistaken in the vile opinion he had conceived of her?' (1301).

Belford correctly predicts Clarissa's response to rape: 'what I apprehend most is, that with her own hand, in resentment of the perpetrated outrage, she (like another Lucretia) will assert the purity of her heart; or, if her piety preserve her from this violence, that wasting grief will soon put a period to her days' (710). In the face of Lovelace's assault, Clarissa can only accept a compromised vision of herself and her authority or die to restore a vision of the integrity of the monarch's two bodies. The patriarchal power that Clarissa concedes as her father's right, despite his failings, becomes her prerogative once death offers itself as the end to which the exercise of power is a means of evacuating the body of its sexual content. As Florian Stuber observes, 'Clarissa herself becomes a Father.'[24] Clarissa claims for herself, most particularly, Job's authority: *'he hath overwhelmed the fatherless, and digged a pit for his friend*: fatherless may *she* well be called, and motherless too, who has been denied all paternal protection and motherly forgiveness' (1176).[25] 'I am nobody's,' Clarissa asserts in her will (1413) – thereby releasing herself from the obligations that attend protection in exchange for the freedom of self-possession only afforded, in life, to men and sovereigns. Lovelace's claim that 'no national point' can be made of Clarissa's death misses the significance of the transfer of power that occurs after the rape (1148).

Clarissa transforms herself, in her dying days, into the emperor of a mystical nation, proving her earlier claims that she is 'no slave in [her] will' (930). The 'LAW' she evokes when Lovelace attempts a second rape now appears as the sovereign's ability to take away life (950); indeed, she evokes the law as she points a knife at her breast. Perversely, Clarissa can transform herself into a supreme (male) monarch only as a result of acknowledging her powerlessness as a woman.[26] 'Chastity is the crown of a woman,' but all monarchs prove kings in Richardson's novel, even the heroine herself (1301). The single life Clarissa once dreamed of proves untenable in a post-rape world: 'would not everyone be able to assign the reason why Clarissa Harlowe chose solitude, and to sequester herself from the world? Would not the look of every creature who beheld me appear as a reproach to me? ... What then, my dear and only friend, can I wish for but death?' (1117). In the moment Richardson creates an association between his heroine's and the king's two bodies, restored to their rightful relation to each other, he also produces the martyr, birthed in death as a self-consuming subject, a snake with a tail in its mouth.

Huis Clos[27]

You are in the world now, you know.
                    Anna Howe to Clarissa, Letter 156, *Clarissa*

So the tyrant dies and his rule is over; the martyr dies and his rule begins.
                    Søren Kierkegaard, *Papers and Journals*[28]

Clarissa and Lovelace represent idealized and perverse forms of monarchical ambition, and they are both defeated in their quests to impose their singular visions on each other.[29] Lovelace's aestheticization of violence is exposed as an excuse for crude misogyny and Clarissa's exercise of power is realized only in its most extreme form, as a death drive. In the defeat of the subject whose sense of entitlement draws on a Restoration vision of sovereign authority, Richardson advances two conflicting ideas. On the one hand, by foregrounding the way in which women are used as objects of exchange by families competing for social and economic status and exposing rape's function as an extension of, rather than an exception to, patriarchal tyranny, Richardson is able to demystify sexual relations and the idea that domesticity provides shelter from the competitiveness and violence of the public sphere. On the other hand, Richardson remystifies sexual relations by sustaining a vision of sexual antagonism that can never be resolved in a political or social fashion, denying even sovereign power as a source of practical, rather than metaphorical, authority. Morden observes that had Clarissa not named Belford as her executor, her will 'would have been no more regarded than if it had been the will of a dead king' (1422).

Richardson attenuates the political discourse shaping both Clarissa's and Lovelace's perspectives, reducing the knowledge Clarissa is forced to learn to an ahistorical and tragic vision of difference. In resigning the political claims of monarchs, Richardson asserts the authority of non-aristocratic male prerogative, made palatable only by the sense that some men's sense of moral obligation can overcome its will-to-power. As Kay notes, 'the specific political objective behind the social criticism is lost' in Richardson's discourse; 'it carries only the sign of personal morality in public life.'[30] What is also lost is the sense of play Lovelace evokes in his description of men and women as sovereigns: 'The women sovereigns are governed by men; the men sovereigns by women – Charming by my soul! For hence we guess at the rudder by which both are governed' (573). And here I mean 'play' in the most serious sense – as an imaginative exercise that allows for the possibilities of new configurations of power. In its refusal of the wit and imagination informing the libertine's plots, the novel articulates its most Puritan tendencies.[31] The only imaginative act, finally, in which Clarissa can engage is the narrative of her own death: 'She'll persuade herself at this rate,' Lovelace suggests, 'that she has nothing to do when all is ready, but to lie down and go to sleep: and such a lively fancy as hers will make a reality of a jest at any time' (1308).[32]

We are left with the darkness of a new social and sexual 'realism,' one that emphasizes the vulnerability of the female subject, either single or married: 'Hence your Symmes's, your Byron's, your Mullins's, your

Wyerley's. ... and your Solmes's, in turn invade you,' Anna remarks early on (84). The first four volumes of the novel meditate on marriage as a potential arena for violation, both emotional and sexual. The Harlowe men terrorize Mrs Harlowe. Solmes's dreams of raping Clarissa – 'Terror and fear, the wretch, the horrid wretch said, looked pretty in a bride' (238) – confirm both Anna's and Clarissa's sense that marriage routinely abjects women: 'Who indeed, as you say, would marry, that can live single?' Anna remarks (134). In the wake of Clarissa's rape, Anna drives home the point more forcefully: 'Oh my dear, these men are a vile race of *reptiles* in *our day*, and mere *bears* in their *own*' (1312, emphasis in text). Clarissa tells Lovelace that 'the married state ... is a state of purity' (703), but no representation of marriage that the novel sustains supports this claim. Lovelace seems closest to the mark when he declares Clarissa unfit for marriage: 'Sacrilege but to touch the hem of her garment! – Excess of delicacy! – ... How can she think to be a wife!' (646).

'Richardson ... seems to construct victimization and aggression as the *only* two alternatives for human behavior,' Lois A. Chaber argues.[33] His representation of a generalized pattern of sexual violation anticipates the conclusions reached by radical feminists such as Catharine A. MacKinnon and Andrea Dworkin in the late twentieth century. 'The male sexual role,' MacKinnon argues, 'centers on aggressive intrusion on those with less power.'[34] As Wendy Brown and others have noted, the vision sustained by MacKinnon and Dworkin refuses, finally, a political response. So pervasive is their sense of men's appetite for violence against women that we are left with a deeply ahistorical, universal, and inflexible account of sexual difference. '"There is no way out" is among students' most frequent response to [MacKinnon's] work,' Brown observes.[35] In his meditations on the uses and abuses of male power, Richardson evokes a Hobbesian world but refuses what Hobbes's political writings, in fact, offer: the re-visioning of the grounds upon which social order is maintained.[36]

We are confronted, then, with a radical critique of the status quo and no means of redress. Richardson's 'huis clos' logic bears consequences not only for Clarissa, but for all the women the novel represents. In particular, it forecloses the possibility that women collectively might effect change. The basis for community outside of the family is, of course, the public sphere and the labour that takes place in that sphere. But Richardson's resistance to the idea of female independence leads him to view that space with suspicion and to associate women's work with perversion.[37] The novel attributes to Betty Barnes, Arabella Harlowe's interfering servant, a kind of evil intent, an appetite for doing harm. A good servant like Clarissa's Hannah proves, literally, incapable of stirring to help her mistress. Belford singles out for insult the mantua-maker and the milliner who provide Mr Brand with his damaging information: 'The two ... not more by *business* led to adorn the person than generally by *scandal* to destroy the *reputations* of those they have a mind to exercise their talents upon!' (1296). The scandal of work extends into the upper classes – Belford cannot imagine Clarissa labouring within a marriage: 'Why should such an angel be plunged so low as into the vulgar offices of domestic life? Were she mine, I should hardly wish to see her a mother unless there were a kind of moral certainty that minds like hers could be propagated. For why, in short, should not the work of bodies be left to *mere* bodies?' (555).

The novel's representation of prostitution brings these issues into sharp focus and expands them into a larger meditation on power. Had Richardson proved less suspicious of women's potential collective agency, his view of Clarissa's exploitation might have extended to the prostitutes and allowed him to view their trade as part of a larger patriarchal system in the terms provided by Carole Pateman: 'prostitution is part of the exercise of the law of male sex-right, one of the ways in which men are ensured access to women's bodies.'[38] Anna Howe moves in this direction when she writes to Belford on the subject of the prostitutes who have terrorized Clarissa: 'see what a guilty commerce with the devils of your sex will bring those to, whose morals ye have ruined! – for these women were once innocent: it was *man* who made them otherwise' (1454).[39] Conversely, Richardson could have imagined the prostitutes as patriarchal lackeys. In a narrative where death announces its heroine's refusal to become a sexual pawn, women who participate in an economy that alienates sexual labour appear complicit, to some, with the men who use sexual transactions, both conventional and illicit, as part of the exercise of patriarchal authority. But *Clarissa* as a whole goes a long way to making sure that the prostitutes represent a class *apart*, neither victims of male violence nor camp guards ready to act on orders. Instead, we can divide the novel's moral terrain between men, women, and prostitutes. Far from appearing to support patriarchal power, the prostitutes threaten it. The danger they represent makes the novel's endorsement of trust in men like Belford and Hickman as the answer to sexism's abuse appear less a concession to necessity than a positive antidote to the problems unleashed on the world by Mrs Sinclair and her myrmidons. The confusion of gender economies that the prostitutes represent proves more dangerous than the maintenance of a gender opposition that the novel, in another frame of reference, identifies as a source of violence and degradation.

Lovelace registers the power the brothel and its inhabitants have to shape Clarissa's sense of identity long before he rapes her: 'I could have told her something that would have humbled her pretty pride in the instant, had she been in a proper place, and proper company about her' (424). The difficulty Clarissa encounters as she tries to identify the cause of her suspicions upon her first meeting of Mrs Sinclair – 'you must not ask me how I like the old gentlewoman' (524) – and her 'nieces' suggests their powers of deception and the threat they represent to Clarissa's trust in the transparency of human relations: 'You know, my dear, that I have an open and free heart, and naturally have as open and free a countenance' (531). It is this trust that authorizes Clarissa's view that 'we may make the world allow for and respect us as we please, if we can be but sturdy in our wills' (54). If Clarissa has a will, the prostitutes are wilful; if Clarissa hopes to impose her views on the world, they are imposters. The difference lies in the prostitutes' willingness to assume a common identity. This kind of collective self-identification refuses Clarissa's belief in her own singularity and represents the most potent threat to the ideal of virtue the novel maintains. 'It is impossible she can get out of thy hands, now that she is in this cursed house,' Belford remarks soon after Clarissa arrives in London (556). Even worse than the libertine, the narrative repeatedly suggests, is the bawd, whose violence expands upon the rake's by turning into a 'trade' men's propensity to act violently toward women (714). The prostitutes' ability to expand one man's individual desire into an economic and psychological 'program' of oppression – a 'worse than masculine violence' (1011) – renders their existence a threat to the social body, an 'infection' (547, 713, 735). Lovelace imagines himself a monarch but unconsciously envies the bawd's authority over Clarissa, dreaming of 'Mother H.' as the means by which he can rape Clarissa a second time (922). He is reduced, finally, to a 'machine' by the prostitutes (658). Like Clarissa, Lovelace has a 'will' that proves ineffectual in the face of larger forces at work.[40] That it is the brothel's women, rather than Lovelace, who rape Clarissa is a thesis advanced perceptively by Judith Wilt: 'They did it, and Lovelace was their tool.'[41] Even in the minutes leading up to her rape, Clarissa looks to Lovelace for protection against Mrs Sinclair: 'With two Hoh-madams she accosted the frighted fair one; who, terrified,

caught hold of my sleeve' (883). The integral role played by the prostitutes, and in particular by Mrs Sinclair, at the moment of sexual assault
proves Wilt's larger claim that the central drama of the novel pits 'not
only Lovelace against Clarissa, but, more deeply, Lovelace and Clarissa
against the women of the house, against "woman."'[42]

At her most abject, Clarissa imagines she has joined the ranks of the
prostitutes. When Lovelace proposes marriage after the rape, Clarissa asks, 'Thinkest thou that I will give a harlot-niece to thy honourable uncle, and to thy *real* aunts; and a cousin to thy cousins from a
brothel?' (909). But having made the grave her final destination – 'my
refuge must be death' (1106) – Clarissa regains her sense of independence. The larger point Richardson makes reflects on all women's collective impulses. Indeed, to share any collective identity is to take on
a taint of scandal. Even at the most intimate level of friendship, the
novel registers a distrust of women's bonds. Anna displays aggressive
traits not unlike those displayed by Sally Martin and Polly Horton, and
Richardson identifies her unwillingness to marry in preference for a
life of female friendship as one of the causes of the tragedy that unfolds. When she first arrives at Mrs Sinclair's, Clarissa writes to Anna:
'Had you married on your mother's last birthday, as she would have
had you, I should not, I dare say, have wanted a refuge that would
have saved me so many mortifications, and so much disgrace' (524). As
soon as she abandons her father's house, Clarissa fears an association
with a community of illicit women. Even before she leaves St Albans,
Clarissa writes of her anxiety about living as an independent woman
in London: 'Who knows but I might pass for a kept mistress?' (335). In
response to Anna's desire to join her in London, Clarissa writes, 'Would
not the world think there was an infection in my fault, if it were to be
followed by Miss Howe?' (550).

When Sally Horton confronts Clarissa in jail, she assumes that she
and Clarissa share an identity as victims of Lovelace's seduction plots:
''bating that he will take advantage where he can of *us* silly credulous
girls, he is a man of honour' (1062, emphasis in text). Belford records
Clarissa's response: 'She lifted up her hands and eyes, instead of speaking: and well she might! For any words she could have used could not
have expressed the anguish she must feel on being comprehended in
the US' (1062). Sally refuses Belford's idealization of Clarissa – 'her lin-
en [was] beyond imagination white' – (1051) in her jailhouse suffering:
'Methinks, miss ... you are a little *soily*, to what we have seen you. Pity
such a nice lady should not have changes of apparel' (1060). Ever prac-

tical, Sally insists on Clarissa's humanity, reminding her of the body and its needs. We could consider Sally's comments on Clarissa's refusal to eat suggestive, were her perspective granted any credibility in the novel: 'Your religion, I think, should teach you that starving yourself is self-murder' (1054). But Sally's comments are reduced to a sordid literalism mirrored in the legal system the prostitutes so adeptly manipulate in their attempts to lure Clarissa back to the brothel in a proceeding Lovelace describes as 'dirtily low' (1047).[43]

That Sally and Polly share Clarissa's class identity – and presumably might have lived out conventional lives were it not for their respective seductions by Lovelace – heightens the sense of urgency surrounding Clarissa's need to distinguish herself from women whom, in a certain light, she resembles.[44] But even more importantly, the 'us' to which Clarissa responds so viscerally reminds us of her original collective aspiration – to share in the moral and aristocratic identity housed in the women of Lovelace's family, upon whose 'great honour' Clarissa relies as a weathervane for her feelings toward Lovelace's proposals until she is raped (167). When Lovelace shows Clarissa letters he pretends to have received from his female relatives, she remarks: 'Why did the man not show them to me last night? Was he afraid of giving me too much pleasure?' (455). The greatest betrayal Clarissa experiences is the deception practised by the courtesans pretending to be Lovelace's aunt and cousin. 'Both are accustomed to ape quality,' Lovelace observes of the women he chooses to play his relatives' parts: 'Both are genteelly descended. Mistresses of themselves, and well educated – yet past pity. True *Spartan* dames; ashamed of nothing but *detection* – always, therefore, upon their guard against that. And in their own conceit, when assuming top parts, the very quality they ape' (875). Like Clarissa, these women claim a status that only belongs to them metaphorically. After her rape Clarissa 'wonders' at her inability to detect the specious characters Lovelace passes off as his relations (902), but the fact remains that she is sufficiently committed, before the assault, to the idea of an aristocratic female community as her own that she cannot detect the fraud playing out in front of her. 'I had not the least suspicion that they were not the ladies they personated,' she later writes to Anna (998). Their mimicry of Clarissa's censoriousness, their promise to act as intermediaries in the family conflict, and their 'air of authority' prove enough to lull Clarissa into a false sense of security: 'Could I help, my dear, being pleased with them?' (1000). Clarissa willingly suspends her disbelief in the charade that unfolds: 'And yet at the time, I thought, highly as they exalted *me*, that in some respects (though I hardly knew in what) they fell short of what I expected *them* to be' (1001). The outrage of discovery masks Clarissa's deep disappointment that the social power she had attributed to Lovelace's aunt and cousin was illusory, that far from securing her within a protective embrace, their attractions only left her more vulnerable to a rake's predations. What Clarissa cannot acknowledge is that the courtesans have staged a play in which she, too, has acted a part in her dreams of female aristocratic authority and, more immediately, in her willingness to pose as Lovelace's wife. The idea that a female education such as she and, she suspects, the courtesans, have had could produce a will to power not yoked to virtue calls into question her profoundest convictions: 'Never were there more cunning, more artful imposters, than these women. Practised creatures, to be sure: yet genteel; and they must have been well educated – Once, perhaps, as much the delight of their parents, as I was of mine: and who knows by what arts ruined, body and mind! – Oh my dear! how pregnant is this reflection!' (1002).[45]

The power Clarissa falsely attributes to 'proper' aristocratic women before her rape belongs to the royal mistress. The novel recognizes this power in its references to Madame de Maintenon, first mistress and then wife to Louis XIV (figure 7). Describing the power of women to press their advantage 'when calamaties ... beget reflection,' Belford observes that 'the royal cully of France, thou knowest, was *Maintenoned* into it by his ill successes in the field' (615). Later Lovelace uses the same term to describe Belton's affair with the sister of a man he kills in a duel: 'she herself thought her brother a coxcomb to busy himself, undesired, in her affairs, and wished for nothing but to be provided for decently and privately in her lying-in; and was willing to take the chance of *Maintenon-ing* his conscience in her favour' (1236).[46] The transformation of the royal mistress into a verb form suggests the power Richardson fears most. In particular, he attributes to the mistress an ability to shape a man's moral conscience for her material advantage. The example of Mme Maintenon suggests that illicit sexual conduct does not bar a woman from entry into marriage and that morality and economics are mutually constitutive. Were Clarissa to enter into a marriage with Lovelace after his assault, comparisons could be drawn between her act of translation and those of a woman like Mme Maintenon. It is precisely to forgo these comparisons that Clarissa separates women of 'family' from those (including herself) she considers sexually contaminated in her refusal of the offer of reconciliation made, after the rape, by Lovelace's aunt: 'indeed, indeed, madam, my heart sincerely repulses the man who, descended from such a family, could be ... so mean as to wish to list into that family a person he was capable of abasing into a companionship with the most abandoned of her sex' (1172).

A latter-day Mme Maintenon appears in the figure of Thomasine, whose narrative appearance coincides with Belford's account of Clarissa's descent into death. Thomasine, mistress to Thomas Belton (whose death bed narrative serves as a foil to Clarissa's), provides Belford with a story on the consequences of immoral living that he recounts to Lovelace. Her masculine name intimates the power she has accrued as a mistress, power that can only be imagined as an encroachment on male prerogative: 'His house is Thomasine's house; not his' (1088). Not only property, but children default to the mistress: 'Siding with the mother, they in a manner expel him' (1089). Thomasine confirms Hobbes's claim that 'in the condition of meer Nature, where there are no Matrimoniall lawes, it cannot be known who is the Father, unlesse it be declared by the Mother: and therefore the right of Dominion over the Child dependeth on her will, and is consequently hers.'[47] James Turner notes that in this passage Hobbes 'imagines women creating a protopolitical language of strong performatives, speech-acts that translate their "will" into "dominion."'[48] Clarissa's dream of translating her will into an exercise of social authority finds its fullest articulation, not in her own acts, but in those of her proxy, the courtesan. Richardson replays Clarissa's script in its perverse form and in doing so reinforces the futility of his heroine's earlier ambitions and the necessity of redirecting her energies. For, as it turns out, the state that Thomasine inhabits is only the 'life of a brute' (1090). To encroach on male prerogative is to contribute to the breakdown of gender hierarchies essential to civil society. The usurpation Thomasine effects takes on a bestial, appetitive aspect. Her sons are 'cubs' and her attempts to secure Belton's property render her 'rapacious' (1187). Like the prostitutes, she appears part of a collective as 'her accomplices' help her in her bid for power (1187).

The sense that the prostitute always represents a power larger than one reminds us of the Restoration pathologization of the Stuart royal mistress as a proliferation of illicit bodies: Charles II's 'Cleavelands, his Nells and his Carwells.'[49] As Clarissa approaches her death, the women who maintain their worldly power appear increasingly indiscriminate as bodies. E.J. Clery notes, 'Mrs. Sinclair and her cohorts seem to violate not only sexual difference, but also the boundaries of the human.'[50] The state of nature Richardson identifies with courtesan authority is most graphically realized by the description Belford provides of a brothel scene late in the narrative, in which Mrs Sinclair appears a 'huge quaggy carcase ... her big eyes goggling and flaming-red as we may suppose those of a salamander' (1388). The women surrounding her bring to Belford's mind 'Virgil's obscene Harpies squirting their ordure upon the Trojan trenchers' (1388). Richardson adds an editorial note to the scene, drawing his readers' attention to his description's intertextuality: 'Whoever has seen Dean Swift's *Lady's Dressing Room* will think this description of Mr. Belford not only more natural but more decent painting, as well as better justified by the design, and the use that may be made of it' (1388). As Brenda Bean has astutely noted, what is missing in Richardson's text is Swift's editorial distance from the truth-claims advanced by the individual describing the scene. Where Swift goes some way toward exploring the inflated expectations that attend cultural standards of feminine excellence, 'Richardson (through Belford) records moral outrage at the depth of woman's treason to standards of female virtue.'[51] Richardson's insistence on the realism of the scene he paints indicates the extent to which the prostitutes' abjection shapes the world Richardson represents in his narrative. For what is striking, in the face of this claim, is the grotesque and exaggerated aspect of the scene's baroque descriptions. The scene lavishly describes Mrs Sinclair's 'mill-post arms,' 'bellows-shaped and various coloured breasts,' and 'huge tongue' (1388). This descriptive excess's ability to pass as the 'real' suggests that Richardson's vision participates in a larger cultural understanding of the prostitute as monstrous.

The rhetorical violence of Belford's attacks on the prostitutes appears justified by the role they have played in Clarissa's downfall. Sally Martin, upon learning of Clarissa's death, claims responsibility: 'She called [Clarissa] the ornament and glory of her sex; acknowledged that her ruin was owing more to their instigations than even (savage as thou art) to thy own vileness: since thou wert inclined to have done her justice more than once, had they not kept up thy profligate spirit to its height' (1378). In assigning blame to the prostitutes, Richardson is able to replace the insult of the Restoration's misogyny with the horror of gender treachery. Every woman may not be, at heart, a rake: but some women, it turns out, are worse than libertines, living beyond the human pale as *'mere* bodies' (555). Mrs Sinclair, Sally, and Polly are finally reduced to, and defeated by, their corrupted parts: the bawd dies of a broken leg,

Sally of 'a fever and surfeit gotten by debauch,' Polly of 'a violent cold, occasioned through carelessness in a salivation' (1491).

Clarissa exemplifies, in an amplified form, the simple lesson Richardson exhorts at the end of the first edition of *Pamela*:

> The poor deluded Female, who, like the once unhappy Miss GODFREY, has given up her Honour, and yielded to the Allurements of her designing Lover, may learn from her Story, to stop at the *first Fault*; and, by resolving to repent and amend, see the Pardon and Blessing which await her Penitence, and a kind Providence ready to extend the Arms of its Mercy to receive and reward her returning Duty. While the abandon'd Prostitute, pursuing the wicked Courses, into which, perhaps, she was at first *inadvertently* drawn, hurries herself into filthy Diseases, and an untimely Death; and, too probably, into everlasting Perdition afterwards.[52]

Two forms of agency are starkly opposed here: that of the penitent and that of the fallen woman who stays the course. Clarissa's 'false step' – leaving her father's house – is recovered by her willingness to embrace death. Terry Castle has argued perceptively that 'Clarissa's physical trauma is epiphanic: it makes her conscious, as nothing else has done, of the politics of meaning in which she has been caught.'[53] But Richardson carefully renders the 'political' a metaphorical, rather than practical, question and renders its material manifestations a source of contamination. *Clarissa* may prove the tragedy of women's exploitation by the world, but it so deeply criminalizes those women who do claim power that we are afforded only religious consolations and the promise, if not the practice, of an attenuated paternalism.

Richardson went to great lengths to defend his 'religious plan' and 'Christian system' in the novel's postscript, and claimed, in a letter to Lady Bradsheigh, that he had written a 'Religious Novel.'[54] In fact, Richardson wrote two religious novels, neither of which readily answers the call of Christian duty. The first, closest to convention, grants the most specious characters some kind of religious affiliation in order to place the novel on the 'proper' side of the secular/religious divide. Richardson claims his rakes are no atheists, but Lovelace's religion merely expresses a willingness to exercise good manners: 'I never was so abandoned to turn into ridicule, or even to treat with levity, things sacred,' Lovelace claims, before going on to compare his refusal to criticize Clarissa's meditations on divinity to his unwillingness to offer 'noisy or tumultuous instances of dislike to a new play' (1145). Belford suggests that the reason neither he nor Lovelace can decipher Clarissa's allegorical letter is because its language draws on the conventions of religious allegory: 'A *religious* meaning is couched under it, and that's the reason that neither you nor I could find it out' (1274, emphasis in text). We are left, in this register, with a social Christianity that pays lip-service only to religious matters.

And then we are left with Clarissa's far more radical antinomian impulses, which bring us to the brink of the courtesan's amoralism and the iconoclasm of the Protestant Whore. Lovelace is attuned to the bid for power embedded in Clarissa's story: 'now she is willing to die as an event which she supposes will cut my heart-strings asunder. And still the more to be revenged puts on the Christian, and forgives me' (1346). Death guarantees the integrity of Clarissa's vision of self-justification in a world that continually fails Protestantism's rigorous standard by falling back on material sanctifications.[55] Clarissa is Protestant in her singularity, her refusal of the earth's institutions and their mediating role. Clarissa's willingness to take on the burden of her singularity, refusing the consolations of a communal standard, reflects her Protestant commitment to the integrity of her own heart and its knowledge of its own, private truth. Her belief in divine grace grants her exemption from moral law, and although Richardson was careful to defend Clarissa against the charge of a self-willed death, the antinomian imperative governing her bid for freedom overrides the sanction against suicide. Like Silvia and Roxana before her, Clarissa stubbornly charts her own lonely path. 'No doubt there is an infinite difference between a tyrant and a martyr,' Kierkegaard observes, 'yet they have one thing in common: compulsion.'[56] Richardson brings into view Protestantism's most interesting tendencies in his vision of Clarissa's fierce spiritual independence. But these impulses are disarmed, finally, by their willingness to naturalize women's victimization under the sign of Christian martyrdom.[57] 'I am nobody's' suggests, finally, *Noli me tangere* – but without a resurrection, the reader is left a doubting Thomas in a world filled with unregenerate magdalens.

Nell Gwyn and the '45

If these *Academicians* [whores] ... do, upon their Arrival at the *Pretender*'s Camp, where they are to be set down, insinuate themselves into the Graces of his *Highlanders*, they will, as a great many Gentlemen here can testify, totally disable them from either firing a Gun or wielding a Broad-sword, and then, we hope, a bloodless Victory may be obtained over them by his Majesty's Forces.

> *The Highlanders Salivated, or the Loyal Association of*
> *M–ll K–g's Midnight Club*[58]

Henry Fielding's engagement with the Restoration is vividly brought to life through *Tom Jones*'s encounter with the '45.[59] While in one register the novel works toward alleviating the tensions governing its immediate historical moment, in another it takes the opportunity afforded by the revival of the Jacobite threat to reflect on the socio-political matrix that shaped the modern novel. The figure of the Restoration courtesan, for Fielding, serves both as a foil against which a new cultural order might be defined, and as a reminder of what the Restoration continues to offer the modern author.[60]

The Jacobite Rebellion of 1745 revisited the question of women's political activism so central to seventeenth-century political and religious debates.[61] The particular dangers afforded by courtesans in relation to these debates appears in a 1723 account of Sally Salisbury's Jacobite sympathies:

> After they had drunk several Flasks, she began a certain young Gentleman's health under the Name of *J— the third*; it was readily pledg'd by three there present; but the fourth drank to the King's Health; whereupon she, on a sudden, snatch'd his own Sword out, and playing it before his Breast, swore she'd let out his little Heart's Blood, if he would not drink it full; which Execution it was believed she would actually have perform'd. Upon which the *Peer* drank it; but went the next Morning very prudently and acquainted his *Majesty* with the whole Matter.[62]

The courtesan's freedom from the social constraints governing other women's lives here emerges as the power to exercise political coercion, but it just as readily appears as a version of England's spirit of liberty in other representations of the period, as when 'Sukey Stichwell' exhorts the whores of London to take up arms against the Jacobite invaders in 1745: 'Let us with all our Might, oppose this Popish *Pretender*, that has already been the Origin of so many Woes to us, and which are but a Prelude to those we must suffer, under his tyrannical Government.'[63]

Fielding's representation of Sophia Western carefully redraws the body of political desire in order to render it entirely male, and, in doing so, attempts to disarm figures like Sally Salisbury and 'Sukey Stichwell.'

In their stead, Tom emerges as the eighteenth-century novel's last, great Protestant Whore.[64] But the project of domesticating the Restoration's controversies remains, finally, incomplete. In the concluding volumes of the novel, Fielding fashions both his hero and his narrator/author as latter-day courtesans whose aesthetic sensibilities serve as an antidote to, rather than an endorsement of, modernity's cultural hegemonies.

Sophia appears in the narrative after a prefatory chapter, one of the 'ornamental parts' Fielding uses to define his aesthetic program.[65] In this prefatory instance, Fielding fits his reflections on aesthetics to the particular occasion of Sophia's introduction: 'we have thought proper to prepare the mind of the reader for her reception, by filling it with every pleasing image which we can draw from the face of nature' (132). He goes on to compare the pomp and ceremony attending Sophia's appearance to a political tradition:

> There is one instance which comes exactly up to my purpose. This is the custom of sending on a basket-woman, who is to precede the pomp at a coronation, and to strew the stage with flowers, before the great personages begin their procession. The ancients would certainly have invoked the goddess Flora for this purpose, and it would have been no difficulty for their priests or politicians to have persuaded the people of the real presence of the deity, though a plain mortal had personated her and performed her office. But we have no such design of imposing on our reader; and therefore those who object to the heathen theology may, if they please, change our goddess into the above-mentioned basket-woman. Our intention, in short, is to introduce our heroine with the utmost solemnity in our power, with an elevation of style, and all other circumstances proper to raise the veneration of our reader. (133)

The striking comparison Fielding draws between his narrative's 'poetical embellishments' and the flowers strewn at a coronation transforms his narrator into a basket-woman. The passage is further complicated by its substitution of Flora for the basket-woman and by the connection Fielding establishes between ancient and modern political practices, both of which, he suggests, bring women's sexual appeal into the public sphere. The original Floralia, hosted by public magistrates looking for votes, honoured Flora *primavera*, mother of flowers (figure 8). They were instigated, according to Ovid's *Fasti*, not by powerful men but by plebians protesting the encroachment on public lands by the rich.[66] Famous for its licentiousness, the Floralia, or Ludi Florales, included performances by prostitutes. Ann B. Shteir notes that 'the association of Flora with prostitutes and bawdy self-display was a foundational feature in later stories about the goddess of flowers, considerably mediated by early Christian criticisms of Roman beliefs and practices.'[67] Indeed, given the central role played by prostitutes in the festivities, one can add 'whore' to the field of associations conjured up by Fielding's 'basket-woman.' That the festival began as a bequest by a courtesan to the city of Rome, and that the myth recounted by Ovid represented nothing more than window-dressing for the festival's true origins, was widely believed by European classicists: 'While the poets of the Renaissance ... were more attracted to Ovid's charming nymph, the scholars found themselves compelled to stress the fact that Ovid's version was only a poetic fiction and that the authentic Flora had, indeed, been a courtesan.'[68] Fielding plays with illicit content residing in the name 'Flora' in a 1728 poem, 'The Masquerade.' Describing the morning after the masquerade's bawdy excesses, the narrator remarks,

> The lover, who has now possess'd,
> From unknown Flora, his request;
> (Who with a pretty, modest grace,
> Discover'd all things but her face:)
> Pulls off her masque in am'rous fury,
> And finds a gentle nymph of Drury.[69]

I will return to the association that appears between Fielding and this particular Flora – *Flora Economica* – below. For now, the gendering of the narrator's style as feminine draws our attention to the continuum that Fielding establishes both between Flora and the narrator, and between Flora, the narrator, and Sophia. The erotic note that the Floralia reference introduces sexualizes the mock-epic convention governing Sophia's introduction, ironizing the narrator's aesthetic claims to 'solemnity' as he displaces the ancients' authority with his plebeian licence.

In the *Tom Jones* passage above, 'our goddess' – i.e., Flora – looks forward to 'our heroine,' even though the former refers to Fielding's art, not to his character. This confusion is deliberate, as becomes apparent when Sophia *does* appear as Flora: 'Do thou, sweet Zephyrus ... lead on those delicious gales, the charms of which call forth the lovely Flora from her chamber ... for lo! adorned with all the charms in which nature can array her ... the lovely Sophia comes' (134). That Sophia should appear as an extension of an artistic practice – one of the 'poetical embellishments' that separate the prosaic from the aesthetic – takes us back to Fielding's refusal of Richardson's aesthetics in *Joseph Andrews*, when he prefaces his description of Fanny with the warning to the reader looking for a correspondence between fiction and the real, '*Quod petis est nusquam.*'[70] The transformation of Sophia into an art form continues in the description that follows: 'Reader, perhaps thou has seen the statue of the *Venus de Medici*. Perhaps, too, thou hast seen the gallery of beauties at Hampton Court ... She was most like the picture of Lady Ranelagh; and, I have heard, more still to the famous Duchess of Mazarine; but most of all, she resembled one whose image never can depart from my breast' (134–5). Fielding establishes Sophia's aesthetic pedigree in the allusions he makes to various English and European standards of beauty and guarantees her integrity by drawing the representation into a circle of intimacy sustained in the allusion to his dead wife that concludes his description. But the description of Sophia functions as much as a joke as a celebration, the humour appearing in the double-edged sword created first by the allusion to Flora and then to the Duchess of Mazarin – a combination made manifest by the close association between representations of Flora and courtesan portraits in seventeenth-century painting (figure 9).[71] Mazarin's claims to fame were not organized around the duchess's looks, but around her licentious conduct. As in the Flora allusion, the courtesan appears alongside the beauty – *meretrix* and *primavera* prove inseparable. The larger Restoration culture Mazarin's beauty and behaviour represent is summed up in Fielding's allusion to Rochester. After listing various beauties whom Sophia resembles, the narrator observes: 'Now if thou hast seen all these, be not afraid of the rude answer which Lord Rochester once gave to a Man, who had seen many things' (134). Fielding alludes to the line that closes 'To all curious Criticks and Admirers of Meeter' – 'If you have seen all this, then kiss mine A-se' – and in doing so evokes a Restoration bawdiness that shifts the description from the sublime to the prosaic, a shift that, as we will see, accompanies Sophia's representation throughout the narrative.[72]

In shuttling Sophia's description between these poles, Fielding achieves two objectives. First, he establishes Sophia's place within a larger mid-eighteenth century aesthetics summed up by Hogarth's 'line of beauty' thesis, developed in *The Analysis of Beauty* (1753). This thesis locates desire at the heart of aesthetic appreciation, refusing the ideal of disinterestedness advanced by Shaftesbury and, later, Joshua Reynolds.[73] Insofar as it views desire as an animating principle, the aesthetic principle Hogarth and Fielding advance draws on the Restoration's practice of linking art and sexuality.[74] The difference – a difference that signals the shifting standard of the mid-eighteenth century – is that only male readers have access to the aesthetic experience both Sophia's looks, and her character, afford. Fielding's aesthetic, like Hogarth's, 'marks women's exclusion from the forms of pleasure which are associated with less chaste forms of beauty.'[75] Sophia's sensual appeal matters most. Her mental attributes, unlike her beauty, require no abstract explication: 'But as there are no perfections of the mind which do not discover themselves in that perfect intimacy to which we intend to introduce our reader with this charming young creature, so it is needless to mention them here: nay, it is a kind of tacit affront to our reader's understanding, and may also rob him also of that pleasure which he will receive in forming his own judgment of her character' (136).

Second, the deflation of aesthetic excellence into the slang of 'ass' empties 'whore' of all but its bodily content – to which all women, proper or improper, can be reduced as objects of readerly, if not practical, desire. By linking Mazarin to the Hampton beauties, most of whom were 'virtuous' women, Fielding attributes a general, rather than specific, sense of whorishness to the earlier period. The political stakes governing debates about Restoration courtesans disappear from view. Instead, female sexuality is integrated into a harmless series of jokes organized around the double meaning of 'muff.' Sophia innocently learns lessons in love through the object that keeps her hands warm. Her servant Honour uses it to translate, for her mistress, Tom's desire: 'He kissed it again and again,' Honour tells Sophia, 'and said it was the prettiest muff in the world' (179). While encouraging the reader to enjoy the wink-wink nudge-nudge humour that appears every time the muff is mentioned, Fielding carefully protects both his heroine's and his hero's literalness. Tom's desire is not the same as the reader's, a fact that preserves the character of Sophia from the taint of illicit sexuality in practice while allowing her to remain an object of the male reader's bawdy fantasy.

Sophia's muff renders her appealing and sets her apart from the remarkably undesirable women who speak their minds in the narrative – most notably, Mrs Western. Mrs Western's political inclinations – 'she was ... very deeply skilled in these matters, and very violent in them' (240) – add weight to the tyrannical influence she attempts to wield over Sophia and represent a marked deviation from the principles of benevolent femininity Fielding attributes to his heroine.[76] As is the case in all of Fielding's writings, educated women in *Tom Jones* represent a particular kind of menace, a sharpened instance of women's universal inclination to manipulate men, one that Fielding contrasts to the intellectual naivety of Sophia: 'Women who, like Mrs. Western, know the world, and have applied themselves to philosophy and politics, would have immediately availed themselves of the present disposition of Mr. Western's mind by throwing in a few artful compliments to his understanding at the expence of his absent adversary; but poor Sophia was all simplicity' (293). The chasm that divides Sophia and the various scheming women who want to use her to gain their ends allows Fielding to demarcate a range of characteristics into a simple opposition of 'Sophia' and 'not-Sophia.'[77] Since all of Sophia's positive attributes appear natural, rather than learned, characteristics that acknowledge their roots in acculturation and education – including an appetite for debates concerning politics and women's rights – prove inimical to the heroine's hardwired features of virtue and integrity. Sophia is capable of committing herself both to daughterly duty and to resistance to a father's tyranny without linking either to a larger intellectual idea.[78]

The separation of women as political or intellectual agents and as virtuous subjects guarantees that when Sophia is mistaken for Jenny Cameron, the confusion can only appear as an occasion for hilarity. Sophia first appears in relation to the Jacobite Rebellion not, however, in the guise of Jenny Cameron, but as the Young Pretender himself. Partridge imagines that Tom is a Jacobite, having heard that Tom was attacked by Northerton for toasting Bonnie Prince Charlie: 'The tall long-sided dame [Fame] ... had related the story of the quarrel between Jones and the officer, with her usual regard to truth. She had, indeed, changed the name of Sophia into that of the Pretender, and had reported that drinking to his health was the cause for which Jones was knocked down' (381–2). Private and public spheres collide here, as they do throughout the narrative.[79] Despite Tom's best efforts to protect Sophia's privacy, Partridge ensures that everyone they meet is acquainted with her name and story. But rather than creating an opening through which Sophia might escape the constraints of a properly private reputation and live up to the heroic character she takes on when she escapes her father's house – becoming an adventurer like the Young Pretender, that is – the confusion created around her status serves, finally, only to remind us of her need for the protection that the domestic sphere can afford if administered properly.

The opposition that appears when Sophia finds herself mistaken for Jenny Cameron is not between Jacobite and Whig politics, as it is when Tom confronts Partridge's allegiance to the Young Pretender, but between 'whore' and 'proper lady.' Significantly, the moment unfolds against the backdrop of the Jacobite Rebellion's most threatening incursions into England:

> While our politic landlord ... was engaged in debating this matter with himself ... news arrived that the rebels had given the duke the slip, and had got a day's march towards London ...
>
> This news determined the opinion of the wise man, and he resolved to make his court to the young lady when she arose; for he had now (he said) discovered that she was no other than Madam Jenny Cameron herself. (502–3)

The political tension of the moment is diffused by Honour's response to the landlord's mistake and the Nell Gwyn allusion that structures the narrative's commentary on it:

> 'Would you imagine that this impudent villain, the master of this house, hath the impudence to tell me, nay, to stand it out to my face, that your ladyship is that nasty, stinking wh-re (Jenny Cameron they call her) that runs about the country with the Pretender? ...
>
> In plain Truth, Honour had as much love for her mistress as most servants have ... But besides this, her pride obliged her to support the character of the lady she waited on ...
>
> On this subject, reader, I must stop a moment, to tell thee a story. 'The famous Nell Gwynn, stepping one day from a house where she had made a short visit, into her coach, saw a great mob assembled, and her footman all bloody and dirty; the fellow being asked by his mistress the reason of his being in that condition, answered, "I have been fighting, madam, with an impudent rascal who called your ladyship a wh-re." "You blockhead," replied Mrs Gwynn, "at this rate you must fight every day of your life; why, you fool, all the world knows it." "Do they?" cries the fellow, in a muttering voice, after he had shut the coach-door, "they shan't call me a whore's footman for all that."' (525–6)

Paradoxically, the moment's ostensible focus on the implications of the label 'whore' successfully delivers Sophia from the taint of scandal. Afraid that the landlord has discovered her true identity as the daughter of Squire Western, Sophia is relieved to find herself mistaken for Jenny Cameron, and Honour's narrative elicits a smile rather than indignation. For Sophia, 'whore' connotes the disgrace of having her name circulated in public – not, as it does for Honour, the intimation of political treachery. Sophia inhabits the sexual ideology of her time, an ideology ostensibly blind to political and class distinctions. Honour proves herself always already a servant, in Fielding's terms, by clinging to the pride she derives from her political affiliation, which involves belonging to a better station than those who serve Jacobites. Fielding insists that Honour will never be more than what she is in the moment when he distinguishes between her obsessions and Sophia's disregard for all thoughts of politics and power.

Fielding mocks Honour's fantasies of privilege by naturalizing the term 'whore.' In recounting the Nell Gwyn story, Fielding turns political argument into a jest, in the same way that his allusions to Flora and Restoration women draw our attention away from the politics at work at a coronation, or in court circles, to a more universal account of Sophia's erotic desirability.[80] Here Nell Gwyn appears in her folk heroine mode, as an antidote to the politically grasping courtesan; she is the mistress who never imagined that her identity added up to anything more than sexual comedy.[81] The anecdote constructs a timeless vision both of sexual conduct – a whore is a whore is a whore – and class identity. Servants are amusing, Fielding implies, in their willingness to fight over issues of status so profoundly not their own. The historical facts of Nell Gwyn's social rise and her involvement in political affairs here disappear in the stability provided by the pairing of 'whore' and 'servant' as terms that anchor, rather than complicate, other social relations. We support Sophia's bid to escape a tyrannical father because we understand that whatever resemblances may appear between her radical quest and the political rebellion abetted by Jenny Cameron, the differences are of kind, not degree. If Cameron was a political operator in the Scottish and English political landscapes of the mid-eighteenth century, Sophia never threatens to exceed her status as a 'Somersetshire Angel' (481).[82] Nell Gwyn's harmlessness, then, cuts both ways: it neutralizes the threat posed by Jenny Cameron and it shores up Sophia's innocence and disinterestedness.[83]

Sophia's representation is larded with allusions to women both sexually and politically resonant, all of which add up, finally, to nothing. Instead, we watch as Sophia becomes less, rather than more, interesting.[84] Sophia's final representation returns us to her first description as a universal aesthetic standard: 'Sophia ... sat at the table like a queen receiving homage, or rather like a superiour being receiving adoration from all around her. But it was an adoration which they gave, not which she exacted: for she was as much distinguished by her modesty and affability as by all her other perfections' (867). April London claims that 'the shift from "Queen" to "superiour Being" attests to the erasure of her personality since it emphasizes not only her passivity but also her relinquishment of any independent title.'[85] Further, Sophia's gracious refusal to insist upon the reverence she is nonetheless given sets her apart from the Duchess of Mazarin and the generation of Restoration courtesans who assumed their right to exact various forms of political and economic obedience from their peers, both male and female. Appropriately, Sophia now represents a domesticated tableau vivant as comparisons to the Hampton beauties' portraits disappear into the fog of the past. It is only two other husbands in this scene, after all, who steal glances at the newest bride. We could argue that Sophia represents an alternative standard of sociability and grace, here, guaranteed to heal the nation after its moment of political strife. That the various parts of Sophia's virtues do not add up, finally, to the sum of this higher ideal, to an allegory of the new species of writing Fielding wants to advance, requires us to consider what, in the end, does.

Tom Jones, Protestant Whore

A Lady Bellaston, disappearing from decent society ... becomes repugnant to that large majority of readers who have no historical sense, who look upon manners, not as ever changing, but as fixed and everlasting.
>   Wilbur Cross, *The History of Henry Fielding*

All those men have their price.
>   Sir Robert Walpole[86]

Tom Jones represents Fielding's 'bloodless Victory' over the threat of Jacobite insurrection. The question that remains is: how does the novel manage to bring its author into view as the sign of its literary achievement? And how does that figure return us to the Protestant Whore? If Richardson translates the Protestant Whore's legacy into a mystical antinomianism, Fielding more readily embraces the materialism that informs both Behn's *Love-Letters* and Defoe's *Roxana*.[87] Tom's declaration of loyalty to the Protestant cause – 'it is the cause of common sense' (381) – ensures his status as a legitimate representative of England's interests, but the more engaging aspect of the novel's religious sensibility – or lack thereof – appears in the narrative's commitment to subjects that evoke a free-thinking tradition.[88] In linking Fielding's scepticism to his interest in whoring (among other illicit topics), I confirm the suspicion voiced by his censorious contemporaries 'that this motely [sic] History of Bastardism, Fornication and Adultery, is highly prejudicial to the Cause of Religion.'[89] This observation supports Fielding's own, more positive assertion: 'Man, therefore, is the highest subject ... which presents itself to the pen of our historian, or of our poet; and, in relating his actions, great care is to be taken that we do not exceed the capacity of the agent we describe' (348). Fielding's attachment to 'Nature' as the principle guiding his narrative renders the novel's questions of virtue, as Michael McKeon has observed, subordinate to those of questions of truth, questions defined not by providence, but by 'the palpable poetic justice of the narrator.'[90] The refusal of a providential episteme in favour of the maxim, 'To natural means alone we are confined' (773), places Fielding in a line of descent from the Restoration's most radical thinkers.[91]

While not as sharply focused as in *Joseph Andrews*, the anticlerical strain in *Tom Jones* links the novel's sceptical perspective to a broader eighteenth-century tradition. Fielding's earlier plays introduce the concerns that the novels explore in detail. *The Debauchees, or, The Jesuit Caught* (1732) sustains an anticlerical discourse that extends beyond the particularity of the Catholic priest who serves as the play's villain, reflecting on the operations of religious belief more generally. 'Thou art a miserable wretch indeed,' Father Martin observes of a man fearing damnation, 'and it is on such miserable wretches depends our power: that superstition which tears thy bowels, feeds ours.'[92] The line of attack that governs *Tom Jones*'s characterization of Thwackum's hypocrisy appears in *Pasquin* (1736), when Queen Common-sense declares,

> But know, I never will adore a priest,
> Who wears pride's face beneath religion's mask,
> And makes a pick-lock of his piety
> To steal away the liberty of mankind.[93]

The juxtaposition of 'liberty' and 'priestcraft' was repeatedly used in the Restoration's religious debates to distinguish not only Protestant and Catholic imperatives, but also freedom of individual conscience and denominational orthodoxy of all stripes. The particular interest in artistic freedom as a means of interrogating religious orthodoxy displayed by the authors studied in earlier chapters rests, I believe, at the heart of *Tom Jones*. J. Paul Hunter argues that 'Fielding's inability to make Tom's acquaintance of "Religion" match his accumulation of "Prudence" may have been both a personal and a historical sign.'[94] I suggest, further, that Fielding demonstrates, in his unwillingness to allow religious conviction to shape his hero's maturation, a suspicion of the period's advocacy of moralism as the sign of a social subject's ethical fitness.

The 'prudence' theme, so exhaustively explored in Fielding criticism, finds its most palpable articulation in Fielding's representation of whoring.[95] The Augustan tradition of bemoaning modernity's alienating tendencies as a species of whoredom (as, for example, in Swift's characterization of 'La Puta' in *Gulliver's Travels*) is largely absent in *Tom Jones*, which goes out of its way to avoid either participating in this tradition or endorsing the emergent sentimentalization of the prostitute as victim.[96] Tom misreads Molly Seagrim's fate in the wake of their sexual relationship – 'He now saw her in all the most shocking postures of death; nay, he considered all the miseries of prostitution to which she would be liable' (191) – and learns, over the course of the narrative, that sexual misconduct need not devolve into abjection. When Tom Nightingale labels Nancy Miller a whore for having had sex with him and refuses to marry her, initially, it is Tom who sets him straight: 'such a shame must proceed from false modesty' (673). Premarital sex neither dooms women to prostitution nor precludes their participation in the marriage plot.[97]

Sex serves as the means by which Tom grows into his knowledge of the world, and his acuity is most finely honed when he whores himself to Lady Bellaston. Since the novel's first appearance, it is this episode, more than any other, that has caused critical consternation. Richardson, naturally, was one of the first to draw attention to the affair's significance for the novel as a whole, describing Fielding's hero as 'a Kept Fellow, the lowest of all Fellows.'[98] The author of a 1749 pamphlet, describing the Bellaston affair, asked, 'Is this corrupted Scene to be called Nature?'[99] Nineteenth-century critics were equally severe: Walter Scott believed Tom 'unnecessarily degraded' by his London sexual escapade and William Forsyth observed: 'It is all very well for Charles Lamb to say that the hearty laugh of "Tom Jones" "clears the air" ... but we must remember that it is the horse-laugh of a youth full of animal spirits and rioting in the exuberance of health, who *sells* himself to Lady Bellaston as her paramour.'[100] Twenty years later, Thackeray struck the same note: 'A hero with a flawed reputation; a hero spunging for a guinea; a hero who can't pay his landlady, and is obliged to let his honour out to hire, is absurd, and his claim to heroic rank untenable.'[101] Most recently, we find John Bender, in his 1998 introduction to the Oxford edition of *Tom Jones* referring to Tom's 'disgraceful London entanglement with Lady Bellaston.'[102]

Critics reflect on Fielding's understanding of this affair in different ways. For detractors like Richardson, Fielding's ability to draw such a low portrait of sexual relations reflects on the author's own propensity for vice. More sympathetic readers view the relationship as one of Tom's stations of the cross, a space of urban corruption through which he must move, with the help of some rather intrusive narrative coincidences, to a happy marriage with Sophia. I follow the lead of the former reading – that is, to link Fielding's authorial persona to Tom's character – but recast that identification in a positive light. In doing so I challenge, necessarily, the latter critical position, which views the affair as an unfortunate interlude. I advance this reading as a way of drawing attention to Fielding's engagement with a point of view that appears, at first glance, most alien from his own. The amorality that attends the representation of Tom's affair with Lady Bellaston links the larger sceptical imperatives governing the narrative to a Restoration world in which accumulation appears as a larger aesthetic principle. Just as the contempt Lady Bellaston shows to questions of reputation signals her willingness to engage in intrigue, so too Fielding's suspension of moral absolutes opens up the field of art-making to new possibilities. 'Moral sense,' within this frame of reference, appears not only unmarketable but also tied to a literal-mindedness inimical to aesthetic sensibility. Rather than identifying the whore appellation as a source of alienation, then, Fielding capitalizes on the appeal of the courtesan's lawlessness.

When he first introduces Lady Bellaston, Fielding's narrator comments:

> I will venture to say the highest life is much the dullest, and affords very little humour or entertainment ... All is vanity and servile imitation. Dressing and cards, eating and drinking, bowing and courtesying, make up the business of their lives.

> Some there are, however, of this rank upon whom passion exercises its tyranny, and hurries them far beyond the bounds which decorum prescribes; of these the ladies are as much distinguished by their noble intrepidity, and a certain superior contempt of reputation, from the frail ones of meaner degree, as a virtuous woman of quality is by the elegance and delicacy of her sentiments from the honest wife of a yeoman and shopkeeper. (649–50)

The description begins as one might expect, casting a cynical eye on the aristocracy's willingness to flout convention and linking it to a more general hypocrisy that separates the 'elegance and delicacy' of corrupt sentiment from the more honest pronouncements of the lower classes. But the representation then moves in an appreciative direction, opposing Lady Bellaston's intrepidity to a more insidious cultural vacuity:

> There is not, indeed, a greater error than that which universally prevails among the vulgar, who, borrowing their opinion from some ignorant satirists, have affixed the character of lewdness to these times. On the contrary, I am convinced there never was less of love intrigue carried on among those persons of condition than now. Our present women have been taught by their mothers to fix their thoughts only on ambition and vanity, and to despise the pleasures of love as unworthy their regard; and being afterwards, by the care of such mothers, married without having husbands, they seem pretty well confirmed in the justness of those sentiments; whence they content themselves, for the dull remainder of life, with the pursuit of more innocent but, I am afraid, more childish amusements, the bare mention of which would ill suit with the dignity of this history. (650)

Here Lady Bellaston remains on Fielding's side, suited in her commitment to 'the pleasures of love' to the dignity of his narrative. Women of the past, Fielding implies, demonstrated a stronger attachment to 'love intrigue' than 'our present women,' whose 'ambition and vanity' in the marriage market require the repression of both plot and desire. The plot that unfolds between Tom and Lady Bellaston thus returns us to an earlier cultural moment, in which women demonstrated a greater propensity for creating interesting narratives. Indeed, the story that unfolds between Tom and Lady Bellaston bears a striking resemblance to the intrigue recounted in Delarivier Manley's *The Lady's Pacquet of Letters* (1707). Beau Wilson's meteoric rise to fame, sponsored, Manley

believed, by the Duchess of Cleveland, finds its mid-century equiva-
lent in the representation of Lady Bellaston's mysterious appearance at
the masquerade and Tom's subsequent enrichment at her hands. Tom's
sudden rise takes the same form as did Beau Wilson's, in the trappings
of dress and affluence: 'by her means he was now become one of the
best-dressed men about town, and was not only relieved from those ridiculous distresses we have before mentioned, but was actually raised
to a state of affluence beyond what he had ever known' (633). Fielding
travels over the same ground as the scandal narrative, refusing only
to indulge in its sexual voyeurism: 'In the evening Jones met his lady
again, and a long conversation again ensued between them; but as it
consisted only of the same ordinary occurrences as before, we shall
avoid mentioning particulars' (632). Sexual 'conversation' appears neither debased nor romanticized, but merely commonplace.

In return for Tom's favours, Lady Bellaston exercises her 'charitable'
faculty: 'though she did not give much in to the hackney charities of
the age, such as building hospitals, &c., [she] was not, however, entirely
void of that Christian virtue; and conceived (very rightly, I think) that a
young fellow of merit, without a shilling in the world, was no improper
object of this virtue' (628). This moment's ironic representation of the
'deserving poor' argument popular at the time particularly outraged
one contemporary critic: 'Fifty Pounds given to *Jones* for his Gallantry
is a most excellent Instance of *Christian Charity*! *Jones's* indeed to *Anderson* is praise-worthy. But this impudent Quality-Whore's is beneath
Censure. Can any thing be more odious, than for a Woman of Figure
to divest herself of her Dignity for a vile Satisfaction, and heap on her
Partner in Guilt so ample a Reward of his Baseness?'[103] Fielding cuts a
fine distinction between 'true' charity and Lady Bellaston's alleviation
of Tom's suffering, which the narrative slyly commends. While criticizing the aristocracy's casual disregard for the poor, Fielding also places
Tom's ability to give to Anderson within a larger cultural nexus that allows prostitution to generate wealth and bankroll a charitable impulse.
Lady Bellaston's private and indulgent act of 'charity,' in other words,
appears on an economic, if not moral, continuum with Tom's gift to
Anderson.[104]

Despite the narrative's declarations regarding Tom's grateful response to Lady Bellaston's generosity, the exchange of money for sexual favours defines the relationship between them as that of client and
prostitute: 'He knew the tacit consideration upon which all her favours
were conferred; and as his necessity obliged him to accept them, so his

honour, he concluded, forced him to pay the price' (634). The narrative is as glad as we are to see Tom relieved from his 'ridiculous distresses' (633) and more sanguine about the means by which that relief is made possible than subsequent critics have proved. That the work Tom undertakes to satisfy Lady Bellaston *is* work may be the detail that most offends readers. Fielding goes out of his way to let us know that the sex itself does not gratify Tom – that, in fact, it repulses him. Returning to the Flora motif, the narrative confronts us with a decaying body as Tom's object: 'She had ... a certain imperfection, which rendered some flowers, though very beautiful to the eye, very improper to be placed in a wilderness of sweets, and what above all others is most disagreeable to the breath of love' (634). Like Roxana, whose final client renders sex 'surfeiting and nauceous' to her, Tom must approach sex instrumentally for the first time in his life.[105] That he does not, like Roxana, own himself a whore as the relationship unfolds appears a form of innocence, lost only when he hears the full story of Lady Bellaston's character: 'he began to look on all the favours he had received rather as wages than benefits, which depreciated not only her, but himself too in his own conceit' (719).

Tom's willingness to turn down the rich Widow Hunt's offer of an advantageous marriage shortly after his relationship with Lady Bellaston has ended might suggest that he has learned that prostitution is distasteful. But the difference between a short-term arrangement and the lengthy contract a marriage implies constitutes, in fact, the crux of the matter. Throughout the narrative, Fielding's protest against parents who barter non-consenting children for profit focuses on this point. Mrs Western views marriage as a market in which Sophia's attractions must be sold to the highest bidder. Even more menacingly, Squire Western appears as a bawd preparing the violation of a girl:

> Western beheld the deplorable condition of his daughter ... [with] the same compunction with a bawd, when some poor innocent whom she hath ensnared into her hands, falls into fits at the first proposal of what is called seeing company. Indeed, this resemblance would be exact, was it not that the bawd hath an interest in what she doth, and the father, though perhaps he may blindly think otherwise, can, in reality, have none in urging his daughter to an almost equal prostitution. (740–1)

Within this configuration, the dispossession a daughter experiences, legally, upon marriage finds no compensation in love and the pleasures of family life. For Fielding, it is the question of duration and coercion that renders the alienation of sexuality, in the instance of marriage, objectionable. The further point to be made – although Fielding does not make it – is that the prostitution effected by the sale of the daughter's sexual favours grants the woman involved no economic agency, which courtesans, unlike their married counterparts, could claim.

This subtext appears in Lady Bellaston's abhorrence of marriage. While her freedom from social constraints can be attributed, in part, to aristocratic privilege, it is also clear that she earns her economic freedom the same way Tom, temporarily, earns his. Honour tells Tom that 'her ladyship meets men at another place ... Much good may it do the gentlewoman with all her riches, if she comes by it in such a wicked manner' (652–3). Lady Bellaston's wealth, in other words, may have as much to do with her work ethic as it does with inheritance and property. At the novel's close we discover that Mrs Fitzpatrick also has learned to profit from her friendship with the Irish peer: 'She lives in reputation at the polite end of the town, and is so good an economist, that she spends three times the income of her fortune without running into debt' (869). The intrepidity Fielding associates with the independence these women maintain suggests the author's interest in, and familiarity with, the courtesan's ability to sustain unconventional and profitable commercial opportunities.[106] Tom is rescued from the fate of Beau Wilson by Sophia, who firsts alleviates his financial distress in the gift of the bank-note he has taken such pains to return to her, and then marries him. But the economic and social portrait Fielding draws in his narration of Tom's moment of whoredom remains unchanged by this marriage. Indeed, rather than repudiating the episode as an aberration, Fielding allows it to stand as a moment of realism among the more contrived episodes of the novel's final volumes, confirming his principle that 'the picture must be after nature herself' (648). Further, rather than separating Tom-the-whore from Tom-the-husband, he links them in the allusion to Restoration libertinism that governs Tom's praise of Sophia's beauty in the final moments of the narrative: 'those eyes ...would fix a Dorimant, a Lord Rochester' (862).

Fielding might have identified with Tom's whoredom – and perhaps it is the possibility of this identification, more than any other aspect of the Lady Bellaston narrative, which has upset critical sensibilities for two hundred and fifty years. His narrator notes that

the slander of a book is, in truth, the slander of the author: for as no one can call another bastard without calling the mother a whore, so neither can any one give the names of sad stuff, horrid nonsense, &c., to a book, without calling the author a blockhead; which though in a moral sense it is a preferable appellation to that of villain, is perhaps rather more injurious to his worldly interest. (494)

Fielding's preference for 'worldly interest' over moral approbation signals his willingness to let his story of a bastard reflect on his material interests as an author/whore. Simon Stern notes that 'despite its economical use of raw materials of fiction, the novel contradicts this tendency in its preference for Tom's "open, generous Disposition," over Blifil's chary stewardship ... After anchoring the story in an economy of scarcity whose tactics he studiously cultivates, Fielding ends by affiliating his text with an aura of luxuriant plenitude.'[107] This affiliation is not limited to an association with Tom's illicit conduct, however, but extends to the novel's other courtesans. If Tom can only imagine himself a reformed male rake, Fielding maintains an openness to wit's transformative powers, including its ability to draw him as a woman. By letting the Restoration to read him as closely as he reads it, Fielding challenges his own confident assertions of mastery, allowing the text to reveal a narrative acumen that undercuts its platitudes and plot contrivances.[108]

Both Fielding and Richardson realized that the political divisions that haunted England in the wake of the '45 remained unresolved. 'That Britons made different choices,' Miranda Burgess observes, 'raised a spectre of national fragmentation with doubly damaging effects, for an internally divided body politics also mean a lack of stable justification for the rule of a contractarian or *de facto* king.'[109] *Clarissa* and *Tom Jones* gain their power from an awareness that the answers to the questions raised by the Restoration and its aftermath could only ever be partial and incomplete. The courtesan manifests a sovereign contempt toward the status quo, turning away from its hypocrisies in order to plumb the turbulent depths of the period's controversies. The Protestant Whore, in both her tragic and comic registers, signifies the novel's heretical tendencies. In their courtesan narratives, Richardson and Fielding remind their readers of the sexual, religious, and political identities that belong not only to the past, but to the present, Whig modernity's alter egos.

Afterword

Spiro Peterson first traced the progress that *Roxana* made after its initial publication, observing the fascination the novel continued to hold for eighteenth-century readers long after Defoe's death. At least six of the editions published after 1724 continued Defoe's story beyond its original ending.[1] The two sequels (1740 and 1775) that narrate happy endings for Defoe's heroine had little impact on other eighteenth-century editions or later readers.[2] Instead, the 1745 sequel, containing a long excoriation of Roxana, served as the basis for the century's most important serializations, revisions, and abridgements of Defoe's novel, and it was this edition that caught the attention of the Romantics: 'The terrors of a guilty mind, haunted with mysterious fears of retribution, have seldom been more powerfully delineated,' William Godwin wrote in 1807.[3] In this narrative, Susan lives to expose Roxana, who, having been suitably punished by her husband, dies in debtors' prison. Roxana's prison story is recounted by her chambermaid Isabel Johnson, whose words close the novel: 'In this Interval she repeated all the Passages of her ill-spent Life to me, and thoroughly repented of every bad Action, especially the little Value she had for her Children, which were honestly born and bred.'[4]

In his prologue to Godwin's *Faulkener*, an 1807 dramatic re-visioning of *Roxana*, Charles Lamb imagines Defoe writing his final novel in a quiet moment of reflection:

In some blest interval of party-strife,
He drew a striking sketch from private life,
Whose moving scenes of intricate distress
We try to-night in a dramatic dress:

A real story of domestic woe,
That asks no aide from music, verse, or show,
But trusts to truth, to nature, and *Defoe*.[5]

The idea that Roxana's story speaks to private, rather than public, affairs tells us much about the different hermeneutics that governed the reception of Defoe's novel after 1750. Of the 1765 edition, M. Wade Mahon remarks: 'The most basic, and most subtle difference between this later version and Defoe's original is not so much that Roxana's point of view has changed but that she inhabits a different kind of world than she did before, a world more like the ones found in later novels.'[6] This world was shaped by mid-century historical watersheds – in particular, the defeat of the Jacobites and the passing of the Hardwicke Marriage Act (1753) – but also by broader transformations, including the advent of secular culture whose coherence depended not on an understanding of human sinfulness and its public manifestations, but on sympathy between individuals.[7]

As Richard H. Popkin and Mark Goldie have observed of the later eighteenth-century *philosophes*, 'Even when they acted dutifully in accord with their own Christian scruples, they often supposed, contrary not only to Hobbes and Mandeville but also scripture, that human nature was fundamentally sociable.'[8] The limits of sympathy concern later writers. Within this context, the gendering of religious controversy takes on a different cast. In the 1755 continuation of *Roxana* (also based on the 1745 edition), we see a shift away from the imperatives governing courtesan narrative in the account of English religious history provided by the Catholic priest who shows Roxana around Canterbury Cathedral:

> That wicked King, so he termed him [Henry VIII], did turn out of the Nunneries, (Places dedicated to God and to Chastity) near Ten-thousand young Women, devoted to Celibacy, in the Streets and Highways of this Kingdom with each a Gown and One Shilling in Money; he did not doubt, he said, but many of them, through the most dire Necessity, were undoubtedly driven to such Practices, as they might and did before abhor and detest.[9]

Instead of focusing on Henry VIII's abuse of religious convention in the royal boudoir, where courtesans became wives, this commentary pits a property-seeking tyrant against poor, disenfranchised women.

Religious controversy shapes itself around an ethics of sexual exploitation, rather than around the fraught moment of political strife that first
produced English Protestantism – a moment defined as much by Tudor
queens as by a king and his mistresses.

This study has traced the iconography of the Protestant Whore as
Restoration court agent, as political observer, as propagandist, and as
entrepreneur. A proxy both for authors and for monarchs, she travels
back and forth between private and public spheres, reminding us of
the conflicts that attended their engagement during the Restoration
and early eighteenth century. On the one hand, the courtesan exercises
her authority as an extension of the court's, a form of 'representative
publicness.'[10] On the other hand, she embodies the voice of England's
citizenry – Nell Gwyn moving from the theatre to the royal boudoir –
staging, in intimate terms, the relationship between an emergent public
sphere and the state. But the courtesan rests uneasily in either register. Her status as an interloper in political affairs and as a maverick
economic subject in civil society renders her, to use Defoe's phrase, 'a
Man-Woman' in both. These tensions are not so much overcome as re-
imagined, in relation to a different set of preoccupations, by the later
novel. After 1750, Roxana's and Clarissa's psychological dramas are
played out in the dark recesses of the Gothic underworld; Silvia's witty
performances stage themselves as the machinations of coquetry against
which virtuous women define their conduct in the pursuit of marital
security; Queen Zarah returns as the louche gambler, ruining family
fortunes. The Stuart monarchy retreats into a past that was put to very
different uses by later novelists.[11]

Nell Gwyn herself emerges as a mostly banal figure in the latter half
of the eighteenth century, her association with the Catholics of Charles
II's court forgotten or forgiven: 'it must be owned, of all this Prince's
Favourites, she was both the most prolific and the least offensive to the
jarring Interests of the Court, or Country. She observed an Evenness
of Conduct, and behaved with so much Mildness, that none were her
Enemies who were Friends to the Kind; and none ever libelled her, but
the malevolent Lord *Wilmot.*'[12] In fiction, her name appears as a sign
of status, rather than status confusion. We find, in Smollett's *Humphry
Clinker* (1771), this moment of conversation between Tabitha and Matthew Bramble, and Mr James Quin, actor:

'Good God, sister, how you talk! I have told you twenty times, that this
gentleman's name is not Gwynn. – ' 'Hoity, toity, brother mine, (she re-

plied) no offence, I hope – Gwynn is an honourable name, of true British extraction – I thought the gentleman had come of Mrs. Helen Gwynn, who was of his own profession; and if so be that were the case, he might be of king Charles's breed, and have royal blood in his veins – ' 'No madam, (answered Quin, with great solemnity) my mother were not a whore of such distinction – True it is, I am sometimes tempted to believe myself of royal descent; for my inclinations are often arbitrary – If I was an absolute prince, at this instant, I believe I should send for the head of your cook in a charger – She has committed felony, on the person of that John Dory; which is mangled in a cruel manner, and even presented without sauce – *O tempora! O mores!*'[13]

Nell Gwyn serves as a guarantor of 'true British extraction' here, her career as an actress serving as the connective tissue that brings together 'royal blood' and the eighteenth-century theatre. 'Whore' – a word expunged from the 1775 edition of *Roxana* – is safely lodged in a comic register, as are allusions to the abuse of power. The Stuart regime no longer appears a threat to Britain's collective security, but rather a glamorous contribution to the theatre's celebrity world. Arbitrary rule has been reduced to the fantasy of exercising domestic tyranny over cooks. Culture replaces politics as the conversational touchstone.[14]

New questions regarding status and authority emerge as the novel turns its attention to the operations of a commercial and imperial culture. But the religio-political agenda that courtesan narrative frames no longer dominates, despite the persistence of religious conflict. The novel, for instance, remains silent on the subject of the Gordon Riots of 1780, one of the eighteenth century's most violent religious uprisings, until 1799, even as it reflects on how religious toleration might work in its representations of marriage.[15] Within the marriage plot, the political import of social conflict takes on a different aspect. As Susan S. Lanser has pointed out, there is no one answer to the question of whether the representation of women's private lives 'may be taken as a *stand-in* for the public realm, and thus an impetus toward a politics, or as a *substitute* for that realm and thus a displacement or deflection of women's public agency.'[16] But certainly, radical and conservative writers alike define women's agency in terms other than those provided by the Protestant Whore's example.[17]

Courtesan narrative opens a window onto a continent of religious controversy and sexual politics that offers no safe harbours for those travelling its coastlines. But the pleasures of the text are manifold. The animated and open-ended disputes I have studied here speak to the dangers and delights of Restoration culture. Courtesan narrative uses the opportunity afforded by Protestantism's doubt to bring strangers into prose fiction's midst: foreigners, antinomians, free-thinkers, rebels. The early novel makes space for these uncanny characters, and in doing so, registers an acute awareness of what difference can mean.

Historical Glossary

1660	Declaration of Breda: Charles Stuart promises 'liberty to tender consciences'
1661	Corporation Act: municipal officers must receive sacrament according to Anglican liturgy
1662	Act of Uniformity: those clergyman not subscribing to all Thirty-Nine Articles are removed from their livings
1662	Declaration of Indulgence: the king capitulates to parliamentary pressure to retract the declaration early in 1663
1664	Conventicle Act: prohibition against Nonconformist meetings of five or more is passed; renewed in stronger language in 1670
1665	Five Mile Act: prevents Dissenting assemblies from gathering at locations within five miles 'of any city, or town corporate, or borough that sends burgesses to the Parliament, within his Majesty's kingdom of England, principality of Wales or of the town of Berwick-upon-Tweed' unless oath of allegiance has been sworn
1672	Declaration of Indulgence: suspends legal penalties against nonconformists and Catholics, although only the former could claim the right to public worship
1673	Declaration rescinded by Parliament, withdrawn by Charles
1673	Test Act: office holders must swear oath of allegiance and receive Anglican sacrament; second Test Act (1678) strengthens language of the first
1678–81	Exclusion Crisis: Parliament attempts to pass into law the exclusion of James, Duke of York the throne; Charles prorogues parliament in 1679 and 1681

1685	Revocation of the Edict of Nantes, which guaranteed civil rights to Huguenots in Catholic France, by Louis XIV
1685	Monmouth Rebellion: James Scott, Duke of Monmouth and illegitimate son of Charles II launches a rebellion against James II; he is captured and executed 15 July 1685
1687, 1688	James II, Declarations of Indulgence: suspension of penal laws, guarantee of freedom of worship, end of oath requirements for holding of public office
1688	invasion of William III, 5 November
1689	William and Mary, 'An Act for exempting their Majesties protestant Subjects, dissenting from the Church of England, from the penalties of certain laws,' known as the Toleration Act: excludes Catholics, attempts to reconcile Dissenting and Anglican religious interests
1701	Act of Settlement: secures Protestant succession to the throne
1707	Act of Security of Church of England: bars Presbyterians from public office
1710	Sacheverell riots during the trial of Henry Sacheverell, whose inflammatory 1709 sermon accused the Whig ministry of failing to protect the Church of England; Sacheverell was suspended from his living for three years, and his sermon ordered burned
1711	Act against Occasional Conformity: to prevent Dissenters from skirting Test Act regulations by taking communion occasionally in the Anglican Church
1714	Schism Act: renders illegal the Dissenters' separate school system
1715	first Jacobite Rising
1717	Bangorian Controversy: Bishop of Bangor publishes *Nature of the Kingdom, or Church, of Christ*, defending individual conscience against Anglican authority; Church of England attempts to discipline Hoadly result in the government's proroguing of convocation
1719	Salters' Hall controversy: Presbyterians meet to protest subscription of belief in the Trinity
1719	Schism and Occasional Acts repealed
1745	second Jacobite Rising

For an introduction to the period's historical landmarks and documents, see the following:

Browning, Andrew, ed. *English Historical Documents*. London: Routledge, 1966, 1996. Taylor and Francis e-library, 2004.

Cook, Chris, and John Stevenson. *Longman Handbook of Modern British History*. 4th ed. London: Longman, 2001.

Fritze, Ronald H., William B. Robison, and Walter Sutton, eds. *Historical Dictionary of Stuart England, 1603–1689*. Westport, CT: Greenwood Press, 1996.

Gregory, Jeremy, and John Stevenson. *The Routledge Companion to Britain in the Eighteenth Century, 1688–1820*. London: Routledge, 2007.

Notes

Introduction

1 'The Hon. Lois Sturt, younger daughter of Lady Alington, is ... considered to resemble the Peter Lely portrait of Nell Gywnn very closely.' *Town and Country*, 14 Dec. 1921. BIBA's 1960s campaign featured an image titled 'Nell Gwyn's Nightshirt.'

2 For a study of the courtesan that looks at earlier material than I examine here, see James Grantham Turner, *Libertines and Radicals in Early Modern London: Sexuality, Politics and Literary Culture, 1630–1685* (Cambridge: Cambridge University Press, 2001).

3 James Granger, *A Biographical History of England*, 2nd ed. (1775), 4:189, recounts the incident as a 'known fact,' though no original source is cited. This anecdote is repeated in almost every Gwyn biography that has been written. These include (in chronological order): Peter Cunningham, *The Story of Nell Gwyn, and the Sayings of Charles II* (1852), ed. Gordon Goodwin (London: A.H. Bullen, 1903); Lewis Melville, *Nell Gwyn: The Story of Her Life* (New York: George H. Doran, 1924); Arthur Irwin Dasent, *Nell Gwynne, 1650–1687; Her Life Story from St. Giles's to St. James's with Some Account of Whitehall and Windsor in the Reign of Charles the Second* (London: Macmillan, 1924); John Harold Wilson, *Nell Gwyn: Royal Mistress* (New York: Pellegrini and Cudahy, 1952); and Charles Beauclerk, *Nell Gwyn: Mistress to a King* (New York: Grove Press, 2005). Roy MacGregor-Hastie argues that the remark was made in November of 1679, when Nell Gwyn went into the streets of London during a moment of anti-Catholic carnival. See his *Nell Gwyn* (London: Robert-Hale, 1987), 156. These sources do not provide primary source material to document their claims. For a consideration of the anecdote's circulation in oral culture before its first print appearance

in 1775, see my '"Known Fact" or Urban Legend?' Nell Gwyn's Oxford Pronouncement,' *Note and Queries* ns 53 (June 2006): 209–10. This anecdote, like the name 'Nell Gwyn,' appears ubiquitous to the point of banality, once known.

4 The work of religious historians proved crucial in developing my thesis concerning the significance of the period's controversies for literary representations of Protestantism. I follow Tony Claydon and Ian McBride in arguing that we ought to think of Restoration and eighteenth-century Protestantism as 'an anxious aspiration,' rather than as a 'triumphal description' (*Protestantism and National Identity: Britain and Ireland, c. 1650–c.1850*, ed. Claydon and McBride [Cambridge: Cambridge University Press, 1998], 27). Of particular importance to my study is their interrogation of the 'Tudor' model of Protestantism and nationality, which stresses the role played by Catholic xenophobia in the emergence of early modern notions of 'Englishness.' They note that 'whilst the basic idea of a protestant Englishness does have much to commend it, the model also has certain problems which must lead to doubts about its effectiveness as a tool of historical analysis' (12). Linda Colley's and J.C.D. Clark's theories of Protestant hegemony in England receive critical scrutiny in Jeremy Black, 'Confessional State or Elect Nation? Religion and Identity in Eighteenth-Century England,' *Protestantism and National Identity*, ed. Claydon and McBride, 53–74. Steven Pincus suggests that the revolutionaries of 1688 understood Protestantism as 'a constituent in, though not constitutive of, English national identity' in 'To Protect English Liberties': The English Nationalist Revolution of 1688,' in *Protestantism and National Identity*, ed. Claydon and McBride, 93. Pincus elaborates on this point in 'Nationalism, Universal Monarchy, and the Glorious Revolution,' in *State/Culture: State-Formation after the Cultural Turn*, ed. George Steinmetz (Ithaca, NY: Cornell University Press, 1999), 182–210. See also J.G.A. Pocock and Gordon J. Schochet, 'Interregnum and Restoration,' *The Varieties of British Political Thought, 1500–1800*, ed. Pocock, with Schochet and Lois G. Schwoerer (Cambridge: Cambridge University Press, 1993), 146–79; Howard Nenner, 'The Later Stuart Age'; and Richard L. Greaves, *Enemies Under His Feet: Radicals and Nonconformists in Britain, 1664–1677* (Stanford: Stanford University Press, 1990).

5 Pettit, *The Visions of the Reformation, or A discovery of the follies and villanies that have been practis'd in popish and fanatical thorough reformations since the reformation of the Church of England* (1683), 20–1.

6 Poole, *Radical Religion from Shakespeare to Milton: Figures of Nonconformity in Early Modern England* (Cambridge: Cambridge University Press, 2000), 4.

7 Defoe, *A Short View of the Present State of the Protestant Religion in Britain, as It is now profest in the Episcopal Church in England, the Presbyterian Church in Scotland, and the Dissenters in Both* (Edinburgh, 1707), 6.

8 Spufford, *Small Books and Pleasant Histories: Popular Fiction and Readership in Seventeenth-Century England* (London: Methuen, 1981), 221.

9 For a detailed account of pornographic writing in England before 1685, see Turner, *Libertines and Radicals in Early Modern London*. My focus on the political and religious, rather than sexual, aspect of courtesan representations distinguishes my study from Bradford K. Mudge's *The Whore's Story: Women, Pornography, and the British Novel, 1684–1830* (Oxford: Oxford University Press, 2000).

10 Turner, *Libertines and Radicals in Early Modern London*, 15.

11 *The Character of a Town-Miss* [1675] (1680), 1, 4.

12 *The Town-Misses Declaration and Apology, Or, an Answer to the Character of a Town-Misse* (1675), 4–5.

13 Laura Brown warns against reading representations as signs of actual power: 'a feminized culture should not be confused with a claim for female power, authority, or autonomy in history.' 'The Feminization of Ideology,' *Ideology and Form in Eighteenth-Century Literature*, ed. David H. Richter (Lubbock, TX: Texas Tech University Press, 1999), 237–38. In the case of the Stuart courtesan, however, we encounter a blurring of boundaries when historical figures become literary tropes. Historians debate the extent to which the Stuart royal mistress's exercised power. See Sonya Wynne, 'The Mistresses of Charles II and Restoration Court Politics, 1660–1685,' Diss. Cambridge University, 1997. London: British Library, 1997. D203331; Wynne, 'The Mistresses of Charles II and Restoration Court Politics,' *The Stuart Court*, ed. Eveline Cruickshanks (Stroud, UK: Sutton, 2000), 171–90; Nancy Klein Maguire, 'The Duchess of Portsmouth: English Royal Consort and French Politician, 1670–1685,' *The Stuart Court and Europe: Essays in Politics and Political Culture*, ed. R. Malcolm Smuts (Cambridge: Cambridge University Press, 1996), 247–73; Rachel Weil, 'The Female Politician in the Late Stuart Age,' *Politics, Transgression, and Representation at the Court of Charles II*, ed. Julia Marciari Alexander and Catharine MacLeod (New Haven, CT: Yale University Press, 2007), 177–92.

14 In stressing this aspect of eighteenth-century politics and culture, I follow those historians who challenge Whig historiography. Paul Kléber Monod, for example, suggests that the eighteenth century 'witnessed not the resolution, but the deepening of social and intellectual contradictions.' *Jacobitism and the English People, 1688–1788* (Cambridge: Cambridge University Press, 1989), 348.

15 'Essay on Criticism,' l. 538, *The Poems of Alexander Pope*, ed. John Butt (New Haven, CT: Yale University Press, 1963), 160.

16 Mikhail Bakhtin, *The Dialogic Imagination: Four Essays*, ed. Michael Holquist, trans. Caryl Emerson and Michael Holquist (Austin: University of Texas Press, 1981), 247. Bakhtin uses this description in reference to the salon world of the French nineteenth-century novel. Courtesan narrative amply demonstrates John Richetti's claim that 'in much eighteenth-century fiction ... [i]ndividualistic identity is still very much involved in communal relationships and social traditions. In such arrangements, public and private intertwine, and public life is sustained by private affiliations and alliances that to modern eyes look scandalous or corrupt.' 'The Public Sphere and the Eighteenth-Century Novel: Social Criticism and Narrative Enactment,' *Eighteenth-Century Life* 16.3 (1992), 117.

17 These authors, more often than not, are grouped according to their antagonistic relation with others members of the coterie. For example, 'The gulf between Defoe the journalist of the bourgeoisie and Aphra Behn the journalist of the court seems impossible to be bridged,' Q.D. Leavis wrote in 1932. The critical consensus has not changed much since the 1930s; William B. Warner describes Defoe's literary project as an effort to subject Behn's aesthetics to 'sustained ethical critique.' Leavis, *Fiction and the Reading Public* (New York: Russell and Russell, 1932), 121. Warner, *Licensing Entertainment: The Elevation of Novel Reading in Britain, 1684–1750* (Berkeley and Los Angeles: University of California Press, 1998), 152. Despite recent attempts to trace the indebtedness of Richardson and Fielding to their predecessors, the sense that the later novels supercede earlier narratives remains, to a large extent, intact.

18 To list but a few of the most influential studies on this subject: Ian Watt, *The Rise of the Novel* (London: Pimlico, 1957, 2000); Michael McKeon, *The Origins of the English Novel* (Baltimore: Johns Hopkins University Press, 1987, 2002); Leopold Damrosch, Jr, *God's Plot and Man's Stories: Studies in the Fictional Imagination from Milton to Fielding* (Chicago: University of Chicago Press, 1985); G.A. Starr, *Daniel Defoe and Spiritual Autobiography* (Princeton: Princeton University Press, 1965); and J. Paul Hunter, *Before Novels: The Cultural Contexts of Eighteenth-Century English Fiction* (New York: W.W. Norton, 1990). I return to the specific readings of Protestantism these critics advance in subsequent chapters.

19 Mah, 'Phantasies of the Public Sphere: Rethinking the Habermas of Historians,' *The Journal of Modern History* 72.1 (March 2000), 176, 169.

20 Watt, *The Rise of the Novel: Studies in Defoe, Richardson, and Fielding*, 74.

21 Ibid., 94.

22 See, for example, Nancy Armstrong, *Desire and Domestic Fiction: A Political History of the Novel* (Oxford: Oxford University Press, 1987) and part 2 of Michael McKeon's *Origins of the English Novel, 1600–1740*.

23 Armstrong, *Desire and Domestic Fiction: A Political History of the Novel* (New York: Oxford University Press, 1987), 8.

24 Ibid., 123. My emphasis on the relevance of Restoration political ideas through the first part of the eighteenth century draws on Steven Pincus and Peter Lake's claim that 'both the Williamite state and the Jacobite state ... could be described as "modern."' Pincus and Lake, 'Rethinking the Public Sphere in Early Modern England,' *Journal for British Studies* 45.2 (April 2006), 287.

25 Melissa Mowry argues in *The Bawdy Politic* that antiroyalist pornography written during the Restoration did not circulate until its publication in *Poems on Affairs of State* in 1697 – and that, as a result, Restoration pornography maintains a singularly antidemocratic perspective. See *Stuart England, 1660–1714: Political Pornography and Prostitution* (Burlington, VT: Ashgate, 2004). I am not persuaded by either claim. On Restoration opposition literature, see Tim Harris, '"There is None that Loves Him but Drunk Whores and Whoremongers": Popular Criticisms of the Restoration Court,' *Politics, Transgression, and Representation at the Court of Charles II*, ed. Julia Marciari Alexander and Catharine MacLeod (New Haven, CT: Yale University Press, 2007), 35–60.

26 Weil, 'Sometimes a Sceptre Is Only a Sceptre: Pornography and Politics in Restoration England,' *The Invention of Pornography: Obscenity and the Origins of Modernity, 1500–1800*, ed. Lynn Hunt (New York: Zone Books, 1993), 132.

27 Recently Kevin Sharpe has claimed that Charles II 'revolutionized the representation of the royal sexual body.' '"Thy Longing Country's Darling and Desire": Aesthetics, Sex, and Politics in the England of Charles II,' *Politics, Transgression, and Representation at the Court of Charles II*, ed. Julia Marciari Alexander and Catharine MacLeod (New Haven, CT: Yale University Press), 12.

28 On this subject, see Lois G. Schwoerer, *The Ingenious Mr. Henry Care, Restoration Publicist* (Baltimore: Johns Hopkins University Press, 2001).

29 James Noggle, *The Skeptical Sublime: Aesthetic Ideology in Pope and the Tory Satirists* (Oxford: Oxford University Press, 2001), 16.

30 See 'libertin/ine,' *Dictionnaire Historique de la Langue Française*, ed. Alain Rey et al. (Paris: Dictionnaries Le Robert, 1992), 1124. For discussions of scepticism's importance to philosophical and literary developments of the late seventeenth and early eighteenth century, see Timothy Dykstal, *The*

Luxury of Skepticism: Politics, Philosophy, and Dialogue in the English Public Sphere, 1660–1740 (Charlottesville: University of Virginia Press, 2001); Sarah Ellenzweig, *The Fringes of Belief: English Literature, Ancient Heresy, and the Politics of Freethinking, 1660–1760* (Stanford: Stanford University Press, 2008); Paul Hammond, 'The King's Two Bodies': *Culture, Politics and Society in Britain 1660–1800*, ed. Jeremy Black and Jeremy Gregory (Manchester: Manchester University Press, 1991); Michael McKeon, *The Origins of the English Novel, 1600–1740* (Baltimore: Johns Hopkins University Press, 1987, 2002); James Noggle, *The Skeptical Sublime: Aesthetic Ideology in Pope and the Tory Satirists* (Oxford: Oxford University Press, 2001); Eve Tavor, *Scepticism, Society and the Eighteenth-Century Novel* (London: Macmillan, 1987).

31 I take the term 'epistemological leisure' from Steven Knapp, who reads the eighteenth century's theorization of literature as part of a larger post-civil war attempt to find a means of containing dangerous beliefs. Knapp, *Personification and the Sublime: Milton to Coleridge* (Cambridge, MA: Harvard University Press, 1985), 141.

32 Steven N. Zwicker makes this observation with reference to Dryden's 'outsider' perspective in the 1690s. Zwicker, *Lines of Authority: Politics and English Literary Culture, 1649–1689* (Ithaca, NY: Cornell University Press, 1993), 199.

33 Rosenthal, *Infamous Commerce: Prostitution in Eighteenth-Century British Literature and Culture* (Ithaca, NY: Cornell University Press, 2006), 4–5.

34 To the extent that I stress the difference between earlier and later configurations of 'whore,' my account differs from Laura Brown's, which emphasizes a continuum. For example, she argues that the evocation of consumption in Restoration discourses 'is a rhetorical precursor to the representation of female commodification and the connection of the female figure with accumulation, exchange, capital, trade, and the whole ethos of a new world of consumption' in the later period. Brown, 'The Feminization of Ideology,' 226.

35 On women's political engagements after 1750, see the essays collected in Amanda Vickery, ed., *Women, Privilege, and Power: British Politics, 1750–Present* (Stanford: Stanford University Press, 2001).

36 Karen O'Brian observes that 'the turn toward social realism in the novel heralded the disengagement of fiction from the kinds of public history espoused by epic and romance.' 'History and the Novel in Eighteenth-Century Britain,' 391. In a similar vein, Everett Zimmerman notes, 'In the late eighteenth century literature becomes associated with poetry and begins gradually to exclude history ... Having established itself as a distinctive form, the novel then accepts its link with poetry even while reserving the

right to make occasional forays into history.' *The Boundaries of Fiction: History and the Eighteenth-Century British Novel* (Ithaca, NY: Cornell University Press, 1996), 29.

37 On this subject, see Helen Thompson, *Ingenuous Subjection: Compliance and Power in the Eighteenth-Century Domestic Novel* (Philadelphia: University of Pennsylvania Press, 2005).

38 The rudeness of Smollett and Sterne, I would suggest, constitutes a species of literary play rather than a politically charged act of intervention.

39 Indeed, Samuel Richardson himself draws the distinction, observing that the triumvirate of Vane, Phillips, and Pilkington 'make the Behn's, the Manley's, and the Heywood's, look white.' *Selected Letters of Samuel Richardson*, ed. John Carroll (Oxford: Clarendon Press, 1964), 173, n68. On later eighteenth-century courtesan stories, see Felicity A. Nussbaum, 'Heteroclites: The Scandalous Memoirs,' *The Autobiographical Subject: Gender and Ideology in Eighteenth-Century England* (Baltimore: Johns Hopkins University Press, 1989), 178–200. See also my reading of Kitty Fisher in *Private Interests: Women, Portraiture, and the Visual Culture of the English Novel, 1709–1791* (Toronto: University of Toronto Press, 2001), 35–40, as well as Marcia Pointon's 'The Lives of Kitty Fisher,' *British Journal for Eighteenth-Century Studies* 27 (2004): 77–97. For a measure of the different stakes governing representations of mistresses and their aristocratic patrons in the second half of the eighteenth century, see John Brewer's insightful analysis of Martha Ray's murder and its cultural significance in *A Sentimental Murder: Love and Madness in the Eighteenth Century* (New York: Farrar, Straus, and Giroux, 2004).

40 Nor do I believe that the Restoration's misogyny was corrected by the evolution of discourses of sympathy toward prostitutes in the eighteenth century. Like Restoration discourses, the language of sympathy can cut in two directions, advancing a misogynous or protofeminist agenda. On the one hand, the prostitute might find herself outside the parameters of new social definitions of the 'deserving poor' and industrious, virtuous 'woman,' as in the 1791 tract *Advice to Unmarried Women*: 'Not content with their humble condition, they [prostitutes] have preferred the wages of sin to the wages of industry, and sacrificed their virtue to their love of dress, to the foolish desire of being finer clothed, of being raised above their companions, and earning their support by an easier service than that of labouring for their bread' (14). *Advice to Unmarried Women: To recover and reclaim the fallen; and to prevent the fall of others, into the snares and consequences of seduction* (1791). On the other hand, she can challenge cultural narratives regarding marriage, particularly those that idealize women's freedom from economic restraint in their choice of husbands. Katherine Binhammer

has identified the complex convergence 'of sex, love, and financial support under a rubric of a post-Hardwicke institution of marriage' in her reading of the Magdalen House narratives. Binhammer, 'The Whore's Love,' *Eighteenth-Century Fiction* 20.4 (summer 2008), 510.

Tony Henderson observes the 'enduring importance of the condemnatory and punitive attitude towards prostitutes' through the late eighteenth and early nineteenth century. Henderson, 'Attitudes towards Prostitution,' *Disorderly Women in Eighteenth-Century London: Prostitution and Control in the Metropolis, 1730–1830* (London: Longman, 1999), 190. See also: Robert Bataille, 'The Magdalen Charity for the Reform of Prostitutes: A Foucauldian Moment,' *Illicit Sex: Identity Politics in Early Modern Culture*, ed. Thomas DiPiero and Pat Gill (Athens: University of Georgia Press, 1997), 109–22; Vern L. Bullough, 'Prostitution and Reform in Eighteenth-Century England,' *Eighteenth-Century Life* 9:3 (1985): 61–74; Vivien Jones, 'Scandalous Femininity: Prostitution and Eighteenth-Century Narrative,' *Shifting the Boundaries: Transformation of the Languages of Public and Private in the Eighteenth Century*, ed. Dario Castiglione and Lesley Sharpe (Exeter: University of Exeter Press, 1995), 54–70; Randolph Trumbach, 'Chapter Six: Prostitution Sentimentalized,' *Sex and the Gender Revolution*, vol. 1, *Heterosexuality and the Third Gender in Enlightenment London* (Chicago: University of Chicago Press, 1998), 169–95.

41 As is perhaps self-evident by this point, I am supportive of sex work and prostitutes' rights. See Anne McClintock, 'Sex Workers and Sex Work: Introduction,' in the special issue of *Social Text* (37 [1993]: 1–10) on this subject, as well as the essays by sex workers and the World Charter for Prostitutes' Rights published in that volume, for a review of the ideas informing feminist support of sex workers and the sex trade. The most forceful reclamation of 'whore' appears in its transformation into the acronym 'W.H.O.R.E.' (Women Helping Ourselves to Rights and Equality) by a Canadian sex trade advocacy website.

42 E.M.W. Tillyard, *Studies in Milton* (New York: Macmillan, 1951), 53. I am grateful to my colleague, John Leonard, for sharing his chapter 'Satan,' forthcoming in a book-length volume on *Paradise Lost* for the revived Milton Variorum Commentary, under the general editorship of Albert C. Labriola and Paul J. Klemp (Duquesne University Press).

43 See, for example, William Warner's comment: 'By editing Roxana's narrative, Defoe subjects the naive absorbed reader to critique and reformation.' William Warner, *Licensing Entertainment*, 152.

44 See Gallagher, *Nobody's Story: The Vanishing Acts of Women Writers in the Marketplace* (Berkeley and Los Angeles: University of California Press, 1994), 1–48.

45 J. Paul Hunter, 'Serious Reflections on Farther Adventures: Resistances to Closure in Eighteenth-Century English Novels,' *Augustan Subjects: Essays in Honor of Martin C. Bottestin*, ed. Albert J. Rivero (Newark: University of Delaware Press, 1997), 292.

1 The Invention of the Protestant Whore

All primary text citations are London publications unless otherwise noted.

1 *The life of Mr. Thomas Hobbes of Malmesbury written by himself in a Latine poem, and now translated into English* (1680), 2. The original reads: 'Atque metum tantum concepit tunc mea mater / Ut paretet geminos, meque metumque simul.' *Thomae Hobbesii Malmesburiensis Vita* (1679). (And then so much fear did my mother conceive, that she gave birth to twins, at once both me and fear.) My thanks to Tom Lockwood for identifying the source of this quotation and for the translation. 'Paretet' should be 'pareret' but the mistake appears in the original.

2 Critics whose work on the subjects of sexuality, religion, and politics have shaped my representation of the period include James Grantham Turner, *Libertines and Radicals in Early Modern London: Sexuality, Politics and Literary Culture, 1630–1685* (Cambridge: Cambridge University Press, 2001); Rachel Weil, *Political Passions: Gender, the Family, and Political Argument in England, 1680–1714* (Manchester: Manchester University Press, 1999); Frances E. Dolan, *Whores of Babylon: Catholicism, Gender, and Seventeenth-Century Print Culture* (Ithaca, NY: Cornell University Press, 1999); Paula McDowell, *The Women of Grub Street: Press, Politics, and Gender in the London Literary Marketplace, 1678–1730* (Oxford: Clarendon Press, 1998); Toni Bowers, *The Politics of Motherhood: British Writing and Culture, 1680–1760* (Cambridge: Cambridge University Press, 1996).

3 In particular, historians tend to separate discourses into categories organized around their profanity content: 'The satirical, obscene, negative language used to decry the court and monarch ... may disclose the deeper fears of Charles II's subjects, but it was not mainstream political discourse,' John Spurr claims. *England in the 1670s: 'This Masquerading Age'* (Oxford: Blackwell Press, 2000), 214. Literary historians have traced the convergence of sexual and religious tropes in their study of Restoration authors, but they less often undertake close readings of political and religious texts. See, for example, Steven N. Zwicker, *Lines of Authority: Politics and English Literary Culture, 1649–1689* (Ithaca, NY: Cornell University Press, 1993); James Anderson Winn, *'When beauty fires the blood': Love and the Arts in the Age of Dryden* (Ann Arbor: University of Michigan Press, 1992); and Kirk

Combe, *A Martyr for Sin: Rochester's Critique of Polity, Sexuality, and Society*
(Newark: University of Delaware Press, 1998) for representative Restoration studies. Cultural historians such as Rachel Weil and James Turner (cited in note 2) provide models for the kind of work this chapter undertakes
in its analysis of non-literary representations.

4 Tim Harris, *London Crowds in the Reign of Charles II: Propaganda and Politics
from the Restoration until the Exclusion Crisis* (Cambridge: Cambridge University Press, 1987), 218.

5 McBride and Claydon, Introduction, *Protestantism and National Identity:
Britain and Ireland, c. 1650–c. 1850* (Cambridge: Cambridge University
Press, 1998), 14.

6 As a denominational shorthand, I am using the term 'Dissenter' here to
refer both to Dissenters (Independents, Baptists, Quakers) and Nonconformists (mainly Presbyterians).

7 According to the medieval theory of the king's two bodies, the body politic is both superior to and larger than the body natural. Furthermore, there
dwells in the body politic 'certain truly mysterious forces which reduce,
or even remove, the imperfections of the fragile human nature.' Ernst H.
Kantorowicz, *The King's Two Bodies: A Study in Mediaeval Political Theology*
(Princeton: Princeton University Press, 1957), 9. In Charles II's case, the
body politic became too closely identified with the body natural, which the
king did not try to shield from scrutiny. Paul Hammond astutely analyses
the dynamics governing the debates surrounding the Restoration monarch
in 'The King's Two Bodies: Representations of Charles II,' *Culture, Politics
and Society in Britain, 1660–1800* (Manchester: Manchester University Press,
1991), 13–48. This chapter reads many of the same satiric portraits of the
king Hammond examines, but focuses more on the religious element and
draws the courtesan into the discussion.

8 Spurr, *The Restoration Church of England, 1646–1689* (New Haven, CT: Yale
University Press, 1991), 378.

9 For a list of the key political events that shaped the Restoration's religious
controversies, see the historical glossary appended to this study. For
historical studies of the religious question in the Restoration period, see
Richard L. Greaves, *Enemies under His Feet: Radicals and Nonconformists in
Britain, 1664–1677* (Stanford: Stanford University Press, 1990); Tim Harris,
Paul Seaward, and Mark Goldie, eds, *The Politics of Religion in Restoration
England* (Oxford: Basil Blackwell, 1990); Ronald Hutton, 'The Religion
of Charles II,' *The Stuart Court and Europe: Essays in Politics and Political
Culture*, ed. R. Malcolm Smuts (Cambridge: Cambridge University Press,
1996), 228–46; Annabel Patterson, 'Parliament and the Control of Religion,

1661–1674,' *The Long Parliament of Charles II* (New Haven, CT: Yale University Press, 2008), 145–62; Jonathan Scott, *England's Troubles: Seventeenth-Century English Political Instability in European Context* (Cambridge: Cambridge University Press, 2000); and John Spurr, *The Restoration Church of England, 1646–1689* (New Haven, CT: Yale University Press, 1991).

10 Patterson, *The Long Parliament of Charles II* (New Haven, CT: Yale University Press, 2008), 146. Jonathan Scott argues that 'If Charles I had seemed an agent of the Counter-Reformation advance, Charles II was one.' 'England's Troubles: Exhuming the Popish Plot,' *The Politics of Religion in Restoration England*, ed. Tim Harris, Paul Seaward, and Mark Goldie, 116. For an opposing view, see Ronald Hutton, 'The Religion of Charles II,' *The Stuart Court and Europe: Essays in Politics and Political Culture*, ed. R. Malcolm Smuts, 228–46.

11 Glanvill, *The Zealous, and Impartial Protestant, Shewing Some great, but less heeded Dangers of Popery, In Order to Thorough and Effectual Security against it* (1681), 2–3.

12 Stephen Colledge [*sic*], 'A Satyrical Sonnet' (1678), Harley MS 7319, fols 35v–37.

13 Indeed, the split between High and Low Church Anglicans that emerged after the Revolution contributed directly to the diminishment of the Church of England's political authority in the eighteenth century.

14 *Aurea Dicta. The King's Gracious Words for the Protestant Religion of the Church of England: Collected from his Majesties Letters, Speeches, Declarations, Directions, and Answers* (1681), 17.

15 Calamy, *A Discourse about a Scrupulous Conscience, Preached at the Parish-Church of St. Mary, Aldermanbury, London* (1683), 17. John Spurr notes that 'Anglican preachers dwelt in morbid detail upon the "controversy" between a wrathful God and an incorrigible nation, and they strove to associate the stability, even fate, of the country with the reformation of national manners.' '"Virtue, Religion, and Government": The Anglican Uses of Providence,' *The Politics of Religion in Restoration England*, ed. Harris, Seaward, Goldie, 30.

16 Tillotson, *The Protestant Religion Vindicated, From the Charge of Singularity and Novelty: in a Sermon Preached Before the King at Whitehall, April 2nd, 1680* (1680), 33.

17 Cawdrey, *A Preparation for Martyrdom, in a Dialogue Betwixt a Minister, and a Gentleman his Parishioner* (1681), 7.

18 Baxter, *The Second Part of the Nonconformists Plea for Peace* (1680), 5.

19 Anon., *The Whore of Babylon's Pockey Priest: Or, a True Narrative of the Apprehension of William Geldon alias Bacon, a Secular Priest of the Church of Rome*

now Prisoner in Newgate. Who Had just before been above two Months in Cure for the French Pox; wherein Is inserted a true Copy of the Apothecaries Bill found in his Chamber, containing the whole Process of that Reverend Fathers Venereal Cure (1679), 10.

20 Baxter, *The Second Part of the Nonconformists Plea for Peace* (1680), 19.

21 *A True-Protestant Catechism, Explaining the Grounds and Methods of the True-Protestant Plot; Set for the Instruction of the Brethren in the Mystery of Whiggism* (1683).

22 Nalson, 'Philerenes,' *Foxes and Fire-brands: or a Speciman of the Danger and Harmony of Popery and Separation* (1680), 4.

23 Dryden, *Absalom and Achitophel, A Poem, The Works of John Dryden*, vol. 2, ed. H.T. Swedenberg, Jr (Berkeley and Los Angeles: University of California Press, 1972), p. 6, l. 45.

24 Saywell, *A Serious Inquiry into the Means of an Happy Union: or, What Reformation is Necessary to prevent Popery, and to avert God's Judgments from the Nation* (1681), 37.

25 Dryden, Preface, *Religio Laici or Layman's Faith, A Poem* (1682), *The Works of John Dryden*, vol. 2, ed. H.T. Swedenberg, Jr (Berkeley and Los Angeles: University of California Press, 1972), 98–122.

    'In 1681 it became possible to characterise the Whigs in religious terms as calvinists who believed that the Church of England was imperfectly reformed and still contained popish elements ... The Tories, on the other hand, regarded the established church, with all its ceremonies, as the true church, and believed that attempts to alter it were part of a popish conspiracy to destroy the principle defense against Rome. Both groups, by externalising the religious threat, either in the form of Popery or dissent, papered over the controversy within the church,' observes Mark Knights, *Politics and Opinion in Crisis, 1678–81* (Cambridge: Cambridge University Press, 1994), 357.

26 Thomas Beverley, *The Whole Duty of Nations* (1681), 36; John Owen, *A Brief and Impartial Account of the Nature of the Protestant Religion: its Present State in the World, its Strength and Weakness, with the Wayes and Indications of the Ruine or Continuance of its Publick National Profession* (1682), 16; Samuel Bolde, *A Plea for Moderation toward Dissenters* (1682), 5; and Joseph Glanvill, *The Zealous, and Impartial Protestant, Shewing Some great, but less heeded Dangers of Popery, In Order to Thorough and Effectual Security against it* (1681), 5.

27 Beverley, *The Whole Duty of Nations*, 61.

28 'Philerenes' [John Nalson], 'Epistle to Mr. Richard Baxter, Mr. William Jenkins, &c.,' *Foxes and Fire-brands*, n.p.

29 George Savile, *A Letter to a Dissenter, Upon Occasion of His Majesties Late Gracious Declaration of Indulgence* (1687), 7.

30 Herbert Croft, *A Short Discourse Concerning the Reading His Majesties Late Declaration in the Churches* (1688), 8–9.

31 On the Church of England and the Revolution, see Mark Goldie, 'The Political Thought of the Anglican Revolution,' *The Revolutions of 1688*, ed. Robert Beddard (Oxford: Oxford University Press, 1991), 102–36, and William Gibson, *The Church of England, 1688--1832: Unity and Accord* (London: Routledge, 2001), chapter 2, 'The Anglican Revolution' (28–69).

32 William Lloyd, 'To the Kingdom in General,' *An Answer to the Bishop of Oxford's Reasons for Abrogating the Test, Impos'd on All Members of Parliament* (1688), 2–3.

33 Parker writes, in his preface to Bramhall's *Vindication*, 'This ensuing Treatise being somewhat superannuated, the Bookseller was very solicitous to have it set off with some Preface, that might recommend it to the present Genius of the Age, and reconcile it to the present Juncture of Affairs. And though I am none of the most Zealous Patrons of the Press, and am at this time as busie and as much concerned as DeWit, or any of the High and Mighty Burgomasters, in Matters of a closer and more comfortable importance to my self and my own Affairs: Yet I could not but yield so far to his importunity, as to improve [illegible word] [...]y fragment of time that I could get into my own disposal, towards the Gratification of his Request.' *Bishop Bramhall's Vindication of Himself and the Episcopal Clergy, from the Presbyterian Charge of Popery, as it is managed by Mr. Baxter in his treatise of the Grotian religion. Together with a preface [by Samuel Parker] shewing what grounds there are of fears and jealousies of Popery* (1672), A2. Marvell responded by using the idea of 'comfortable importance' to refer to Parker's mistress in the *Rehearsal Transpros'd*: 'A man would guess that this Giant had promised his *Comfortable Importance* a Simarre of the beards of all the *Orthodox Theologues* in Christendom.' A 'Simarre' refers to '*Cymar*: a loose robe or undergarment for women; also a bishop's gown.' *Rehearsal Transpros'd*, ed. Annabel Patterson, *The Prose Works of Andrew Marvell*, vol. 1 (1672–1673) (New Haven, CT: Yale University Press, 2003), p. 65, n143.

34 Burnet, *The Ill-Effects of the Animosities among Protestants in England Detected* (1688), 12.

35 I take my spelling of 'Walters' (also spelled 'Walter' in other sources) from Ferguson's pamphlets. Although Ferguson's name does not appear on the first pamphlet, it does on the second, which resembles its predecessor so closely I assume a common author. I follow Rachel Weil's lead in using 'Whig' somewhat anachronistically; the terms Whig and Tory 'should be taken as loose but convenient ideological designations, and do not necessarily denote membership in a "modern" party organization' in this period. Weil, *Political Passions*, p. 44, n1. For an astute reading of Ferguson's

activities as a propagandist – both Whig and, later, Jacobite – see Melinda S. Zook, 'Turncoats and Double Agents in Restoration and Revolutionary England: The Case of Robert Ferguson, the Plotter,' *Eighteenth-Century Studies* 42.3 (2009): 363–78.

36 Ferguson, *A Letter to a Person of Honour, concerning the Black Box* (1680), 1.
37 Ferguson, *A Letter to a Person of Honour, concerning the Kings disavowing the having been Married to the D. of M.'s Mother* (1680), 5, 11. A year later, Dryden revalued the monarch's 'promiscuous scatterings' by identifying the king's impulsiveness with his generosity:

> Then Israel's monarch, after Heaven's own heart,
> His vigorous warmth did variously impart
> To wives and slaves; and wide as his command
> Scattered his Maker's image through the land.

Absalom and Achitophel, A Poem, The Works of John Dryden, 2:5, ll. 7–10.
38 Ferguson, *A Letter ... concerning the Kings disavowing the having been Married to the D. of M.'s Mother*, 1.
39 Ferguson, *A Letter ... concerning the Black Box*, 6.
40 Ferguson, *A Letter ... concerning the Black Box*, 3.
41 Lawrence, *Of the profound Popery of the Common Lawyers, in Transubstantiation of two persons into one person, and the mischiefs thereof*, (1680), 67. This treatise was published with the longer *Marriage by the Morall Law of God Vindicated. Against all Ceremonial Laws of Popes and Bishops destructive to Filiation Aliment and Succession and the Government of Familyes and Kingdoms* (1680). Both Rachel Weil and Mark Goldie offer insightful commentary on Lawrence's work. See Goldie, 'Contextualizing Dryden's Absalom: William Lawrence, the Laws of Marriage, and the Case for King Monmouth,' *Religion, Literature and Politics in Post-Reformation England, 1540–1688* (Cambridge: Cambridge University Press, 1996), 208–30; Weil, *Political Passions*, 54–8.
42 Lawrence, *Of the profound Popery of the Common Lawyers*, 66–7.
43 Lawrence, *Marriage by the Morall Law of God Vindicated*, 91.
44 Weil, *Political Passions*, 57.
45 Ferguson, *A Letter to a Person of Honour*, 6
46 Weil, 'Sometimes a Sceptre is only a Sceptre: Pornography and Politics in Restoration England.' *The Invention of Pornography: Obscenity and the Origins of Modernity, 1500–1800*, ed. Lynn Hunt (New York: Zone, 1993), 132.
47 Weil sees the attention to whores working as a means of deflecting attention away from the king toward his royal mistresses in political pornography, but I argue that 'whore' too often appears in descriptions of the

monarch himself for it to stand only as a sign of female degradation of the regime. See Weil, 'Sometimes a Sceptre is only a Sceptre,' 152.

48 Paul Hammond analyses the effect of Charles's behaviour on public opinion in 'The King's Two Bodies: Representations of Charles II,' 13–48.

49 Harley MS 7319, fols 33v–35, 'The Whore of Babylon' (1678); alternately, Harley MS 7317, fols 67–68v, 'On the Dutchess of Portsmouth,' n.d.

50 Portsmouth, in fact, often emerges as a more astute political operator than the king himself, so abjected does he appear by sexual desire, which seldom defines representations of the French mistress. Portsmouth is loyal to France, but Charles's sexual appetite directly impedes any capacity to recognize the large issues facing England.

51 Maguire, 'The Duchess of Portsmouth: English Royal Consort and French Politician, 1670–85.' *The Stuart Court and Europe: Essays in Politics and Political Culture*, ed. R. Malcolm Smuts (Cambridge: Cambridge University Press, 1996), p. 247. Rachel Weil has recently reframed the question of the Stuart royal mistress's political prerogative: 'We might be skeptical of claims that Portsmouth really influenced the king, or that he needed her as a conduit to Louis XIV, or that she controlled access to him ... But the relevant point is that people thought she had such powers.' 'The Female Politician in the Late Stuart Age,' *Politics, Transgression, and Representation at the Court of Charles II*, ed. Julia Marciari Alexander and Catharine MacLeod (New Haven, CT: Yale University Press, 2007), 185.

52 *Articles of High-Treason and other High Crimes and Misdemeanors Against the Dutches of Portsmouth* [1680].

53 'Upon his Majesties being made free of the Citty,' Marvell, *Poems and Letters*, 1:191, l. 54. Attribution is uncertain; the work was first published in *State Poems* (1697).

54 Turner, *Libertines and Radicals in Early Modern London: Sexuality, Politics and Literary Culture, 1630–1685* (Cambridge: Cambridge University Press, 2001), 256.

55 Hart and Stevenson, *Heaven and the Flesh: Imagery of Desire from the Renaissance to the Rococo* (Cambridge: Cambridge University Press, 1995), 71–2. Hart and Stevenson speculate that 'Tompson's picture seems to have been executed neither for Nell Gwyn herself nor for members of the court, but as a commentary for unimplicated male connoisseurs, invited to imagine the intimate life of Charles II and the erotic forces that beset him' (71).

56 Rochester, 'if buizy love intrenches, / There's a sweet soft Page of mine / Can doe the Trick worth Forty wenches.' 'Love to a Woman,' ll. 14–16. *The Works of John Wilmot, Earl of Rochester*, ed. Harold Love (Oxford: Oxford University Press, 1999), 38.

57 'Satyr' (1677), Harley MS 7319, fols 26–8.

58 'A Ballad called the Haymarket Hectors.' *Poems on Affairs of State: Augustan Satirical Verse, 1660-1714* (hereafter cited as *POAS*), 7 vols. Gen. ed. George de F. Lord. Vol. 1, ed. de F. Lord (New Haven, CT: Yale University Press, 1963–75), p. 171, ll. 49–54. The ballad recounts the slitting of Coventry's nose after he alluded somewhat insultingly to Nell Gwyn in a session of Parliament.

59 'The Lady of Pleasure or The Life of Nelly truly Shown From Hop-gard'n Cellar to the Throne Till into th' Grave She tumbled down' (1686?) Harley MS 7319, fols 269–72v; a note to this poem suggests it was written five or six years after date that appears on MS.

60 *POAS*, vol. 1, ed. de F. Lord, p. 183, l. 98.

61 'A Letany for St. Omers' (1682).

62 *Madam Gwins Answer to the Dutchess of Portsmouths Letter* (1682).

63 Marvell, 'The Kings Vowes,' *Poems and Letters*, 1:175, ll. 64–6.

64 A letter from Henry Coventry to Essex written in 1677 suggests how deeply implicated Nell Gwyn became in state affairs: 'Whereas the King hath referred a Pencon in Lord Rochester's name to the Lord Lieutenant of Ireland for granting certain lands ... to the use of Mrs Gwyn these lands are likely to be disposed of otherwise then the King intends by the Court of claymes. It is therefore humbly desire[d] his Ma[jesty] will be please[d] to order Mr Secretary to write to the Lieutenant to take private order with the comm[oners] of the Court of Claymes that the hearing of all causes concerning the said lands named in the schedule may be deferred and that the other causes may be finished before these be meddled with.' *Essex Papers*, vol. 1, *1672–1679*, ed. Osmund Airy (Camden Society, 1890), 145.

65 'On the Prorogation,' *POAS*, vol.1, ed. de F. Lord, p. 179, l.13.

66 Portsmouth's anus, the poem continues, 'So powerful is of late, / Although it's both blind and dumb, / It rules both Church and State.' 'Satire,' *POAS*, vol. 2, ed. Elias F. Mengel, Jr, p. 291, ll. 22–3.

67 *Smith's Protestant Intelligence, Domestick and Foreign* (17–21 March, 28–31 March, 4–7 April 1681, 1681).

68 Dryden, 'Epilogue,' *Tyrannick Love, or the Royal Martyr. A Tragedy. The Works of John Dryden*, vol. 10, ed. Maximillian Novak (Berkeley and Los Angeles: University of California Press, 1970), p. 193, ll. 29–30.

69 Untitled Song (MS Don.b.8, p. 504) quoted in John Harold Wilson, ed. *Court Satires of the Restoration* (Columbus: Ohio State University Press, 1976), 248.

70 Indeed, in a satire that inverts Nelly's dream of sleeping with Charles

every night, Portsmouth appears as the political agency governing the
court's daytime drama:

> You govern every Council meeting,
> Making th' Fools do as you think fitting:
> Your Royal Cully has command,
> Only from you at second hand;
> He does but at the Helm appear,
> Sit there and sleeps while your Slaves steer:

'Portsmouth's Looking Glass.' *Poems on Affairs of State* (1697).

71 'Nell Gwynne,' *POAS*, vol. 1, ed. de F. Lord, 420.
72 *Madame de Sévigné: Correspondance*, 3 vols, ed. Roger Duchêne (Paris: Gallimard, 1974), '"puisqu'elle est de si grande qualité, pourquoi s'est-elle faite
  p ... ? Elle devrait mourir de honte. Pour moi, c'est mon métier, je ne me
  pique d'autre chose"' (vol. 2, p. 99; translation mine).
73 'The Earl of Rochester's Verses For Which He Was Banished,' *POAS*, vol. 1,
  ed. de F. Lord, p. 424, ll. 28–31.
74 Love provides substantial evidence to link the 'Protestant Whore' of this
  poem to Gwyn, providing further evidence for the presence of a well-
  known identification between Gwyn and the Protestant interest in Restoration England. Love, 'Nell Gwyn and Rochester's "By All Love's Soft, Yet
  Mighty Pow'rs,"' *Notes and Queries* 49.3 (2002), 355–7.
75 *A Pleasant Battle Between Two Lap Dogs of the Utopian Court* (1681), 3.
76 'A Satyrical Sonnet' (1678), Harley MS 7319.
77 *The Dutchess of Portsmouths and Count Coningsmarks Farwel to England*
  (1682) betrays the fear that Portsmouth only represents the tip of an ice-
  berg: 'Long have we lookt for the Duchesses departure, but she has stuck
  to us like Birdlime, she has been long a Mote in the Kingsdoms Eye, and
  now the true Protestants cry out, blessed be God our Plague is removed!
  But whilst they sing this Song, millions of skulking Papists are praying to
  the Virgin *Mary*, and to all the Saints, even to Saint *Coleman*, and Saint *Sta-*
  ly, for her safe journey and her speedy return.' 'Millions' of papists could
  only populate England if they were masquerading as its Protestant
  majority.
78 *POAS*, vol. 2, ed. Mengel, Jr, pp. 243–4, ll. 40–55.
79 *POAS*, vol. 2, ed. Mengel, Jr., 244.
80 'The Ladies' March,' ll. 63–4, *Court Satires of the Restoration*, ed. John
  Harold Wilson (Columbus, OH: Ohio State University Press, 1976), 58.
81 'True Protestant,' used satirically, referred to Whig dissenters (*POAS*, vol.

3, ed. Howard H. Schless, 197); 'the Protestant Joyner' was the title given to Stephen College, whose zealous ballad and pamphlet publications on the subject of the Popish Plot led to his conviction on charges of treason; College was executed in 1681.

82　No copy of this sermon appears to be extant. But we find reference to it in Tenison's memoirs. It seems that the Earl of Jersey tried to prejudice Queen Mary against Tenison in the early days of her reign: 'he [the earl] represented to her Majesty, who was speaking in Terms of Respect about Dr. *Tennison*, that he had some Weeks before deliver'd a notable Funeral Sermon, in praise of Mrs. *Eleanor Gwyn*, one of King *Charles* the Second's late Concubines. *What then*, said the Queen, in a sort of Discomposure, which she was the least subject to of any Lady breathing. *I have heard as much. This is a Sign that the poor unfortunate Woman died Penitent; for if I can read a Man's Heart through his Looks, had not she made a truly Pious and Christian End, the Doctor could never have been induc'd to speak well of her.' Memoirs of the Life and Times of ... T. Tennison, late Archbishop of Canterbury ... Together with his last Will and Testament, etc.* 3rd ed. [1716], 20.

83　Charles H. Hinnant makes a compelling case for reading *The London Jilt; Or, the Politick Whore* (1683) as a precursor to *Moll Flanders* and *Roxana*. His reading attends to the 'questions of feeling and desire' the narrative raises, rather than politics and religion. *The London Jilt*'s subtitle evokes the protagonist's canniness, not affairs of state. Hinnant, Introduction, *The London Jilt; or, the Politick Whore* (Peterborough, ON: Broadview Press, 2008), 29. The connections Hinnant establishes confirm my claim that courtesan narrative drew on a wide range of storytelling traditions, including whore biography and the picaresque.

84　Here I follow James Turner, who concludes his reading of *The Parliament of Women* by observing: 'In all early modern *pornographia*, and most fully in those mocking 'petitions' and 'parliaments' that voice a feminist politics in an attempt to embalm it in absurdity, history reverses the famous aphorism that Karl Marx wielded against Louis Napoleon: world-changing ideas make their first appearance as farce.' *Libertines and Radicals*, 274.

85　*The Whore's Rhetorick* (1683): Fascimile Reproduction, with an introduction by James R. Irvine and G. Jack Gravlee (Delmar, NY: Scholars' Fascimiles and Reprints, 1979), 25. Future references will be cited parenthetically.

86　*The Parliament of Women, Or, a Compleat History of the Proceedings and Debates, of a particular Junto, of Ladies and Gentlewomen, With a design to alter the Government of the world By way of a Satyr* (1684), 7. Future references will be cited parenthetically.

87　For another reading of *The Whore's Rhetorick* and the evolution of the English novel, see James Turner, '*The Whore's Rhetorick*: Narrative, Pornography, and the Origins of the Novel,' *Studies in Eighteenth-Century Culture* 24 (1995): 297–306.

88 These comments are translated directly from the Italian original, Ferrante Pallavicino's *La retorica delle puttane* (1642).

89 *Erotopolis* (1684) makes a related observation about boarding schools, claiming that girls emerge from their confines only to travel directly into Bettyland, i.e., whoredom, 'and never more return into their own Country' (152).

90 The author of *Erotopolis* takes a different view of the romance's import. The shepherdesses of Bettyland are 'deeply Learn'd, for having nothing else to do as they sit upon the Plains, they are always reading *Cassandra, Ibrahim Bassa, Grand Cyrus, Amadis de Gaule, Hero and Leander, the School of Venus,* and the rest of these classick Authors: by which they are mightily improved both in Practice and Discourse. Put them to their shifts and they are the best in the world at an Intreague or stratagem' (59–60).

2 'No Neuters in Treason'

1 Janet Todd, ed., *The Secret Life of Aphra Behn* (London: Pandora, 2000), 496, n14; Todd also describes Silvia's character as 'an amalgamation of the royal whores as delivered in satire, with Barbara, Duchess of Cleveland, prevailing,' 497, n22.

2 *The Third Part of the Growth of Popery and Arbitrary Government in England* (1683), 61. Here I follow Toni Bowers's thesis regarding amatory fiction: 'It is neither accidental nor simply predictable that amatory fiction's most common plots are plots of seduction and betrayal, that it so obsessively represents false oaths, failed promises, and broken vows ... The problem of broken vows constituted a significant and prolonged crisis in English culture at the end of the seventeenth century.' 'Sex, Lies, and Invisibility: Amatory Fiction from the Restoration to Mid-Century,' *The Columbia History of the British Novel*, ed. John Richetti et al. (New York: Columbia University Press, 1994), 63.

3 Weil, *Political Passions: Gender, the Family and Political Argument in England, 1680–1714* (Manchester: Manchester University Press, 1999), 232. Rachel Carnell offers a similar assessment of the uses of prose fiction for partisan politics, suggesting that 'the development of novelistic realism corresponds ... with the competition among different versions of political selfhood, each of which sought to be perceived as universal selfhood.' *Partisan Politics, Narrative Realism, and the Rise of the British Novel* (New York: Palgrave Macmillan, 2006), 4.

4 On the topic of sexual difference and its political import, my argument resembles that advanced by Ellen Pollak in her chapter on Behn in *Incest and the English Novel, 1684–1814* (Baltimore: Johns Hopkins University Press, 2003), 59–85: 'what Behn's complex structuring of her tale makes evident is the profound interimplication – indeed the mutually constitutive nature – of sexuality and politics' (73).

5 This line of investigation departs from the critical commonplace that Defoe's and Richardson's novels 'are among the first that self-consciously present the rise of gender as political categories and the poignancy of the invasion of public opinion into private spaces.' Paula R. Backscheider, 'The Rise of Gender as Political Category,' *Revising Women: Eighteenth-Century 'Women's Fiction' and Social Engagement*, ed. Paula R. Backscheider (Baltimore: Johns Hopkins University Press, 2000), 56. For an excellent account of earlier political romances, see Paul Salzman, *English Prose Fiction, 1558–1700* (Oxford: Oxford University Press, 1985).

6 *The Secret History of the Rye-House Plot; and of Monmouth's Rebellion. Written by Ford, Lord Grey in 1685. Now first published from a manuscript, sign'd by himself* (1754). Janet Todd, whose biography of Behn provides the most detailed account of the affair that inspired *Love-Letters*, notes only that 'after 1685 the historical Lady Henrietta Berkeley seems to have crept back to England into the bosom of her family and church.' *The Secret Life of Aphra Behn* (London: Pandora, 2000), 496, n18.

7 Dorrit Cohn, *The Distinction of Fiction* (Baltimore: Johns Hopkins University Press, 1999), 152.

8 McKeon, *The Secret History of Domesticity: Public, Private, and the Division of Knowledge* (Baltimore: Johns Hopkins University Press, 2005), 516.

9 I follow Natania Meeker's reading of Lucretius here. *Voluptuous Philosophy: Literary Materialism in the French Enlightenment* (New York: Fordham University Press, 2006), 224. We know that Behn was an admirer of Lucretius. Her poem commending Thomas Creech's translation of *De Rerum Natura* praises Lucretius's Reason, which 'Pierces, Conquers, and Compells / Beyond poor Feeble Faith's Dull Oracles.' Behn, *The Works of Aphra Behn*, ed. Janet Todd, 7 vols (Columbus: Ohio State University Press, 1992–6), 1:29, no. 11, ll. 55–6 (variants).

10 Behn writes what Mayer describes as 'humanist modern history,' which has its roots in Machiavelli. But while Behn spends moments reading into the hearts of great men, she spends the vast majority of her time inside the mind of her purely fictional character. For a definition of humanist historiography, see Robert Mayer, *History and the Early English Novel: Matters of Fact from Bacon to Defoe* (Cambridge: Cambridge University Press,

1997), 25. I agree with the illuminating account of the emergence of historical fiction provided by Mayer in his study, but I am not persuaded by his
reasons for his excluding Behn from an emergent tradition of historical
fiction. Discounting *Love-Letters*, among other works, from the canon of
historical fiction, Mayer claims, 'in these texts one finds no confronta-
tion with readerly expectations engendered by the narratives being read'
(153). See also Jane Spencer, 'Not being a historian: Women Telling Tales in
Restoration and Eighteenth-Century England,' *Contexts of Pre-Novel Narrative*, ed. Roy Eriksen (New York: Mouton de Gruyter, 1994), 319–40. On
French historiography and women's writing, see Faith E. Beasley, *Revising
Memory: Women's Fiction and Memoirs in Seventeenth-Century France* (New
Brunswick, NJ: Rutgers University Press, 1990).

11 Aravamudan, *Tropicopolitans: Colonialism and Agency, 1688–1804* (Durham:
Duke University Press, 1999), 42.

12 'The abject *porne* and the sublime *cortegiana honesta* or royal mistress –
more like the ancient Greek hetaira – between them define all sexual
transgression, gendered female even when the wild libertines are ostensibly male.' Turner, *Libertines and Radicals in Early Modern London: Sexuality,
Politics and Literary Culture, 1630–1685* (Cambridge: Cambridge University
Press, 2000), xii.

13 Sévigné writes appreciatively in response to her daughter's account of the
Mancini sisters: 'Your description of Madame Colonne and her sisters is
divine. It awakens us despite ourselves: it's an admirable painting' (La description que vous me faites de Mme Colonne et de sa sœur est une chose
divine; elle réveille malgré qu'on en ait; c'est une peinture admirable), Sevigné, *Lettres de Madame de Sevigné*, 3 vols, ed. Emile Gérard-Gailly (Paris:
Gallimard, 1953–7), 1:573. Future references will be cited parenthetically.
Translations are mine, here and elsewhere in the chapter.

14 On the evolution of the literary portrait in France, see Joan DeJean, *Tender
Geographies: Women and the Origins of the Novel in France* (New York: Columbia University Press, 1991), 48–9, 82. Following DeJean, I use only the
family name of the French women writers I discuss here; see *Tender Geographies*, 2.

15 Behn's dedications also resemble English dedications authored by her
male contemporaries. I stress the French connection here to draw attention
to the aesthetics of female intimacy at work in both the Mazarin and Gwyn
dedications, and their import for the image of woman authorship Behn
wants to create. For an account of Wycherley's dedication to the Duchess of Cleveland, see Turner, *Libertines and Radicals*, 201–10. On Dryden's
dedication to the same, see James Winn, 'When *beauty fires the blood*': *Love*

and the Arts in the Age of Dryden (Ann Arbor: University of Michigan Press, 1992), 61–5.

16 Madame de La Fayette (Marie Madeleine Pioche de la Vergne), 'Portraite de Mme La Marquise de Sévigné Par Mme La Comtesse de la Fayette Sous le Nom d'Un Inconnu,' Œuvres Complètes, ed. Roger Duchêne (Paris: François Bourin, 1990), 9. Translations are mine.

17 Behn strengthens the French connection between her work and that of her French contemporaries by setting *Love-Letters* in the sixteenth-century French court, also the setting for Lafayette's *La Princesse de Clèves*.

18 'To Mrs. Ellen Gwin,' *The Feign'd Curtizens, The Works of Aphra Behn*, 6:86–7. Future references will be cited parenthetically.

19 The courtesan here anticipates the development of character Deidre Shauna Lynch attributes to the eighteenth-century novel, including 'characters' quality of eerie thing-hood' and its relation to the evolution of print culture. *The Economy of Character: Novels, Market Culture, and the Business of Inner Meaning* (Chicago: University of Chicago Press, 1998), 18. Hortense Mancini learned the hard facts of her status as an economic agent quickly after she fled her husband: 'It is a great Truth that I never dreamed that I should ever want money, but experience hath taught me it is commonly the first thing, that is wanting, especially to those, that having always lived in great plenty of it, never know the necessity and importance of discreetly manag[ing] it.' M. L'Abbé de Saint-Réal (César Vichard), *The memoires of the Dutchess Mazarine. Written in French by her own hand, and done into English by P. Porter, Esq; Together with the reasons of her coming into England. Likewise, a letter containing a true character of her person and conversation* (1676), 66.

20 Roy MacGregor-Hastie attributes Nell Gwyn's 'Protestant Whore' pronouncement to an appearance at the November 1679 anniversary celebrations of Queen Elizabeth's accession. No documentation supports this claim, but the prevalence of these celebrations alerts us to Elizabeth's importance as a Protestant icon during the Restoration. For an account of the 1679 celebrations, see MacGregor-Hastie, *Nell Gwyn* (London: Robert Hale, 1987), 156.

21 Nothing could be further from the truth than the story this sentence tells. Gwyn hoped for a title for herself for as long as Charles II lived, and anecdote recounts that she held her son by the heel over a bridge, threatening to drown him if the king did not grant him, and his brother, titles. For this narrative, see the Gwyn biographies listed in chapter 1.

22 DeJean notes: 'For centuries, historians have debated the seriousness of the threat to the monarchy posed by the Fronde, the name used to characterize a series of popular uprisings that took place between 1648 and 1653 with

the backing of an almost constantly shifting alliance of parliamentarians and nobility of the highest ranks.' *Tender Geographies*, 36.

23 For a full biographical portrait of Mancini, see Bryan Bevin, *The Duchess Hortense: Cardinal Mazarin's Wanton Niece* (London: Rubicon, 1987).

24 *The memoires of the Dutchess Mazarine*, 17.

25 The Fronde, as DeJean has observed, was a war fought extensively by aristocratic women, a fact that shaped the literary culture that arose in its wake. See *Tender Geographies*, 36–42. Commenting on Scudéry's first novel, published during the years of the Fronde rebellion, DeJean notes, 'The bond forged ... between prose fiction and political subversion marks the origin of the modern French novel' (45).

26 Sévigné records the remark in a letter to her daughter: 'To everything people said to Madame Mazarin in order to oblige her to reunite with her husband, she would always respond, laughing, as during the civil war, "No Mazarin, no Mazarin."' (Sur tout ce qu'on disoit ici à Mme. Mazarin pour l'obliger de se remettre avec son mari, elle répondait toujours en riant, comme pendant la guerre civile: 'Point de Mazarin, point de Mazarin.') *Lettres*, 1:209.

27 *Tender Geographies*, 112.

28 Ibid., 111.

29 Invited to England by Ralph Montagu, a member of Charles II's Privy Council, Mancini was championed by English courtiers hoping to weaken the influence of the king's most powerful royal mistress, Louise de Kéroualle, Duchess of Portsmouth. But the Duchess of Mazarin remained faithful only to her own pleasures and seems to have lost any real political influence she might have wielded almost immediately by taking up with a variety of lovers other than the king. This fact did not stop her being implicated in both the Popish and the Rye House Plots.

30 'Mme de Mazarin court les champs de son côté; on la croit en Angleterre: il n'y a, comme vous savez, ni foi, ni loi, ne prêtre; mais je crois qu'elle ne voudroit pas, comme dit la chanson, qu'on en eût chassé le Roi.'

31 Sévigné's interest in Mazarin may have been premised on this understanding of the courtesan's actions. Sévigné identifies herself, or rather, her writing, as libertine in interesting ways: 'I am so libertine when I write, that the first turn I take reigns the whole course of my letter' (Je suis tellement libertine quand j'écris, que le premier tour que je prends règne tout du long de ma lettre) (2:436). Writing in the aftermath of James II's arrival in France, Sévigné marks the seriousness of the political situation with the freedoms of her pen: 'You see a little where the libertinism of my pen takes me; but consider that the conversations are full of these great events'

(Voyez un peu où me porte le libertinage de ma plume; mais vous jugez bien que les conversations sont pleines de ces grands événements) (3:303).

32 *Poems on Affairs of State: Augustan Satirical Verse, 1660–1714.* 7 vols. Gen. ed. George de F. Lord. 'Rochester's Farewell,' vol. 2 (ed. Elias F. Mengel), p. 224, l.124 and ll. 134–5.

33 *POAS*, 'Queries,' 2:296–7, ll. 76–9.

34 A striking articulation of this internationalism/sexual polymorphousness equation appears in Benedetto Gennari's *Hortense Mancini, Duchess of Mazarin* (figure 5). For a reading of the colonial and racial discourses at work in this painting, see Aravamudan, *Tropicopolitans*, 37–8. I will return to this image, and the Protestant Whore's relation to English imperialism, in chapter 4.

35 'To the Most Illustrious Princess, The Duchess of Mazarine,' Behn, *The History of the Nun, Works* 3:208–9. Future references will be cited parenthetically.

36 Saint-Evrémond writes, rather more directly, in a letter to Mme Harvey, 'Tout sexes pour Hortense a fourni des aman[t]s' (all sexes have furnished Hortense with lovers). *Œuvres ... avec la vie de l'auteur, par monsieur Des Maizeaux ... Nouvelle édition.* 9 vols, ed. Pierre Des Maizeaux (Amsterdam, 1753), v. 37. At least one satire of the period portrays her affair with the king's daughter as the defining moment of her career at court ('Rochester's Farewell,' *POAS* 2:223–5).

37 Todd, *Secret Life of Aphra Behn*, 394.

38 Published posthumously. 'Les incertitudes de la Philosophie ne sont guères plus grandes que celles de l'Histoire; & ceux qui l'ont beaucoup lue, disent que l'on accommode l'Histoire à peu près comme les viandes dans une cuisine. Chaque Nation les apprête à sa manière: de sorte que la même chose est mise en autant de ragouts différents, qu'il y a de Pays au monde; & Presque toujours on trouve plus agréables ceux qui sont conformes à sa coutume. Il faut être fort simple, dit un bel esprit, pour étudier l'Histoire avec l'espérance d'y découvrir ce qui s'est passé; c'est bien assez qu'on sache ce qu'en ont dit tels ou tels Auteurs; & ce n'est pas tant l'Histoire des Faits qu'on doit chercher, que l'Histoire des Opinions & des Relations.' *Les Œuvres de M. L'Abbé de Saint Réal, nouvelle édition, rangeé dans un meilleur ordre, & augmentée* (Paris, 1745), 3:20. It appears that Vichard is drawing on Pierre Bayle here (the 'bel esprit' he mentions), for a very similar passage appears in Bayle's *Les Nouvelles de la Republique des lettres*: 'L'on accomode l'histoire à peu près comme les viandes dans une cuisine. Chaque nation les apprête à sa manière, de sorte que la même chose est mise en autant de ragoûts différents, qu'il y a de pays au

monde, et presque toujours on trouve plus agréables ceux qui sont conformes à sa coutume. Voilà, ou peu s'en faut, le sort de l'histoire; chaque
nation, chaque religion, chaque secte prend les mêmes faits tout crus où
ils se peuvent trouver, les accommode et les assaisonne selon son goût, et
puis ils semblent à chaque lecteur vrais ou faux, selon qu'ils conviennent
ou qu'ils répugnent à ses préjugés.' Pierre Bayle, *Les Nouvelles de la Republique des lettres* (mars 1686, art 4), republished in Bayle's *Œuvres diverses*
(La Haye, 1737), 1:510. My thanks to Jillian Richardson at the University
of Ottawa for locating the Vichard citation, which I originally read in
Michaud's *Biographie Universelle* (40:95), and for drawing my attention to
the Bayle connection.

39 It is unclear what kind of relationship Gwyn and Monmouth actually enjoyed; they were only a year apart in age, after all. In 1679, John Stewkeley
wrote, 'Nell Gwin begg'd hard of his Majestie to see him [Monmouth],
telling him he was grown pale, wan, lean & long-visaged merely because
he was in disfavour; but the King bid her be quiet for he would not see
him.' *Memoirs of the Verney Family, From the Restoration to the Revolution,
1660–1696,* 4 vols. Compiled by Margaret M. Verney (London: Longmans,
1899), 4:265.

40 *A New Vision of Lady Gr–y's, Concerning her Sister, the Lady Henrietta Berkeley.
In a Letter to Madam Fan——* (1682), single sheet.

41 *POAS,* 2:122.

42 'Epilogue to the Same. Spoken by the Lady Slingsby' [1682], *The Prologues
and Epilogues of the Restoration, 1660–1700* (Part Two: 1677–1690), ed. Pierre
Danchin (Nancy: Université Nancy, 1981), pp. 424–5, ll. 7–8, 17–18.

43 Goreau, *Reconstructing Aphra: A Social Biography of Aphra Behn* (New York:
Dial Press, 1980), 251–2.

44 Melinda S. Zook analyses the range of representations of Monmouth Behn
produced in her political poetry. See 'The Political Poetry of Aphra Behn,'
The Cambridge Companion to Aphra Behn, ed. Derek Hughes and Janet Todd
(Cambridge: Cambridge University Press, 2004), 46–67.

45 Payne, '"And Poets Shall by Patron-Princes Live": Aphra Behn and Patronage': *Curtain Calls: British and American Women and the Theatre,* ed. Mary
Anne Schofield and Cecilia Macheski (Athens, OH: Ohio University Press,
1991), 111.

46 Aphra Behn, *Love-Letters between a Nobleman and His Sister,* ed. Janet Todd
(London: Penguin, 1996), 3–4. Future references will be cited parenthetically.

47 Todd, Introduction, *Love-Letters,* xiv.

48 Ibid.

49 As James Turner notes, 'Behn never lets us forget the different situations of the man and the woman.' *Schooling Sex: Libertine Literature and Erotic Education in Italy, France, and England, 1534–1685* (Oxford: Oxford University Press, 2003), 382.

50 King, 'Spying Upon the Conjuror: Haywood, Curiosity, and "the Novel" in the 1720s,' *Studies in the Novel* 30.2 (1998): 183. Benedict, *Curiosity: A Cultural History of Early Modern Inquiry* (Chicago: University of Chicago Press, 2001), 139.

51 It also, as Helen Thompson notes, 'portends the novel's capacity abruptly to evacuate – and to reinvest – the romantic signifiers which are here only strategically drained of content.' '"Thou monarch of my Panting Soul": Hobbesian Obligation and the Durability of Romance in Aphra Behn's *Love-Letters,*' *British Women's Writing in the Long Eighteenth Century: Authorship, Politics and History,* ed. Jennie Batchelor and Cora Kaplan (New York: Palgrave MacMillan, 2005), 119, n15.

52 Benedict, 'The Curious Genre: Female Inquiry in Amatory Fiction,' *Studies in the Novel* 30.2 (1998): 206.

53 Behn's willingness to rewrite scripture echoes contemporary developments in Continental intellectual history: French Jesuit Richard Simon's commentary on the fallacies of the Hebrew scriptures was translated as *A Critical History of the Old Testament* in 1682. Behn returned to this tradition in the preface to her translation of Fontanelle's *La pluralité des Mondes* (1686) in 1688. Robert Markley examines Behn's preface in 'Global Analogies: Cosmology, Geosymmetry, and Skepticism in Some Works of Aphra Behn,' *Science, Literature and Rhetoric in Early Modern England,* ed. Juliet Cummins and David Burchell (Aldershot: Ashgate, 2007), 203.

54 As Ros Ballaster notes, 'The power of the writer lies in her ability to interpret and manipulate the reader's desire, and it is this lesson that Behn's Sylvia must learn if she is to prosper.' *Seductive Forms: Women's Amatory Fiction from 1684–1740* (Oxford: Clarendon Press, 1992), 111.

55 Ballaster, *Seductive Forms,* 109–10. Michael McKeon advances a similar claim, arguing that Silvia learns how to tell her story from the narrator: 'Silvia learns from the example of Behn's narrator how to practice the gendered 'Arts of Woman' with the ethical latitude normally accorded men.' *The Secret History of Domesticity: Public, Private and the Division of Knowledge,* 535. But both Silvia and the narrator learn first from servants. In volume 3, we discover that the narrator has learned much from another servant of Silvia's: 'I have heard her Page say, from whom I have had a great part of the Truths of her Life, that he never saw *Silvia* in so pleasant a Humour all his life before' (388).

56 'Behn superimpose[s] the sexual upon the political in such a way to make
each an allegory for the other,' Bradford K. Mudge claims in *The Whore's
Story: Women, Pornography, and the British Novel, 1684–1830* (Oxford: Oxford University Press, 2000), 126. See also Angeline Goreau, *Reconstructing
Aphra: A Social Biography of Aphra Behn* (London: Dial Press, 1980), 274–7;
Donald A. Wehrs, '*Eros*, Ethics, Identity: Royalist Feminism and the Politics of Desire in Aphra Behn's *Love-Letters*,' *Studies in English Literature
1500–1900* 32.3 (1992): 461–78; Janet Todd describes Silvia as 'the shameless
mirror image of a Whig capitalist' in 'Who is Silvia? What is she? Feminine
Identity in Aphra Behn's *Love-Letters between a Nobleman and His Sister*,'
Aphra Behn Studies, ed. Janet Todd (Cambridge: Cambridge University
Press, 1996), 202. John Richetti deems Silvia an even worse nightmare than
the duke; see '*Love Letters between a Nobleman and His Sister*: Aphra Behn
and Amatory Fiction,' *Augustan Subjects: Essays in Honor of Martin C. Battestin*, ed. Albert J. Rivero (Newark: University of Delaware, 1997), 13–28.
57 John Richetti claims that the closing pages of *Love-Letters* offers us a 'romanticized, tragic portrait of Monmouth.' The impetus of the third volume, I believe, is to undermine Monmouth thoroughly by drawing on all
the well-known facts of his superstition, his indecisiveness, and his stupid-
ity. '*Love Letters between a Nobleman and His Sister*: Aphra Behn and Amatory Fiction,' 27.
58 Various Continental anticlerical discourses, authored by both Catholics
and Protestants, were circulating at this time, and Behn was likely interested in all of them. Huguenot Pierre Bayle's ideas, in particular, resonate
with Behn's. Bayle grounds his religious scepticism in the deceptively
simple premise that '*there are misfortunes without comets, and comets without
misfortunes*,' *Various Thoughts on the Occasion of a Comet* (1683), trans. Robert
C. Bartlett (Albany, NY: State University of New York, 2000), 62 (emphasis
in text). According to Bayle human history reveals an inverse proportion
of religious activism to the kind of behaviour a benevolent deity might
endorse: 'Persecutions, prisons, gallows, and, in general, all the violence
used in favor of the sound religion are but criminal excess that God does
not care to bless' (288).

 That Behn was reading Bayle in the early 1680s is suggested by her addition of a marginal note to *The History of Oracles*, which identifies June
1686 as the issue of Bayle's *Nouvelles de la Republique des lettres* to which
Fontanelle is referring in his remarks. In addition to writing his own study
on the subject, Bayle reviewed, in 1684, a 1681 Latin publication by Antony
Van Dale, titled *de Oraculis Ethnicorum*. Fontenelle subsequently published
The History of Oracles as a popularized version of Van Dale's scholarly text

in 1687. Behn's translation of Fontenelle's work was published in London in 1688. While Behn's lack of Latin would have prevented her from reading the Van Dale text, she may well have read Bayle's review of it, and Bayle's *Miscellaneous Reflections* may have inspired her to translate Fontenelle. For a consideration of Huguenot historiography, see Hugh Trevor-Roper, 'A Huguenot Historian: Paul Rapin,' *Huguenots in Britain and Their French Background, 1550–1800*, ed. Irene Scouloudi (London: Macmillan, 1987), 3–19.

59 Here we are reintroduced to Robert Ferguson, Whig propagandist and author of the Black Box Affair pamphlets.

60 Rivero, '"Hieroglifick'd" History in Aphra Behn's *Love-Letters between a Nobleman and His Sister*,' *Studies in the Novel* 30.2 (1998), 134.

61 In her illuminating reading of Octavio's induction earlier in the narrative, Helen Thompson observes how Behn 'recuperates the origins of the "Idea" of heaven itself'; *Love-Letters* frames her entrance into narrative as the necessary effect of a crisis attending the political workings of post-Hobbesian matter.'"Thou monarch of my Panting Soul": Hobbesian Obligation and the Durability of Romance in Aphra Behn's *Love-Letters*,' 116–17.

62 Melinda S. Zook draws a more tentative version of my conclusion: 'Behn may well have perceived – as did others – that James was pushing Protestant England to the brink of revolution.' 'Contextualizing Aphra Behn: Plays, Politics, and Party, 1679–1689,' *Women Writers and the Early Modern British Political Tradition*, ed. Hilda Smith (Cambridge: Cambridge University Press, 1995), 90. Paul Kléber Monod points out the dilemma facing Nonjuror royalists in 1688: 'Passive obedience and non-resistance were useless in dealing with a monarch like James II, who was determined to pursue unpopular policies that threatened the Church of England. The Nonjurors could not deny that James had a right to act as he did, but few of them could stomach his goal of reintegrating Roman Catholics into political life.' *Jacobitism and the English People, 1688–1788* (Cambridge: Cambridge University Press, 1989), 22.

63 *The Trial of Ford, Lord Grey of Werk*, 58.

64 Adee, *A Plot for the Crown*, 20.

65 Derek Hughes observes: 'Behn sees history as fragmented and delusive; particularly in works written as James II's reign, and her own life, drew to their close.' 'Aphra Behn and the Uses of History,' *The Female Wits: Women and Gender in Restoration Literature and Culture*, ed. Pilar Cuder Dominguez, Zenon Luis Martinez, and Juan Antonio Prieto Pablos (Huelva: Universidad de Huelva, 2006), 181.

66 Q.D. Leavis attributed this neutrality to inexperience on Behn's part: 'Her

touch is always light and cool. She is so innocent of literary devices that she never even seems to have decided whether she is writing comedy or tragedy; there is no poetic justice.' *Fiction and the Reading Public* (London: Chatto and Windus, 1932), 120. More recently, Ros Ballaster attributes it to the cynicism of the fallen world Behn describes, in which narrative can only imply 'the chaotic, haphazard, and contingent nature of desire, political, social and economic.' '"The story of the heart": *Love-Letters between a Noble-man and His Sister*,' *Cambridge Companion to Aphra Behn*, ed. Hughes and Todd, 149.

67 Behn, *Works*, 4:171.

68 Laura J. Rosenthal makes a similar claim in her reading of *Oroonoko*, linking the sophistication of Behn's narrative technique to the novel's 'subtle ironies,' which call into question the cultural and political agenda advanced by the novel's young narrator. Rosenthal, '*Oroonoko*: Reception, Ideology, Narrative Strategy,' *Cambridge Companion to Aphra Behn*, ed. Hughes and Todd, 164. Robert Markley observes the philosophical continuum linking *Oroonoko* and Behn's translation of Fontanelle: 'Any effort to assess her contribution to the history of the novel must consider the ways in which *Oroonoko* fits into a complex tradition of radical skepticism.' 'Global Analogies: Cosmology, Geosymmetry, and Skepticism in some Works of Aphra Behn,' 212.

69 Pollak, *Incest and the English Novel, 1684–1814*, 85.

3 The Secret History of Women's Political Desire, 1690–1714

1 Astell, *Some Reflections Upon Marriage, Occasion'd by the Duke & Duchess of Mazarine's Case; Which is also consider'd* (1700), 8.

2 Eve Tavor Bannet describes the period's condemnation of Anne's 'bedroom' politics: 'pamphlets and secret histories ... repeatedly represented the queen conducting government business in her bedroom and consulting her "bedroom" women about it – [she was] damned by associations of the sovereign's bedchamber with deception and ambition, as much as by virtue of the fact that it was not a closet.' '"Secret history": Or, talebearing inside and outside the secretorie,' *The Uses of History in Early Modern England*, ed. Pauline Kewes (San Marino, CA: Huntington Library, 2006), 386.

3 In tracing the gendered contours of the rise of the politics of oligarchy, my analysis of the period follows Jonathan Scott's reading of the Revolution of 1688/9: 'Parliaments might have won the religious and political struggle of the troubles, and with it the capacity to enshrine certain "liberties" in law, but against their power there was now no protection. This state ... was

one not of citizenship but subjection.' Scott, *England's Troubles: Seventeenth-Century English Political Instability in European Context* (Cambridge: Cambridge University Press, 2000), 496.

4 I take this phrase from Mark Goldie's account of 'the amphibious régimes of William and Anne.' 'The Political Thought of the Anglican Revolution,' *The Revolutions of 1688*, ed. Robert Beddard (Oxford: Oxford University Press, 1991), 104.

5 Stephens, *An Account of the Growth of Deism* (1696), 10. 'Far from "delivering" the Established Church from its time of troubles,' Robert Beddard argues, 'William of Orange plunged it headlong into internecine strife and partial disintegration.' 'The Unexpected Whig Revolution of 1688,' *The Revolutions of 1688*, 95.

6 On Anglican efforts to reconstitute 'the politically and religiously intolerant polity they had nurtured in the early 1680s,' see Mark Goldie, 'The Political Thought of the Anglican Revolution,' 135. After 1689, Dissenters were perceived by some as a more immediate threat to church integrity than the Catholics. Latitudinarians, Richard Ashcraft suggests, led the way in stirring up animosities and 'often served as the shock troops of persecution in the war against nonconformity.'Ashcraft, 'Latitudinarianism and Toleration: Historical Myth versus Political History,' *Philosophy, Science, and Religion in England, 1640–1700*, ed. Richard Kroll, Richard Ashcraft, and Perez Zagorin (Cambridge: Cambridge University Press, 1992), 160.

7 (Attribution uncertain, possibly Defoe), *A Dialogue Betwixt Whig and Tory, Aliàs Williamite and Jacobite. Wherein the Principles and Practices of each Party are fairly and impartially stated; that thereby Mistakes and Prejudices may be removed from amongst us, and all those who prefer English Liberty, and Protestant Religion, to French Slavery and Popery, may be inform'd how to choose fit and proper Instruments for our Preservation in these Times of Danger* (1693), 27–8.

8 Rose, *England in the 1690s: Revolution, Religion, and War* (London: Blackwell, 1999), 264. Mark Goldie and Clare Jackson trace the rise of Whig Jacobitism in the 1690s: 'Whig Jacobites denounced the Revolution as unfinished business: a defaced palimpsest of unfulfilled expectations and betrayed promises.' 'Williamite Tyranny and the Whig Jacobites,' *Redefining William III: The Impact of the King-Stadholder in International Context*, ed. Esther Mijers and David Onnekink (Burlington, VT: Ashgate, 2007), 181.

9 de Krey, 'Revolution *redivivus*: 1688–1689 and the Radical Tradition in Seventeenth-Century London Politics,' *The Revolution of 1688–89*, ed. Lois G. Schwoerer (Cambridge: Cambridge University Press, 1992), 216.

10 Gary S. de Krey argues that '"Protestant union" was abandoned for the sake of political union: the act of toleration accepted and institutional-

ized the mutual distrust of Anglicans and dissenters.' 'Reformation in
the Restoration Crisis, 1679–1682,' *Religion, Literature, and Politics in Post-
Reformation England, 1540–1688*, ed. Donna B. Hamilton and Richard Strier
(Cambridge: Cambridge University Press, 1996), 248.

11 *An Enquiry after Religion: Or, A View of the Idolatry, Superstition, Bigottry and
Hipocrisie of all Churches and Sects throughout the World* (1691), 17.

12 Ashcraft suggests this defensiveness was a product of 'deep-rooted fears
and prejudices directed against Catholicism,' 'Latitudinarianism and Toleration,' 152.

13 Locke, *A Letter Concerning Toleration*, trans. William Popple [1689], *A Letter
Concerning Toleration in Focus*, ed. John Horton and Susan Mendes (London: Routledge, 1991), 15–16. Interestingly, the debate over the church's
and state's relation to morality has been revived in the twenty-first century by a polemical sermon delivered by the archbishop of Canterbury,
Rowan Williams. Williams argues that in a polity governed by globaliza-
tion and multinational market economies, the Church of England needs to
assume, again, its central place in the life of the citizenry: 'In the heyday
of the welfarist nation state, there was a reasonable cause for saying that
public morality was taken for granted ... Because of its abandonment of
a clear morality for the public sphere, the market state is in danger of
linking its legitimacy ... to its ability to maximise varieties of personal
insurance.' William goes on to advocate the church as the guarantor of a
meaningful public sphere, a space that will enable 'telling a certain story,
witnessing to certain non-negotiable things about humanity and about
the context in which humanity lives. A really secular society would be one
where there were no more such spaces left.' 'The Richard Dimbleby
Lecture 2002,' Westminster School, London, 19 December 2002. http://
www.anglicancommunion.org/acns/articles/32/25/acns3236.html.

14 Isaacs, 'The Anglican Hierarchy and the Reformation of Manners, 1688–
1738,' *Journal of Ecclesiastical History* 33.3 (1982), 409. See also Rose, *England
in the 1690s*, 205–9.

15 Reformer John Dunton took up the issue of prostitution directly in *The
Night-Walker; or, Evening Rambles in Search after Lewd Women* (1696). In his
address to the Duchess of Cleveland in the October issue, Dunton warns:
'You may assure your self Madam, that those who record the Proceedings
of the present Age, will not miss to take notice of your self; N[ell] G[wyn]
and the D—ss of P[ortsmouth] as having been companions in Debauchery
to a certain P— now gone to his place; and there's no way to retrieve your
Honour, but by a publick Repentance, and leaving a Testimony behind
you to the World, that you abominate your former Course of Life ...'

'Epistle Dedicatory,' *The Night-Walker* (October 1696, n.p.) (New York: Garland, 1985). For commentary on Dunton's participation in the ideologies promoted by the Society for the Reformation of Manners see Laura J. Rosenthal, *Infamous Commerce: Prostitution in Eighteenth-Century British Literature and Culture* (Ithaca, NY: Cornell University Press, 2006), 52–7. The moral reformers eventually lost out to critics – most notably Mandeville – who refused to believe 'that the policing of personal morals was a central element of an effective politics of virtue.' Shelley Burtt, *Virtue Transformed: Political Argument in England, 1688–1740* (Cambridge: Cambridge University Press, 1992), 63.

16 Melinda S. Zook provides an excellent account of these two portraits in 'History's Mary: The Propagation of Queen Mary II, 1689–1694,' *Women and Sovereignty*, ed. Louise Olga Fradenburg (Edinburgh: Edinburgh University Press, 1992), 170–91. Rachel Weil also provides a detailed account of the symbolic uses to which Mary was put in the aftermath of the Revolution in 'Strange Paradox of Power: Images of Mary II,' in *Political Passions: Gender, the Family and Political Argument in England, 1680–1714* (Manchester: Manchester University Press, 1999), 105–20. My discussion draws attention to the religious elements at work in the representations Zook and Weil analyse. See also W.M. Spellman, 'Queen Mary II: Image and Substance during the Glorious Revolution,' *Political Rhetoric, Power, and Renaissance Women*, ed. Carole Levin and Patricia A. Sullivan (Albany, NY: State University of New York Press, 1995), 243–56. For a broader consideration of the religious aspect of Williamite ideology, see Tony Claydon, *William III and the Godly Revolution* (Cambridge: Cambridge University Press, 1996).

17 'An Ode on Her Highness, the Princess of Orange' (The Hague, 1688). 'A woman of deep, sometimes morbid piety, the Queen had been shocked by the state of the nation's religious life upon her return to England in 1689,' Rose notes. *England in the 1690s*, 203.

18 Burnet, BL Add MS 63057B, fol. 158.

19 By the King and Queen, *A Proclamation Against Vitious, Debauched, and Profane Persons* (21 January 1691/2). W.A. Speck imagines this providential historiography as Mary's psychological compensation for the betrayal of her father: 'The notion that God had weighed her father in the balance and found him wanting and that she and her husband were instruments to avenge divine wrath was psychologically crucial to reconcile her actions in the Revolution with her conscience.' 'William – and Mary?' *The Revolution of 1688–1689: Changing Perspectives*, ed. Lois G. Schwoerer (Cambridge: Cambridge University Press, 1992), 142.

20 Lloyd, *A Sermon Preached Before her Majesty, on May 29, being the Anniversary of the Restauration of the King and Royal Family* (1692), 11.

21 'A Poem on the Death of the Queen,' by a Gentlewoman of Quality (1694/5), 3; T.D'Urfey, *Gloriana. A Funeral Pindarique Poem: Sacred to the Blessed Memory of that Ever-admired and most Excellent Princess, Our Late Gracious Soveraign Lady Queen Mary* (1695), 19; T.N., Gent., 'A Poem on the Queen' (1695), 1; 'A Funeral Eclogue, Sacred to the Memory of Her Most Serene Majesty. Our Late Gracious Queen Mary' (1694/5), 7; and William Walsh, 'A Funeral Elegy Upon the Death of the Queen' (1695), 5.

22 John Cumming, *A Sermon Preached on Occasion of the Death of our late Gracious & Memorable Sovereign, Queen Mary* (1695), 15–16.

23 Burnet, *An Essay on the Memory of the Late Queen* (1696), 26–8.

24 Mark Knights observes that 'the differences in the ways Whigs and Tories wrote history or thought of the past, in the first age of party, are surprisingly few. Indeed, the partisans shared similar conspiratorial outlooks and anxieties about key words and slogans. Yet, the parties offered different interpretations.' 'The Tory Interpretation of History in the Rage of Parties,' *The Uses of History in Early Modern England*, 347.

25 'The Female Parricide,' *Poems on Affairs of State*, vol. 5, ed. William J. Cameron (New Haven, CT: Yale University Press, 1971), p. 157, l. 5; 'A Litany for the Reducing of Ireland,' *POAS*, vol. 5, p. 221, l. 41; Arthur Mainwairing, 'Tarquin and Tullia,' *POAS*, vol. 5, p. 52, ll. 111–12.

26 *A Collection of the Best Poems, Lampoons, Songs, & Satyrs from the Revolution 1688 to 1692* (manuscript), 13.

27 Behn, 'A Congratulatory Poem on Her Sacred Majesty Queen Mary upon Her Arrival in England' (1689), ll. 62, 95, 99. *Works*, ed. Janet Todd (London: William Pickering and Chatto; Columbus: Ohio State University Press, 1992–6), 1:294–9.

28 Weil, *Political Passions*, 148.

29 Nathaniel Crouch, *The Secret History, of the Last Four Monarchs of Great Britain: Viz. James I, Charles I, Charles II, James II, To which is added, An Appendix, Containing the Later Reign of James the Second* (1693), 61.

30 *Amours of the Sultana of Barbary, a Novel in Two Parts* (1689), 53.

31 *Secret History of the Dutchess of Portsmouth: Giving an Account of the Intreagues of the Court, during her Ministry. And of the Death of K.C.II* (1690), 132.

32 David Jones, *Secret History of Whitehall, From the Restoration of Charles II. Down to the Abdication of the late K. James* (1697), 79–80.

33 *Love Letters between Polydorus and Messalina, Late Queen of Albion* (1689), 39–40. *The Second Part of the Amours of Messalina Late Queen of Albion*.

Wherein the Secret Court Intrigues of the Four last Years Reign are furthur pur-sued; Particularly the Imposture of the Child. By a Woman of Quality, a Late Confidant of Q. Messalina (attrib. Gregorio Leti) (1689), 61.

34 *The Amours of the Sultana of Barbary. A Novel in Two Parts* (1689), 15–16.

35 *The Secret History of the Dutchess of Portsmouth: Giving an Account of the In-treagues of the Court, during her Ministry. And of the Death of K.C.II* (1690), 76.

36 Bannet, '"Secret history": Or, talebearing inside and outside the secretorie,' 387.

37 Patterson, 'Marvell and Secret History,' *Marvell and Liberty,* ed. Warren Chernaik and Martin Dzelnais (London: Macmillan Press, 1999), 46. More literary accounts of the secret history genre, to which I will return below, appear in Michael McKeon, *The Origins of the English Novel, 1600–1740* (Baltimore: The Johns Hopkins University Press, 2002), 54–5; John Richetti, *Popular Fiction before Richardson: Narrative Patterns, 1700–1739* (Oxford: Clarendon Press, 1969), chapter 4; Jerry C. Beasley, *Novels of the 1740s* (Athens, GA: University of Georgia Press, 1982), 53–4.

38 Mayer, *History and the Early English Novel: Matters of Fact from Bacon to De-foe* (Cambridge: Cambridge University Press, 1997), 111.

39 Ibid., 153.

40 Duke of Buckingham, John Sheffield, *The character of Charles II, King of Eng-land, with a short account of his being poyson'd* (1696), 6–7.

41 Ogg, *England in the Reigns of James II and William III* (Oxford: Clarendon Press, 1955), 537.

42 Two excellent accounts of Queen Anne's reign place their emphases else-where: Toni Bowers traces Anne's attempts to identify herself as a symbol-ic mother of the nation after the death of her last surviving child. Unable to expand maternal codes into indices of an inherent right to rule, Queen Anne found herself on the defensive, arguing her own legitimacy in the face of patriarchal conventions that failed to recognize her political con-tribution to the nation's future. Bowers, 'Queen Anne Makes Provision,' *Refiguring Revolutions: Aesthetics and Politics from the English Revolution to the Romantic Revolution,* ed. Kevin Sharpe and Steven N. Zwicker (Berkeley and Los Angeles: University of California Press, 1998), 57–74. Rachel Weil views Anne's difficulties through the lens of England's transition from pre-modern to modern forms of political authority and focuses her attention on the debilitating scandals surrounding Anne's intimate relations with the women of her court. Weil, *Political Passions,* 162–86.

43 *Memoirs of Sarah, Duchess of Malborough together with her Characters of her Contemporaries and her Opinions* (1742) (London: Routledge, 1830), ed. Wil-liam King (New York: Kraus Reprint, 1969), 5.

44 'A New Ballad to the Tune of Fair Rosamund,' quoted in David Brontë Green, *Sarah Duchess of Marlborough* (New York: Scribner, 1967), 322.

45 *Tudor and Stuart Proclamations: 1485–1714* (no. 4814, 26 March 1702), calendared by Robert Steele. 2 vols (Oxford: Clarendon, 1910), 1:518.

46 *A Collection of Queen Anne's Speeches, Messages, &c. From Her Accession to the Throne, to Her Demise* (1714), 7.

47 Wilson, *The Importance of the Reign of Queen Anne in English Church History* (Oxford: Blackwell, 1911), 35.

48 Swift, of course, provides the most well-known literary response to Anne's religious attachments and the religious controversies of the period in *Tale of a Tub* and book 1 of *Gulliver's Travels*.

49 *A Collection of Queen Anne's Speeches, Messages, &c. From her Accession to the Throne, to Her Demise* (1714), 19.

50 Speech to Parliament, 5 April 1710. *Collection*, 37.

51 Bowers, 'Queen Anne Makes Provision,' *Refiguring Revolutions*, 60.

52 Bowers, *The Politics of Motherhood: British Writing and Culture* (Cambridge: Cambridge University Press, 1996), 75–89.

53 Harley MS 6914, f. 106.

54 Quoted (and modernized) in Weil, *Political Passions*, 206; original reprinted in Appendix III, Green, *Sarah Duchess of Marlborough*, 318–21.

55 *A Collection of all the Dialogues Written by Mr. Thomas Brown* (1704), A2.

56 Thomas Brown, *A Continuation or Second Part of the Letters from the Dead to the Living* (1703), 160–1.

57 Robert ('Beau') Feilding, 'An Elegy On the Death of the Dutchess of Cleveland, who Died on Sunday Night last October, 9, 1709. At her House in Chiswick, in the 65th Year of her Age' (1709).

58 Brown, *Continuation*, 307–8.

59 *Memoirs*, ed. King, 192. On the correspondence between Anne and Mary regarding Sarah Churchill, see Frances Harris, *A Passion for Government: The Life of Sarah, Duchess of Malborough* (Oxford: Clarendon Press, 1991), 44.

60 Indeed, the particular kind of power-mongering that the narrative describes speaks not so much to a particular 'Whig' ideology (the Churchills had earlier associated themselves with moderate Tories), as to a system of power that E.P. Thompson sees emerging, after 1688, among 'great agrarian magnates, privileged merchant capitalists, and their hangers-on, who manipulated the organs of the State in their own private interest ... It should be seen less as government by aristocracy ... than as a *parasitism*.' 'The Peculiarities of the English,' *Socialist Register* (1965), 322–3.

61 J.A. Downie has written a persuasive account for rethinking the usual attribution of *Queen Zarah* to Delarivier Manley: 'What if Delarivier Manley

Did *Not* Write *The Secret History of Queen Zarah*?' *The Library: The Transactions of the Bibliographic Society* 5.3 (2004): 247–64. Rachel Carnell has
recently expanded upon Downie's thesis and supports his arguments for
identifying Joseph Browne as a more likely candidate for authorship. Despite the evidence Downie and Carnell provide, I believe there are good
reasons to think Manley wrote this narrative. First, Manley's intimate
knowledge of the Duchess of Cleveland means that she had a wealth of
detail upon which to draw her in her representation of the young Sarah
Jennings, John Churchill, and Barbara Villiers. Second, neither Carnell nor
Downie can explain, to my satisfaction, why Manley did not protest the
attribution of *Zarah* to her in 1711: 'The fact that Manley seems not to have
publicly protested against the 1711 title page of *Queen Zarah* could mean
that she simply did not notice the work's appearance.' Carnell, *A Political
Biography of Delarivier Manley* (London: Pickering and Chatto, 2008), 142.
Third, I disagree with Downie's claim that the work 'is entirely committed to party politics, rather than sexual politics' (262). As the reading that
follows shows, these two realms of 'politicking' are very closely related.
Finally, I find the similarities between this work and *The New Atalantis*
striking. However, Downie and Carnell have made a convincing argument
against attribution based on other factors, and because I am uncertain, my
argument does not figure Manley into its analysis of the text, to which I
refer only as '*Zarah*.' For a defence of a Manley attribution, see Ruth Her-
man, *The Business of a Woman: The Political Writings of Delarivier Manley*
(Newark: University of Delaware Press, 2003), 63–5.

I am concerned that this narrative's de-attribution could lead to its critical neglect. J.A. Downie describes *Zarah* as a 'much less accomplished performance than the *New Atalantis*' (263), and Carnell notes: 'The impression
is given, especially in the second part, of a work cobbled together with
ever increasing haste' (143). *Zarah* strikes me as a spirited and engaging
contribution to the political debates of the eighteenth century's first
decade.

62 *The Second Part, or a Continuation of the Secret History of Queen Zarah, and the
Zarazians; Being a Looking-glass for —— in the Kingdom of Albigion. Faithfully
Translated from the Italian Copy now lodg'd in the Vatican at Rome, and never
before Printed in any Language*, ed. Patricia Köster, *The Novels of Mary Delarivier Manley 1705–1714* (Gainsville, FL: Scholars' Facsimiles and Reprints,
1971), 1:138 (Future references will be marked parenthetically by page
number to this volume. Parts I and II of *Queen Zarah* take up pp. 1–262 of
volume 1. Another, more readily available edition of the first part of *Queen
Zarah* appears in *Popular Fiction by Women, 1660–1730: An Anthology*, ed.

Paula Backscheider and John Richetti (Oxford: Clarendon Press, 1996), 45–80).

63 This act moved to bar nonconformists from taking communion in the Anglican Church only occasionally, a practice which enabled many leading Dissenters to hold public office. The Act of Occasional Conformity was defeated twice in 1703 (January and December) and again in 1704; it eventually passed in 1711.

64 [William Cobbett] *Cobbett's Parliamentary History of England. From the Norman Conquest, in 1066, to the Year 1803.* 36 vols. (London: R. Bagshaw, 1810), 6:335.

65 See Frances Harris, *A Passion for Government: The Life of Sarah, Duchess of Marlborough* (Oxford: Clarendon Press, 1991), 19–25. Harris notes that Sarah Jenyns had her mother sent away from court when she perceived Mrs Jenyns might prove an obstacle in her pursuit of John Churchill.

66 John J. Richetti, *Popular Fiction before Richardson*, 132.

67 McDowell notes that Sarah Churchill 'was ahead of her time in recognizing the "public" as an increasingly important conceptual entity in British political life.' *Women of Grub Street*, 270.

68 Here (and through to the passage ending 'it is high time, after this long Digression') *Zarah* draws on Abbé Morvan de Bellegarde's *Lettres Curieuses de littérature et de morale*, from which the work's preface is also lifted. Rachel Carnell has analysed the significance of the adaptation of Bellegarde's work for volume 2 of *Zarah* in 'More Borrowing from Bellegarde in Delarivier Manley's *Queen Zarah and the Zarazians*,' *Notes and Queries* 51.4 (winter 2004): 377–9. In this particular passage (and elsewhere in *Zarah*), the author pauses to make an interjection regarding female character that is not in Bellegarde's original: another reason, to my mind, to think that Manley may have authored this text.

69 Arthur Mainwaring to Sarah Churchill (19 January 1710), BL Add MS 61460, fol. 165; Blenheim E25.

70 Bucholz, *The Augustan Court: Queen Anne and the Decline of Court Culture* (Stanford: Stanford University Press, 1993), 250–1.

71 Kirkpatrick, *Advice to Protestants: Being a Prefatory Address to all Her Majesty's Protestant Subjects* (Dublin, 1714), 8–9.

72 Gilburt Burnet, *The New Preface and Additional Chapter to the Third Edition of the Pastoral Care* (1713), 6.

73 G.V. Bennett claims that the High Church moment extinguished itself in the Sacheverell riots, despite the hopes that attended the Tory victory of 1710: 'In spite of her new Tory ministers and her gracious expressions of favour for the clergy, it was unreal and fanciful to imagine that Anne was

about to inaugurate a period of Anglican reaction. One facet of her character was an acid dislike of factious clergymen or of any discord in religion.' 'Conflict in the Church,' *Britain after the Glorious Revolution, 1689–1714*, ed. Geoffrey Holmes (London: Macmillan, 1969), 167.

74 Anon., *The Life, Character, and Death of the most Illustrious Pattern of Female Virtue, the Lady Jane Gray, Who was Beheaded in the Tower at 16 Years of Age, for her stedfast Adherence to the Protestant Religion* (1714), 9. Eighteenth-century authors use 'Gray,' but the *DNB* uses 'Grey.' The first edition of this text, housed at the British Library, has written in manuscript below the last line of the title, 'a damned Lye'; the same hand also notes Dudley as co-conspirator alongside Grey, thus refusing the gendered import of the narrative.

Interestingly, the story had been retold twenty years earlier, in John Banks's *The Innocent Usurper; or, the Death of the Lady Jane Gray. A Tragedy* (pub. 1694). But at that time, the play did not escape the censor's notice, who probably detected the possibility of the play being read as a critique of Mary II. It was never performed in this period. For a brief discussion of this play, see Robert Hume's *The Development of English Drama in the Late Seventeenth Century* (Oxford: Clarendon Press, 1976), 217.

75 'To the Countess of Salisbury,' *The Force of Religion; or, Vanquish'd Love* (1715), n.p.

76 Gildon, *Remarks on Mr. Rowe's Tragedy of the Lady Jane Gray, and all his other Plays* (1715), 10, 12; Anon., *Remarks on the Tragedy of the Lady Jane Gray: in a Letter to Mr. Rowe* (1715), 19. For an insightful study of Nicholas Rowe's *Lady Jane Gray* and *Jane Shore* see Jean I. Marsden, *Fatal Desire: Women, Sexuality, and the English Stage, 1660–1720* (Ithaca, NY: Cornell University Press, 2006). Of the intersection of Rowe's Whig affiliations and the sexual politics of *Jane Shore*, Brett Wilson observes: 'At issue in Rowe's Whiggish tragedy is the signification of Jane's body, whose feminine gender must remain intact to serve as an index of her mistreatment, but whose sexuality must be wiped out to keep her a figure of sympathetic identification.' 'Jane Shore and the Jacobites: Nicholas Rowe, the Pretender, and the National She-Tragedy,' *ELH* 72.4 (2005), 835.

77 For a full account of the reception history of the Jane Shore story, see Maria M. Scott, *Re-presenting 'Jane' Shore: Harlot and Heroine* (Aldershot: Ashgate, 2005).

78 Preface,*The Unfortunate Concubines: The History of Fair Rosamond, Mistress to Henry II; and Jane Shore, Concubine to Edward IV; Kings of England. Shewing how they came to be so. With Their Lives, Remarkable Actions, and Unhappy Ends* (1708), ii–iii.

79 *The Life and Death of Jane Shore; Containing the whole Account of her Amorous Intrigues with King Edward the IVth. And the Lord Hastings: Her Penitence, Punishment and Poverty.* (1714), 10.

80 John Dunton, *King Abigail: or, The Secret Reign of the She-Favorite, Detected and Applied; in a Sermon Upon these Words, 'And Women rule over them'* (1715), 'To the Reader,' A2. Future references will be cited parenthetically. This John Dunton is the moral reformer whose commentary on prostitution was noted above (see note 15).

4 'A House Divided'

1 Benjamin Hoadly, *The Nature of the Kingdom, or Church, of Christ* (1717), 7.
2 For a detailed account of the Bangorian crisis, see Andrew Starkie, *The Church of England and the Bangorian Controversy, 1716–1721* (Woodbridge, Suffolk: Boydell Press, 2007). See also Edwin R. Bingham, 'The Political Apprenticeship of Benjamin Hoadly,' *Church History* 16.3 (1947): 154–65; Gerald B. Switzer, 'The Suppression of Convocation in the Church of England,' *Church History* 1.3 (1932): 150–62; and the inflammatory essay on Hoadly by Herbert M. Vaughan, in Vaughan, *From Anne to Victoria: Fourteen Biographical Studies between 1702 and 1901* (Port Washington, NY: Kennikat Press, 1931), 56–71. Vaughan describes Hoadly as a 'mean, cringing, pompous, unpleasant personage,' one of the first 'ecclesiastical cormorants' of the eighteenth century, whose work threatened 'to reduce the whole Christian Church to the level of the Mohammedan Faith' (71, 70, 63). The influence of Hoadly on Defoe's work has been traced by Maximillian E. Novak, 'Sincerity, Delusion, and Character in the Fiction of Defoe and the "Sincerity Crisis" of his Time,' *Augustan Studies: Essays in Honor of Irvin Ehrenpreis*, ed. Douglas Lane Patey and Timothy Keegan (Newark: University of Delaware Press, 1985), 109–26. Novak claims that 'it was the Bangorian Controversy and the debate over sincerity that turned Defoe toward a type of fiction that fused a vivid presentation of a real world of things, people, and events with a focus on the inner life' (123). Paula Backscheider briefly touches on Defoe's relation to Hoadly in her review essay, 'Firing off the Canon,' *Novel: A Forum on Fiction* 24.1 (1990): 115–18.
3 Novak makes this point: 'What was most startling was the way in which the battle between bishops of the Church of England was carried forth in the daily press. There may have been a precedent for the use of newspapers for this purpose but none comes easily to mind.' '*A Vindication of the Press*' and the Defoe Canon,' *Studies in English Literature, 1500–1900* 27.3 (1987): 402.

4 Novak discusses this incident in 'Defoe, the Occult, and the Deist Offensive during the Reign of George I,' *Deism, Masonry, and the Enlightenment: Essays Honoring Alfred Owen Aldridge*, ed. J.A. Leo Lamay (Newark: University of Delaware Press; London: Associated University Presses, 1987), 93–108.

5 Defoe, *A Short View of the Present State of the Protestant Religion in Britain as It is now profest in the Episcopal Church in England, the Presbyterian Church in Scotland, and the Dissenters in Both* (Edinburgh 1707), 25.

6 Defoe, *The Pernicious Consequences of the Clergy's Intermedling with Affairs of State: with Reasons Humbly offer'd for passing a Bill to Incapicitate them from the Like Practice for the Future* [1714], 29.

7 Novak, *Daniel Defoe: Master of Fictions* (Oxford: Oxford University Press, 2001), 524.

8 Starr, *Defoe and Spiritual Autobiography* (Princeton, NJ: Princeton University Press, 1965), xi.

9 Novak argues 'Defoe participated in these controversies mainly in an ironic, mocking role. Although he mainly agreed with Hoadly and defended him, he also noted that the Dissenters had held similar ideas about sincerity for decades' ('The Deist Offensive,' 95). I suggest that this ironic mode finds expression as a Protestant scepticism in Defoe's fiction.

10 My interest in thinking about the political and economic as mutually constitutive terms in Defoe follows Carol Kay's lead: 'The economic power that so many critics have thought to be Defoe's only concern was chiefly interesting to him as a means to political power.' *Political Constructions: Defoe, Richardson, and Sterne in Relation to Hobbes, Hume, and Burke* (Ithaca, NY: Cornell University Press, 1988), 13.

11 Faller, *Crime and Defoe: A New Kind of Writing* (Cambridge: Cambridge University Press, 1993), 244.

12 Defoe, *Roxana* (1724), ed. David Blewett (London: Penguin, 1982), 104–5. Future references will be cited parenthetically.

13 I agree with John Richetti's claim that 'the organizing narrative premise of Defoe's *Roxana* is the unbridgeable gap between the private confessional mode of the narrative and the public world in which the heroine has made her name and fortune ... The resulting subjectivity is in effect quite spooky, incommunicable except in the silent reading world of her narrative.' 'The Public Sphere and the Eighteenth-Century Novel: Social Criticism and Narrative Enactment,' *Eighteenth-Century Life* 16.3 (1992): 121.

14 Novak first made this point; see *Realism, Myth, and History in Defoe's Fiction* (Lincoln: University of Nebraska Press, 1983), 115. It seems fitting that the cover of the Penguin edition of the novel features a portrait of the Duchess of Portsmouth, rather than of Nell Gwyn. Gwyn's popularization was

furthered, in the years Defoe's career spanned, by publications such as
Joke Upon Joke (1721), which includes verses on Nell Gwyn, and Alexander
Smith's 'Nell Gwin, Concubine to King Charles II,' *The School of Venus, or,
Cupid Restor'd to Sight; being a History of Cuckolds and Cuckold Makers* (1716).
Etherege's poems, 'Madam Nelly's Complaint' and 'The Lady of Pleasure:
A Satyr' appeared in *The Works of George Villiers … Duke of Buckingham*
(1715).

15 Defoe, *Royal Religion; Being some Enquiry after the Piety of Princes. With Remarks on a Book, Entituled, A Form of Prayers us'd by King William* (1704), 20.

16 *The Letters of Daniel Defoe*, ed. George Harris Healey (Oxford: Clarendon
Press, 1955), 45.

17 Charles II announced his patronage of Huguenot refugees fleeing France
in 1681, even before Louis XIV's revocation of the Edict of Nantes in 1685.
Bernard Cottret has noted that during this period, 'to express sympathy
for the poor refugees ... became in England a mark of good citizenship and
devotion to the Protestant cause.' Cottret, *The Huguenots in England: Immigration and Settlement c. 1550–1700* (Cambridge: Cambridge University
Press, 1985), 187. On their side, Huguenots served as 'England's cultural
intermediaries' in their capacity as translators and commentators on European culture and politics. Graham C. Gibbs, 'Huguenot Contributions
to England's Intellectual Life, and England's Intellectual Commerce with
Europe, c. 1680–1720,' *Huguenots in Britain and Their French Background,
1550–1800*, ed. Irene Scouloudi (London: Macmillan, 1987), 35. Nonetheless, the appeal of an international Protestant identity did not always overcome the fear of French incursions into English culture, and Huguenots
were often identified as closeted Catholics trying to take advantage of
English hospitality. They were caught in the wave of anti-French sentiment
that swept over England between 1679 and 1681, a feeling sharpened by
economic rivalry and jealousy over the Huguenots' commercial acumen.
Eveline Cruickshanks observes that Restoration Tories viewed the Huguenots as 'the scum of all Europe.' 'Religion and Royal Succession: The Rage
of Party,' *Britain in the First Age of Party, 1680–1750: Essays Presented to Geoffrey Holmes*, ed. Clyve Jones (London: Hambledon Press, 1987), 22.

The Huguenots' plight in France also drew attention to the more general
problem of religious toleration. English denunciations of French persecutions could readily be turned back on their speakers in light of England's
anti-Catholic laws. If the English government often proved lax in enforcing
these laws, public sentiment in the 1680s was moving in the opposite direction in anticipation of James II's reign as a Catholic monarch. For many
defenders of anti-Catholic policy (including some prominent Huguenot
figures), the issue was uncomplicated, with Protestantism standing for a

higher principle of freedom. But many writers of the period recognized the special challenge posed by the Huguenot refugees. We witness English unease with recent Huguenot arrivals in one contemporary account: 'Jacques Dugua, having come recently from France, according to him for religious reasons, buried his wife two weeks ago and has nevertheless married a young English woman with whom he can't converse.' ('Jacques Dugua etant venu depuis peu de France a ce qu'il dit pour la religion ... enterra sa femme il y a quinze jours & s'est neamoins marié deja à une fille Angloise a qui il ne sauroit parler.') *Livres d'actes de 1679 à 1692* (MS 7), 87. From the Library of the French Protestant Church of London, Soho Square. Translation mine.

18 Watt, *Rise of the Novel: Studies in Defoe, Richardson, and Fielding* (1957) (London: Pimlico, 2000), 80.

19 Marvell, 'Last Instructors to a Painter,' ll. 895–8, *Poems and Letters of Andrew Marvell*, 3rd ed., vol. 1, H.M. Margoliouth (Oxford: Clarendon Press, 1952), 141–65.

20 *The Letters of Daniel Defoe*, ed. George Harris Healey (Oxford: Clarendon Press, 1955), 36.

21 Steven Pincus and Peter Lake note the connection between the seventeenth-century French and English states: 'The French and Jacobite states were ... decidedly new and in their own ways decidedly modern. They had the resources to fight wars on a scale unimaginable in the sixteenth century; they had new mechanisms to manipulate and agitate public opinion (the newly extensive post office, for example); and they had large bureaucracies that professionalized and nationalized governance.' 'Rethinking the Public Sphere in Early Modern England,' *Journal of British Studies* 45.2 (2006): 287.

22 For an extremely insightful reading of the Jew, and the ways in which Roxana's characterization draws on anti-Semitic discourses, see Laura J. Rosenthal, 'Whore, Turk, and Jew: Defoe's *Roxana*,' *Infamous Commerce: Prostitution in Eighteenth-Century British Literature and Culture* (Ithaca, NY: Cornell University Press, 2006), 70–96.

23 Flynn, *The Body in Swift and Defoe* (Cambridge: Cambridge University Press, 1990), 82.

24 William Law observed: 'I will no more say your Lordship is in the interest of the Quakers, or Socinians, or Papists, than I would charge you with being in the interest of the Church of England, for as your doctrines equally support them all, he ought to ask your Lordship's pardon, who should declare you more a friend to one than the other.' *William Law's Defence of Church Principles: Three Letters to the Bishop of Bangor, 1717–1719,*

ed. J.O. Nash and Charles Gore, 2nd ed. (Edinburgh: John Grant, 1909), 146.

25 'Libertine,' *Oxford English Dictionary Online* (Oxford University Press, 2005). http://dictionary.oed.com (6/22/09).

26 Anon., c. 1687. London BL Add. MS 32,095, fols 363–80. From the Malet Collection. State Papers and Historical Documents 1087–1762.

27 Aravamudan, *Tropicopolitans: Colonialism and Agency, 1688–1804* (Durham: Duke University Press, 1999), 37–8.

28 For an excellent reading of Mignard's portrait of the Duchess of Portsmouth, see Joseph Roach, *Cities of the Dead: Circum-Atlantic Performance* (New York: Columbia University Press, 1996), 127–30. See also Kim F. Hall's readings of the Restoration courtesan portraits featuring black attendants: *Things of Darkness: Economies of Race and Gender in Early Modern England* (Ithaca, NY: Cornell University Press, 1995), 247–53. Sander Gilman has traced the evolution of representations of the black servant forward from the eighteenth to the nineteenth century. See 'Black Bodies, White Bodies: Toward an Iconography of Female Sexuality in Late Nineteenth-Century Art, Medicine, and Literature,' *Critical Inquiry* 12.1 (autumn 1985), 204–42.

29 The National Portrait Gallery chose not to buy the painting in 1995, when it came on to the art market. One practical reason for the Gallery's decision may have been the portrait's size: at 90 × 70 inches, it would have dwarfed the small room that houses portraits of Charles and James II in the Gallery.

30 Susan Shifrin undertakes a reading of Mancini's representations as Cleopatra in '"Subdued by a Famous Roman Dame": Picturing Foreignness, Notoriety, and Prerogative in the Portraits of Hortense Mancini, Duchess of Mazarin,' *Politics, Transgression, and Representation at the Court of Charles II*, ed. Julia Marciari Alexander and Catharine MacLeod (New Haven, CT: Yale University Press, 2007), 145–51. 'The Dutchess of Mazarines Farewel to England' (1680) refers to Mazarin as '*Egypts* Queen' (2).

31 Shifrin, '"Subdued by a Famous Roman Dame,"'166.

32 *Poems on Affairs of State*, vol. 2, ed. Elias F. Mengel, Jr (New Haven, CT: Yale University Press, 1965), p. 225, ll. 154–7. For an account of Gennari's own description of the Moors' presence in the portrait and the racialization of the Diana/Achtaeon iconography that governs the painting, see Shifrin, 'A Copy of My Countenance,' 201.

33 'Colin,' *Poems on Affairs of State*, vol. 2, p. 172, ll. 82–3.

34 For speculation regarding Mancini's possible collaboration in the portrait's composition, see Shifrin, 'A Copy of my Countenance,' 202.

35 Shawn Lisa Maurer explores the significance of Clayton's Amazonian al-

lusion in '"I wou'd be a *Man-Woman"*: *Roxana*'s Amazonian Threat to the Ideology of Marriage,' *Texas Studies in Literature and Language* 46.3 (fall 2004): 363–86. Unlike Maurer, I read Defoe's representation of the Amazonian figure in a positive light.

36 The connection between the Ottoman Empire and the French despotism so often associated with Louise de Kéroualle was well established by the early eighteenth century. Among the arguments used against Louis XIV in the years after 1689 was that of the French king 'as a "Great Turk." This became possible because the last substantial Ottoman incursion into Europe coincided with Louis' aggression.' Tony Claydon, *Europe and the Making of England, 1660–1760* (Cambridge: Cambridge University Press, 2007), 172.

37 Nussbaum, *Torrid Zones*, 36. In referring to subjects of the Ottoman Empire under the generic term of 'Turk,' Defoe follows an early modern English xenophobic tradition: 'many of the figures – whether real historical people or literary characters – referred to as "Turks" were not Turks in any sense, but rather Muslims, European converts, or characters from just about anywhere who behaved in certain ways.' Gerald Maclean, *Looking East: English Writing and the Ottoman Empire before 1800* (London: Palgrave Macmillan, 2007), 8. On representations of the Turk in early modern England, see Nabil Matar, *Turks, Moors, and Englishmen in the Age of Discovery* (New York: Columbia University Press, 1999) and also Matar's *Islam in Britain, 1558–1685* (Cambridge: Cambridge University Press, 1998).

38 Carol Houlihan Flynn has suggested that the Turkish women captured by the Maltese ship 'were already subordinated to the demands of the seraglio,' and the sexual power Roxana inherits from them represents 'the confined freedom of the seraglio where women are locked up the better to display their charms.' *The Body in Swift and Defoe* (Cambridge: Cambridge University Press, 1990), 84.

39 Some of the works representing 'Roxana's' that circulated in England include: Madeleine de Scudéry's *Ibrahim, or the Illustrious Bassa* (1652), Gauthier de Costes de la Calprenède's *Cassandra* (1652), William Davenant's *Siege of Rhodes* (1659), Nathaniel Lee's *The Rival Queens* (1677), Racine's *Bajazet* (1672, adapted by Charles Johnson in 1717 as *The Sultaness*), and Montesquieu's *Persian Letters* (1722). Petulant, in Act I, scene i, of Congreve's *Way of the World*, refers to 'Roxolanas' as a plural common noun meaning 'courtesans.' Female authority was associated with the Ottoman state in a more general sense, as well. Gerald Maclean notes that the seventeenth-century Ottoman Empire fascinated the English in part because it witnessed 'the so-called "reign of the women" under Valide Kösem.' *Looking East*, 217. For a detailed account of the history of 'Roxane's' place in the

English imagination, see Ros Ballaster, 'Performing *Roxane*: The Oriental Woman as the Sign of Luxury in Eighteenth-Century Fictions,' *Luxury in the Eighteenth Century: Debates, Desires and Delectable Goods*, ed. Maxine Berg and Elizabeth Eger (New York: Palgrave Macmillan, 2003), 165–77.

40 Novak has observed that Restoration debates over the Ottoman siege of Vienna set a young Defoe against the Whigs who wanted to see the Ottoman rulers, and their Protestant Hungarian allies, defeat the Roman Catholic Austrian monarchy. *Daniel Defoe: Master of Fictions*, 65–6.

41 Felicity Nussbaum describes this moment as the culmination of Roxana's self-alienation. *Torrid Zones*, 36.

42 *Oxford English Dictionary Online* (Oxford University Press, 2005). http://dictionary.oed.com (6/21/09).

43 Novak turns to the representation of anal intercourse in satiric characterizations of Charles II's relationship with Louise de Kéroualle as a possible source for Defoe's representation of Roxana's sexual practices. See 'The Unmentionable and Ineffable in Defoe's Fiction,' *Studies in the Literary Imagination* 15 (1982): 85–102. We can make a more general observation – that anal intercourse and vaginal intercourse with a prostitute conventionally amount to the same thing in the popular imagination of the period: the death of the subject's social coherence. In his reading of the eighteenth-century fascination with anal eroticism, Cameron McFarlane analyses the period's representation of the sodomite as 'a terrifying and unnatural figure bent on the destruction of the social order,' a characterization that could equally apply to the figure of the prostitute. McFarlane, *The Sodomite in Fiction and Satire, 1660–1750* (New York: Columbia University Press, 1997), 106.

44 Cynthia Wall, 'Gendering Rooms: Domestic Architecture and Literary Acts,' *Eighteenth-Century Fiction* 5.4 (1993): 354.

45 As Leo Bersani has observed in his reading of nineteenth- and twentieth-century representations of prostitutes, convention deems that: 'Prostitutes publicize (indeed, sell) the inherent aptitude of women for uninterrupted sex.' 'Is the Rectum a Grave?' *October* 43 (1987): 211.

46 *The Diary of John Evelyn*, ed. E.S. DeBeer, 6 vols. *Kalendarium, 1650–1672*, 1–5 March, 1671 (Oxford: Clarendon Press, 1955), 3:573.

47 The moment that Roxana's client finds Amy in bed with his mistress plays out this possibility: 'how do I know what *Amy* is?' he asks, 'It may be Mr. *Amy* for all I know' (228).

48 Earlier in the narrative, Roxana initiates her sexual relationship with the Dutch merchant (a prostitute/client relationship, unbeknownst to him) by leaving her door unlatched: 'I shut my Door, that is, latch'd it, for I seldom

lock'd or bolted it, and went to-Bed; I had not been in-Bed a Minute, but he comes in his Gown, to the Door, and opens it a little way' (182).

49 For an account of the illicit activities of Charles II's page of the bedchamber, William Chiffinch, see the *DNB* entry on Chiffinch: http://www .oxforddnb.com/view/article/5281. *Oxford Dictionary of National Biography* (Oxford University Press, 2004–7).

50 *Review*, 11 June 1713, vol. I [ix], p. 214.

51 This doubling back in the narrative echoes a larger temporal doubling that structures the novel. Roxana names 1683 as the year of her arrival in England as a young Huguenot child; but her performance in front of the king, when she is approaching middle age, occurs in the same decade. The effect is the creation of a religious/sexual palimpsest twice marked 'Restoration.' Ros Ballaster observes: 'If this inconsistency produces a rent in the realist fabric of the text, it serves to bring together two periods of ostentatious luxury with very different class associations.' 'Performing *Roxane*,' 166.

52 Here my argument follows that advanced by Felicity Nussbaum: 'The impossibility of reconciling maternity with sexual freedom is painfully clear in *Roxana*.' *Torrid Zones*, 40. Toni Bowers also traces the powerful conflict that emerges in the novel's concluding pages between the imperatives of economic authority and maternal responsibility: 'Motherhood threatens Roxana's survival, but so does maternal abdication. There is no escape.' *The Politics of Motherhood: British Writing and Culture, 1680–1760* (Cambridge: Cambridge University Press, 1996), 116. Historically, this conflict was not always so: James Turner notes the case of Catherine Sedley, who began her career as a mistress, but then married well. She remarked to her sons: 'if any body call either of you the son of a whore, you must bear it for you are so, but if they call you bastards, fight till you die.' Quoted in Turner, *Libertines and Radicals in Early Modern London: Sexuality, Politics and Literary Culture, 1630–1685* (Cambridge: Cambridge University Press, 2001), 250.

53 In reading against the idea of Roxana's disastrous relationship with her daughter as the punishment Defoe wants to inflict on his heroine, I am reading in the same vein as John Richetti, who argues that 'Roxana remains existentially free for us as readers in a special way by running deliberately into her own moral-psychological necessity.' *Defoe's Narratives: Situation and Structures* (Oxford: Clarendon Press, 1975), 226.

54 Jesse Molesworth notes that 'Susan's hunger for narrative consequence reveals itself in an obsession with the details of Roxana's story.' '"A Dreadful Course of Calamities": *Roxana's* Ending Reconsidered,' *ELH* 74.2 (2007): 500. It will become clear, in what follows, that I do not, as a reader, have

much sympathy for Roxana's daughter; nor do I think Defoe imagines that her quest is 'natural,' outside of the fact that Susan does not consciously understand herself to be involved in a complex struggle for power. In refusing the daughter's claims, I am resisting readings advanced by critics such as Lincoln B. Faller, who argues that 'Roxana's daughter loves her (poor creature!) and means her no harm.' Faller, *Crime and Defoe*, 235.

55 The first Levant Company ship set sail from England to Turkey in 1582. Its name? *The Great Susan*. Thanks to my student, Patrick Casey, for unearthing this resonant historical detail.

56 Deleuze and Guattari, *Anti-Oedipus: Capitalism and Schizophrenia*, trans. Robert Hurley, Mark Seem, and Helen R. Lane, preface by Michel Foucault (Minneapolis: University of Minnesota Press, 1983), 263.

57 Here my argument moves in the opposite direction to that of Rebecca Shapiro: 'Susan's desire ... conflicts with the increasingly capitalistic social structures in eighteenth-century England.' 'The "Unnatural" Mother-Daughter Relationship in Daniel Defoe's *Roxana*.' *The Literary Mother: Essays on Representations of Maternity and Child Care*, ed. Susan C. Staub (Jefferson, NC: McFarland, 2007), 44.

58 Nussbaum draws our attention to the homoerotic aspect of this encounter. See *Torrid Zones*, 38–9.

59 Marshall, *The Figure of Theater: Shaftesbury, Defoe, Adam Smith, and George Eliot* (New York: Columbia University Press, 1986), 152.

60 The attention *Roxana* grants to secrets links her narrative back to the 'histories' we encountered in chapter 3. Manley's scandal narrative *The Lady's Pacquet of Letters* describes the contest for power between the Duchess of Cleveland, named by the narrative as the benefactor of the unknown Beau Wilson, as a struggle over the secret of identity that the duchess is determined to keep to herself. Wilson's desire to unravel that mystery is reminiscent of other early modern accounts of curiosity:

> My Happiness is so imperfect, that I know not how, properly, it can be call'd such; if I am to be undone by the Sin of Knowledge, 'twas the loss of Paradise, and must be mine. Whether push'd on by my evil Genius, or some more irresistable unaccountable Power, I am resolv'd this Night shall end my Pain; (if you do not think fit yourself to oblige me with the discovery) thus (clasping your lovely Body in my Arms) will I expect the Morning, Day will confess the Charmer; but if your Face happen to be unknown to me (as 'tis scarce possible, since the late opportunities I have had of seeing those few Persons who have it in their Power to do as you have done) I'll follow you this moment, like your Shadow, till I

explore that Secret you have so long, so disobligingly, and so religiously kept; and to which you can have no other Motive, but vile distrust of my Honour, or have too great an opinion of my Vanity.

Like Roxana, the duchess can only interpret the desire for knowledge as a direct assault on her powers: 'W— shall never see me more, that Vainglorious Fool, who, even to my self, cou'd not forbear boasting of his good Fortune. Will he be more discreet to others? No 'tis impossible, the Wretch must die, that's certain; but the manner, ay, there's the difficulty.' Countess d'Aulnoy, *Memoirs of the Court of England ... To which is added, The Lady's Pacquet of Letters* (1707), 537, 541.

61 Marshall, *The Figure of Theater*, 153.
62 Starr, *Defoe and Casuistry* (Princeton: Princeton University Press, 1971).
63 Monod, Paul Kléber, *Jacobitism and the English People, 1688–1788* (Cambridge: Cambridge University Press, 1989), 158.
64 Thompson, *Models of Value: Eighteenth-Century Political Economy and the Novel* (Durham: Duke University Press, 1996), 118. Robert Clark pursues the problem of the economic from an alternate angle; Defoe's emphasis on the economic, he claims, ensured that women 'could not escape subjection to patriarchal definitions.' Clark, Introduction, *Roxana*, Everyman Edition (London: Dent and Charles E. Tuttle, 1998), xxxviii.
65 Here I draw on Jonathan Culler's reading of the Oedipus myth as a template for all successful narrative. Culler observes: 'Oedipus himself and all his readers are convinced of his guilt but our conviction does not come from the revelation of the deed. Instead of the revelation of a prior deed determining meaning, we could say that it is meaning, the convergence of meaning in the narrative discourse, that leads us to posit this deed as its appropriate manifestation.' Culler, *The Pursuit of Signs: Semiotics, Literature, Deconstruction* (Ithaca, NY: Cornell University Press, 1981), 174. On Roxana's accumulation of 'the materials of remorse,' see John Richetti, 'An Emerging New Canon of the British Eighteenth-Century Novel: Feminist Criticism, the Means of Cultural Production, and the Question of Value,' *A Companion to the Eighteenth-Century English Novel and Culture*, ed. Paula R. Backscheider and Catherine Ingrassia (Oxford: Blackwell, 2005), 380.
66 Starr, *Defoe and Spiritual Autobiography*, 165.
67 Liz Bellamy observes a similar tension in the formal operations of *Conjugal Lewdness*: 'the narrative form seems to function in opposition to the moral intentions of the tale.' Introduction, *Conjugal Lewdness* (1727), *Religious and Didactic Writings of Daniel Defoe*, vol. 5, ed. Liz Bellamy (London: Pickering and Chatto, 2006), 17.

68 Snow, 'Arguments to the Self in Defoe's *Roxana*,' *Studies in English Literature 1500–1900* 34.3 (1994): 524.
69 Molesworth, '"A Dreadful Course of Calamities": *Roxana*'s Ending Reconsidered,' 503.
70 Here I refuse the idea that the novel's ending represents a failure: 'Because [Roxana] cannot take stock of herself or accomplish a serious personal reckoning, she likewise cannot bring this spiritual autobiography to a meaningful close.' D. Christopher Gabbard, 'The Dutch Wives' Good Husbandry: Defoe's *Roxana* and Financial Literacy,' *Eighteenth-Century Studies* 37.2 (2004): 248.
71 Hoppit, *A Land of Liberty?* 241.
72 McKeon, *The Origins of the English Novel, 1660–1740* (Baltimore: Johns Hopkins University Press, 1987, 2002), 323, 336. In his recent biography of Defoe, Novak points out that 'Max Weber and R.H. Tawney used Baxter's writing to argue for the Protestant basis of capitalism ... Defoe seems to have come out against Williams and Baxter, and this should be remembered in view of attempts to impose the Weber-Tawney thesis on Defoe's fictional heroes and heroines.' *Daniel Defoe: Master of Fictions* (Oxford: Oxford University Press, 2001), 126.
73 Joseph Glanvill, *The Zealous, and Impartial Protestant, Shewing Some great, but less heeded Dangers of Popery, In Order to Thorough and Effectual Security Against it* (1681), 5.

5 A World of One's Own

1 Malborough, Sarah Churchill, Duchess of. *The Opinions of Sarah Duchess-Dowager of Malborough. Published from original MSS* (Edinburgh, 1788), 120.
2 Margaret Cavendish, *The Blazing World and Other Writings*, ed. Kate Lilley (London: Penguin, 1994), 124.
3 On women's manipulation of the patronage system that arose alongside parliamentary politics, see Elaine Chalus, '"To Serve my friends": Women and Political Patronage in Eighteenth-Century England,' *Women, Privilege, and Power: British Politics, 1750 to the Present*, ed. Amanda Vickery (Stanford: Stanford University Press, 2001), 57–88. For a consideration of women's activities as public agents in the republic of letters, see Betty A. Schellenberg, *The Professionalization of Women Writers in Eighteenth-Century Britain* (Cambridge: Cambridge University Press, 2005).
4 'Embracing the Absolute: The Politics of the Female Subject in Seventeenth-Century England,' *Genders* 1 (1988): 25.
5 Feminist critics have considered *Clarissa*'s political import from a number

of different perspectives. For example, Susan S. Lanser suggests, 'Clarissa dies for women's rights: sacrificing herself in a dramatic display of the consequences of sexual subjugation, she resurrects her subjectivity and her social power through words.' Lanser, 'The Novel Body Politic,' *A Companion to the Eighteenth-Century English Novel and Culture*, ed. Paula R. Backscheider and Catherine Ingrassia (Oxford: Blackwell, 2005), 492.

6 Samuel Richardson, *Clarissa, or the History of a Young Lady* (1748–9), ed. Angus Ross (London: Penguin, 1985), 358. Future references will be noted parenthetically.

7 The consensus regarding Clarissa's rational asexuality as an effective antidote to libertine misogyny is well-represented by Jocelyn Harris's assertion that 'the contained body, the nonsexual body, the chaste and Platonic body is the safer paradigm, for women ... It is not bourgeois shame that makes Richardson draw these powerful scenes, but a genuine and laudable desire to guard women from the consequences of sexual anarchy.' 'Grotesque, Classical and Pornographic Bodies in *Clarissa*,' *New Essays on Samuel Richardson*, ed. Albert J. Rivero (New York: St Martin's, 1996), 110.

8 Katherine Binhammer traces how Richardson's narrative modes grant Clarissa alternative ways of knowing herself and the world. Clarissa's plot, she observes, 'suggests the possibility that women's knowledge is not always reduced to carnality or the absence of it, and that she can have an ontological status which is not sexed.' 'Knowing Love: The Epistemology of *Clarissa*,' *ELH* 74.4 (2007): 859–79.

9 Recently, Laura J. Rosenthal has described *Clarissa* as 'an averted prostitute narrative,' linking the novel to earlier eighteenth-century whore biographies and astutely demonstrating how it raises 'extreme versions of questions fundamental to selfhood in commercial culture.' *Infamous Commerce: Prostitution in Eighteenth-Century British Literature and Culture* (Ithaca, NY: Cornell University Press, 2006), 130.

10 *The Trial of Ford, Lord Grey of Werk, &c.* [1682] (1716), 78.

11 Eaves and Kimpel, *Samuel Richardson: A Biography* (Oxford: Clarendon Press, 1971), 35.

12 See Margaret Anne Doody, 'Richardson's Politics,' *Eighteenth-Century Fiction* 2.2 (January 1990): 113–26; Tom Keymer, *Richardson's 'Clarissa' and the Eighteenth-Century Reader* (Cambridge: Cambridge University Press, 1992), 116–20; Toni Bowers, *The Politics of Motherhood: British Writing and Culture, 1680-1760* (Cambridge: Cambridge University Press, 1996), 201–3.

13 Doody, 'Richardson's Politics,' 122. That the Harlowe men both have the name James sets allusions to the tyranny practised by the historical Stuart family in opposition to the idealized Jacobite doctrine the novel advances.

This association works differently in *Sir Charles Grandison*, where many of the novel's benevolent characters have Jacobite names. In that comic novel, as Margaret Doody points out, Richardson describes 'what 'Bonnie Prince Charlie,' the last Stuart hope, should have been but was not.' 'Samuel Richardson: Fiction and Knowledge,' *The Cambridge Companion to the Eighteenth-Century Novel*, ed. John Richetti (Cambridge: Cambridge University Press, 1996), 111. *Grandison*, I suggest, marks the novel's shift into a nostalgic register. *Clarissa* engages Jacobitism as a contemporary and pressingly relevant political discourse. Paul Kléber Monod's rejection of the idea of Jacobitism as 'a reactionary attitude, a yearning for the order and stability of a mythical past' coincides with J.C.D. Clark's claim that 'since it can be shown that dynastic allegiance, whether to the Hanoverians or the Stuarts, had little or nothing to do with nostalgia, the marked absence of nostalgia in early eighteenth-century culture is not evidence of the absence of Jacobitism.' Monod, *Jacobitism and the English People, 1688–1788* (Cambridge: Cambridge University Press, 1989), 92. Clark, 'Religious Affiliation and Dynastic Allegiance in Eighteenth-Century England: Edmund Burke, Thomas Paine and Samuel Johnson,' *ELH* 64.4 (1997): 1049.

14 Monod, *Jacobitism and the English People*, 92.

15 My reading of *Clarissa*'s Jacobite inflection moves in the opposite direction to those taken by Tom Keymer and Morris Golden, who see Lovelace as the Young Pretender waging war against the innocent nation (Clarissa). While Richardson may have distanced himself publicly from his earlier Jacobite tendencies in the 1730s and 1740s, *Clarissa* reflects a profound disenchantment with the period's new social and political realities. See Golden, 'Public Context and Imagining Self in *Clarissa*,' *Studies in English Literature, 1500–1900* 25.3 (1985): 575–98; and Keymer, *Richardson's Clarissa and the Eighteenth-Century Reader* (Cambridge: Cambridge University Press, 1992) 169–76. On the place of rape in Jacobite discourse, see Howard Erskine-Hill, 'Literature and the Jacobite Cause: Was There a Rhetoric of Jacobitism?' *Ideology and Conspiracy*, 49–70. On virginity and rape in Jacobite poetics, see Ronald Paulson, '*The Rape of the Lock*: A Jacobite Aesthetics,' *Acts of Narrative*, ed. Carol Jacobs and Henry Sussman (Stanford: Stanford University Press, 2003), 130–45. On the Jacobite imagery of the virgin Astraea, see Murray G.H. Pittock, *Jacobitism* (London: Macmillan Press, 1998), 71–2.

16 Bowers observes that 'what is at stake [is] ... the purity of conscience and the moral justification of the Augustan body politic.' *The Politics of Motherhood*, 202.

17 I use the term 'antinomian' loosely here, to refer to Clarissa's willingness

to define social strictures on her own terms. As the novel progresses, Clarissa's antinomianism takes on its more precise religious meaning, as the dominion of the law of grace over moral law.

18 Kay, 'Sympathy, Sex, and Authority in Richardson and Hume,' *Studies in Eighteenth-Century Culture* 12 (1983): 89.

19 Kay describes this tension between the individual and communal standards in Richardson's work: '[Richardson's] perfectionistic protagonists at times suffer to achieve a merger of debilitating, trivial conformity and weird singularity.' 'Sympathy, Sex, and Authority in Richardson and Hume,'79.

20 I have discussed this passage, and Clarissa's understanding of class, in an earlier work. See *Private Interests: Women, Portraiture, and the Visual Culture of the English Novel, 1709–1791* (Toronto: University of Toronto Press, 2001), 83.

21 Michael McKeon, among others, has noted Clarissa's conservatism, including her recognition that 'if Lovelace is for his part a vile aristocrat, he is at least the real thing.' *The Origins of the English Novel, 1660–1740* (Baltimore: Johns Hopkins University Press, 1987, 2002), 418.

22 In her study, *Enlightened Virginity in Eighteenth-Century Literature,* Corrinne Harol traces the evolution of 'the virtuous, and highly marriageable heroine, of sentimental fiction' as the de-corporealized version of the more problematical seventeenth- and early eighteenth-century virgin (New York: Palgrave Macmillan, 2006), 12. Harol views the anachronisms that colour Clarissa's representation from a different perspective than mine: 'On the one hand, *Clarissa* looks far backward, to a patriarchy based in authority and obedience and to a religious model of virginity based in transcendence. On the other hand, it looks forward to feminist critiques of eighteenth-century ideas about female sexuality and its importance to property and inheritance.' *Enlightened Virginity*, 169. I locate the charge of *Clarissa*'s critique in its alignment of the problematical virgin Harol identifies with a past political tradition – that is to say, in its ability to bring the past forward.

23 Ian Watt characterizes Clarissa's anxieties as a form of sexual self-loathing: 'sexual intercourse, apparently, means death for the woman.' *The Rise of the Novel: Studies in Defoe, Richardson, and Fielding* (1957) (London: Pimlico, 2000), 232.

24 Stuber, 'On Fathers and Authority in *Clarissa*,' *Studies in English Literature, 1500–1900* 25.3 (1985), 574.

25 Here I draw on Erik Leborgne's insightful article, 'Clarissa Harlot or Clarissa Hallowed? L'échiquier moral de Clarisse,' *Littératures* 48 (2003): 35–48:

'The identification with Job can be read as a revalorization of the paternal imago. In addressing her posthumous letters to all her family members, Clarissa occupies, on the level of fantasy, the place of a father with moral authority and whose word is incontestable – the exact opposite of the iniquitous father of Harlowe Place' (L'identification à Job peut ... se lire comme une revalorisation de l'*imago* paternelle. En adressant des lettres posthumes à tous les siens, Clarissa occupe, sur le plan de fantasme, la place d'un père à l'autorité morale et à la parole incontestable – l'exacte antithèse du père inique de Harlowe Place) (45, my translation). I am less interested in the psychoanalytic than political resonances of Clarissa's bid for power.

26 As Peggy Thompson argues, 'without denying the perspective from which Clarissa's pain is a passion – purposeful and redemptive – we can recognize how the ... theories of atonement evoked in the novel (and its scholarship) contribute to Clarissa's identity as a passive woman who derives meaning and importance only from her victimization by men.' 'Abuse and Atonement: The Passion of Clarissa Harlowe,' *Eighteenth-Century Fiction* 11.3 (April 1999): 270. See also, Lois A. Chaber, 'Christian Form and Anti-Feminism in *Clarissa*,' *Eighteenth-Century Fiction* 15.3–4 (2003): 507–37. Frances Ferguson makes a related point in her account of how Clarissa's unconscious state at the moment of rape reduces her to the status of a child: 'Clarissa's achievement – and her plight – is to become the living embodiment of a legally stipulated state of infancy in which the contradiction can never be overcome and not even consent itself can count to override nonconsent.' 'Rape and the Rise of the Novel,' *Representations* 20 (fall 1987): 110.

27 I want to evoke the multiple connotations of this expression, including, 'no exit' (toutes portes fermées); 'in camera'; and 'the talks are continuing behind closed doors' (les négociations se poursuivrent à huis clos). *Le Grand Robert de la Langue Francaise*, 2nd ed., vol. 5, ed. Alain Ray (Montreal: Le Robert, 1994), 274–5. *Collins-Robert French-English Dictionary*, 2nd ed. (New York: HarperCollins, 1993), 336.

28 Kierkegaard, *Papers and Journals: A Selection*, trans. and ed. Alastair Hanay (London: Penguin, 1996), 352. My thanks to Kelly McGuire for directing me to this source.

29 As Margaret Doody notes, 'The personal imperial principle manifested in Lovelace's will, and Clarissa's Christian morality are curiously parallel. Both acknowledge, in quite different ways, the freedom of the will, the sovereignty of the self.' *A Natural Passion: A Study of the Novels of Samuel Richardson* (Oxford: Clarendon Press, 1974), 124. Corrinne Harol makes a re-

lated observation: 'Clarissa and Lovelace are both anachronistic characters: a libertine and a celibate caught in a modern world, that is, in a novel.' *Enlightened Virginity*, 172.

30 Kay, *Political Constructions*, 130.

31 'The Puritan fear of play – both verbal wit and fictive invention – reflects a deep commitment to reading God's story rather than substituting one's own, but it also reflects a fear that the self might find freedom in play,' observes Leopold Damrosch, Jr, *God's Plot and Man's Stories: Studies in the Fictional Imagination from Milton to Fielding* (Chicago: University of Chicago Press, 1985), 264.

32 I agree with William Warner's observation that 'Clarissa's final significa-tion of herself as virtue can only be ventured through her death. This is her last and most crucial act as an artist.' *Reading* Clarissa: *The Struggles of Interpretation* (New Haven, CT: Yale University Press, 1979), 26.

33 'Christian Form and Anti-Feminism in *Clarissa*,' *Eighteenth-Century Fiction* 15.3–4 (April–July 2003): 512.

34 MacKinnon, *Towards a Feminist Theory of the State* (Cambridge, MA: Har-vard University Press, 1989), 127.

35 Brown, *States of Injury: Power and Freedom in Late Modernity* (Princeton: Princeton University Press, 1995), 91.

36 Miranda Burgess argues that 'Richardson turns Jacobite nostalgia to Lockean liberal ends, but only at a price, for violence overtakes the text, overshadowing the ghosts of sentimental theory.' *British Fiction and the Pro-duction of Social Order, 1740–1830* (Cambridge: Cambridge University Press, 2000), 71.

37 Rosenthal argues that women's work is invariably reduced to a species of prostitution: 'The possibility of nonsexual labour [in *Clarissa*] ... remains almost beyond representation.' *Infamous Commerce*, 149.

38 Pateman, *The Sexual Contract* (Stanford: Stanford University Press, 1988), 194.

39 Richardson's support of the Magdalen House and his willingness to print *The Histories of Some of the Penitents in the Magdalen House* (1760) suggest that the author, in a different arena, agreed with Anna's view of prostitu-tion as a form of male tyranny. See William M. Sale, *Samuel Richardson: Master Printer* (Ithaca, NY: Cornell University Press, 1950), 120.

40 Nowhere are Lovelace's delusions of power more marked than in his frequent recourse to the marriage plot as his back-up plan – 'I can marry her when I will' (647). That convention, finally, is less powerful than the destructive forces unleashed by the prostitutes marks the darkness of the novel's vision of modernity. As Margaret Doody has observed, the novel

is 'startlingly pessimistic.' 'Samuel Richardson: Fiction and Knowledge,' *The Cambridge Companion to the Eighteenth-Century Novel*, ed. John Richetti (Cambridge: Cambridge University Press, 1996), 109.

41 Judith Wilt, 'He Could Go No Farther: A Modest Proposal about Lovelace and Clarissa,' *PMLA* 92.1 (1977): 27.

42 Ibid., 25.

43 Clarissa's understanding that the law operates in concert with, rather than in opposition to, her oppressors motivates her refusal to take Lovelace to court for rape: 'It would no doubt have been a ready retort from *every* mouth, that I ought not to have thrown myself into the power of such a man, and that I ought to take for my pains what had befallen me' (1253, emphasis in text). Instead of relying on the courts for justice, Clarissa draws on her own moral strength: 'My will is unviolated' (1254).

44 Lovelace describes Sally and Polly as 'creatures who, brought up too high for their fortunes, and to a taste of pleasure and the public diversions, had fallen an easy prey to his seducing arts' (534). Although Clarissa's fortune is sufficient for a match superior to her birth, Lovelace thinks the Harlowes beneath him, as we have seen. In her sense of social entitlement, Clarissa, like Sally and Polly, has been brought up 'too high.'

45 Clarissa's use of 'pregnant,' here, is resonant. That is, Clarissa's recognition that her life story might resemble that of a courtesan, here, would take on a larger dimension should her body be reduced, by a pregnancy, to the materiality she associates with the prostitute. I discuss the spectre of a pregnant Clarissa elsewhere. See *Private Interests*, 107–9.

46 Madame Maintenon reappears in *Sir Charles Grandison* in a similarly perfidious role. *The History of Sir Charles Grandison*, 3 vols, ed. Jocelyn Harris (Oxford: Oxford University Press, 1972), 1:412.

47 Thomas Hobbes, *Leviathan* (1651), ed. C.B. Macpherson (London: Penguin, 1968, 1985), 254.

48 Turner, *Libertines and Radicals in Early Modern London: Sexuality, Politics and Literary Culture, 1630–1685* (Cambridge: Cambridge University Press, 2001), 88.

49 'Upon his Majesties being made free of the Citty,' Marvell, *Poems and Letters*, 1:191, l. 54. Attribution is uncertain; the work was first published in *State Poems* (1697).

50 Clery, *The Feminization Debate in Eighteenth-Century England: Literature, Commerce, and Luxury* (New York: Palgrave Macmillan, 2004), 121.

51 Bean, 'Sight and Self-Disclosure: Richardson's Revision of Swift's "The Lady's Dressing Room,"' *Eighteenth-Century Life* ns 14.1 (1990): 9. For further analysis of the brothel scene, see Rosenthal, *Infamous Commerce*, 266–7

and Jocelyn Harris, 'Grotesque, Classical and Pornographic Bodies in *Clarissa*,' *New Essays on Samuel Richardson*, ed. Albert J. Rivero (New York: St Martin's, 1996), 101–16.

52 *Pamela*, ed. Thomas Keymer and Alice Wakely (Oxford: Oxford University Press, 2001), 501.

53 Castle, *Clarissa's Ciphers: Meaning and Disruption in Richardson's 'Clarissa'* (Ithaca, NY: Cornell University Press, 1982), 109.

54 Richardson to Lady Bradsheigh, quoted in *Selected Letters of Samuel Richardson*, ed. John Carroll (Oxford: Clarendon Press, 1965), 88.

55 Christopher Hill made this point fifty years ago; the standards of Clarissa's society, he noted, 'are those of the market: justification by faith was for Sundays only.' 'Clarissa Harlowe and Her Times,' *Essays in Criticism* 5 (1955): 332.

56 Kierkegaard, *Papers and Journals*, 352.

57 Feminist theologian Sheila Collins has observed that in their willingness to identify with the 'Christ event as normative for their lives, women have participated in their own crucifixion.' *A Different Heaven and Earth* (Valley Forge, PA.: Judson Press, 1974), 89.

58 *The Highlanders Salivated, or the Loyal Association of M–ll K–g's Midnight Club: with the serious Address of the Ladies of Drury, to the Batter'd strolling Nymphs of their Community* (1746), 24.

59 Thomas R. Cleary's claim that *Tom Jones* 'is not primarily a political work' suggests a more narrow definition of 'political' than I am using here. *Henry Fielding: Political Writer* (Waterloo, ON: Wilfred Laurier University Press, 1984), 264. I am indebted to prévious work on Fielding and the '45, most obviously, in terms of my feminist perspective, to Jill Campbell's *Natural Masques: Gender and Identity in Fielding's Plays and Novels* (Stanford: Stanford University Press, 1995), but also John Allen Stevenson's *The Real History of Tom Jones* (New York: Palgrave Macmillan, 2005), as well as Peter J. Carlton's essays, cited below.

60 'The Church, like the Walpole ministry, was condemned as fallen and corrupt.' Jeremy Black, 'Introduction: An Age of Political Stability?' *Britain in the Age of Walpole* (London: Macmillan, 1984), 12.

61 Jill Campbell notes that 'the specter of female self-assertion, of female demands for equality and social change, may appear as a feared attendant in the train of either Jacobite or Whig political claims.' *Natural Masques*, 145. On women's Jacobite activism, see Pittock, *Jacobitism*, 78–82.

62 *The Genuine History of Mrs. Sarah Prydden, Usually Called, Sally Salisbury, and her Gallants. Regularly Containing, the Real Story of her Life* (1723), 51–2.

63 *The Highlanders Salivated, or the Loyal Association of M–ll K–ng's Midnight*

Club ... To which is prefixed, The Speech of Miss Sukey Stichwell, Chairwoman of the said Club, on the Melancholy Situation of Affairs (1746), 14–15.

64 In reading Tom as a descendent of Behn's Silvia and Defoe's Roxana I depart, needless to say, from the idea of a moral Tom and of a religious Fielding. This reading has been most thoroughly advanced by Martin C. Battestin. See Battestin's General Introduction, *The History of Tom Jones, a Foundling*, 2 vols (Middletown, CT: Wesleyan University Press, 1975), xvii–lxi, and notes to that edition; also, *The Providence of Wit: Aspects of Form in Augustan Literature and the Arts* (Oxford: Clarendon Press, 1974), 141–92; and *The Moral Basis of Fielding's Art: A Study of Joseph Andrews* (Middletown, CT: Wesleyan University Press, 1959), 14–25.

65 Fielding, *The History of Tom Jones, a Foundling* (1749), ed. John Bender and Simon Stern (Oxford: Oxford University Press, 1996), 132. Future references will be cited parenthetically.

66 On the Flora myth and Floralia, see T.P. Wiseman, *The Myths of Rome* (Exeter: University of Exeter Press, 2004), 1–10 and 'The Games of Flora,' *The Art of Ancient Spectacle*, ed. Bettina Bergmann and Christine Kondoleon (Studies in the History of Art 56) (New Haven, CT: Yale University Press, 1999), 195–203.

67 Shteir, '*Flora primavera* or *Flora meretrix*? Iconography, Gender, and Science,' *Studies in Eighteenth-Century Culture* 36 (2007): 152. I am indebted not only to this article, which led me to other Flora source material, but also to conversations with Professor Shteir for enriching my reading of Fielding's use of the Flora allusion.

68 Julius S. Held, 'Flora, Goddess and Courtesan,' *Essays in Honor of Erwin Panofsky*, 2 vols, ed. Millard Meiss (New York: New York University Press, 1961), 1:210.

69 'The Masquerade' (1728), *Political Operas 1: Satire and Allegory*, selected and arranged by Walter H. Rubsamen (New York: Garland Publishing, 1974), *The Ballad Opera*, vol. 20 (of 28), p. 10, ll. 375–80, facsimile text of poem.

70 'What you seek is nowhere.' Fielding, *Joseph Andrews* (1742), ed. Martin C. Battestin (Middletown, CT: Wesleyan University Press, 1967), 152.

71 On this subject, see Ursula Weber-Woelk, '"Flora la belle Rommaine": Studien zur Ikonographie der Göttin Flora im 17. Jahrhundert' (PhD diss., Cologne, 1995). Held remarks, of Titian's *Flora*, 'the picture ... should be considered as an important piece of evidence for the respect and admiration paid to the leading courtesans during the Renaissance.' 'Flora, Goddess and Courtesan' (213).

The Flora portrait I reproduce here (figure 9) represents, I believe, Hortense Mancini. The Hermitage lists the portrait as representing Gabriela

244 Notes to pages 163–5

Mancini, sister-in-law to Hortense, but other portraits of Hortense Mancini establish the likeness. Susan Shifrin reproduces the prototype portrait of Hortense Mancini upon which, she believes, this Flora image is based, in '"Subdued by a Famous Roman Dame": Picturing Foreignness, Notoriety, and Prerogative in the Portraits of Hortense Mancini, Duchess of Mazarin,' *Politics, Transgression, and Representation at the Court of Charles II*, ed. Julia Marciari Alexander and Catharine MacLeod (New Haven, CT: Yale University Press, 2007), 151.

72 'To all curious Criticks and Admirers of Meeter,' *The Works of John Wilmot Earl of Rochester*, ed. Harold Love (Oxford: Oxford University Press, 1999), 270. This poem is linked to Rochester by its inclusion in the 1680 anthology, *Poems on several occasions by the Right Honourable, the E. of R—*, a collection of poems by Rochester and other authors of libertine verse. The link between Sophia and 'whorish' women is intensified by Fielding's allusion to this poem, which lists, as one of the 'things' the speaker has seen, the sexual appeal of 'Anstrudder' ('Or have you seen our Gallants, keep a pudder, / With Fair and Grace, and Grace, and Fair Anstrudder,' ll. 11–12), remarked in other court poems of the period for her illicit sexual conduct. She may have been the daughter of Sir Philip Anstruther, royalist. My thanks to John H. O'Neill for this insight.

73 I have discussed Hogarth's aesthetic theory elsewhere. See Conway, *Private Interests*, 153–4. See also Ronald Paulson's Introduction, *The Analysis of Beauty* (New Haven, CT: Yale University Press, 1997), xvii–lxiii, and Robert W. Jones, *Gender and the Formation of Taste in Eighteenth-Century Britain* (Cambridge: Cambridge University Press, 1998), 49–56.

74 Robert Jones attributes the aesthetic's interest in the palpable to an emergent discourse of sensibility, but I stress Hogarth's ironic relation to the aesthetic, to the creation of what Paulson describes as 'a practical aesthetics' closer in spirit to Restoration modes than mid-century discourses. Paulson, Introduction, xxxiii.

75 Jones, *Gender and the Formation of Taste in Eighteenth-Century Britain*, 52.

76 Betty Rizzo notes that Fielding's 'more libidinous and scolding viragos, like Fortune, seem modelled in part on the Restoration heroines of Manley and Aphra Behn.' 'The Gendering of Divinity in *Tom Jones*,' *Studies in Eighteenth-Century Culture* 24 (1995), 266.

77 Rizzo suggests that Sophia comes to resemble, by degrees, her less outstanding peers. By the end of the novel, she observes, 'Sophia has apparently learned to habitually lie, flatter, and manipulate ... Paradoxically, all Sophia needed to become perfect as a wife was to become detectably inferior to her husband.' 'The Gendering of Divinity in *Tom Jones*,' 273–4.

78 I am not persuaded by Angela J. Smallwood's reading of Sophia as the sign of Fielding's progressive attitudes toward women. *Fielding and the Woman Question:The Novels of Henry Fielding and the Feminist Debate, 1700–1750* (New York: St Martin's, 1989), 152.

79 As Campbell has observed, 'the features of private identity (including one's gender) ... are as much characterized by confusion, multiple reference, and fluidity as the features of this novel's political world.' *Natural Masques*, 166.

80 Fielding is drawing on a Cambridge Jest Book (probably a now non-extant 1746 edition) in his telling of this story, which was recounted as early as 1674 in that year's *Cambridge Jests*. The 1674 version does not name Nell Gwyn, alluding only to 'A notable Strumpet.' See Tom Keymer, '*Tom Jones*, Nell Gwyn, and the Cambridge Jest Book' *Notes and Queries* 51.4 (December 2004); 408–9.

81 Just as Jenny Cameron turns into Nell, we can imagine Flora MacDonald, another Jacobite rebel, becoming the basket-woman strewing flowers before the coronation, comic relief in times of political strife.

82 Campbell, *Natural Masques*, 142.

83 Sophia's domestication imitates the novel's de-politicization of its past. In particular, Fielding dismisses the political aspect of the French romance tradition, rewriting its allegorical dimension as a cover for sexual intrigue: 'to say truth, I have often suspected that those very enchanters with which romance everywhere abounds were in reality no other than the husbands of those days; and matrimony itself was, perhaps, the enchanted castle in which the nymphs were said to be confined' (529). Fielding identifies Behn not as a fellow free-thinker and political writer, but as the author of mindless amatory fiction, suitable for idle Irish men: 'This young fellow lay in bed reading one of Mrs. Behn's novels; for he had been instructed by a friend, that he would find no more effectual method of recommending himself to the ladies than the improving his understanding, and filling his mind with good literature' (458).

84 'As the arrangement in which Sophia dwindled into a wife and its ramifications were tendentious, Fielding failed to underscore them.' Rizzo, 'The Gendering of Divinity in *Tom Jones*,' 274.

85 London, 'Controlling the Text: Women in *Tom Jones*.' In *Women and Early Fiction*, ed. Jerry C. Beasley, special issue of *Studies in the Novel* 19.3 (1987): 331.

86 Walpole, quoted in William Coxe, *Memoirs of the Life and Administration of Sir Robert Walpole*, 3 vols (1798), 1:757.

87 J.C.D. Clark argues that 'it was not Lockeian contractarianism but Hoad-

leian latitudinarianism which provoked the most bitter domestic ideo-
logical conflict of the century.' Clark, *English Society 1688–1832: Ideology,
Social Structure and Political Practice during the Ancien Regime* (Cambridge:
Cambridge University Press, 1985), 302. On Fielding's interest in Hoadly's
ideas and his friendship with Hoadly's sons, see Battestin, *A Henry Fielding
Companion* (Westport, CT: Greenwood, 2000), 79–80.

88 That Tom, an appealing bastard wandering the English countryside,
should resemble both the Catholic Young Pretender and the Protestant
Duke of Monmouth drives home the idea that religious affiliation, in the
end, matters less than sociability. For differing views on the significance
of Tom's resemblance to Bonnie Prince Charlie, see McKeon, *Origins of the
English Novel*, 418; John Stevenson, 'Tom Jones and the Stuarts' *ELH* 61
(1994): 571–95; Peter J. Carlton, 'The Mitigated Truth: Tom Jones's Double
Heroism,' *Studies in the Novel* 19.4 (1987): 397–409, and '*Tom Jones* and the
'45 Once Again,' *Studies in the Novel* 20.4 (1988): 361–73. On the subject of
the Duke of Monmouth, see Richard Braverman, 'Rebellion Redux: Figuring Whig History in *Tom Jones*,' *Clio* 24.3 (1995), 265–6.

89 'Aretine' goes on to highlight the anticlerical strain of thinking that colours
Tom Jones, noting the 'the gross Ridicule and Abuse which are wantonly
thrown on religious Characters. Who reviles the Clergy may be well said
to be upon the very Threshold of Immorality and Irreligion ... ' 'Aretine,'
from a letter to 'Selim Slim' (*Old England*, 27 May 1749); quoted in Thomas
Lockwood and Ronald Paulson, eds, *Henry Fielding, the Critical Heritage*
(London: Routledge,1969), 168.

90 McKeon, *Origins of the English Novel*, 407–8. John Richetti makes a similar
claim: 'What matters most ... is the narrator's authority and the deferred
truthful wholeness it always delivers.' 'The Old Order and the New Novel
of the Mid-Eighteenth Century: Narrative Authority in Fielding and Smollett,' *Eighteenth-Century Fiction* 3.2 (1990): 191.

91 Leopold Damrosch Jr argues, '*Tom Jones* is a romance that accommodates
the world to human desires ... There is no longer any question of demonstrating the ultimate order of things, or of proving that Fortune is really
Providence after all.' Like McKeon, and most famously Claude Rawson,
Damrosch views Fielding as anticipating secular modernity, registering
what Rawson describes as 'the Augustan ideal under stress.' My reading
suggests that Fielding's novel marks the end-point, not of an epistemology
of order and providence, but of seventeenth-century doubt, which takes on
a new form in the Enlightenment tradition. Damrosch, *God's Plot and Man's
Stories: Studies in the Fictional Imagination from Milton to Fielding* (Chicago:
University of Chicago Press, 1985), 301. See also Rawson, *Henry Fielding*

and the Augustan Ideal under Stress (Atlantic Highlands, NJ: Humanities
Press International, 1991), 53–66. Simon Dickie traces the debate surrounding Fielding's free-thinking and anticlerical tendencies in '*Joseph Andrews*
and the Great Laughter Debate,' *Studies in Eighteenth-Century Culture*, vol.
34, ed. Catherine Ingrassia and Jeffrey S. Ravel (Baltimore: Johns Hopkins
University Press, 2005), 304–7.

92 *The Debauchees or, The Jesuit Caught, The Plays of Henry Fielding*, 3 vols., ed.
Thomas Lockwood (Oxford: Oxford University Press, 2004–), 2:215.

93 *Pasquin, The Works of Henry Fielding*, 10 vols, ed. Leslie Stephen (1882),
10:177. Battestin documents Fielding's flirtation with free-thinking ideas,
but argues that this interest was short-lived (see Battestin, with Ruthe R.
Battestin, *Henry Fielding: A Life* [London: Routledge, 1989], 151–60). As will
become evident as my reading of *Tom Jones* unfolds, I do not believe that
Fielding outgrew his earlier scepticism.

94 Hunter, *Occasional Form: Henry Fielding and the Chains of Circumstance* (Baltimore: Johns Hopkins University Press, 1975), 190.

95 Here I follow George A. Drake's line of argument regarding Fielding's
representation of 'prudence': 'Fielding's ambiguous use of the word "prudence" may reflect his ambivalence about the real possibilities of true prudence and judgement, as would his coyness in enunciating the doctrine.
Prudence and judgment seem to be limited by the existing state of *manners*
...' 'Historical Space in the "History of": Between Public and Private in *Tom
Jones*' *ELH* 66.3 (1999): 731. On this topic see also Eleanor Hutchens, *Irony
in Tom Jones* (University, AL: University of Alabama Press, 1965), 101–18;
Glenn W. Hatfield, *Henry Fielding and the Language of Irony* (Chicago: University of Chicago Press, 1968), 179–96; Martin C. Battestin, *The Providence
of Wit: Aspects of Form in Augustan Literature and the Arts* (Oxford: Clarendon Press, 1974), 164–92; and Frederick G. Ribble, 'Aristotle and the "Prudence" Theme of *Tom Jones*,' *Eighteenth-Century Studies* 15.2 (1981): 26–47.

96 From a biographical perspective, we can identify several factors that appear to have shaped Fielding's representations. Bertrand Goldgar has
examined Fielding's complex relation to prostitutes as individuals, and
prostitution as a profession, noting that 'on the one hand, his attitude toward the young women brought into his court was one of great sympathy;
on the other hand, when required to look at such problems from a societal
rather than personal viewpoint ... he called for every effort to check the
progress of prostitution and suppress its practice.' Goldgar, 'Fielding and
the Whores of London' *Philological Quarterly* 64.2 (1985): 270. Thomas
Lockwood describes a more personal investment in Fielding's identification with the prostitute's amoralism in his recent reading of *Shamela*: 'It

seems to me obvious that Fielding ... identifies devotedly with his character in spirit, for the reckless freedom from hypocritical respectability she represents.' Lockwood, '*Shamela*,' *The Cambridge Companion to Henry Fielding*, ed. Claude Rawson (Cambridge: Cambridge University Press, 2007), 47. One can also speculate about the attraction of whoring to Fielding from an economic standpoint. 'As a professional who owned only his literary and then his legal skills,' John Richetti observes, Fielding 'was dependent, to put it crudely, on the patronage of the rich and powerful.' 'The Old Order and the New Novel in the Mid-Eighteenth Century: Narrative Authority in Fielding and Smollett,' 187. Fielding was chronically short of money and the sense of urgency around the need to procure ready cash, not once but over and over again, vividly manifest in the exigencies of London's sex trade, would have been all too familiar. As Battestin notes, '[Fielding's] ability to run through money at speed was extraordinary – almost a talent.' *Henry Fielding: A Life*, 447.

97   The arc of Jenny Jones's career proves this claim most forcefully.
98   Richardson, Letter to Astraea and Minerva Hill, *Selected Letters of Samuel Richardson*, ed. John Carroll (Oxford: Clarendon Press, 1964), 127.
99   Orbilius, *An examen of The history of Tom Jones, a foundling. In two letters to a friend* (1750 [1749]), 88.
100   Scott, 'Prefatory Memoir to Fielding,' *The Novels of Henry Fielding, Esq.* (1821), xix. William Forsyth, *The Novels and Novelists of the Eighteenth Century, in Illustration of the Manners and Morals of the Age* (1871), 261. Emphasis in text.
101   W.M. Thackeray, 'Hogarth, Smollett, and Fielding,' *The Four Georges: The English Humourists of the Eighteenth Century* (London: Smith, Elder, 1869), 320.
102   Bender, Introduction, *Tom Jones*, xxvi.
103   *An examen of The history of Tom Jones, a foundling. In two letters to a friend*, 88.
104   Rosenthal documents contemporary preoccupations with male 'keeping' in her chapter on *Tom Jones*. See *Infamous Commerce*, 154–78.
105   Defoe, *Roxana, The Fortunate Mistress* (1724), ed. David Blewett (London: Penguin, 1982), 241.
106   Here I differ from James Thompson, who argues that Fielding attempts 'to change the new narrative of profit, accumulation, and improvement back into an older dynastic vision of the stable hereditary estate.' *Models of Value: Eighteenth-Century Political Economy and the Novel* (Durham: Duke University Press, 1996), 140.
107   Stern, '*Tom Jones* and the Economics of Copyright,' *Eighteenth-Century Fiction* 9.4 (1997): 440, 442.

108 J. Paul Hunter arrives at a similar conclusion from a different direction: 'Fielding's symmetry seems to me ... evidence of his resistance to a meaningful and persuasive sense of narrative closure, a resistance that possibly tells us something about him as a believer, philosopher, or magistrate and that certainly tells us a lot about him as a novelist trying to practice in a species in the process of defining itself.' 'Serious Reflections on Farther Adventures: Resistances to Closure in Eighteenth-Century English Novels,' *Augustan Subjects: Essays in Honor of Martin C. Battestin*, ed. Albert J. Rivero (Newark: University of Delaware Press, 1997), 285.

109 Burgess, *British Fiction and the Production of Social Order, 1740–1830* (Cambridge: Cambridge University Press, 2000), 58.

Afterword

1 Peterson, 'Defoe's *Roxana* and Its Eighteenth-Century Sequels: A Critical and Bibliographical Study,' unpublished PhD dissertation, Harvard University, 1953. P.N. Furbank and W.R. Owens provide a more recent overview of the editions and identify two editions – 1735 and 1742 – no longer extant in 'The "Lost" Continuation of *Roxana*,' *Eighteenth-Century Fiction* 9.3 (1997): 299–308. John Mullan notes that the alterations made by later publishers constitute 'responses to some of *Roxana*'s most disturbing insights.' Introduction, *Roxana* (Oxford: Oxford University Press, 1996), x. For a reading of the ideological and narrative implications of the 1765 *Roxana*, see M. Wade Mahon, 'The Rhetoric of Virtuous Reading in Defoe's *Roxana* and the 1765 Continuation,' *Reader: Essays in Reader-Oriented Theory, Criticism, and Pedagogy* 49 (2003): 10–43. Robert J. Griffin situates the *Roxana* continuations in the broader context of book history: 'What seems clear ... is that eighteenth-century publishers exploited the opportunities of an abrupt ending and hired anonymous writers to fill in the blanks ... The different ways the blanks were filled tell us, if not about the author, then at least how publishers perceived the desires of actual customers in the marketplace.' 'The Text in Motion: Eighteenth-Century *Roxanas*,' *ELH* 72.2 (2005): 393.

2 They do, nonetheless, reflect shifts in the period's standards, including the possibility of a sympathetic reading of the prostitute's story: the 1775 edition manages to expunge the word 'whore' from the narrative, marry Roxana to a husband who forgives her her past life as a mistress, and effect a reconciliation between Roxana and her children – no small achievement.

3 Godwin, Preface, *Faulkener: A Tragedy* (1807), vi. For an account of the

reception and circulation of *Roxana* among Godwin, Lamb, and later, Hazlitt, see Furbank and Owens, 'The "Lost" Continuation of Defoe's *Roxana*.'

4 Cited from the 1765 edition – the edition the Romantics identified as the '1745' text. There is only one extant copy of the 1745 edition, which is housed at the Newberry Library in Chicago. *The life and adventures of Roxana, the fortunate mistress, or, most unhappy wife* (1765), 144. Godwin picks up this theme in his characterization Roxana as Countess Orsini in his play, *Faulkener: A Tragedy* (1807). At the end of the play, the Countess proclaims: 'I have grievously erred; but all seeing Heaven can tell, never for a moment did I cease to be a mother.' Godwin, *Faulkener: A Tragedy*, 74.

5 Lamb, 'Prologue,' *Faulkener: A Tragedy* (1807), n.p.

6 Mahon, 'The Rhetoric of Virtuous Reading in Defoe's *Roxana* and the 1765 Continuation,' 27.

7 The separation of sexuality from discourses of sinfulness is particularly apparent in Cleland's 1748 pornographic novel, *Memoirs of a Woman of Pleasure* (*Fanny Hill*). Its treatment of Fanny's sexuality as secular and apolitical marks a mid-century shift in courtesan representations.

8 Popkin and Goldie, 'Scepticism, Priestcraft, and Toleration,' *The Cambridge History of Eighteenth-Century Political Thought* (Cambridge: Cambridge University Press, 2006), 109.

9 *The life and adventures of Roxana, the fortunate mistress; or, most unhappy wife* (1755), 377–8. The 1755 edition adds to the 1745 text excerpts from Defoe's *Tour* – but this excerpt is not from that work.

10 I refer to Jürgen Habermas here only in a suggestive fashion, although I believe the figure of the courtesan complicates his thoughts on gender and the public sphere in a number of interesting ways. For his account of 'representative publicness' and his description of the public sphere, see parts 1 and 2 of *The Structural Transformation of the Public Sphere: An Inquiry into a Category of Bourgeois Society*, trans. Thomas Burger (Cambridge, MA: MIT Press, 1989, 1992). For feminist responses to Habermas, see the essays collected in *Feminists Read Habermas: Gendering the Subject of Discourse*, ed. Johanna Meehan (London: Routledge, 1995).

11 It is beyond the scope of this study to examine the representations of the Stuart monarchy by Scott and other later novelists, or to pursue the intriguing thesis advanced by Clare Jackson and Mark Goldie: 'As Whig Jacobite arguments fused with republican and utopian visions, Jacobitism proved able, ultimately, to consort with Jacobinism, as a movement once dedicated to restoring the House of Stuart gave way to a movement enshrining the universal rights of the citizen.' 'Williamite Tyranny and the

Whig Jacobites,' *Redefining William III: The Impact of the King-Stadholder in International Context*, ed. Esther Mijers and David Onnekink (Burlington, VT: Ashgate, 2007), 178. Laura Brown makes a related claim in her reading of how seventeenth-century discourses inform feminism in the late eighteenth century: 'In a new revolutionary period those images, produced by common liberationist political logic, make the tropes of one radical discourse of one revolutionary period available to another.' 'The Feminization of Ideology,' *Ideology and Form in Eighteenth-Century Literature*, ed. David H. Richter (Lubbock, TX: Texas Tech University Press, 1999), 238.

12 *Memoirs of the Life of Eleanor Gwinn, a Celebrated Courtezan in the Reign of Charles II and Mistress to that Monarch* (1752), 43.

13 Recounted in a letter from Matthew Bramble's nephew, Jeremy Melford, to Sir Watkin Phillips. Tobias Smollett, *The Expedition of Humphry Clinker* (1771), ed. James L. Thorson (New York: W.W. Norton, 1983), 50.

14 Anthony S. Jarrell argues that this shift redefined the function of literature at the end of the eighteenth century: 'The move toward a private, individual realm of literature helped redirect the powerful effects of print and subordinate politics to culture.' *Britain's Bloodless Revolutions: 1688 and the Romantic Reform of Literature* (New York: Palgrave Macmillan, 2005), 58.

15 Carol Houlihan Flynn reflects on this silence in 'Whatever Happened to the Gordon Riots?' *A Companion to the Eighteenth-Century English Novel and Culture*, ed. Paula R. Backscheider and Catherine Ingrassia (Oxford: Blackwell, 2005), 459–80. Richardson's *Sir Charles Grandison* set the stage for the later eighteenth-century novel's consideration of marriage and religious difference after attempts to pass the Jewish Naturalization Act stirred up toleration debates in 1753.

16 Lanser, 'The Novel Body Politic,' *A Companion to the Eighteenth-Century English Novel and Culture*, ed. Paula R. Backscheider and Catherine Ingrassia (Oxford: Blackwell, 2005), 494–5.

17 Roxanne Eberle analyses later representations of sexual misconduct in *Chastity and Transgression in Women's Writing, 1792–1897*, noting that 'radical women writers argue that even if a woman is technically "unchaste" – due to forcible rape, dastardly seduction, or even willing compliance – she can still be virtuous, and hence a model of British womanhood' (New York: Palgrave, 2002), 6.

Bibliography

Manuscript Sources

British Library, London

Add. MS 32,095, fols 363–80. State Papers and Historical Documents 1087–
    1762.
Add. MS 61,460, fol. 165. Arthur Mainwaring to Sarah Churchill. 1710.
Add. MS 63,057B, fol. 158. Gilbert Burnet, 'History of My Own Times.' c.
    1697–1700.
Harleian MS 6914 fol.106. 'On the Duchess of Malbrough.' 1703.
Harleian MS 7317 fols 67–8v. 'On the Dutchess of Portsmouth.' n.d.
Harleian MS 7319:
    fols 269–72v. 'The Lady of Pleasure or the Life of Nelly truly Shown From
        Hop-gard'n Cellar to the Throne Till into th' Grave She tumbled down.'
        1686(?).
    fols 33v–5. 'The Whore of Babylon.' 1678.
    fols 26–8. 'Satyr,' Mr. Lacy. 1677.
    fols 35v–7. 'A Satirical Satyr.' Stephen Colledge. 1678.

Huntington Library, San Marino, California

MS EL 8770. 'A Collection of the Best Poems, Lampoons, Songs, & Satyrs from
    the Revolution 1688 to 1692.'

Library of the French Protestant Church, London

MS 7. Livres d'actes de 1679 à 1692.

Printed Primary Sources

Unless otherwise noted, place of publication is London.

Adee, Nicholas. *A Plot for the Crown, in a Visitation Sermon at Cricklade, May the Fifteenth, 1682. Being a Parallel between the Heir and Husband-men in the Parable, and the Rightful Prince, and his Excluders in Parliament.* 1685.

Advice to Unmarried Women: To recover and reclaim the fallen; and to prevent the fall of others, into the snares and consequences of seduction. 1791.

The Amours of the Sultana of Barbary. A Novel in Two Parts. 1689.

An Appeal from the City to the Country, for the Preservation of Her Majesty's Person, Liberty, Property, and the Protestant Religion. Remonstrating, the Dangers and Miseries of an Arbitrary and Tyrannical Power, which the People of Great Britain may (if not timely prevented) be involv'd in, by the fiery Principles, and pernicious Doctrines, of Dr. Sachervell, and His High Church Faction. 1710.

Articles of High-Treason and other High Crimes and Misdemeanors Against the Dutches of Portsmouth. [1680].

Aulnoy, Countess d' (Marie-Catherine La Mothe). *Memoirs of the Court of England ... To which is added, The Lady's Pacquet of Letters.* 1707.

Aurea Dicta. The King's Gracious Words for the Protestant Religion of the Church of England: Collected from his Majesties Letters, Speeches, Declarations, Directions, and Answers. 1681.

Banks, John. *The Innocent Usurper; or, the Death of the lady Jane Gray. A Tragedy.* 1694.

Baxter, Richard. *The Second Part of the Nonconformists Plea for Peace.* 1680.

Bayle, Pierre. *Bayle: Political Writings.* Ed. Sally L. Jenkinson. Cambridge: Cambridge University Press, 2000.

– *Various Thoughts on the Occasion of a Comet.* 1683. Trans. Robert C. Bartlett. Albany, NY: State University of New York Press, 2000.

Behn, Aphra. *Love-letters between a Nobleman and his Sister.* 1684–7. Ed. Janet Todd. London: Penguin, 1996.

– *The Works of Aphra Behn.* 7 vols. Ed. Janet Todd. London: William Pickering and Chatto; Columbus: Ohio State University Press, 1992–6.

Beverley, Thomas. *The Whole Duty of Nations. Or, National True Religion Argued and Perswaded Upon the Greatest Motives of Scripture and Reason.* 1681.

Bolde, Samuel. *A Plea for Moderation toward Dissenters.* 1682.

Bousset, James Benign. *The History of the Variations of the Protestant Churches.* 2 vols. Paris, 1718. 6th ed. Antwerp, 1742.

Brémond, Gabriel de. *The Apology: or, the Genuine Memoirs of Madam Maria Manchini, Constabless of Colonna, eldest Sister to the Duchess of Mazarin. Writ-*

ten in Spanish by her own Hand, and afterwards made into English by a Person of Quality. 1679.

Brown, Thomas. *A Collection of all the Dialogues Written by Mr. Thomas Brown.* 1704.

– *A Continuation or Second Part of the Letters from the Dead to the Living.* 1703.

Buckingham, John Sheffield, Duke of. *The Character of Charles II, King of England, with a short account of his being poyson'd.* 1696.

Burnet, Gilbert. *An Essay on the Memory of the Late Queen.* 1696.

– *The Ill-Effects of the Animosities among Protestants in England Detected.* 1688.

– *The New Preface and Additional Chapter to the Third Edition of the Pastoral Care.* 1713.

Burrough, Edward. *An alarm to all flesh with an invitation to the true seeker forthwith to flye for his life (clearly) out of the short-lived Babylon into the life ... also, a word of encouragement to the faithful to be faithful still.* 1660.

Calamy, Benjamin. *A Discourse about a Scrupulous Conscience, Preached at the Parish-Church of St. Mary, Aldermanbury, London.* 1683.

Cavendish, Margaret. *The Blazing World and Other Writings.* Ed. Kate Lilley. London: Penguin, 1994.

Cawdrey, Zachary. *A Preparation for Martyrdom, in a Dialogue Betwixt a Minister, and a Gentleman his Parishoner.* 1681.

The Character of a Town-Miss. [1675]. 1680.

Churchill, Sarah (Duchess of Malborough). *An Account of the Conduct of the Dowager Duchess of Malborough, From her first coming to Court, to the Year 1710.* 1742. Rpt. as *Memoirs of Sarah, Duchess of Malborough, together with her Characters of her Contemporaries and her Opinions.* Ed. and intro. William King. George Routledge and Sons, 1830. Rpt. New York: Kraus, 1969.

– *The Opinions of Sarah Duchess-Dowager of Malborough. Published from original MSS.* Edinburgh. 1788.

Cobbett, William. *Cobbett's Parliamentary History of England. From the Norman Conquest, in 1066, to the Year 1803.* 36 vols. London: R. Bagshaw, 1810.

A Collection of Queen Anne's Speeches, Messages, &c. From Her Accession to the Throne, to her Demise. 1714.

A Collection of State Songs, Poems, &c. that have been publish'd since the rebellion. 1716.

Coxe, William. *Memoirs of the Life and Administration of Sir Robert Walpole.* 3 vols. 1798.

Croft, Herbert. *A Short Discourse Concerning the Reading His Majesties Late Declaration in the Churches.* 1688.

Crouch, Nathaniel. *The Secret History ... of the Last Four Monarchs of Great Brit-*

ain: Viz. James I, Charles I, Charles II, James II, To which is added, An Appendix, Containing the Later Reign of James the Second. 1693.

Cumming, John. A Sermon Preached on Occasion of the Death of our late Gracious & Memorable Sovereign, Queen Mary. 1695.

Defoe, Daniel. Conjugal Lewdness. 1727. Ed. Liz Bellamy. Vol. 5 of Religious and Didactic Writings of Daniel Defoe. 10 vols. Ed. W.R. Owens and P.N. Furbank. London: Pickering and Chatto, 2006.

– Defoe's Review, reproduced from the original editions, with an introduction and bibliographical notes by Arthur Wellesley Secord. New York: Published for the Facsimile Text Society by Columbia University Press, 1938.

– A Dialogue Betwixt Whig and Tory, Alias Williamite and Jacobite. Wherein the Principles and Practices of each Party are fairly and impartially stated; that thereby Mistakes and Prejudices may be removed from amongst us, and all those who prefer English Liberty, and Protestant Religion, to French Slavery and Popery, may be inform'd how to choose fit and proper Instruments for our Preservation in these Times of Danger. 1693.

– The Letters of Daniel Defoe. Ed. George Harris Healey. Oxford: Clarendon Press, 1955.

– The Pernicious Consequences of the Clergy's Intermedling with Affairs of State: with Reasons Humbly offer'd for passing a Bill to Incapacitate them from the Like Practice for the Future. [1714].

– Roxana, The Fortunate Mistress. 1724. Ed. David Blewitt. London: Penguin, 1982.

– Royal Religion: Being some Enquiry after the Piety of Princes. With Remarks on a Book, Entituled, A Form of Prayers us'd by King William. 1704.

– A Short View of the Present State of the Protestant Religion in Britain as It is Now profest in the Episcopal Church in England, the Presbyterian Church in Scotland, and the Dissenters in Both. Edinburgh, 1707.

Dryden, John. The Works of John Dryden. General editors, Edward Niles Hooker, H.T. Swedenberg, Jr. Berkeley and Los Angeles: University of California Press, 1956–96.

Dunton, John. King Abigail: or, The Secret Reign of the She-Favorite, Detected and Applied; in a Sermon Upon these Words, 'And Women rule over them.' 1715.

– The Night-walker: or, Evening Rambles in Search after Lewd Women. 1696. Ed. Randolph Trumbach. Facsimile. New York: Garland, 1985.

D'Urfey, Thomas, Gloriana. A Funeral Pindarique Poem: Sacred to the Blessed Memory of that Ever-admired and most Excellent Princess, Our Late Gracious Soveraign [sic] Lady Queen Mary. 1695.

The Dutchess of Portsmouths and Count Coningsmarks Farwel to England. 1682.

An Enquiry after Religion: Or, A View of the Idolatry, Superstition, Bigotry and Hi-
pocrisie of all Churches and Sects throughout the World. 1691.

Erotopolis. The Present State of Bettyland. 1684.

Essex Papers. Vol. 1, *1672–1679.* Ed. Osmund Airy. Camden Society, 1890.

Ferguson, Robert. *A Letter to a Person of Honour, concerning the Black Box.* 1680.

– *A Letter to a Person of Honour, concerning the Kings disavowing the having been*
Married to the D. of M.'s Mother. 1680.

Feilding, Robert ('Beau'). 'An Elegy On the Death of the Dutchess of Cleveland, who Died on Sunday Night last October, 9, 1709. At her House in
Chiswick, in the 65th Year of her Age.' 1709.

Fielding, Henry. *The History of Tom Jones, a Foundling.* 1749. Ed. John Bender
and Simon Stern. Oxford: Oxford University Press, 1996.

– *Joseph Andrews.* 1742. Ed. Martin C. Battestin. Wesleyan, CT: Wesleyan University Press, 1967.

– *The Plays of Henry Fielding.* 3 vols. Ed. Thomas Lockwood. Oxford: Oxford
University Press, 2004–.

– *The Works of Henry Fielding.* 10 vols. Ed. Leslie Stephen. London, 1882.

Forsyth, William. *The Novels and Novelists of the Eighteenth Century, in Illustra-*
tion of the Manners and Morals of the Age. London: John Murray, 1871.

'A Funeral Eclogue, Sacred to the Memory of Her Most Serene Majesty. Our
Late Gracious Queen Mary.' 1694/5.

A Gentlewoman of Quality. 'A Poem on the Death of the Queen.' 1694/5.

The Genuine History of Mrs. Sarah Prydden, Usually Called, Sally Salisbury, and
her Gallants. Regularly Containing, The real Story of her Life. 1723.

Gildon, Charles. *Remarks on Mr. Rowe's Tragedy of the Lady Jane Gray.* 1715.

Glanvill, Joseph. *The Zealous, and Impartial Protestant, Shewing Some great,*
but less heeded Dangers of Popery, In Order to Thorough and Effectual Security
against it. 1681.

Granger, James. *A Biographical History of England.* 2nd ed. 1775.

The Highlanders Salivated, or the Loyal Association of M–ll K–ng's Midnight Club:
with the serious Address of the Ladies of Drury, to the batter'd strolling Nymphs of
their Community. 1746.

The history of Mademoiselle de Beleau: or, the new Roxana, the fortunate mistress,
afterwards Countess of Wintselsheim. Published by Mr. Daniel De Foe. And
from papers found, since his decease, it appears was greatly altered by himself.
1775.

Hoadly, Benjamin. *The Nature of the Kingdom, or Church, of Christ.* 1717.

Hobbes, Thomas. *Leviathan.* 1651. Ed. C.B. Macpherson. London: Penguin,
1968, 1985.

– *Thomae Hobbesii Malmesburiensis Vita.* 1679.

Hollands Leaguer: Or, An Historical Discourse of the Life and Actions of Doná Britanica Hollandia the Arch-Mistris of the wicked women of Eutopia. 1632.

Joke Upon Joke. 1721.

Jones, David. *Secret History of Whitehall, From the Restoration of Charles II. Down to the Abdication of the late K. James.* 1697.

Kirkpatrick, James. *Advice to Protestants: Being a Prefatory Address to all Her Majesty's Protestant Subjects.* Dublin, 1714.

LaFayette, Marie Madeleine Pioche De La Vergne. *Oeuvres Complètes.* Ed. Roger Duchêne. Paris: François Bourin, 1990.

Law, William. *William Law's Defence of Church Principles: Three Letters to the Bishop of Bangor, 1717–1719.* Ed. J.O. Nash and Charles Gore. 2nd ed. Edinburgh: John Grant, 1909.

Lawrence, William. *Marriage by the Morall Law of God Vindicated. Against all Ceremonial Laws of Popes and Bishops destructive to Filiation Aliment and Succession and the Government of Familyes and Kingdoms.* 1680.

– *Of the profound Popery of the Common Lawyers, in Transubstantiation of two persons into one person, and the mischiefs thereof.* 1680.

Leslie, Charles. *An Answer to a Book Intituled, The State of the Protestants in Ireland Under the late King James's Government.* 1692.

'A Letany for St. Omers.' 1682.

The life and adventures of Roxana, the fortunate mistress; or, most unhappy wife. 1755.

The Life, Character, and Death of the most Illustrious Pattern of Female Virtue, the Lady Jane Gray, Who was Beheaded in the Tower at 16 Years of Age, for her stedfast Adherence to the Protestant Religion. 1714.

The Life and Character of Jane Shore, collected From our best Historians, chiefly from the Writings of Sir Thomas More ... Humbly offer'd to the Readers and Spectators of her Tragedy, Written by Mr. Rowe. 1714.

The Life and Death of Jane Shore; Containing the whole Account of her Amorous Intrigues with King Edward IVth. And the Lord Hastings: Her Penitence, Punishment, and Poverty. 1714.

Lloyd, William. *A Sermon Preached Before her Majesty, on May 29, being the Anniversary of the Restauration of the King and Royal Family.* 1692.

– 'To the Kingdom in General.' *An Answer to the Bishop of Oxford's Reasons for Abrogating the Test, Impos'd on All Members of Parliament.* 1688.

Locke, John. *A Letter Concerning Toleration.* Trans. William Popple. 1689. In *A Letter Concerning Toleration in Focus,* ed. John Horton and Susan Mendes. London: Routledge, 1991.

Lockwood, Thomas, and Ronald Paulson, eds. *Henry Fielding: The Critical Heritage.* London: Routledge, 1969.

Madam Gwins Answer to the Dutchess of Portsmouths Letter. 1682.

Manley, Delarivier. *The New Atlantis.* 1709. Ed. Ros Ballaster. Harmondsworth: Penguin, 1992.

– [attribution uncertain]. *The Secret History of Queen Zarah, and the Zarazians; Being a Looking-glass for — in the Kingdom of Albigion.* And *The Second Part, or a Continuation of the Secret History of Queen Zarah.* 1705. In *The Novels of Mary Delarivier Manley 1705–1714.* Vol. 1. Ed. Patricia Köster. Gainsville, FL: Scholars' Facsimilies and Reprints, 1971.

Marvell, Andrew. *Poems and Letters of Andrew Marvell.* 3rd ed. Vol.1. Ed. H.M. Margoliouth. Oxford: Clarendon Press, 1971.

– *Prose Works of Andrew Marvell.* Vol. 1. Ed. Annabel Patterson. New Haven, CT: Yale University Press, 2003.

– *A Seasonable Discourse, Shewing the Unreasonableness and Mischiefs of Impositions in Matters of Religion, Recommended to Serious Consideration.* 1687.

Memoirs of the Life and Times of … T. Tennison, late Archbishop of Canterbury … Together with his last Will and Testament, etc. 3rd ed. [1716].

Memoirs of the Life of Eleanor Gwinn. 1752.

Memoirs of the Lives of King Edward IV. And Jane Shore. Extracted from the best Historians. 1714.

A Memorial for the 30th of January: or, Fanatick Loyalty. 1716.

Nalson, John. *Foxes and Fire-brands: or a Speciman of the Danger and Harmony of Popery and Separation.* 1680.

A New Vision of Lady Gr—y's, Concerning her Sister, the Lady Henrietta Berkeley. In a Letter to Madam Fan — . 1682.

'An Ode on Her Highness, the Princess of Orange.' The Hague, 1688.

Owen, John. *A Brief and Impartial Account of the Nature of the Protestant Religion: its Present State in the World, its Strength and Weakness, with the Wayes and Indications of the Ruine or Continuance of its Publick National Profession.* 1682.

Parker, Samuel. 'A Preface to the Reader.' *Bishop Bramhall's Vindication of Himself and the Episcopal Clergy, from the Presbyterian Charge of Popery, as it is managed by Mr. Baxter in his treatise of the Grotian religion. Together with a preface [by Samuel Parker] shewing what grounds there are of fears and jealousies of Popery.* 1672.

The Parliament of Women, Or, a Compleat History of the Proceedings and Debates, of a particular Junto, of Ladies and Gentlewomen, With a design to alter the Government of the world. By way of a Satyr. 1684.

Pettit, Edward. *The Visions of the Reformation, or A discovery of the follies and villanies that have been practis'd popish and fanatical thorough reformations since the reformation of the Church of England.* 1683.

A Pleasant Battle Between Two Lap Dogs of the Utopian Court. 1681.

Poems on Affairs of State: Augustan Satirical Verse, 1660–1714. 7 vols. Gen. ed.
George de F. Lord. New Haven, CT: Yale University Press, 1963–75.
Political Operas 1: Satire and Allegory. Selected and arranged by Walter H. Rub-
samen. New York: Garland Publishing, 1974.
*A Review of the Tragedy of Jane Shore. Consisting of Observations on the Characters,
Manners, Stile, and Sentiments.* 1714.
Richardson, Samuel. *Clarissa, or the History of a Young Lady.* 1747–8. Ed. Angus
Ross. London: Penguin, 1985.
– *Pamela.* 1740. Ed. Thomas Keymer and Alice Wakely. Oxford: Oxford Uni-
versity Press, 2001.
– *Selected Letters of Samuel Richardson.* Ed. John Carroll. Oxford: Clarendon
Press, 1965.
Rowe, Nicholas. *Three Plays.* Ed. J.R. Sutherland. London: Scholartis Press,
1929.
Saint-Evrémond, Charles Marguetel de Saint Denis. *The Works of Monsieur de
St. Evremond, Made English from the French Original,* 3 vols. 2nd ed. 1728.
– *Œuvres ... avec la vie de l'auteur, par monsieur Des Maizeaux ... Nouvelle édi-
tion.* 9 vols. Ed. Pierre Des Maizeaux. Amsterdam, 1753.
Savile, George. *A Letter to a Dissenter, Upon Occasion of His Majesties Late Gra-
cious Declaration of Indulgence.* 1687.
Saywell, William. *A Serious Inquiry into the Means of an Happy Union; or, What
Reformation is Necessary to prevent Popery, and to avert God's Judgments from the
Nation.* 1681.
Scott, Walter. 'Prefatory Memoir to Fielding.' *The Novels of Henry Fielding, Esq.*
London: James Ballantyne, 1821.
*The Secret History of the Dutchess of Portsmouth: Giving an Account of the In-
treagues of the Court, during her Ministry. And of the Death of K.C.II.* 1690.
*The Secret History of the Rye-House Plot; and of Monmouth's Rebellion. Written by
Ford, Lord Grey in 1685. Now first published from a manuscript, sign'd by himself.*
1754.
Sévigné, Marie de Rabutin-Chantal. *Lettres de Madame de Sevigné.* 3 vols. Ed.
Emile Gérard-Gailly. Paris: Gallimard, 1953–7.
– *Correspondance.* 3 vols. Ed. Roger Duchêne. Paris: Gallimard, 1974–8.
Smith, Alexander. 'Nell Gwin, Concubine to King Charles II.' *The School of Ve-
nus, or, Cupid Restor'd to Sight; being a History of Cuckolds and Cuckold Makers.*
1716.
Smith's Protestant Intelligence, Domestick and Foreign. 17–21 March, 28–31
March, 4–7 April, 1681.
Stephens, William. *An Account of the Growth of Deism.* 1696.
The Third Part of the Growth of Popery and Arbitrary Government in England. 1683.

Tillotson, John. *The Protestant Religion Vindicated, From the Charge of Singularity and Novelty: in a Sermon Preached Before the King at Whitehall, April 2nd, 1680.* 1680.

The Town-Misses Declaration and Apology; Or, an Answer to the Character of a Town-Misse. 1675.

The Trial of Ford, Lord Grey of Werk, &c. [1682]. 1716.

A True-Protestant Catechism, Explaining the Grounds and Methods of the True-Protestant Plot; Set for the Instruction of the Brethren in the Mystery of Whiggism. 1683.

Tudor and Stuart Proclamations: 1485–1714. Calendared by Robert Steele. 2 vols. Oxford: Clarendon Press, 1910.

The Unfortunate Concubines: The History of Fair Rosamond, Mistress to Henry II; and Jane Shore, Concubine to Edward IV; King of England. Shewing how they came to be so. With Their Lives, Remarkable Actions, and Unhappy Ends. 1708.

Verney, Margaret M. *Memoirs of the Verney Family, From the Restoration to the Revolution, 1660–1696.* Compiled by Margaret M. Verney. 4 vols. London: Longmans, 1899.

Vichard de St. Réal, César. '*Lettre. Sur l'Etude & Sur les Sciences.*'In *Les Œuvres de M. L'Abbé de Saint Réal. Nouvelle Édition, Rangeé dans un meilleur ordre, & augmentée.* Vol. 3, 17–24. Paris, 1745.

– *The memoires of the Dutchess Mazarine. Written in French by her own hand, and done into English by P. Porter, Esq; Together with the reasons of her coming into England. Likewise, a letter containing a true character of her person and conversation.* 1676.

Walsh, William. 'A Funeral Elegy Upon the Death of the Queen.' 1695.

The Whore of Babylon's Pockey Priest; Or, a True Narrative of the Apprehension of William Geldon alias Bacon, a Secular Priest of the Church of Rome now Prisoner in Newgate. Who Had just before been above two months in Cure for the French Pox; wherein Is inserted a true Copy of the Apothecaries Bill found in his Chamber, containing the whole Process of that Reverend Fathers Venereal Cure. 1679.

The Whore's Rhetorick. 1683. Fascimile reproduction. Intro. James R. Irvine and G. Jack Gravlee. Delmar, NY: Scholars' Fascimiles and Reprints, 1979.

Wilson, John Harold, ed. *Court Satires of the Restoration.* Columbus: Ohio State University Press, 1976.

A Woman of Quality, A Late Confidant of Q. Messalina [attrib. Gregorio Leti]. *Love Letters between Polydorus and Messalina, Late Queen of Albion.* 1689.

– *The Second Part of the Amours of Messalina Late Queen of Albion. Wherein the Secret Court Intrigues of the Four last Years Resign are further pursued; Particularly the Imposture of the Child.* 1689.

Young, Edward. *The Force of Religion; or, Vanquish'd Love.* 1715.

Secondary Sources

Aikins, Janet E. 'To Know Jane Shore, "think on all time backward."' *Papers on Language and Literature* 18.3 (1982): 258–77.

Alexander, Julia Marciari, and Catharine MacLeod, eds. *Politics, Transgression, and Representation at the Court of Charles II*. New Haven, CT: Yale University Press, 2007.

Aravamudan, Srinivas. *Tropicopolitans: Colonialism and Agency, 1688–1804*. Durham: Duke University Press, 1999.

Armstrong, Nancy. *Desire and Domestic Fiction: A Political History of the Novel*. New York: Oxford University Press, 1987.

Ashcraft, Richard. 'Latitudinarianism and Toleration: Historical Myths versus Political History.' In *Philosophy, Science, and Religion in England, 1640–1700*, ed. Richard Kroll, Richard Ashcraft, and Perez Zagorin, 151–77. Cambridge: Cambridge University Press, 1992.

Backscheider, Paula R. 'Firing off the Canon.' *Novel: A Forum on Fiction* 24.1 (1990): 115–18.

– 'The Rise of Gender as Political Category.' In *Revising Women: Eighteenth-Century 'Women's Fiction' and Social Engagement*, ed. Paula R. Backscheider, 31–57. Baltimore: Johns Hopkins University Press, 2000.

– and Catherine Ingrassia, eds. *A Companion to the Eighteenth-Century English Novel and Culture*. Oxford: Blackwell, 2005.

Bakhtin, Mikhail. *The Dialogic Imagination: Four Essays*. Ed. Michael Holquist. Trans. Caryl Emerson and Michael Holquist. Austin: University of Texas Press, 1981.

Ballaster, Ros. 'Performing *Roxane*: The Oriental Woman as the Sign of Luxury in Eighteenth-Century Fictions.' In *Luxury in the Eighteenth Century: Debates, Desires and Delectable Goods*, ed. Maxine Berg and Elizabeth Eger, 165–77. New York: Palgrave Macmillan, 2003.

– *Seductive Forms: Women's Amatory Fiction from 1684–1740*. Oxford: Clarendon Press, 1992.

– '"The story of the heart": *Love-Letters between a Noble-man and His Sister*.' In *Cambridge Companion to Aphra Behn*, ed. Hughes and Todd, 135–50.

Bannet, Eve Tavor. '"Secret history": Or, talebearing inside and outside the secretorie.' In *The Uses of History in Early Modern England*, ed. Pauline Kewes, 367–88. San Marino, CA: Huntington Library, 2006.

Barthes, Roland. *Le Plaisir du Texte*. Paris: Editions du Seuil, 1973.

– *The Pleasure of the Text*. Trans. Richard Miller. New York: Hill and Wang, 1975.

Bataille, Robert. 'The Magdalen Charity for the Reform of Prostitutes: A Foucauldian Moment.' In *Illicit Sex: Identity Politics in Early Modern Culture*, ed. Thomas DiPero and Pat Gill, 109–22. Athens: University of Georgia Press, 1997.

Battestin, Martin C. General Introduction. In *The History of Tom Jones, a Foundling*. 2 vols. Middletown, CT: Wesleyan University Press, 1975.

– *A Henry Fielding Companion*. Westport, CT: Greenwood, 2000.

– *Henry Fielding: A Life*. London: Routledge, 1989.

– *The Moral Basis of Fielding's Art: A Study of Joseph Andrews*. Middletown, CT: Wesleyan University Press, 1959.

– *The Providence of Wit: Aspects of Form in Augustan Literature and the Arts*. Oxford: Clarendon Press, 1974.

Bean, Brenda. 'Sight and Self-Disclosure: Richardson's Revision of Swift's "The Lady's Dressing Room."' *Eighteenth-Century Life* ns 14.1 (1990): 1–23.

Beasley, Faith E. *Revising Memory: Women's Fiction and Memoirs in Seventeenth-Century France*. New Brunswick, NJ: Rutgers University Press, 1990.

Beasley, Jerry C. *Novels of the 1740s*. Athens, GA: University of Georgia Press, 1982.

Beddard, Robert. 'The Unexpected Whig Revolution of 1688.' In *Revolutions of 1688*, ed. Robert Beddard, 11–101. Oxford: Oxford University Press, 1991.

Bender, John. Introduction. In *Tom Jones*, ed. John Bender and Simon Stern. Oxford: Oxford University Press, 1996.

Benedict, Barbara M. *Curiosity: A Cultural History of Early Modern Inquiry*. Chicago: University of Chicago Press, 2001.

– 'The Curious Genre: Female Inquiry in Amatory Fiction.' *Studies in the Novel* 30.2 (1998): 194–210.

Bennett, G.V. 'Conflict in the Church.' In *Britain after the Glorious Revolution, 1689–1714*, ed. Geoffrey Holmes, 155–75. London: Macmillan, 1969.

Bersani, Leo. 'Is the Rectum a Grave?' *October* 43 (1987): 197–222.

Bevin, Bryan. *The Duchess Hortense: Cardinal Mazarin's Wanton Niece*. London: Rubicon, 1987.

Bingham, Edward R. 'The Political Apprenticeship of Benjamin Hoadly.' *Church History* 16.3 (1947): 154–65.

Binhammer, Katherine. 'Knowing Love: The Epistemology of *Clarissa*.' *ELH* 74.4 (2007): 859–79.

– 'The Whore's Love.' *Eighteenth-Century Fiction* 20.4 (2008): 507–34.

Black, Jeremy. 'Confessional State or Elect Nation? Religion and Identity in Eighteenth-Century England.' In *Protestantism and National Identity: Britain and Ireland, c. 1650– c.1850*, ed. Tony Claydon and Ian McBride, 53–74. Cambridge: Cambridge University Press, 1998.

Bowers, Toni. *The Politics of Motherhood: British Writing and Culture*. Cambridge: Cambridge University Press, 1996.

– 'Queen Anne Makes Provision.' In *Refiguring Revolutions: Aesthetics and Poli-*

tics from the English Revolution to the Romantic Revolution, ed. Kevin Sharpe and Steven N. Zwicker, 57–74. Berkeley and Los Angeles: University of California Press, 1998.

– 'Sex, Lies, and Invisibility: Amatory Fiction from the Restoration to Mid-Century.' In *The Columbia History of the British Novel*, ed. John Richetti et al., 50–72. New York: Columbia University Press, 1994.

Braverman, Richard. 'Rebellion Redux: Figuring Whig History in *Tom Jones*.' *Clio* 24.3 (1995): 251–68.

Brewer, John. *A Sentimental Murder: Love and Madness in the Eighteenth Century*. New York: Farrar, Straus, and Giroux, 2004.

Brown, Laura. 'The Feminization of Ideology.' In *Ideology and Form in Eighteenth-Century Literature*, ed. David H. Richter, 223–40. Lubbock, TX: Texas Tech University Press, 1999.

Brown, Wendy. *States of Injury: Power and Freedom in Late Modernity*. Princeton: Princeton University Press, 1995.

Bucholz, R.O. *The Augustan Court: Queen Anne and the Decline of Court Culture*. Stanford: Stanford University Press, 1993.

Bullough, Vern L. 'Prostitution and Reform in Eighteenth-Century England.' *Eighteenth-Century Life* 9.3 (1985): 61–74.

Burgess, Miranda. *British Fiction and the Production of Social Order, 1740–1830*. Cambridge: Cambridge University Press, 2000.

Burtt, Shelley. *Virtue Transformed: Political Argument in England, 1688–1740*. Cambridge: Cambridge University Press, 1992.

Campbell, Jill. *Natural Masques: Gender and Identity in Fielding's Plays and Novels*. Stanford: Stanford University Press, 1995.

Carlton, Peter J. 'The Mitigated Truth: Tom Jones's Double Heroism.' *Studies in the Novel* 19.4 (1987): 397–409.

– '*Tom Jones* and the '45 Once Again.' *Studies in the Novel* 20.4 (1988): 361–73.

Carnell, Rachel. *Partisan Politics, Narrative Realism, and the Rise of the British Novel*. New York: Palgrave and Macmillan, 2006.

– *A Political Biography of Delarivier Manley*. London: Pickering and Chatto, 2008.

Castle, Terry. *Clarissa's Ciphers: Meaning and Disruption in Richardson's 'Clarissa.'* Ithaca, NY: Cornell University Press, 1982.

Chaber, Lois A. 'Christian Form and Anti-Feminism in *Clarissa*.' *Eighteenth-Century Fiction* 15.3–4 (2003): 507–37.

Chalus, Elaine. '"To Serve my friends": Women and Political Patronage in Eighteenth-Century England.' In *Women, Privilege, and Power: British Politics, 1750 to the Present*, ed. Amanda Vickery, 57–88.

Clark, J.C.D. *English Society 1688–1832: Ideology, Social Structure and Political Practice during the Ancien Regime.* Cambridge: Cambridge University Press, 1985.

– 'Religious Affiliation and Dynastic Allegiance in Eighteenth-Century England: Edmund Burke, Thomas Paine and Samuel Johnson.' *ELH* 64.4 (1997): 1029–67.

Clark, Robert. Introduction, *Roxana*, Everyman edition. London: Dent and Charles E. Tuttle, 1998.

Claydon, Tony. *Europe and the Making of England, 1660–1760.* Cambridge: Cambridge University Press, 2007.

– *William III and the Godly Revolution.* Cambridge: Cambridge University Press, 1996.

Claydon, Tony, and Ian McBride, eds. *Protestantism and National Identity: Britain and Ireland, c. 1650–c. 1850.* Cambridge: Cambridge University Press, 1998.

Cleary, Thomas R. *Henry Fielding: Political Writer.* Waterloo, ON: Wilfred Laurier University Press, 1984.

Clifton, Robin. *The Last Popular Rebellion: The Western Rising of 1685.* London: St Martin's, 1984.

Cohn, Dorrit. *The Distinction of Fiction.* Baltimore: Johns Hopkins University Press, 1999.

Collins, Sheila. *A Different Heaven and Earth.* Valley Forge, PA.: Judson Press, 1974.

Combe, Kirk. *A Martyr for Sin : Rochester's Critique of Polity, Sexuality, and Society.* Newark: University of Delaware Press, 1998

Conway, Alison. *Private Interests: Women, Portraiture, and the Visual Culture of the English Novel, 1709–1791.* Toronto: University of Toronto Press, 2001.

Cottegnies, Line. '"Aphra Behn Unmasqued"' A. Behn's Translation of La Rouchefoucauld's *Réflexions*.' In *Aphra Behn: Identity, Alterity, Ambiguity*, ed. Mary Ann O'Donnell, Bernard Dhuicq, and Guyonne Leduc, 12–29. Paris: L'Harmattan, 2000.

Cottret, Bernard. *The Huguenots in England: Immigration and Settlement, c. 1550–1700.* Cambridge: Cambridge University Press, 1985.

Crane, Julie. 'Defoe's *Roxana*: The Making and Unmaking of a Heroine.' *Modern Language Review* 102.1 (2007): 11–25.

Cranston, Maurice. 'John Locke and the Case for Toleration.' In *John Locke: A Letter Concerning Toleration in Focus*, ed. John Horton and Susan Mendus, 78–97. London: Routledge, 1991.

Cross, Wilbur L. *The History of Henry Fielding.* 2 vols. New Haven, CT: Yale and Oxford University Presses, 1918.

Cruickshanks, Eveline, ed. *Ideology and Conspiracy: Aspects of Jacobitism, 1689–1759*. Edinburgh: John Donald Publishers, 1982.

– 'Religion and Royal Succession: The Rage of Party.' In *Britain in the First Age of Party, 1680–1750: Essays Presented to Geoffrey Holmes*, ed. Clyve Jones, 19–43. London: Hambledon Press, 1987.

Culler, Jonathan. *The Pursuit of Signs: Semiotics, Literature, Deconstruction*. Ithaca, NY: Cornell University Press, 1981.

Cunningham, Peter. *The Story of Nell Gwyn, and the Sayings of Charles II*. 1882. Ed. Gordon Goodwin. London: Bullen, 1903.

Damrosch, Leopold, Jr. *God's Plot and Man's Stories: Studies in the Fictional Imagination from Milton to Fielding*. Chicago: University of Chicago Press, 1985.

Dasent, Arthur Irwin. *Nell Gwynne, 1650–1687, her life story from St. Giles's to St. James's with some account of Whitehall and Windsor in the reign of Charles the Second*. London: Macmillan, 1924.

DeJean, Joan. *Tender Geographies: Women and the Origins of the Novel in France*. New York: Columbia University Press, 1991.

Deleuze, Gilles. *The Logic of Sense*. Trans. Mark Lester with Charles Stivall. New York: Columbia University Press, 1990.

Deleuze, Gilles, and Felix Guttari. *Anti-Oedipus: Capitalism and Schizophrenia*. Trans. Robert Hurley, Mark Seem, and Helen R. Lane. Pref. by Michel Foucault. Minneapolis: University of Minnesota Press, 1983.

Dhuicq, Bernard. 'France and Roman Catholicism: Intertextuality in Aphra Behn's Works.' In *Aphra Behn: Identity, Alterity, Ambiguity*, ed. Mary Ann O'Donnell, Bernard Dhuicq, and Guyonne Leduc, 1–12. Paris: L'Harmattan, 2000.

Dickie, Simon. '*Joseph Andrews* and the Great Laughter Debate.' In *Studies in Eighteenth-Century Culture*, vol. 34, ed. Catherine Ingrassia and Jeffrey S. Ravel, 271–332. Baltimore: Johns Hopkins University Press, 2005.

Dictionnaire Historique de la Langue Française. Ed. Alain Rey, et al. Paris: Dictionnaires Le Robert, 1992.

Dolan, Frances E. *Whores of Babylon: Catholicism, Gender, and Seventeenth-Century Print Culture*. Ithaca, NY: Cornell University Press, 1999.

Doody, Margaret Anne. 'Gender, Literature, and Gendering Literature in the Restoration.' In *Cambridge Companion to English Literature*, ed. Steven N. Zwicker, 58–81. Cambridge: Cambridge University Press, 1998.

– *A Natural Passion: A Study of the Novels of Samuel Richardson*. Oxford: Clarendon Press, 1974.

– 'Richardson's Politics.' *Eighteenth-Century Fiction* 2.2 (January 1990): 113–26.

– 'Samuel Richardson: Fiction and Knowledge.' In *The Cambridge Companion to the Eighteenth-Century Novel*, ed. John Richetti, 90–119. Cambridge: Cambridge University Press, 1996.

Downie, J.A. 'What if Delarivier Manley Did *Not* Write *The Secret History of Queen Zarah*?' *The Library: The Transactions of the Bibliographic Society* 5.3 (2004): 247–64.

Drake, George A. 'Historical Space in the "History of": Between Public and Private in *Tom Jones*.' *ELH* 66.3 (1999): 707–37.

Duchovnay, Gerald. 'Aphra Behn's Religion.' *Notes and Queries* 23 (1976): 235–7.

Eaves, T.C. Duncan, and Ben D. Kimpel. *Samuel Richardson: A Biography*. Oxford: Clarendon Press, 1971.

Erskine-Hill, Howard. 'Literature and the Jacobite Cause: Was There a Rhetoric of Jacobitism?' In *Ideology and Conspiracy*, ed. Cruickshanks. 49–70.

Faller, Lincoln B. *Crime and Defoe: A New Kind of Writing*. Cambridge: Cambridge University Press, 1993.

Feldwick, Arlen, and Cary J. Nederman. '"Religion Set the World at Odds": Deism and the Climate of Religious Tolerance in the Works of Aphra Behn.' In *Beyond the Persecuting Society: Religious Toleration before the Enlightenment*, ed. John Christian Laursen and Cary J. Nederman, 216–31. Philadelphia: University of Pennsylvania Press, 1998.

Flynn, Carol Houlihan. *The Body in Swift and Defoe*. Cambridge: Cambridge University Press, 1990.

– 'Richardson and His Readers: An Introduction to the Essays.' In *Clarissa and Her Readers: New Essays for the Clarissa Project*, ed. Carol Houlihan Flynn and Edward Copeland, 1–18. New York: AMS, 1999.

Forneron, Henri. *Louise de Kéroualle, Duchess of Portsmouth, 1649–1734*. Paris, 1886.

Furbank, P.N., and W.R. Owens. 'The "Lost" Continuation of *Roxana*.' *Eighteenth-Century Fiction* 9.3 (1997): 299–308.

Gabbard, D. Christopher. 'The Dutch Wives' Good Husbandry: Defoe's *Roxana* and Financial Literacy.' *Eighteenth-Century Studies* 37.2 (2004): 237–51.

Gallagher, Catherine. 'Embracing the Absolute: The Politics of the Female Subject in Seventeenth-Century England.' *Genders* 1 (1988): 24–39.

– *Nobody's Story: The Vanishing Acts of Women Writers in the Marketplace*. Berkeley and Los Angeles: University of California Press, 1994.

Gibbs, Graham C. 'Huguenot Contributions to England's Intellectual Life, and England's Intellectual Commerce with Europe, c. 1680–1720.' In *Huguenots in Britain and Their French Background, 1550–1800*, ed. Irene Scouloudi, 20–41. London: Macmillan, 1987.

Gibson, William. *The Church of England, 1688–1832: Unity and Accord*. London: Routledge, 2001.

Gilman, Sander. 'Black Bodies, White Bodies: Toward an Iconography of Female Sexuality in Late Nineteenth-Century Art, Medicine, and Literature.' *Critical Inquiry* 12.1 (1985): 204–42.

Golden, Morris. 'Public Context and Imagining Self in *Clarissa*.' *Studies in English Literature, 1500–1900* 25.3 (1985): 575–98.

Goldgar, Bertrand. 'Fielding and the Whores of London.' *Philological Quarterly* 64.2 (1985): 265–73.

– *Walpole and the Wits: The Relation of Politics to Literature, 1722–1742.* Lincoln, NB: University of Nebraska Press, 1976.

Goldie, Mark. 'Contextualizing Dryden's Absalom: William Lawrence, The Laws of Marriage, and the Case for King Monmouth.' In *Religion, Literature, and Politics in Post-Reformation England, 1540–1688*, ed. Donna B. Hamilton and Richard Strier, 208–30. Cambridge: Cambridge University Press, 1996.

– 'The Political Thought of the Anglican Revolution.' In *The Revolutions of 1688*, ed. Robert Beddard, 102–36. Oxford: Oxford University Press, 1991.

– and Clare Jackson. 'Williamite Tyranny and the Whig Jacobites.' In *Redefining William III: The Impact of the King-Stadholder in International Context*, ed. Esther Mijers and David Onnekink, 177–200. Burlington, VT: Ashgate, 2007.

– and Richard H. Popkin. 'Scepticism, Priestcraft, and Toleration.' In *The Cambridge History of Eighteenth-Century Political Thought*, ed. Mark Goldie and Robert Wokler. Cambridge: Cambridge University Press, 2006. 79-109.

Goreau, Angeline. *Reconstructing Aphra: A Social Biography of Aphra Behn.* New York: Dial Press, 1980.

Greaves, Richard L. *Enemies under His Feet: Radicals and Nonconformists in Britain, 1664–1677.* Stanford: Stanford University Press, 1990.

Green, David. *Sarah Duchess of Marlborough.* New York: Charles Scribner's Sons, 1967.

Griffin, Robert J. 'The Text in Motion: Eighteenth-Century *Roxanas*.' *ELH* 72.2 (2005): 387–406.

Gwynn, Robin. *Huguenot Heritage: The History and Contribution of the Huguenots in Britain.* 2nd rev. ed. Brighton: Sussex Academic Press, 2001.

Hall, Kim F. *Things of Darkness: Economies of Race and Gender in Early Modern England.* Ithaca, NY: Cornell University Press, 1995.

Hammond, Paul. 'The King's Two Bodies: Representations of Charles II.' In *Culture, Politics and Society in Britain, 1660–1800*, ed. Jeremy Black and Jeremy Gregory, 13–48. Manchester: Manchester University Press, 1991.

Harol, Corrinne. *Enlightened Virginity in Eighteenth-Century Literature.* London: Palgrave Macmillan, 2006.

Harris, Frances. *A Passion for Government: The Life of Sarah, Duchess of Malborough.* Oxford: Clarendon Press, 1991.

Harris, Jocelyn. 'Grotesque, Classical and Pornographic Bodies in *Clarissa.*' In *New Essays on Samuel Richardson*, ed. Albert J. Rivero, 101–16. New York: St Martin's, 1996.

Harris, Tim. *London Crowds in the Reign of Charles II: Propaganda and Politics from the Restoration until the Exclusion Crisis.* Cambridge: Cambridge University Press, 1987.

– Paul Seward, and Mark Goldie, eds. *The Politics of Religion in Restoration England.* Oxford: Basil Blackwell, 1990.

Hart, Clive, and Kay Gilliland Stevenson. *Heaven and the Flesh: Imagery of Desire from the Renaissance to the Rococo.* Cambridge: Cambridge University Press, 1995.

Hatfield, Glenn W. *Henry Fielding and the Language of Irony.* Chicago: University of Chicago Press, 1968.

Held, Julius S. 'Flora, Goddess and Courtesan.' In *Essays in Honor of Erwin Panofsky*, 2 vols, ed. Millard Meiss, 1:201–18. New York: New York University Press, 1961.

Helgerson, Richard. *Adulterous Alliances: Home, State, and History in Early Modern European Drama and Painting.* Chicago: University of Chicago Press, 2000.

Henderson, Tony. *Disorderly Women in Eighteenth-Century London: Prostitution and Control in the Metropolis, 1730–1830.* London: Longman, 1999.

Hill, Christopher. 'Clarissa Harlowe and her Times.' *Essays in Criticism* 5 (1995): 315–40.

Hinnant, Charles. Introduction. *The London Jilt; or, the Politick Whore.* Peterborough, ON: Broadview Press, 2008.

Hoppit, Julian. *A Land of Liberty? England 1689–1727.* Oxford: Clarendon Press, 2000.

Hughes, Derek. 'Aphra Behn and the Uses of History.' In *The Female Wits: Women and Gender in Restoration Literature and Culture*, ed. Pilar Cuder Dominguez, Zenon Luis Martinez, and Juan Antonio Prieto Pablos, 177–89. Huelva: Universidad de Huelva, 2006.

– and Janet Todd, eds. *The Cambridge Companion to Aphra Behn.* Cambridge: Cambridge University Press, 2004.

Hume, Robert. *The Development of English Drama in the Late Seventeenth Century.* Oxford: Clarendon Press, 1976.

Hunter, J. Paul. *Before Novels: The Cultural Contexts of Eighteenth-Century English Fiction.* New York: W.W. Norton, 1990.

– *Occasional Form: Henry Fielding and the Chains of Circumstance.* Baltimore: Johns Hopkins University Press, 1975.

– 'Serious Reflections on Farther Adventures: Resistances to Closure in Eighteenth-Century English Novels.' In *Augustan Subjects: Essays in Honor of Mar-*

tin C. Battestin, ed. Albert J. Rivero, 276–94. Newark: University of Delaware Press, 1997.

Hutchens, Eleanor. *Irony in Tom Jones*. University, AL: University of Alabama Press, 1965.

Hutton, Ronald. 'The Religion of Charles II.' In *The Stuart Court and Europe: Essays in Politics and Political Culture*, ed. Ronald Smuts, 228–46. Cambridge: Cambridge University Press, 1996.

Isaacs, Tina. 'The Anglican Hierarchy and the Reformation of Manners 1688–1738.' *Journal of Ecclesiastical History* 33.3 (1982): 391–411.

Israel, Jonathan I. *Radical Enlightenment: Philosophy and the Making of Modernity 1650–1750*. Oxford: Oxford University Press, 2001.

Jones, Robert W. *Gender and the Formation of Taste in Eighteenth-Century Britain*. Cambridge: Cambridge University Press, 1998.

Jones, Vivien. 'Scandalous Femininity: Prostitution and Eighteenth-Century Narrative.' In *Shifting Boundaries: Transformation of the Languages of Public and Private in the Eighteenth Century*, ed. Dario Castiglione and Lesley Sharpe, 54–70. Exeter: University of Exeter Press, 1995.

Kantorowicz, Ernst H. *The King's Two Bodies: A Study in Mediaeval Political Theology*. Princeton: Princeton University Press, 1957.

Kay, Carol. *Political Constructions: Defoe, Richardson, and Sterne in Relation to Hobbes, Hume, and Burke*. Ithaca, NY: Cornell University Press, 1988.

– 'Sympathy, Sex, and Authority in Richardson and Hume.' *Studies in Eighteenth-Century Culture* 12 (1983): 77–92.

Kewes, Paulina, ed. *The Uses of History in Early Modern England*. San Marino, CA: Huntington Library, 2006.

– '"The State is out of Tune": Nicholas Rowe's *Jane Shore* and the Succession Crisis of 1713–14.' *Huntington Library Quarterly* 64.3–4 (2001): 283–308.

Keymer, Tom. *Richardson's 'Clarissa' and the Eighteenth-Century Reader*. Cambridge: Cambridge University Press, 1992.

– '*Tom Jones*, Nell Gwyn, and the Cambridge Jest Book.' *Notes and Queries* 51.4 (December 2004): 408–9.

Kierkegaard, Søren. *Papers and Journals: A Selection*. Ed. and trans. Alastair Hanay. London: Penguin, 1996.

King, Kathryn R. *Jane Barker, Exile: A Literary Career, 1675–1725*. Oxford: Oxford University Press, 2000.

– 'Spying Upon the Conjuror: Haywood, Curiosity, and "the Novel" in the 1720s.' *Studies in the Novel* 30.2 (1998): 178–93.

Knapp, Steven. *Personification and the Sublime: Milton to Coleridge*. Cambridge, MA: Harvard University Press, 1985.

Knights, Mark. *Politics and Opinion in Crisis, 1678–81*. Cambridge: Cambridge University Press, 1994.

de Krey, Gary S. 'Revolution *redivivus*: 1688–1689 and the Radical Tradition in Seventeenth-Century London Politics.' In *The Revolution of 1688–89*, ed. Lois G. Schwoerer, 198–217. Cambridge: Cambridge University Press, 1996.

Kristeva, Julia. 'Stabat Mater.' In *Tales of Love*. Trans. Leon S. Roudiez, 234–63. New York: Columbia University Press, 1987.

Lanser, Susan S. 'The Novel Body Politic.' In *A Companion to the Eighteenth-Century English Novel and Culture*, ed. Paula R. Backscheider and Catherine Ingrassia, 480–503. Oxford: Blackwell, 2005.

Laursen, John Christian. 'Baylean Liberalism: Tolerance Requires Nontoler-ance.' In *Beyond the Persecuting Society: Religious Toleration before the Enlightenment*, ed. John Christian Laursen and Cary J. Nederman, 197–215. Philadelphia: University of Pennsylvania Press, 1998.

Leavis, Q.D. *Fiction and the Reading Public*. London: Chatto and Windus, 1932; New York: Russell and Russell, 1965.

Leborgne, Erik. 'Clarissa Harlot or Clarissa Hallowed? L'échiquier moral de Clarisse.' *Littératures* 48 (2003): 35–48.

Lockwood, Thomas. 'Shamela.' In *The Critical Companion to Henry Fielding*, ed. Claude Rawson, 38–49. Cambridge: Cambridge University Press, 2007.

London, April. 'Controlling the Text: Women in *Tom Jones*.' *Women and Early Fiction*, ed. Jerry C. Beasley. Special issue of *Studies in the Novel* 19.3 (1987): 323–33.

Love, Harold. *English Clandestine Satire, 1660–1702*. Oxford: Oxford University Press, 2004.

– 'Nell Gwyn and Rochester's "By Al Love's Soft, Yet Mighty Pow'rs."' *Notes and Queries* 49.3 (2002): 355–7.

– ed. *The Works of John Wilmot, Earl of Rochester*. Oxford: Oxford University Press, 1999.

Lynch, Deidre Shauna. *The Economy of Character: Novels, Market Culture, and the Business of Inner Meaning*. Chicago: University of Chicago Press, 1998.

MacGregor-Hastie, Roy. *Nell Gwyn*. London: Robert-Hale, 1987.

MacKinnon, Catharine A. *Towards a Feminist Theory of the State*. Cambridge, MA: Harvard University Press, 1989.

Maclean, Gerald. 'Literature, Culture, and Society in Restoration England.' In *Culture and Society in the Stuart Restoration: Literature, Drama, History*, ed. Gerald Maclean, 3–30. Cambridge: Cambridge University Press, 1995.

– *Looking East: English Writing and the Ottoman Empire before 1800*. New York: Palgrave Macmillan, 2007.

Maguire, Nancy Klein. 'The Duchess of Portsmouth: English Royal Consort and French Politician, 1670–85.' In *The Stuart Court and Europe: Essays in Politics and Political Culture*, ed. R. Malcolm Smuts, 247–73. Cambridge: Cambridge University Press, 1996.

Mahon, M. Wade. 'The Rhetoric of Virtuous Reading in Defoe's *Roxana* and the 1765 Continuation.' *Reader: Essays in Reader-Oriented Theory, Criticism, and Pedagogy* 49 (2003): 10–43.

Markley, Robert. 'Global Analogies: Cosmology, Geosymmetry, and Skepticism in Some Works of Aphra Behn.' In *Science, Literature and Rhetoric in Early Modern England*, ed. Juliet Cummins and David Burchell, 189–212. Aldershot: Ashgate, 2007.

Marsden, Jean. 'Sex, Politics, and She-Tragedy: Reconfiguring Lady Jane Grey.' *Studies in English Literature 1500–1900* 42.3 (2002): 501–22.

Marshall, David. *The Figure of Theater: Shaftesbury, Defoe, Adam Smith, and George Eliot*. New York: Columbia University Press, 1986.

Marshall, John. *John Locke: Resistance, Religion, and Responsibility*. Cambridge: Cambridge University Press, 1994.

Matar, Nabil. *Islam in Britain, 1558–1685*. Cambridge: Cambridge University Press, 1998.

– *Turks, Moors, and Englishmen in the Age of Discovery*. New York: Columbia University Press, 1999.

Maurer, Shawn Lisa. '"I wou'd be a *Man-Woman*": *Roxana*'s Amazonian Threat to the Ideology of Marriage.' *Texas Studies in Literature and Language* 46.3 (2004): 363–86.

Mayer, Robert. *History and the Early English Novel: Matters of Fact from Bacon to Defoe*. Cambridge: Cambridge University Press, 1997.

McClintock, Anne. 'Sex Workers and Sex Work: Introduction.' *Social Text* 37 (1993): 1–10.

McDowell, Paula. *The Women of Grub Street: Press, Politics, and Gender in the London Literary Marketplace, 1678–1730*. Oxford: Clarendon Press, 1998.

McFarlane, Cameron. *The Sodomite in Fiction and Satire, 1660–1750*. New York: Columbia University Press, 1997.

McKeon, Michael. 'Historicizing Absalom and Achitophel.' In *The New Eighteenth Century: Theory, Politics, English Literature*, ed. Felicity Nussbaum and Laura Brown, 23–40. New York: Routledge, 1987.

– *The Origins of the English Novel, 1600–1740*. Re-issued with a new introduction. Baltimore: Johns Hopkins University Press, 2002.

– *The Secret History of Domesticity: Public, Private and the Division of Knowledge*. Baltimore: Johns Hopkins University Press, 2005.

Meeker, Natania. *Voluptuous Philosophy: Literary Materialism in the French Enlightenment*. New York: Fordham University Press, 2006.

Melville, Lewis. *Nell Gwyn: The Story of Her Life*. New York: George H. Doran, 1924.

Mijers, Esther, and David Onnekink, eds. *Redefining William III: The Impact*

.*of the King-Stadholder in International Context*. Burlington, VT: Ashgate, 2007.

Miller, J. Hillis. *Fiction and Repetition: Seven English Novels*. Cambridge, MA: Harvard University Press, 1982.

Molesworth, Jesse. '"A Dreadful Course of Calamities": *Roxana's* Ending Reconsidered.' *ELH* 74.2 (2007): 493–508.

Monod, Paul Kléber. *Jacobitism and the English People, 1688–1788*. Cambridge: Cambridge University Press, 1989.

Mowry, Melissa. *The Bawdy Politic in Stuart England, 1660–1714*. Burlington, VT: Ashgate, 2004.

Mudge, Bradford K. *The Whore's Story: Women, Pornography, and the British Novel, 1684–1830*. Oxford: Oxford University Press, 2000.

Mullan, John. Introduction. *Roxana* (1724). Oxford: Oxford University Press, 1996.

Nenner, Howard. 'The Later Stuart Age.' In *The Varieties of British Political Thought, 1500–1800*, ed. J.G.A. Pocock and Lois G. Schwoerer, 180–208. Cambridge: Cambridge University Press, 1993.

Noggle, James. *The Skeptical Sublime: Aesthetic Ideology in Pope and the Tory Satirists*. Oxford: Oxford University Press, 2001.

Novak, Maximillian E. *Daniel Defoe: Master of Fictions*. Oxford: Oxford University Press, 2001.

– 'Defoe, the Occult, and the Deist Offensive during the Reign of George I.' In *Deism, Masonry, and the Enlightenment: Essays Honoring Alfred Owen Aldridge*, ed. J.A. Leo Lamay, 93–108. Newark: University of Delaware Press; London: Associated University Presses, 1987.

– *Realism, Myth, and History in Defoe's Fiction*. Lincoln: University of Nebraska Press, 1983.

– 'Sincerity, Delusion, and Character in the Fiction of Defoe and the "Sincerity Crisis" of his Time.' In *Augustan Studies: Essays in Honor of Irvin Ehrenpreis*, ed. Douglas Lane Patey and Timothy Keegan, 109–26. Newark: University of Delaware Press, 1985.

– 'The Unmentionable and Ineffable in Defoe's Fiction.' *Studies in the Literary Imagination* 15 (1982), 85–102.

– '*A Vindication of the Press* and the Defoe Canon.' *Studies in English Literature, 1500–1900* 27.3 (1987): 399–411.

Nussbaum, Felicity. *Torrid Zones: Maternity, Sexuality, and Empire in Eighteenth-Century English Narratives*. Baltimore: Johns Hopkins University Press, 1995.

O'Brian, Karen. 'History and the Novel in Eighteenth-Century Britain.' In *The Uses of History in Early Modern England*, ed. Paulina Kewes, 389–405. San Marino, CA: Huntington Library, 2006.

Ogg, David. *England in the Reigns of James II and William III*. Oxford: Clarendon Press, 1955.

Pateman, Carole. *The Sexual Contract*. Stanford: Stanford University Press, 1988.

Patterson, Annabel. *The Long Parliament of Charles II*. New Haven, CT: Yale University Press, 2008.

– 'Marvell and Secret History.' In *Marvell and Liberty*, ed. Warren Chernaik and Martin Dzelnais, 23–49. London: Macmillan, 1999.

Paulson, Ronald. Introduction. *The Analysis of Beauty*. New Haven, CT: Yale University Press, 1997.

– '*The Rape of the Lock*: A Jacobite Aesthetics.' In *Acts of Narrative*, ed. Carol Jacobs and Henry Sussman, 130–45. Stanford: Stanford University Press, 2003.

Payne, Deborah C. '"And Poets Shall by Patron-Princes Live": Aphra Behn and Patronage.' In *Curtain Calls: British and American Women and the Theatre*, ed. Mary Anne Schofield and Cecilia Macheski, 105–19. Athens: Ohio University Press, 1991.

Peterson, Spiro. 'Defoe's *Roxana* and Its Eighteenth-Century Sequels: A Critical and Bibliographical Study.' PhD diss., Harvard University, 1953.

Pettegrew, Andrew. *Marian Protestantism: Six Studies*. Aldershot: Scholars Press and Ashgate, 1996.

Pincus, Steven. 'Nationalism, Universal Monarchy, and the Glorious Revolution.' In *State/Culture: State-Formation after the Cultural Turn*, ed. George Steinmetz, 182–210. Ithaca, NY: Cornell University Press, 1999.

– '"To Protect English Liberties": The English Nationalist Revolution of 1688.' In *Protestantism and National Identity: Britain and Ireland, c. 1650–c. 1850*, ed. Tony Claydon and Ian McBride, 53–74. Cambridge: Cambridge University Press, 1998.

– and Peter Lake. 'Rethinking the Public Sphere in Early Modern England.' *Journal of British Studies* 45.2 (2006): 270–92.

Pittock, Murray G.H. *Jacobitism*. London: Macmillan Press, 1998.

Pocock, J.G.A., and Gordon J. Schochet. 'Interregnum and Restoration.' In *The Varieties of British Political Thought, 1500–1800*, ed. J.G.A. Pocock and Lois G. Schwoerer, 146–79. Cambridge: Cambridge University Press, 1993.

Pollak, Ellen. *Incest and the English Novel, 1684–1814*. Baltimore: Johns Hopkins University Press, 2003.

Poole, Kristen. *Radical Religion from Shakespeare to Milton: Figures of Nonconformity in Early Modern England*. Cambridge: Cambridge University Press, 2000.

Poovey, Mary. *The Proper Lady and the Woman Writer*. Chicago: University of Chicago Press, 1988.

Prytula, Nina. '"Great-Breasted and Fierce": Fielding's Amazonian Heroines.' *Eighteenth-Century Studies* 35.2 (2002): 173–93.

Rawson, Claude Julien. *Henry Fielding and the Augustan Ideal under Stress.* Atlantic Highlands, NJ: Humanities Press International, 1991.

Ribble, Frederick G. 'Aristotle and the "Prudence" Theme of *Tom Jones*.' *Eighteenth-Century Studies* 15.2 (1981): 26–47.

Richetti, John. *Defoe's Narratives: Situation and Structures.* Oxford: Clarendon Press, 1975.

– '*Love Letters between a Nobleman and His Sister*: Aphra Behn and Amatory Fiction.' In *Augustan Subjects: Essays in Honor of Martin C. Battestin*, ed. Albert J. Rivero, 13–28. Newark: University of Delaware, 1997.

– 'The Old Order and the New Novel of the Mid-Eighteenth Century: Narrative Authority in Fielding and Smollett.' *Eighteenth-Century Fiction* 3.2 (1990): 183–96.

– *Popular Fiction before Richardson: Narrative Patterns, 1700–1739.* Oxford: Clarendon Press, 1969.

– 'The Public Sphere and the Eighteenth-Century Novel: Social Criticism and Narrative Enactment.' *Eighteenth-Century Life* 16.3 (1992): 114–29.

Rivero, Albert J. '"Hieroglifick'd" History in Aphra Behn's *Love-Letters between a Nobleman and His Sister*.' *Studies in the Novel* 30.2 (1998): 126–38.

Rizzo, Betty. 'The Gendering of Divinity in *Tom Jones*.' *Studies in Eighteenth-Century Culture* 24 (1995): 259–77.

Roach, Joseph. *Cities of the Dead: Circum-Atlantic Performance.* New York: Columbia University Press, 1996.

Rose, Craig. *England in the 1690s: Revolution, Religion, and War.* London: Blackwell, 1999.

Rosenthal, Laura. *Infamous Commerce: Prostitution in Eighteenth-Century British Literature and Culture.* Ithaca, NY: Cornell University Press, 2006.

– Introduction. *Nightwalkers: Prostitute Narratives from the Eighteenth Century.* Peterborough, ON: Broadview Press, 2008.

– '*Oroonoko*: Reception, Ideology, Narrative Strategy.' In *Cambridge Companion to Aphra Behn*, ed. Hughes and Todd, 135–50.

Sale, William M. *Samuel Richardson: Master Printer.* Ithaca, NY: Cornell University Press, 1950.

Salzman, Paul. *English Prose Fiction, 1558–1700.* Oxford: Oxford University Press, 1985.

Schellenberg, Betty A. *The Professionalization of Women Writers in Eighteenth-Century Britain.* Cambridge: Cambridge University Press, 2005.

Scott, Jonathan. 'England's Troubles: Exhuming the Popish Plot.' In *The Politics of Religion in Restoration England*, ed. Tim Harris, Paul Seaward, and Mark Goldie, 107–31. Oxford: Basil Blackwell Press, 1990.

– *England's Troubles: Seventeenth-Century English Political Instability in European Context*. Cambridge: Cambridge University Press, 2000.

Scott, Maria M. *Representing 'Jane' Shore: Harlot and Heroine*. Aldershot: Ashgate, 2005.

Shapiro, Rebecca. 'The "Unnatural" Mother-Daughter Relationship in Daniel Defoe's *Roxana*.' In *The Literary Mother: Essays on Representations of Maternity and Child Care*, ed. Susan C. Staub, 33–47. Jefferson, NC: McFarland, 2007.

Sharpe, Kevin. '"Thy Longing Country's Darling and Desire": Aesthetics, Sex, and Politics in the England of Charles II.' In *Politics, Transgression, and Representation at the Court of Charles II*, ed. Julia Marciari Alexander and Catharine MacLeod, 1–34.

Shell, Alison. 'Popish Plots: *The Feign'd Courtezans* in Context.' In *Aphra Behn Studies*, ed. Janet Todd, 31–49. Cambridge: Cambridge University Press, 1996.

Shifrin, Susan. '"A Copy of My Countenance": Biography, Iconography, and Likeness in the *Portraits of the Duchess of Mazarin and Her Circle*.' PhD dissertation, Bryn Mawr College, 1998. UMI, 1998.

– '"Subdued by a Famous Roman Dame": Picturing Foreignness, Notoriety, and Prerogative in the Portraits of Hortense Mancini, Duchess of Mazarin.' In *Politics, Transgression, and Representation at the Court of Charles II*, ed. Julia Marciari Alexander and Catharine MacLeod, 145–51.

Shteir, Ann B. '*Flora primavera* or *Flora meretrix*? Iconography, Gender, and Science.' *Studies in Eighteenth-Century Culture* 36 (2007): 147–68.

Smallwood, Angela J. *Fielding and the Woman Question: The Novels of Henry Fielding and the Feminist Debate, 1700–1750*. New York: St Martin's, 1989.

Smith, Charles Saumarez. Forward. *Painted Ladies: Women at the Court of Charles II*, ed. Catharine MacLeod and Julia Marciari Alexander. London: National Portrait Gallery, in association with Yale Center for British Art, 2001.

Snow, Malinda. 'Arguments to the Self in Defoe's *Roxana*.' *Studies in English Literature 1500–1900* 34.3 (1994): 523–34.

Sollers, Philippe. 'What is Libertinage?' Trans. Roger Celestin. In *Libertinage and Modernity*. Special issue of *Yale French Studies*, ed. Catherine Cusset. 94 (1998): 199–212.

Speck, W.A. 'William – and Mary?' In *The Revolution of 1688–89: Changing Perspectives*, ed. Lois G. Schwoerer, 131–46. Cambridge: Cambridge University Press, 1992.

Spencer, Jane. 'Not Being a Historian: Women Telling Tales in Restoration and Eighteenth-Century England.' In *Contexts of Pre-Novel Narrative*, ed. Roy Eriksen, 319–40. New York: Mouton de Gruyter, 1994.

– *The Rise of the Woman Novelist: From Aphra Behn to Jane Austen*. London: Basil Blackwell, 1986.

Spufford, Margaret. *Small Books and Pleasant Histories: Popular Fiction and Readership in Seventeenth-Century England*. London: Methuen, 1981.

Spurr, John. *England in the 1670s: 'This Masquerading Age.'* Oxford: Blackwell Press, 2000.

– *The Restoration Church of England, 1646–1689*. New Haven: Yale University Press, 1991.

– '"Virtue, Religion, and Government": The Anglican Uses of Providence.' In *The Politics of Religion in Restoration England*, ed. Tim Harris, Paul Seaward, and Mark Goldie, 29–47. Oxford: Basil Blackwell Press, 1990.

Starkie, Andrew. *The Church of England and the Bangorian Controversy, 1716–1721*. Woodbridge, Suffolk: Boydell Press, 2007

Starr, G.A. *Defoe and Casuistry*. Princeton: Princeton University Press, 1971.

– *Defoe and Spiritual Autobiography*. Princeton: Princeton University Press, 1965.

Staves, Susan. *Players' Scepters: Fictions of Authority in the Restoration*. Lincoln: University of Nebraska Press, 1979.

Stern, Simon. '*Tom Jones* and the Economics of Copyright.' *Eighteenth-Century Fiction* 9.4 (1997): 429–45.

Stevenson, John Allen. *The Real History of Tom Jones*. New York: Palgrave Macmillan, 2005.

– 'Tom Jones and the Stuarts.' *ELH* 61.3 (1994): 571–95.

Stuber, Florian. 'On Fathers and Authority in *Clarissa*.' *Studies in English Literature, 1500– 1900* 25.3 (1985): 557–74.

Switzer, Gerald B. 'The Suppression of Convocation in the Church of England.' *Church History* 1.3 (1932): 150–62.

Tannenbaum, Amie G., and Donald G. Tannenbaum. 'John Locke and Pierre Bayle on Religious Toleration: An Enquiry.' *Studies on Voltaire and the Eighteenth Century: Transactions of the Eighth International Congress of the Enlightenment* 303 (1992): 418–21.

Thompson, E.P. 'The Peculiarities of the English.' *Socialist Register* (1965): 311–62.

Thompson, Helen. *Ingenuous Subjection: Compliance and Power in the Eighteenth-Century Domestic Novel*. Philadelphia: University of Pennsylvania Press, 2005.

– '"Thou monarch of my Panting Soul": Hobbesian Obligation and the Durability of Romance in Aphra Behn's *Love-letters*.' In *British Women's Writing in the Long Eighteenth Century: Authorship, Politics and History*, ed. Jennie Batchelor and Cora Kaplan, 107– 20. New York: Palgrave MacMillan, 2005.

Thompson, James. *Models of Value: Eighteenth-Century Political Economy and the Novel*. Durham: Duke University Press, 1996.

Thompson, Peggy. 'Abuse and Atonement: The Passion of Clarissa Harlowe.' *Eighteenth-Century Fiction* 11.3 (1999): 255–70.

Tillyard, E.M.W. *Studies in Milton*. New York: Macmillan, 1951.

Todd, Janet. *The Critical Fortunes of Aphra Behn*. Columbia, SC: Camden House, 1998.

– Introduction. *Love-Letters between a Nobleman and His Sister*, by Aphra Behn, ed. Janet Todd. London: Penguin, 1996.

– ed. *The Secret Life of Aphra Behn*. London: Pandora, 2000.

– 'Who is Silvia? What is she? Feminine Identity in Aphra Behn's *Love-Letters between a Nobleman and His Sister*.' In *Aphra Behn Studies*, ed. Janet Todd, 199–218. Cambridge: Cambridge University Press, 1996.

– and Derek Hughes, eds. *The Cambridge Companion to Aphra Behn*. Cambridge: Cambridge University Press, 2004.

Trevor-Roper, Hugh. 'A Huguenot Historian: Paul Rapin.' In *Huguenots in Britain and Their French Background, 1550–1800*, ed. Irene Scouloudi, 3–19. London: Macmillan, 1987.

Trumbach, Randolph. *Sex and the Gender Revolution*, vol. 1, *Heterosexuality and the Third Gender in Enlightenment London*. Chicago: University of Chicago Press, 1998.

Tumbleson, Raymond D. *Catholicism in the English Protestant Imagination: Nationalism, Religion, and Literature, 1600–1745*. Cambridge: Cambridge University Press, 1998.

Turner, James Grantham. *Libertines and Radicals in Early Modern London: Sexuality, Politics and Literary Culture, 1630–1685*. Cambridge: Cambridge University Press, 2001.

– 'The Libertine Sublime: Love and Death in Restoration England.' *Studies in Eighteenth-Century Culture* 19 (1989): 99–115.

– '*The Whore's Rhetorick*: Narrative, Pornography, and the Origins of the Novel.' *Studies in Eighteenth-Century Culture* 24 (1995): 297–306.

Valenze, Deborah M. *Prophetic Sons and Daughters: Female Preaching and Popular Religion in Industrial England*. Princeton: Princeton University Press, 1985.

Vaughan, Herbert M. *From Anne to Victoria: Fourteen Biographical Studies between 1702 and 1901*. Port Washington, NY: Kennikat Press, 1931.

Vermeule, Blakey. *The Party of Humanity: Writing Moral Psychology in Eighteenth-Century Britain*. Baltimore: Johns Hopkins University Press, 2000.

Vickery, Amanda. *The Gentleman's Daughter: Women's Lives in Georgian England*. New Haven, CT: Yale University Press, 1998.

– ed. *Women, Privilege, and Power: British Politics, 1750 to the Present*. Stanford: Stanford University Press, 2001.

Wall, Cynthia. 'Gendering Rooms: Domestic Architecture and Literary Acts.' *Eighteenth-Century Fiction* 5.4 (1993): 349–72.

Warner, William B. *Licensing Entertainment: The Elevation of Novel Reading in Britain, 1684–1750*. Berkeley and Los Angeles: University of California Press, 1998.

– *Reading* Clarissa: *The Struggles of Interpretation*. New Haven, CT: Yale University Press, 1979.

Watt, Ian. *The Rise of the Novel: Studies in Defoe, Richardson, and Fielding*. London: Pimlico, 2000.

Weber, Harold. *Paper Bullets: Print and Kingship under Charles II*. Lexington, KY: University of Kentucky Press, 1996.

Weber-Woelk, Ursula. '"Flora la belle Rommaine": Studien zur Ikonographie der Göttin Flora Im 17. Jahrhundert.' PhD dissertation, Cologne, 1995.

Wehrs, Donald A. '*Eros*, Ethics, Identity: Royalist Feminism and the Politics of Desire in Aphra Behn's *Love-Letters*.' *Studies in English Literature 1500–1900* 32.3 (1992): 461–78.

Weil, Rachel. *Political Passions: Gender, the Family, and Political Argument in England, 1680–1714*. Manchester: Manchester University Press, 1999.

– 'Sometimes a Sceptre is only a Sceptre: Pornography and Politics in Restoration England.' In *The Invention of Pornography: Obscenity and the Origins of Modernity, 1500–1800*, ed. Lynn Hunt, 125–56. New York: Zone, 1993.

– 'The Female Politician in the Late Stuart Age.' In *Politics, Transgression, and Representation at the Court of Charles II*, ed. Julia Marciari Alexander and Catharine MacLeod, 177–92. New Haven, CT: Yale University Press, 2007.

Williams, Rowan. 'The Richard Dimbledy Lecture 2002.' Westminster School, London. 19 December 2002. http://www.anglicancommunion.org/acns/articles/32/25/acns3236.html.

Wilson, Brett. 'Jane Shore and the Jacobites: Nicholas Rowe, the Pretender, and the National She-Tragedy,' *ELH* 72.4 (2005): 823–43.

Wilson, Frederick. *The Importance of the Reign of Queen Anne in English Church History*. Oxford: Blackwell, 1911.

Wilson, John Harold. *Court Satires of the Restoration*. Columbus, OH: Ohio State University Press, 1976.

– *Nell Gwynn, Royal Mistress*. New York: Pellegrini & Cudahy, 1952.

Wilt, Judith. 'He Could Go No Farther: A Modest Proposal about Lovelace and Clarissa.' *PMLA* 92.1 (1977): 19–32.

Winn, James Anderson. '*When beauty fires the blood*': Love and the Arts in the Age of Dryden. Ann Arbor: University of Michigan Press, 1992.

Wiseman, Susan. *Conspiracy and Virtue: Women, Writing, and Politics in Seventeenth-Century England*. Oxford: Oxford University Press, 2006.

Wiseman, T.P. 'The Games of Flora.' In *The Art of Ancient Spectacle*, ed. Bettina Bergmann and Christine Kondoleon, 195–203. New Haven: Yale University Press, 1999.

– *The Myths of Rome*. Exeter: University of Exeter Press, 2004.

Wynne, Sonya M. *The Mistresses of Charles II and Restoration Court Politics, 1660–1685*. Diss. Cambridge University, 1997.

Zimmerman, Everett. *The Boundaries of Fiction: History and the Eighteenth-Century British Novel*. Ithaca, NY: Cornell University Press, 1996.

Zook, Melinda S. 'Contextualizing Aphra Behn: Plays, Politics, and Party, 1679–1689.' In *Women Writers and the Early Modern British Political Tradition*, ed. Hilda Smith, 75– 93. Cambridge: Cambridge University Press, 1995.

– 'History's Mary: The Propagation of Queen Mary II, 1689–1694.' In *Women and Sovereignty*, ed. Louise Olga Fradenburg, 170–91. Edinburgh: Edinburgh University Press, 1992.

– 'The Political Poetry of Aphra Behn.' In *The Cambridge Companion to Aphra Behn*, ed. Hughes and Todd, 46–67. Cambridge: Cambridge University Press, 2004.

– 'Turncoats and Double Agents in Restoration and Revolutionary England: The Case of Robert Ferguson, the Plotter.' *Eighteenth-Century Studies* 42.3 (2009): 363–78.

Zwicker, Steven N. *Lines of Authority: Politics and English Literary Culture, 1649–1689*. Ithaca, NY: Cornell University Press, 1993.

Index